Antislavery, Abolition, and the Atlantic World

R. J. M. BLACKETT AND

JAMES BREWER STEWART,

EDITORS

EMANCIPATING
NEW YORK

THE POLITICS OF SLAVERY
AND FREEDOM

1777–1827

David N. Gellman

LOUISIANA STATE UNIVERSITY PRESS

BATON ROUGE

PUBLISHED BY LOUISIANA STATE UNIVERSITY PRESS
Copyright © 2006 by Louisiana State University Press
All rights reserved
Manufactured in the United States of America
FIRST PRINTING

DESIGNER: *Amanda McDonald Scallan*
TYPEFACE: *New Caledonia*
TYPESETTER: *G&S Typesetters, Inc.*
PRINTER AND BINDER: *Edward Brothers, Inc.*

Library of Congress Cataloging-in-Publication Data

Gellman, David Nathaniel.
  Emancipating New York : the politics of slavery and freedom, 1777–1827 /
David N. Gellman.
    p. cm. — (Antislavery, abolition, and the Atlantic world)
  Includes bibliographical references and index.
  ISBN-13: 978-0-8071-3174-9 (cloth : alk. paper)
  ISBN-10: 0-8071-3174-1 (cloth : alk. paper)
    1. Antislavery movements—New York (State)—History.   2. Slaves—
Emancipation—New York (State)   3. New York (State)—Politics and
government—1775–1865.   4. Slavery—New York (State)—History.
5. Abolitionists—New York (State)—Political activity.   6. New York (State)—
Race relations.   I. Title.   II. Series.
E445.N56G45 2006
306.3′620974709034—dc22

                                                              2005035621

for Monica

CONTENTS

ACKNOWLEDGMENTS

As I have imagined finishing this book through the years of research and writing, I have relished the prospect of thanking all those who have supported and encouraged me.

I first began to formulate a notion of what being a historian actually meant while an undergraduate at Amherst College. Thesis advisors N. Gordon Levin and Sean Redding gave me a feel for thinking big. Robert Gross's American Studies seminar on Shays's Rebellion during my senior year led me to realize that we really do not know everything about early America that we need to know. Ever since, Bob has served as a model, friend, and supporter.

This book began life as a dissertation. At Northwestern, T. H. Breen was a tireless advisor who set high standards. James Oakes provided an example of provocative scholarship on slavery. James Campbell offered his insight from close range and from afar; only years later, did I come to appreciate the full value of his nine-page single-spaced commentary faxed from South Africa.

I have experienced phenomenal generosity as I have transformed this project into a book, especially from series editors Richard J. M. Blackett and James Brewer Stewart. Richard offered a valuable critique and issued memorable marching orders over lunch at a conference in California. Jim recruited the manuscript to the series, conveyed his optimism that I would make the necessary changes, and offered important insights. From the first, Jim extended his unique, warm collegiality, making me, a novice then holding a mere term appointment, feel as if I shared something essential with a professor of great scholarly accomplishment.

Fellow historians have offered much thoughtful commentary and provided indications that I might be on the right track. In addition to my dissertation committee and series editors, the manuscript is significantly better for having been read by Dickson D. Bruce Jr., Graham Russell Hodges, and Joanne Pope Melish. Various draft chapters, conference papers, and article manuscripts received helpful responses from W. Andrew Achenbaum, David Brion Davis, Jay Fliegelman, Thelma Wills Foote, Patrick Griffin, John Larson, Tim Lockley, Lynda Morgan, Michael Morrison, Steven Reich, Michael Vorenberg, Alfred Young, and the members of the Newberry Library's Seminar in Early American History. John Brooke more than once offered welcome encouragement.

Rand Dotson and George Roupe at LSU Press have guided the manuscript to publication. Copyeditor Julia Ridley Smith tightened the prose. Mary Lee Eggart, from LSU's Department of Geography and Anthropology, made three helpful maps. Portions of this book have appeared previously as "Pirates, Sugar, Debtors, and Slaves: Political Economy and the Case for Gradual Abolition in New York," *Slavery and Abolition* 22, no. 2 (2001): 51–68; and "Race, the Public Sphere, and Abolition in Late Eighteenth-Century New York," *Journal of the Early Republic* 20 (Winter 2000): 607–36. I thank the publishers of *Slavery and Abolition* (www.tandf.co.uk) and the University of Pennsylvania Press for graciously permitting me to reprint this material.

Daniel Albert and David Quigley belong to a special, hybrid category. Friends to me long before any of us became historians, they have helped sustain this project through their intellect and example, as well as their many thoughtful suggestions. Dan has listened to me complain, even when I was in no position to do so. Dave went so far as to coedit a document reader with me.

The night I arrived in Greencastle for my interview at DePauw University marked the beginning of several rewarding relationships. Yung-chen Chiang, Julia Bruggemann, Rod Clifford, Bob Dewey, John Dittmer, Mac Dixon-Fyle, Glen Kuecker, Tiyi Morris, John Schlotterbeck, Barbara Steinson, Barbara Whitehead—thank you for sharing your lives as teacher-scholars in DePauw's Department of History. Special thanks are due also to fellow basement dwellers Mary Giles and Bob Hershberger.

I am grateful to the institutions where I conducted my research and those which have provided the time, money, and facilities to enable me to finish my writing. Northwestern University Library, especially Peter Burtch and his staff in the microform room, provided me with a superb home base. Even short visits to various New York archives turned up research gems. These archives include the Troy Public Library; the New York State Library in Albany; the Adriance Library in Poughkeepsie; the New York Public Library Rare Book and Manuscript Room; the New-York Historical Society; the Haviland Records Room in New York City, which houses the Archives of the New York Yearly Meeting—Religious Society of Friends; the Nassau County Historical Society, Hofstra University; and the Long Island Room of the Queensborough Public Library. Travel to these sites was made possible through the generous support of the Society of Colonial Wars, Illinois Chapter. A John and Janice Fisher Time-Out course release at DePauw, funded under the auspices of the Faculty Development Committee, provided time for revisions. More broadly, Dean Neal Abraham and President Robert Bottoms have my deep appreciation for encouraging faculty scholarship. I also thank my students at DePauw for practicing history with me. History major and work-study student Nicholas Gaffney gave several chapters a careful reading as I prepared to make final revisions. Marilyn Culler cheerfully agreed to take my picture.

My brief eastward forays would have been considerably less pleasurable without the friendly hospitality of Melissa Hayes Albert and Dan Albert, Megan DeMott and David Quigley, Melissa Favreault, Stephen and Christina Gellman, Jim and Katherine Perkins, Paul Schwartzberg and Lisa Waldman, and Neil and Marcie Sullivan. I also have benefited from many personal kindnesses as I have worked on this project. In particular, I extend thanks to Claire Dunnett, Dave Dunnett, Frank Fennell, Kay Fennell, Mark Fennell, Jenny Fennell, Lindsay Freylack, Zach Grammel, Jane Matthews, Ken Matthews, and Lee Willer.

The certainty that Benet D. Gellman and Adell Wade would have approved of this work has fortified me in my determination to publish it.

My brother Stephen blazed all the right trails—history major, sports fandom, Springsteen, and parenthood. My mother has saved everything I ever wrote, expressed boundless confidence in me, and provided all manner of support; I am deeply grateful.

While revising this study, I regularly encountered passages originally composed before the birth of my children. Because of Hannah and Ben, I know with great assurance that time never stands still but rather rushes ahead to new discoveries and unanticipated joys. This book is better for the intellectual influence of my wife Monica, to whom it is dedicated. I treasure most what she has taught me that transcends books—about community, about humane professionalism, and, above all, about love.

EMANCIPATING NEW YORK

INTRODUCTION

New York, the state with the highest concentration and largest number of slaves north of Maryland, finally designated freedom as a birthright on July 5, 1799. The "Act for the gradual abolition of slavery" implemented a maddeningly indirect program of emancipation for African American New Yorkers born any time after the nation's twenty-third birthday. The law declared the children of slave mothers to be free but obligated those children to endure a period of service to their mothers' masters extending well into adulthood. Gradual abolition nonetheless had profound consequences for New York and the nation, for enslaved blacks as well as for free whites. New York's emancipation act guaranteed the emergence of a historically rare and protean slaveless democracy in the half of the United States that lay north of the Mason-Dixon Line.[1] Subsequently, the fast-growing Empire State would become a cornerstone of the proverbial American "house divided against itself," occupying a terrain contested by free blacks, abolitionists of every kind, southern apologists, and cultural innovators of "whiteness."[2]

Slavery in New York collapsed during the generation following the passage of the gradual abolition law, yet how New Yorkers decided to abolish slavery at all is, at best, partially understood. The ultimate rejection of slavery within New York's borders occurred as part of a much wider movement to abolish slavery in the Revolutionary-era North and an even broader transatlantic movement to dismantle the international slave trade and many of the assumptions upon which that trade rested. Slavery discourse in New York reflected and elaborated upon those wider discussions of liberty and humanitarianism. Because New York was one of the last northern states to act against slavery within its borders, the story of abolition there throws into particularly sharp relief the ambivalence toward slavery of Revolutionary-era white Americans.[3] At stake in New York's prolonged debate over slavery during the final two decades of the eighteenth century were fundamental propositions about citizenship, the proper dimension of the public sphere, the regional and partisan identities of New Yorkers, and the political economy of prosperity, poverty, and productivity. Moreover, emerging and highly contested ideas about race shaped and were shaped by the extended debate over slavery.

This book explains the abolition of slavery in New York as a product of organized white opposition, of changes in the political structure, and of black resistance. But the explanation for the abolition of slavery relies even more upon an analysis of the vigorous public discourse about slavery, race, and citizenship that kept the problem of slavery before the public for the better part of two decades. Slavery became a negative reference point in measuring the presence or absence of justice in a state formulating a postindependence economic and political identity. In the process, the institution of slavery lost its legitimacy, and the public overcame racialized concerns about citizenship that had undermined the case for abolition. Some white New Yorkers even found ways to conceive of African American equality in positive terms. Caught in a web of antislavery discourse which spanned the Atlantic world, New Yorkers finally reached the inescapable conclusion that slavery comported neither with their ideals nor their interests. New Yorkers defined the contours of an American public discourse about freedom, slavery, race, and citizenship that would shape events well beyond the official end of New York slavery in 1827, a full generation after the passage of the state's original gradual emancipation law.

I.

Although never a "slave society" on the order of Virginia, South Carolina, or Louisiana and by the mid-nineteenth century not even a "society with slaves," New York state is well cast for a leading role in the history of race in America.[4] Black life in New York City—which would become the nation's first and greatest metropolis in the nineteenth century—has attracted considerable scholarly interest in recent years. Social historians of northern African American life have unearthed a wealth of data, often concentrating on Manhattan and surrounding areas before and after the commencement of gradual abolition. We now know a great deal about family formation, residential living patterns, occupational structure, and even the dress and demeanor of northern free blacks in general and of black residents of New York City in particular. Often confined to the worst housing and lowest-status jobs, New York City's emerging free black population nonetheless founded a variety of religious and cultural institutions that met the needs of the community and served as a base for antebellum black political protest.[5] The terms and timing of abolition reshaped antebellum black life in the countryside as well, giving rise to a diversity of northern black experiences scholars are just beginning to appreciate.[6] Thus, the process by which northern abolition was contested, approved, and secured in New York state demands detailed investigation. That investigation, moreover, must resist the temptation to follow so many existing studies by focusing on greater New York City, rather than the whole state of New York. The prospect of gradual abolition attracted attention in all parts of the state and could only be achieved by negotiating the complexities of state politics.

New York state's centrality within nineteenth-century racial, sectional, and cultural politics makes the early national-era debate over emancipation especially significant. Over the past decade, historians have increasingly emphasized the crucial role that the antebellum North in general—and often New York in particular—played in the intertwined histories of race and African American identity. Among other things, New York was the birthplace and hothouse of the blackface minstrel stage. Scholars such as Eric Lott and David Roediger have found in the staged emulation and disparagement of African Americans a powerful institution and metaphor through which to understand the nature of nineteenth-century white supremacy. The characters of the minstrel stage harnessed New York's cultural power to a national project of herrenvolk democracy, which New York itself practiced by simultaneously enfranchising most white men and disfranchising most black men in its 1821 state constitution.[7]

Subsequently, city and state became crucial, dynamic sites of democratic and national politics during the antebellum period. The size of New York's electorate and the ambitions of its politicians necessarily involved the Empire State in national slavery politics. At the federal level, New Yorkers supplied the South with political allies essential for the "Slave Power" to dominate national political life. In response, others launched antislavery and free-soil political parties, precursors to a broader reaction in parts of New York against proslavery politicians.[8]

Despite segregationist and prosouthern impulses, antebellum New York also provided a home and a critical base of operations to the antebellum abolitionist movement. Indeed, Sojourner Truth, the most powerful symbol of black feminism and antislavery in the nineteenth century, was born a slave in Ulster County, New York. The nation's first African American newspaper, *Freedom's Journal*, was founded in New York. Frederick Douglass made his home in Rochester, where he launched a series of abolitionist periodicals. Lewis and Arthur Tappan headquartered their benevolent empire of reform and its prominent abolitionist subsidiary there. Moreover, popular energy for abolitionism was sustained in part by western New York's famous "burned over" district of Christian revivalist fervor. Friendships that expressed the potential and pitfalls of interracial brotherhood were forged in New York among such figures as black physician-activist James McCune Smith and white landowner-philanthropist Gerrit Smith.[9] The timing, character, and nature of New York's abolition of slavery shaped the world in which these and thousands of less-prominent opponents of slavery operated.

II.

The story of abolition in New York state, for which, improbably, no book-length historical narrative has been published, challenges emerging models of northern emancipation. Similarities and differences between New York and elsewhere are equally telling. To clarify how New Yorkers abolished slavery in the first place, this book maintains that New York occupied a critical position in the arc of northern abolitionism running from early national-era Pennsylvania through antebellum New England. Nothing approaching the Garrisonian-inspired abolitionist mass mobilization that began in the 1830s occurred in the late eighteenth century. Nonetheless, support for statewide abolition was generated publicly rather than being orchestrated quietly by early national-era elites.[10] Moreover, New Yorkers clearly felt compelled to respond to regional, national, and international challenges to slavery.

Despite telling continuities with movements in other states and at other times, emancipation in New York also carried with it special significance and was conditioned by circumstances particular to the state itself. Among the crucial differences between New York and its neighbors was the impressive size and scope of slavery in the Hudson River valley, Manhattan, and Long Island. As Part I of this study indicates, slavery played an important role in the development of the colony's diverse regions. Into the early independence period, New Yorkers held a larger number of slaves than the other states north of Maryland and a greater percentage of slaves as well.[11] Moreover, the fact that in New York slavery survived the initial ideological and military blows of the American Revolution, meant that the discussion of slavery's future in the state took place in a much different context than in Pennsylvania, which abolished slavery in 1780, or Connecticut and Rhode Island, where legislatures passed gradual abolition schemes in 1784. While Quaker activists in New York played a prominent role in opposing slavery, Quakers were a much more marginal group in New York than Pennsylvania. The mechanism for abolition was quite different as well in Massachusetts. No New York court would have dared to pronounce a blanket condemnation of slavery as the Supreme Judicial Court did in that state. In nineteenth-century New York, debating the memory of slavery was far more important than in New England, where the process of eliminating a more modest institution began earlier and the project of repressing the slave past was more feasible.[12]

The timing of New York's abolition facilitates an examination of the relationship between slavery and American political culture.[13] The delayed beginning of gradual abolition in New York precludes ascribing emancipation to Revolutionary fervor or the inevitable realization of Revolutionary ideals. As established in Part II, those ideals were hotly contested and dramatically reshaped during the final years of the eighteenth century, often in ways not immediately and not obviously favorable to emancipationist goals.

New Yorkers worked out their stance toward the future of slavery in their state amid dramatic events taking place in the United States and the broader Atlantic world. The ratification of the U.S. Constitution, the confirmation of the Jay Treaty, the intensifying partisan competition between Republicans and Federalists, the slave revolution in St. Domingue, and the initial parliamentary campaign against the British slave trade all shaped slavery discourse in New York. These events and many others encouraged New Yorkers to think about their own continuing practice of domestic slavery and their relationship to the new nation. Indeed, independence from British rule prompted New Yorkers, like other Americans, to contemplate their place in the world, their ambitions for economic power and prosperity, and the balance between individual opportunity and social order. Discussions of slavery—metaphoric and actual—bubbled up to the surface in all these contexts.

New York's newspapers in particular recorded a variety of responses to slavery. This brisk newspaper discourse testifies to the perceptiveness of slavery's opponents, who used a burgeoning print culture to bring abolitionist initiatives and successes elsewhere to bear on the politics of abolition in New York. It also demonstrates that print culture's role in defining political life, far from reaching its peak during the colonial crisis, was accelerating, in part because momentous issues like slavery remained unresolved and vitally connected to so many other controversies that defined the new republic.[14]

Historians of the early-national period have barely scratched the surface in understanding the reciprocal meanings that slavery had for a broad range of issues central to American political discourse and what those issues meant for the discourse over slavery and abolition. Grappling with slavery required blacks and whites, slaves and masters, slaveholders and nonslaveholders to define their identities with a regard to a variety of subjects that ranged well beyond slavery itself. By conducting a close and extensive reading of newspapers and other published materials and placing that reading in the context of legislative, Manumission Society, and census records, an interpretation that captures the dynamic interaction of slavery with other issues is possible. Ultimately, for a range of New Yorkers, slavery increasingly seemed incompatible with popular ideas about freedom, economic growth, regional identity, social justice, and race.

III.

At every stage of the contest over slavery, New Yorkers advanced explicit and implicit arguments about citizenship and the public sphere. Concerns about who should participate actively in the governance of city, state, and nation had to be resolved in practice as well as in principle in the new republic.[15] As a result, ideas about race became embroiled in discussions of citizenship and the public sphere, with clear implications for slavery itself.

Dating back to the seventeenth century, racial bondage acted as a foil for the concept of freedom. Subsequently, the concept of citizenship which emerged after U.S. independence specifically hinged on the right to vote and the competence to earn a living. The ability to participate publicly in political debate and cultural discussions constituted a third aspect of citizenship.[16]

In all three instances, slavery represented a powerful antithesis, as a concept and as a material reality.[17] Even before the large-scale economic transformations of the nineteenth century, slavery equated with economic and social dependence, which ran counter to citizenship.[18] Citizens worked—ideally for themselves, but definitely not for people who literally or figuratively owned them. Citizens bore an obligation to stay clear of public and charitable support, or the permanent direction of a person of superior "social standing."[19] Voting, the most concrete political manifestation of citizenship, remained closely linked to property holding in New York and elsewhere after independence. Only those holding a sufficient amount of property could vote. Thus, marital property law, along with gendered assumptions about work and autonomy, combined with franchise rules to distinguished propertied males alone as possessing the full measure of citizenship.[20]

Also vital to achieving full citizenship was the ability to contribute to public discourse. Print culture—especially newspapers—proliferated across New York in the late eighteenth century, opening to scrutiny and debate all manner of social and political questions.[21] Newspapers claimed for themselves the roles of informants, educators, and political arbiters. The public opinion these papers helped to formulate was the cornerstone of politics in a republican society. Meanwhile, the intensity of politics in the early-national period further enlarged the role of the engaged citizenry in public life.[22] Defining who was entitled to contribute to this burgeoning public discourse helped to mark the borders between citizenship, subordination, and slavery.[23]

The dynamic, expanding, contentious "public sphere" of the late eighteenth century was where New Yorkers weighed propositions regarding black citizenship, in conjunction with many other debates about policy and participation. The growth of the political public made the question of whose voice legitimately belonged in the public sphere all the more important. If the "citizen" constituted the appropriate unit of the public sphere and public opinion registered the citizen's opinion, then what types of people comprised the citizenry became critical. Stigmatizing potential participants in the public sphere provided one way of making more exclusive its implicit universality.[24] Conversely, if outsiders pushed their way into the pages of public discourse—or even threatened to do so—they had the potential to liberalize, if not universalize, the emerging public sphere. The prolonged debate over whether to eliminate slavery and alter the racial order necessarily addressed itself to the redefinition of citizenship and the public sphere decades before a self-conscious free-black abolitionist leadership emerged by addressing these same questions.[25] Significantly, white-owned newspapers did not preclude and sometimes even encouraged the egalitarian imagination of their readers.

How African Americans voices should look and sound in print was something that blacks and whites worked out in response to one another. As a recent study has argued, in the eighteenth and early nineteenth centuries, this interracial literary dialogue involved northerners as much or more than southerners. Poets, such as Jupiter Hammon and Phillis Wheatley, and memoirists, such as Venture Smith and John Jea, constructed influential models of the printed African American persona. Whites with a variety of motives eagerly participated in the literary construction of the black voice.[26] Heightening the political significance of black voicings in late-eighteenth-century New York was the fact that the abolition of slavery had yet to receive legal sanction and that slavery was a subject of national and international debate.

Remarks about slavery and race, whether voiced as literary fictions or expressed in the context of broader discussions of political and economic development, bolstered the direct attacks on the morality of slavery which were appearing at the same time and in the same places. Such an antislavery discourse, to borrow a phrase from historian Seymour Drescher's work on English abolitionism, produced "a structure of opinion" against slavery.[27] This structure of opinion sustained an environment in which white New Yorkers came to regard gradual abolition as plausible, desirable, even necessary.

IV.

Public opinion about race, citizenship, and the public sphere shaped and reflected the strategies pursued by a variety of people with an interest in or influence over the future of slavery in New York. Slaves, slaveholders, humanitarian antislavery activists, and political officeholders played critical roles in the struggle for gradual abolition. The power to register opinions on, let alone to rewrite, the state's laws varied, but every act of resistance, like every vote cast in the legislature or article published in a newspaper, constituted a strand in a vast web of resistance, ideology, and calculation that enveloped the issue of slavery in New York and determined its fate. People acted because others spoke out, and people spoke because others acted.

African American New Yorkers had the primary stake in the prospect of their own freedom and searched for ways to advance that cause individually and collectively. From the Revolution to the passage of the gradual abolition law and beyond, black New Yorkers asserted their aspirations through various forms of resistance, putting pressure on the institution of slavery in New York. African Americans also expressed views of race and citizenship which underscored the legitimacy of black freedom and the urgency of emancipation. Black participation on both sides of the Revolutionary conflict signaled the ambitions of New York's enslaved population. The wartime contributions to the loyalist cause in particular was punctuated by the departure from New York City of thousands of American slaves in 1783. Following the end of the war, blacks continued to resist the conditions of slavery by running away in increasing numbers. African Americans in New York also protested their bondage on individual legal grounds in ways that prodded antislavery activists to work harder on their behalf. Once gradual abolition officially commenced, slaves sought leverage with their masters to accelerate the pace of black freedom. Moreover, throughout the era, African American New Yorkers sought to maintain and deepen the bonds of family and community attachment as a counterweight to the burdens imposed upon them through slavery.[28]

As recent social historians have already constructed an excellent portrait of black life during the final years of New York slavery, this study emphasizes instead how African American actions helped to shape the contours of public and political debates.[29] Black agency in bringing about an end to slavery in New York was real. But that agency also was bounded by the power that whites, individually and collectively, maintained over them, particularly after the British conceded defeat in the Revolutionary War. Slave owners, white lawmakers, and white citizens at large were not forcibly compelled to release slaves from bondage. Private manumissions and public laws followed a timetable that whites negotiated among themselves as much as with slaves, who, given their own choice, clearly preferred freedom.

As with slaves, the power of the dedicated group of New York City–based antislavery advocates had a real, albeit circumscribed, influence on prospects for abolition. Some members of the New York Manumission Society (NYMS) had enormous power and influence, such as John Jay, the organization's founding president, who became U.S. Supreme Court chief justice and governor of New York. Collectively, the organization helped keep the issue of slavery before the public and the legislature. The NYMS also assisted individual African Americans to advance their freedom claims, helping to enforce laws that limited at the margins the scope and power of slavery in the state. In addition, the society took the lead in providing formal education for blacks in New York City.

The NYMS embodied the strengths and weaknesses of elite eighteenth-century northern abolitionism. The organization demonstrated unmistakable commitment to the ultimate goal of abolition and helped keep the issue before the public after slavery survived the initial revolutionary ideological challenge. As the national tide of abolitionist sentiment ebbed in the 1790s, these activists pressed on. But the organization did not have the ability to effect its will unilaterally any more than the slaves themselves did.[30]

Ultimately, the authority to abolish slavery rested with the state's elected officials. New York's constitution ensured that, at least in the lower house of the legislature, a majority of males were directly represented.[31] More importantly, the governmental structure ensured that property holders, including those in the state's diverse slaveholding regions, would have a significant influence in determining slavery's future.

Over the course of two decades, the legislature weighed a range of questions arising from the broader discourse about slavery. The consideration of a number of issues circulating in newspapers and pamphlets registered on the legislature's decade-and-a-half of indecision, and in the final outcome of the gradual abolition debate. Uncertainty over the place of blacks in New York's public political life doomed the initial push for a gradual abolition law in the 1780s. An even more complicated relationship emerged in the late 1790s involving proposed gradual abolition legislation, wide-ranging public reservations about slavery, publicly expressed concerns over the citizenship of the economically disadvantaged, and partisan passions. By the end of the eighteenth century, a fortuitous combination of ideological discourse, activism, and electoral alignment produced the legislative victory essential to the eventual extinction of slavery in New York. As Part III of this study illustrates, it remained for black and white New Yorkers in the succeeding three decades to sort out the further implementation of abolition as well as the meaning of abolition's cultural and political legacy. During the period between 1800 and 1827, New Yorkers dismantled slavery. Free blacks then sought to define abolition as a triumph that would serve as a foundation for the spread of freedom in New York and the rest of the nation, even as whites erected a regime that denied blacks full citizenship, including the franchise, and popularized the notion that racial inferiority marred African Americans, slave and free.

The story told in these pages holds significance first and foremost because emancipation in New York was a crucial event in the broader history of American abolitionism and, indeed, U.S. history between the Revolution and the Civil War. Both the white supremacy and the egalitarianism that emerged in the nineteenth century were prefigured in the prolonged debate over slavery. Moreover, the state's abolition act was on the leading edge of a transformation in thinking about such diverse issues as regional identity, the power of the state to punish and confine, the organization of labor, economic expansion, the meaning of race, and the nature of citizenship.[32] New York enacted abolition before the grim logic of "racial modernity" intervened; gradualism also enabled white supremacy to emerge before black freedom and its underlying egalitarian logic could fully take root.[33] Even so, emancipation helped to secure the transformation of New York, once the heartland of northern slavery, into the most dynamic northern free-labor state during the antebellum period. New York also became a place where African Americans could articulate, if not often realize, their version of freedom.

In telling this story, I have one further goal. The narrative treats slavery in New York as an essential aspect of the formation of a new political culture. This study thus cuts against the grain of major recent syntheses of the early-national period which minimize the subject of racial bondage. We will only profit from heightened popular interest in the Founding Fathers if we recognize how central slavery was to the ideas, attitudes, and conditions with which they grappled.[34] By connecting slavery to critical questions about citizenship, the public sphere, and political identity, this study demonstrates how and why historians must construct syntheses that emphasize race and slavery.[35] Examining how a past public debated issues of racial justice in a politically and culturally tempestuous era might even help us to understand the public debates over national identity, race, and diversity taking place in our own turbulent times.

I

NO EXIT

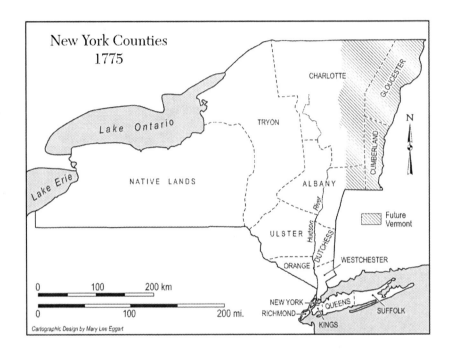

New York Counties
1775

Lake Ontario

Lake Erie

NATIVE LANDS

CHARLOTTE

TRYON

GLOUCESTER

CUMBERLAND

ALBANY

Hudson River

ULSTER

DUTCHESS

WESTCHESTER

ORANGE

N

Future
Vermont

0   100   200 km

0   100   200 mi.

NEW YORK

QUEENS

RICHMOND

SUFFOLK

KINGS

Cartographic Design by Mary Lee Eggart

1

Labor, Law, and Resistance in the Eighteenth Century

For some, freedom arrived as a murmur rather than a shout.

On November 17, 1783, Rachel Willis, her husband Samuel, and their three young children gathered aboard the *Nesbit*, joining 150 other Americans of African descent. The ship prepared to weigh anchor for Nova Scotia as part of the nearly complete British evacuation of New York City. Two years after Cornwallis's surrender to Washington at Yorktown and two months after the signing of the Peace of Paris, the war between the United States and Britain was over. For Rachel Willis of Long Island, New York, a new era of independence and freedom beckoned in Canada. She and her fellow passengers did not wish to tarry in order to see whether the rights successfully claimed by white former colonists would extend to black Americans as well.[1]

A range of possibilities existed for African Americans as American independence finally dawned in New York City. On the same newspaper page that announced the mustering of the *Nesbit*'s passengers, Col. Frederick Weissenfels offered a five-dollar reward for Dina, "a strong and well built" teenage slave who had fled her home on Fair Street. Weissenfels knew Dina well enough to describe her petticoat, her hat, and her hair, dyed a "reddish cast." The colonel issued the customary warning to ship captains and "other persons" not to aid Dina, who, like thousands of African Americans before and after her in New York, was chattel, the legally held property of a white master.

Just below the reward offered for fifteen-year-old Dina, another advertisement indicated the tenuous alternatives to flight or bondage. "WANTED" was "a Cook . . . white or black; a good recommendation . . . required."[2] The future did not preclude mobility and choice and did not necessarily, at least at the bottom of the social hierarchy, prescribe roles on strictly racial lines. But even such a circumscribed version of freedom remained a chimera in November 1783. With the occupation of its major port finally at an end, New Yorkers had an agenda freighted with unfinished business. Translating revolutionary ideals into postcolonial realities was but one of many priorities. New Yorkers sought to rebuild an economy, not only resuming in earnest the ordinary business of getting and spending, but doing so amid the wreckage of fire and neglect in Manhattan and without access to the West Indian markets upon which provincial commerce had relied. New Yorkers also had to find out how a political system designed in the crucible of civil war between patriots and loyalists, masters and slaves, British officials and colonial subjects, would function in a time of peace and confederation.[3]

Dina and Rachel Willis, along with thousands like them, could expect at best incremental change, despite the bold pronouncements about human equality borrowed from the Declaration of Independence and incorporated in the new state's constitution.[4] To be sure, the long conflict between American colonies and the British mother country gave rise to rhetoric that highlighted slavery's injustice, and the chaos of war provided opportunities for slaves to intensify their resistance to their condition as human property. But the economic, social, and geographic roots for continued enslavement of New Yorkers of African descent had spread widely during the eighteenth century. Even the flood of revolutionary ideology did not have the force to dislodge slavery after a century and a half of growth and development. Understanding the debate over abolition in New York state requires a consideration not only of the ideas and events of the American Revolution but also a look at the structure and distinguishing characteristics of slavery in various corners of the fractious mid-eighteenth-century English colony.

New York, according to the leading historian of colonial American slavery, had taken significant steps toward becoming a "slave society" by the middle of the eighteenth century. As New Yorkers unsuspectingly lurched into a continental showdown with British authority, black bondage remained a deeply ingrained aspect of the world whites sought to defend from what they deemed to be British infringements on colonial rights. Mid-eighteenth-century New York bore the distinct characteristics of other New World slave societies. Individually and in gangs, blacks labored on docks and farms, worked as artisans, and catered to the personal needs of the rich. Dutch slave owners found their annual Pinkster holiday gatherings punctuated by the rhythms and musical styles of their black slaves. Although most slaves came to New York via the West Indies, by midcentury members of some of the province's most prominent families, including the Schuylers and the Livingstons, had helped to Africanize New York by increasingly importing directly from Africa. Overall, from 1700 to 1774, ships brought an estimated 6,800 to 8,000 blacks to New York, forming the basis for a slave population that comprised approximately 12 percent of the province's total population.[5]

More broadly, the New York City merchant class had attained its luxuries and the province much of its wealth through trade with the sugar colonies of the West Indies. Meanwhile, a host of Hudson River valley farmers worked busily alongside their black slaves to produce the wheat to feed West Indian slavery. From the farm villages of Long Island to the artisan shops of Manhattan, slaveholding was a widespread practice. Slaveholding, it should be noted, hardly provided a source of enduring unity for the province's whites, who were deeply divided by ethnicity, unequal access to land, and political alliance. Nor did planter wealth pile up as high in New York as it did in England's tobacco, rice, and sugar-producing American colonies. Nonetheless, slavery clearly provided a variety of whites, Dutch and English, quasi-feudal lords and ordinary farmers, with a means to generate wealth and to spend it.[6]

On the rare occasion when whites in colonial New York confronted the efficacy of slavery, the questions had to do with the dangers the presence of slaves posed, not the injustice of the institution itself. The prosecution of an alleged 1741 conspiracy by Manhattan's slaves to burn down and take over the city revealed that white New Yorkers yielded nothing to southern colonists when it came to delivering brutal justice to would-be insurrectionists. Thirty blacks were hanged or burned at the stake, while over seventy others were transported out of the province. The insurrection scare and the subsequent trials dramatized the kind of coercive rule that slave owners and government authorities together legally wielded over bondspeople throughout British North America.[7]

I.

During the eighteenth century, New Yorkers practiced the full range of white oppression and black resistance characteristic of slavery elsewhere along the Atlantic seaboard. A 1730 law, building on several prior pieces of legislation, served as the legal foundation for slavery in New York through the 1780s. Slaves enjoyed none of the safeguards, including protection from abusive masters, accorded to bound laborers in laws enacted in the seventeenth century. During the early eighteenth century, authorities strengthened prohibitions against engaging slaves in minor commercial transactions. Other than for the purpose of work, slaves could not gather legally in groups larger than three. Legislators provided a procedure for public whipping and, in case of severe offense, execution. State law also enjoined slaves from carrying all manner of weapons. In the early 1700s, the colony also began to govern manumission, previously a subject left to owners and their servants. Provincial law required masters to post substantial bonded sums to cover the potential costs to towns should a freed person require public assistance. Even then, manumission offered limited freedom. The colony viewed free blacks as dangerous consorts for enslaved blacks, who might be punished for even acts of minor friendship.[8]

Like those in other English colonies, New York's political leaders legislated distinctions between African American slavery and more general categories of unfree labor. While not clearly articulating a notion of "race," starting in the late seventeenth century, New York law distinguished servitude according to continental origin, skin color, and familial descent. Laws defined indentured servitude as an arrangement voluntarily entered under registered terms, thus imposing a time limit on the tenure of service by whites. In 1679, authorities outlawed the enslavement of Indians born in New York. Although Indians from outside the colony might be made slaves, the definition of life service became more closely identified with men and women of African origin.[9]

The legal resemblance to the Virginia Tidewater and the Carolina low country notwithstanding, New York never crossed the threshold from *society with slaves* to *slave society,* especially if the latter term is defined as a society in which the structure of political, economic, and social power derives its fundamental characteristics from the existence of slavery.[10] Yet a brief survey of the province during the middle two quarters of the eighteenth century reveals that slavery enjoyed a robust presence in the colony and that many white New Yorkers had a stake in an institution that identified the bodies of certain people with inherited life servitude.

II.

The geography of African bondage in colonial New York produced variations on a single theme: widespread slaveholding as a means of supplementing household labor and helping to make up for demographic shortfalls in a colony that failed to attract sufficient numbers of free, white laborers. In each of colonial New York's three regions—Long Island, New York City, and the Hudson River valley—slaves and slaveholders molded a unique provincial society in which race-based power intersected with ethnic diversity as well as hierarchies of inherited wealth, prestige, and influence.

Slavery on Long Island provided a flexible labor system requiring African Americans to contribute to agriculture, craft, and maritime activities. Apportioned as Suffolk County on its eastern two-thirds, and Queens and Kings Counties on the western edge adjacent to Manhattan, Long Island contained substantial numbers of English settlers even before England seized control of the province. New England migrants brought with them their Puritan community-based institutions and values, including an acceptance, however qualified, of black slavery. The town of East Hampton in the late seventeenth and early eighteenth centuries was a "triracial society," employing native Indians in various aspects of the burgeoning whaling industry, while acquiring a small number of blacks for domestic service. Exhibiting the diverse uses of slaves on Long Island, Henry Lloyd, son of a wealthy landowner from Queens, chided his father in 1759 for not purchasing a black man recommended to him. The slave "was not only usd to a farm but might have done all your Smith work & if you had a demand for Square Timber," he would have cut that, too. Without a cash crop like rice or tobacco, masters on Long Island did not trade or work their slaves with the urgent aggressiveness of other American slave societies. Nonetheless, blacks, living at close quarters with whites, provided a labor pool from which white Long Islanders drew throughout the eighteenth century.[11]

Slaves represented a large portion of Long Island's population during the colonial period. Through the middle decades of the eighteenth century, slaves comprised over 10 percent of Suffolk County, hovering between 1,000 and 1,500 in number. Queens County, its European inhabitants including Dutch and English of multiple faiths, maintained an even larger slave population. During the decades preceding the Revolutionary War, the slave presence climbed above 20 percent, or about two thousand persons. Moving east, Kings County, with a smaller total population than its Long Island neighbors, contained an even larger proportion of slaves, over 30 percent, giving it the highest concentration of slaves amongst New York counties. The population of Staten Island's Richmond County was approximately 20 percent slave for much of the second half of the eighteenth century.[12]

A bustling transatlantic port, New York City provided a more open and volatile atmosphere for slavery than Long Island. The slave population in the city climbed to over two thousand by the mid-1740s, and surpassed three thousand by 1771. The proportion of blacks on Manhattan crested at 20 percent of all inhabitants during the 1740s, the decade of the alleged slave conspiracy. The proportion of slaves subsequently declined to approximately 14 percent by 1771. Women made up a larger proportion of the adult slave population than men, particularly after midcentury, reflecting the demand for female domestics. Black men helped fulfill a dynamic seaport economy's demand for unskilled labor, although they also became skilled artisans or participated in the retail sector.[13]

Relatively urban, New York City provided unique opportunities for blacks to associate. African Americans participated actively in the petty commerce of the city, and markets provided a gathering place in which to socialize.

Certain taverns that served black slaves also provided opportunities for community bonding. These conditions contributed to what white authorities perceived as black unruliness. Despite attempts to limit black gatherings, nighttime movements, and commerce, all these activities continued to characterize city life.[14]

The practical limitations on strict white governance did not erase the hardships of slavery. Manumission, let alone upward mobility, was rare. Not only did individual masters exercise great latitude over punishment, but the law also applied corporal penalties more broadly than on white malefactors. The city provided unusual opportunities for physical movement but not permanent familial and communal sites similar to the slave quarters of the plantation south.[15] As one careful student of the slave family in New York has concluded, "family life involved an ever-changing network of long-distance relationships" due to the small numbers of slaves owned by individual whites and disruptions such as sale or a master's death.[16]

The counties arrayed along the Hudson River north of Manhattan represented a third, highly varied, regional setting. The parceling out of portions of the region into quasi-feudal estates conferred great power on a small number of families. In such places, tenant farmers worked plots owned by landlords. During the Dutch and English periods, the Hudson River valley constituted a frontier, bordering on French-allied Indian territory. These factors lessened the appeal to potential settlers. The importation of enslaved blacks, via New York City, from the West Indies and, increasingly, from Africa, augmented the valley's labor force. In addition to farm work in this grain region, African colonials contributed their labor to milling, iron manufacture, and river commerce. As on Long Island, Hudson Valley masters preferred black males over females to fulfill these needs. Despite the large size of a few individual slaveholdings, African Americans did not form a plantation labor force. Still, if any of New York's regions bears comparison to the southern colonies in terms of slavery, it is the Hudson River valley, with its coerced labor, wealthy landed elite, and staple agricultural production.[17]

The region's five counties illustrate the extent of slavery's spread in the colony. Albany County had the largest slave population in the Hudson River valley and, after midcentury, the largest slave population in the entire province. By the early 1770s almost four thousand African Americans inhabited this northerly jurisdiction. Yet slaves as a percentage of Albany County's population fell from 15 percent in 1756 to 9 percent in 1771 as white immigration to the region boomed. At midcentury, slaves made up as much as a fifth of Ulster County's population, where slavery was widespread among yeoman households.[18] The slave population of Westchester County, north of New York City, increased to over 15 percent by 1771. In sum, the European settlers of the Hudson River valley knew racial bondage well and took advantage of its perceived benefits. As the province had grown during the eighteenth century, so too had African slavery.

III.

The precise dynamic of the master-slave relationship may have varied from region to region—indeed, household to household—but bondage throughout the colony generated similar antagonisms and scars. The patterns of slave resistance established during the colonial period persisted in the independence era, contributing to the emerging movement for abolition. Indeed, the discourse regarding slavery, which New Yorkers would find unavoidable after the war, was grounded in decades of social experience.

The particular characteristics of slavery in New York help to illuminate the cruel and all-too-human dilemmas experienced throughout the Atlantic slave system. The urban setting of New York City, the small average size of individual slaveholdings throughout the colony, and New York's relative distance from the main centers of American slavery placed masters and slaves in intimate conflict.[19] No matter how well disposed an individual master might feel toward his or her slaves, slavery's harsh inequity revealed itself. Henry Lloyd II urged his nephew in Queens to care well for elderly slaves and not to overwork them, promising to reimburse his nephew for his costs. Yet he also urged that one male slave be sold "for the most he will fetch if he continues sullen." [20]

For slaves, the threat of sale southward may have represented a horror sufficient to keep them under control. The Scottish writer Anne Grant shared youthful memories from Albany of slaves shipped to Jamaica for persistently bad behavior. Grant commented, "the culprit was carefully watched on his way to New York, lest he should evade the sentence by self-destruction." Two African-born matriarchs serving in the Schuyler household spared their masters the need to discipline young slaves by "inflict[ing]" their own reproofs, "with a view to prevent the dreaded sentence of expulsion." Expressing a self-serving ambivalence, Henry Lloyd reflected on his decision to sell a slave woman and her family locally for less than he could have had he "sent [her] to Carolina against her will, though by what I can learn of the treatment Negroes meet with at the plantation she was design'd for is Such as that Some of those I have Sent prefer their Scituation to that they have left." [21]

Despite, or perhaps because of, the precarious nature of their situation, slaves in New York challenged slavery with individual and collective acts of resistance. Throughout the eighteenth century, slaves, generally young men, ran away from their masters. Some followed family members in the wake of sales, others pursued a more permanent freedom strategy by fleeing to Indian tribes or to the French. New York City provided another popular destination, where the relative anonymity might provide protection. In addition, the city, as a major Atlantic port, offered the possibility of maritime employment, which might remove a runaway even farther from his master.

Running away represented an assertion of freedom far in advance of organized antislavery efforts. The increased likelihood of achieving that freedom and the cost that running away inflicted on those New York farmers whose few slaves constituted a major material asset made it an effective means of challenging the institution.[22] Resistance by runaways, most typically between the age of sixteen and twenty-five, was inscribed hundreds of times in the public newspapers that registered their disappearance. Summer, when the work regimen was hardest, was the most common date of departure. Runaways brought varying degrees of knowledge and experience about life in New York to the quest for freedom. A few, like Philip Livingston's unnamed "Negro Man, lately imported from Africa," advertised in November 1752, knew neither Dutch nor English and may have lacked a clear plan. Others, such as the mulatto Tom, who departed from Poughkeepsie in 1755, could read, write, and play the fiddle, as well as forge a pass. Some runaways may have had extensive contact with the world beyond their masters' homes: Jacobus from Ulster County had worked as a sailor and undoubtedly anticipated that more such work was available.[23]

Slaves also took emphatic collective measures against slavery. The 1712 Manhattan rebellion was the first major slave revolt on the Anglo-American mainland. Under the leadership of slaves from Africa, a group of twenty-four put a building to flames. They used previously stashed weapons to kill and wound several whites who came to extinguish the fire. Their presumed goal of stoking a broader uprising failed, as armed whites arrived to drive the provocateurs into retreat. Authorities imprisoned large numbers of blacks, not all of whom had participated in the conspiracy. Eighteen people were executed by such means as live burning, starvation in chains, breaking on the wheel, and hanging.[24]

The precarious nature of mid-eighteenth-century race relations was demonstrated openly in 1741. White officials in New York City uncovered an alleged conspiracy that laid open the physical and social insecurity permeating this English colony. The proof for the plot rested on evidence of an organized burglary ring and a series of arsons. Authorities, who encouraged certain black and white informants to provide key testimony, failed to secure confessions from many of the accused conspirators and extracted admissions of guilt from others under great duress. The accused conspirators received group rather than individual trials and lacked legal counsel. Nonetheless, the investigation did confirm the extensive secretive networks among the city's blacks. Surreptitious meetings allowed blacks not only to socialize but also to engage in small crimes, and enabled some to assert their leadership skills and to forge alliances with disgruntled or marginal whites, such as the tavern keeper John Hughson.

At the core of the 1741 episode was a small group of slaves, apparently led by Caesar Varick, Prince Auboyneau, Quaco Roosevelt, and Cuffee Philipse. They had bold plans to use arson as a means of expanding their operations, fencing stolen goods while enjoying the satisfaction of disrupting white authority. The subsequent trials exposed through the application of the broad definition of conspiracy contained within the colony's slavery laws that a much wider circle of slaves had expressed hostility toward white New Yorkers. As some slaves planned to extend their fencing activities, other slaves spoke to one another about their hopes for launching widespread assaults on white Manhattan.

The prosecution and punishment of alleged black plotters was driven by white officials' desire to repress the spirit of resistance among the city's black population, whether or not blacks acted upon their hostility toward white authority. Memories of 1712 and concerns that the Spanish, with whom England was at war, might attack New York City, heightened the hopes of some blacks and haunted white jurists. In a city that, despite English rule, had an ethnically disparate population and a discordant political history, African American slaves made an inviting target upon which to project tensions in times of trouble.[25]

While the 1741 episode was singular in terms of the response it generated, white fears of black conspiracy resurfaced. Fear of alliance between French Acadian refugees and black slaves arose in eastern Long Island. In 1761 rumors of a slave plot circulated in Schenectady. Clearly, some white New Yorkers worried that a disgruntled internal labor force multiplied the dangers to a colony beset by war and rivalry with European and Indian neighbors.[26]

Regardless of the efficacy of the conspiracies that haunted white masters from time to time, African American New Yorkers clearly collaborated on projects of cultural resistance and innovation. Organized attempts by England's Society for the Propagation of the Gospel in Foreign Parts to Christianize slaves had little success. Through much of the eighteenth century, and beyond, black New Yorkers preferred their own syncretic blend of African and Christian religious expression and the adaptation of European customs to their own purposes. The celebration of Pinkster offers the most dramatic example of the alteration of a European religious custom for the purposes of African American cultural expression. What had been a Dutch celebration of the Pentecost became an African American celebration by the late eighteenth century. African-inflected dance and the selection of a presiding festival "king" attracted black participants and white spectators from many miles around to open-air gatherings.[27] Less formal—and less open—gatherings of black New Yorkers at night and on Sundays enabled African Americans to maintain and elaborate on distinctive forms of sociability, music, clothing, dance, and even gesture. The adaptation of African funereal customs and constitution of West African–style secret societies were important conduits for the maintenance of old-world identities across space and time. The high number of runaway adds singling out the musical talents of fugitives suggests that black New Yorkers took pleasure in developing their own musical styles. Similarly, colorful and, to white observers, discordant combinations in black people's clothing suggested the development of distinct African American visual sensibilities.[28]

As slavery spread throughout provincial New York, whites and blacks adapted African bondage to the diverse economic and social circumstances of the colony that ranged northward up the Hudson River and along the three eastern coastal islands. Throughout the colonial period, African Americans seized opportunities to resist the conditions of their enslavement and to define cultural space for themselves in ways that evoked cultural memories of Africa and fit New World circumstances. Meanwhile, masters sought to mold black labor to the needs of the province's port city and its agricultural hinterlands. In small, private ways, such as the threat of sale out of the colony, and in openly violent public acts, such as the suppression of slave conspiracies, whites enforced the law of slavery and its underlying spirit of coercive mastery.

Collectively and individually, whites of great and modest means assumed their right to the profits of slavery and the social authority that went with it. The conditions surrounding the conspiracy trials of 1741 raised the concerns of a few prominent whites about the safety of maintaining the institution. But slavery, the slave trade, and the direct and indirect profits that derived from it had become a normative part of life in the province, as in the rest of the Atlantic during the colonial period. It was sanctioned by law and across generations as a means of extracting labor in a world that was cruel, violent, contentious, and uncertain.[29] For New Yorkers, black and white, the pathos of slavery was largely the pathos of everyday life. The burden of that pathos was, of course, borne unequally. But, for the most part, like colonial status itself, the institution was not subjected to a sustained, public critique. The white colonists' deeply vested interest in slavery, however, would be tested—and opportunities for black resistance dramatically multiplied—with the coming of an imperial crisis of unforeseen dimensions.

2

Unfinished Revolutions

The Revolutionary War changed everything and nothing for the institution of slavery in New York. The strained, paradoxical equilibrium was captured, perhaps unintentionally, in the essays of Hector St. John de Crèvecoeur. Writing as the emblematic "American Farmer," the French immigrant to Orange County imagined a "new man" emerging in America. This American archetype would be European in blood lines, always ambitious, and often prosperous. Unlike the English, who "have no trees to cut down, no fences to make, no negroes to buy and to clothe," white American farmers proudly worked, "careful and anxious to get as much as they can" for themselves.[1]

In terms that might describe New York or Virginia, New Jersey or Georgia, a bountiful prosperity characterized the life of the fortunate American farmer. Crèvecoeur's narrator described his own felicitous situation: "Every year I kill from 1500 to 2000 weight of pork, 1200 of beef . . . of fowls my wife has always a great stock: what can I wish more? My negroes are tolerably faithful and healthy." For this New Yorker, writing more generally as an American, black slaves were emblematic of their master's and their nation's good fortune. Crèvecoeur painted a portrait in which citizenship and slavery, self-possessive ambition and the possession of others, all helped to define a world of promise and possibility.[2]

The timing and circumstances of Crèvecoeur's publication partook of a reality far more jarring than these passages suggest. In 1778, the transplanted Frenchman departed his beloved Pine Hill estate in war-torn Orange County. Perhaps because of his loyalist sympathies, he chose this moment to seek passage to France, where he hoped to renew ties to his relatives. After passing several difficult months in British-occupied Manhattan, the "American Farmer" made his way to Europe. The prosperity and citizenship of which he optimistically wrote was a thing of the past and perhaps the future, but not the present, when his essays were first published in London in 1782.[3] Financially strapped masters struggled to feed and clothe the blacks as well as the whites in their households; moreover, the thousands of blacks who escaped to freedom or fought for the British proved to be not even "tolerably faithful." Still, Crèvecoeur's description resonated well enough. At the end of the Revolutionary War, slavery remained ingrained in the state's economic and social identity, just as it remained a fundamental part of the new nation's identity. Descriptions of America's freedoms clashed with the reality of slavery and the implicit color-coding of national identity.[4]

The fight to create a new political order while preserving many of the old privileges had been a tempestuous affair with, as Crèvecoeur well knew, many casualties. The tremors that brought revolution to North America's eastern seaboard colonies also stimulated new thinking about slavery in the Atlantic world. The tidal wave of armed conflict ultimately swept the British from thirteen colonies; while individual slaves sailed off from New York when the conflict fully ebbed, slavery's foundation remained in place. Yet because the Revolution fundamentally altered the political, economic, cultural, and even moral climate of New York, the seeds of an enduring antislavery discourse were now embedded in that foundation—with unsettling long-term consequences.

I.

Even as the Atlantic slave trade blended into the stream of colonial life from Albany, New York, to Savannah, Georgia, other transatlantic currents began subtly to erode the acceptance of slavery. The effects of the antislavery undertow were barely detectable for most of the prerevolutionary period. Nonetheless, Anglo-American Quakers and major British intellectual figures raised questions about New World slavery and other institutions embraced by European imperial powers. The spread of potentially subversive ideas helped set the stage for events that would disrupt political life and challenge slavery in New York and throughout mainland North America.[5] Specifically, the emerging commitment of Quakers to abolition, the influence of English and Scottish Enlightenment critiques, and the egalitarian impulses of the Great Awakening all had subtle yet profound effects on New York slavery.

Prior to 1750 in America, most overt questioning of racial slavery emerged from within Quaker circles. The Society of Friends defined itself as a discrete community striving for moral purity through open-ended self-questioning, a disposition that made Quakers less likely than other groups to accept existing social arrangements. Moreover, the sect's pacifism encouraged a critique of slavery, given that institution's philosophical and sometimes actual origin in the taking of captives in warfare and the violently coercive nature of slavery itself.[6]

As early as 1693, New York Quakers publicly registered their concerns, as one despised group speaking out on behalf of another.[7] Contributing to the province's-oft-remarked-upon religious diversity, Quakers were politically marginalized in colonial New York. Authorities used the Quaker prohibition against oath taking to deny Friends the franchise until the 1730s, and throughout the colonial period they were barred from major public offices and from testifying in court. Like those in the Quaker colony of Pennsylvania and in New England, some New York Friends in the early eighteenth century doubted whether they should continue to own slaves. The New York Meeting, however, did not reach consensus on the matter. Thus, Quakers in New York, like their brethren in neighboring colonies, continued to own, buy, and sell slaves.[8]

Pennsylvania Friends led the way among American Quakers in denouncing and renouncing slavery. During the 1750s, Quaker political authority collapsed in Pennsylvania when the group's pacifism clashed with the exigencies of the Seven Years' War. Deprived of political power, the society emphasized its moral authority and purity. Thus, in 1758 the Philadelphia Yearly Meeting expressed its desire that Friends manumit their slaves and forbade the further purchase or sale of slaves. Itinerant Quaker revivalists linked antislavery Friends on both sides of the Atlantic, helping to sustain the Pennsylvania Quaker commitment to emancipation.[9]

New York Friends resolved to confront slavery just as the American colonial crisis came to a head. Although not as large or influential a community as their brethren in Philadelphia, New York Quakers, including those in the slaveholding regions of New York City and Western Long Island, established an antislavery precedent for their province. Indeed, the response of the New York Yearly Meeting to manumission foreshadowed organized opposition to slavery in the state after the Revolutionary War.

New York's Yearly Meeting deliberated for several years before forging communal consensus on a full-blown rejection of slavery. The 1767 meeting temporized when confronted with a question, originating in Dutchess County, as to whether "it is consistent with a Christian spirit to keep" slaves. Fearing the exacerbation of internal "strife among us," the 1768 yearly meeting nonetheless viewed African Americans as "Rational Creatures and by nature born free." The question then became whether to implement complete emancipation, which might include those "too young & some too old to procure a livelihood." Prompted by their consciences as well as the antislavery path adopted in Philadelphia, the New York Yearly Meeting in 1771 decided that Quakers should not sell their own blacks as slaves. The meeting also selected several members to encourage New York Friends to manumit slaves "suitable for" freedom, while educating and taking adequate care of those deemed unready. In succeeding years, the yearly meetings recorded a strengthened commitment to combat slavery among Friends.[10]

By 1776, the yearly meeting indicated its expectation that New York Quakers would manumit slaves at adulthood. A stern warning went out that "friends can have no Unity" with those who held slaves. In the early 1780s, the meeting took the next step, suggesting that freeing slaves did not fulfill a Quaker's responsibility; education for young blacks and "a Settlement between" freed people and their former masters also became a part of the Friends' program. It had taken approximately two decades for New York's Quakers to develop their own concept of gradual abolition, including concern for the place free blacks might occupy in society.[11]

The process by which New York Quakers came to renounce slavery and to address its consequences for slaves and society overlapped with a broader debate barely underway among New York's revolutionary leaders. The yearly meeting had laid the groundwork for Quaker leadership in the subsequent battle over gradual abolition. Quakers helped to destabilize the institution in New York by their exemplary willingness to emancipate their own slaves, as well as their emerging desire to join with other New Yorkers to demand that the new state's government act to make the Quaker commitment to abolition the law of the land.[12]

II.

Quakers were not the only white North American colonists who began to question the institution of slavery. A vast and still-growing literature has debated the influence of Lockean liberalism, the Scottish Enlightenment, and Christian revivalism on American revolutionaries, as well as Anglo-American opponents of slavery. While the influence of figures like John Locke, David Hume, and George Whitefield on American slavery is indirect and not without ambiguity, black and white Americans began to talk earnestly, sometimes even urgently, about African American freedom in terms that echoed these thinkers. Such talk represented a complex amalgam of ideas and experience.

The ideas of English philosopher John Locke fortified opposition to slavery, along with broader propositions about the fundamental basis of human government and the right to resist political tyranny. Locke's belief in the inherent right of persons to enter society as self-possessing individuals rendered chattel slavery anomalous in the eyes of many of his disciples. Locke also offered an educational psychology suggesting that the differences among men stemmed from environmental not inborn causes. While Locke did not extend the implication of his ideas to Africans being enslaved during his time—indeed he managed to fashion a problematic accommodation of slavery—many American patriots recognized that they could not easily mount a philosophical defense of slavery, at least not on the same grounds that they were advancing arguments for their own revolt against unjust authority.[13]

Scottish thinkers David Hume and Adam Smith helped American nationalists to conceptualize what types of institutions belonged in a free and prosperous society built on a Lockean foundation of rights.[14] Hume voiced a belief, later made famous by Thomas Jefferson, that slavery had a negative effect on slaveholders, particularly children, who "are only qualified to be, themselves, slaves and tyrants; and in every future intercourse, either with their inferiors or superiors, are apt to forget the natural equality of mankind." At the same time, Hume also expressed racially prejudicial attitudes about the abilities of Africans which would lend strength to a scientifically expressed racism in the postwar period.[15]

Hume and Smith also emphasized slavery's depressive effect on the economic development of nations, a sentiment which subsequent New Yorkers would echo. Individual and national industry only progressed if workers received compensation commensurate with their efforts. Slaves, as Smith elaborated, lacked reasons to work harder, more efficiently, or more inventively. Masters, moreover, paid for the care and discipline that free people would have to manage for themselves. Free persons, moreover, handled these expenses more efficiently.[16] According to Hume, slavery made the classical world more brutish than the modern world, and less populous, less wealthy, and less happy. Such conceptualizations helped to sharpen Lockean notions of rights and environment by describing them in primarily economic terms.[17]

Assaults on the logic of slavery were hardly confined to professorial essays. Popular transatlantic religious energies reached far beyond the international Quaker network, helping to prepare the ground for attacks on slavery in the decades prior to the American Revolution. The revivals of the Great Awakening not only challenged the localized monopolies of various established colonial churches but also made the first extensive Christian inroads into the African American community at large. Itinerant preachers, often inspired by the American tours of English revivalist George Whitefield, brought their message to the people out-of-doors, rejected traditional religious classifications and hierarchies, and prized religious feeling over doctrine and study. Revivals attracted significant numbers of black converts and implicitly leveled the spiritual playing field for blacks and whites, undermining notions that individuals were destined to occupy a lowly station in life, temporally as well as spiritually.[18]

The egalitarian Christianity of the Great Awakening, moreover, foreshadowed the political challenge to hierarchy and established authority which would fuel the imperial conflict. Fused with the secular urgency of the American quest for independence, the Great Awakening's emphasis on casting aside sin, personal choice, and even anticipation of millennial transformation, may have encouraged Revolutionary-era Americans to reflect more intensively on the evils of slavery and the opportunity to modify or even dispense with the practice.[19]

III.

Ideas, of course, are as likely to produce hypocrites and temporizers as they are liberators, as two New Yorkers with virtually the same name make clear. The black itinerant preacher John Jea, who grew up a slave on a Dutch-owned farm in New York during the 1770s and 1780s, poignantly recalled "a day of fasting, prayer, and thanksgiving . . . commanded by General Washington, to pray to Almighty God to withdraw his anger from us. . . ." As Jea bitterly remarked, the slaves "were obliged to fast, but were not exempted from work. . . ."[20] John Jay, a leading New York patriot and a slaveholder, drew on the metaphorical power of bondage in his 1774 "Address to the People of Great Britain," which he wrote on behalf of the Continental Congress, referring to Britain's "forging chains for her friends and children" and acting as an "advocate for slavery and oppression." Jay invoked the metaphor in his personal correspondence as well. Trying to persuade an acquaintance not to side with loyalists, he asked her how she would feel "being the Mother of Slaves" should the British win: "For who are Slaves but those, who in all Cases without Exception are bound to obey the uncontroulable Mandates of a Man. . . . Slaves Madam! can have no Property—they toil not for themselves. . . ."[21]

As one scholar of the Revolutionary-era press has argued, the metaphor of political enslavement had the potential to remind white American readers that Britain's great offense was treating them as lowly Negroes, hence implicitly accentuating a racialized discourse.[22] Even so, neither whites nor blacks were content to leave the metaphor at that. By the time the white John Jay expressed his sentiments, he and others already had made the connection between the rhetorical uses of slavery and the evils of real human bondage. Indeed, as early as 1764, Massachusetts lawyer and patriot firebrand James Otis had written, "the Colonists are by the law of nature free born, as indeed all men are, white or black." Ten years later, Philadelphian Richard Wells rejected any attempt by his countrymen to "reconcile the exercise of SLAVERY with our *professions of freedom.*"[23]

Lest whites try to reconcile the irreconcilable, African Americans seized upon revolutionary rhetoric to make their own public appeals for freedom. In Boston, seedbed of the Revolution, slaves in the 1770s repeatedly petitioned the governor and provincial legislature, explaining, "We expect great things from men who have made such a noble stand against the designs of their fellow men to enslave them." In poetry and prose, blacks claimed their natural rights in the same language that whites claimed theirs. Indeed, any deprivations experienced by colonists were more than matched by those of slaves. One petitioner proclaimed, "We have no Property! We have no Wives! No children! We have no City! No Country!" Phillis Wheatley, the famous slave poet of Boston, chided white patriots for their hypocrisy:

> how, presumptuous shall we hope to find
> Divine acceptance with th' Almighty mind—
> While yet (O deed ungenerous!) they disgrace
> And hold in bondage Afric's blameless race![24]

Whether voiced as flattery or reprimand, black petitioners made clear that the step from white grievances to their own was quite short.

Such sentiments by African Americans were not confined to New England. Slave poet Jupiter Hammon of Long Island, New York, wrote from a position of spiritual equality in his Revolutionary-era poems, instructing his "Dear Master":

> 'Tis God alone can give us peace;
> It's not the pow'r of man:
> When virtuous pow'r shall increase,
> 'Twill beautify the land.

Hammon's critique gained additional poignancy from his firsthand experience of the displacement and tragedy of war. His patriot master Joseph Lloyd had fled to Connecticut to avoid the British occupation of Long Island, with Hammon in tow. In 1780, distraught over news of an apparent patriot defeat in the south, Lloyd committed suicide. Thus, Hammon's dialogue can be read as a rebuke of the misplaced hopes of war as well as an assertion of spiritual equality.[25]

While Hammon's personal concerns were with sanctification in the next world rather than freedom in this world, others offered more temporal interpretations of the conflict's potential. In the South Carolina countryside, a black slave preacher captured the hope raised by the revolutionary crisis and pervasive talk of liberty, telling his listeners, "The old King had reced a Book from our Lord by which he was to Alter the World (meaning to set the Negroes free) but for not doing so, was now gone to Hell & in Punishmt." A new king had arrived who would set the slaves free.[26]

As the drafting of the Declaration of Independence illustrates, the "contagion of liberty," spread widely but not uncontrollably. The clarion call of human equality in Jefferson's self-evident truths would for the next ninety years be taken up by those who sought to abolish slavery. Yet the Continental Congress edited out language denouncing the slave trade as "a cruel war against human nature itself," fomented and sustained by the British. At the same time it strengthened Jefferson's complaint that the king had encouraged American slaves to rebel against their masters—a reference to Lord Dunmore's invitation that Virginia slaves seize their freedom and run to British lines.[27] The preamble's inspiring, high-minded principles notwithstanding, the cause of independence and the cause of freedom were not the same thing.

New York state's 1777 constitution, deliberated upon in the Hudson Valley town of Kingston while the British occupied New York City and hovered menacingly to the north and west, recapitulated the Continental Congress's high principles and its deference to slaveholding interests. Indeed, the new state's charter literally reproduced the Declaration of Independence as part of its own lengthy preamble.[28] At the New York convention, Gouverneur Morris attempted to convince his fellow delegates to endorse gradual abolition as a goal for the new state government.

As an advocate for gradual abolition, Morris was a unique figure, emblematic of the nascent campaign against slavery in New York. Morris's father, Lewis, had been a wealthy landowner and possessor of perhaps more slaves than any man in the state, owning forty-six in 1762. Upon his death, the elder Morris left one slave to Gouverneur, with provisions for a second to accrue to him upon his mother's death. Reflecting his aristocratic legacy, the younger Morris was among the most conservative members of the revolutionary leadership, later advocating that U.S. senators serve for life. Even in the 1770s, Morris was less impressed than many of his peers with egalitarian revolutionary rhetoric. Yet slavery to him symbolized the most egregious aspects of aristocracy, which granted privileges irrespective of talent. His views may have been shaped by the bitterness among his siblings over the complicated terms of his father's will.[29]

On April 17, just three days before the new constitution was accepted by the provincial congress, Morris offered a provision proclaiming that "a regard to the rights of human nature and the principles of our holy religion, loudly call upon us to dispense the blessings of freedom to all mankind" but acknowledging that "at present" freeing New York's slaves would be "productive of great dangers." The solution, according to Morris's proposed language, was to urge "future Legislatures of the State . . . to take the most effectual measures consistent with the public safety, and the private property of individuals, for abolishing domestic slavery . . . so that in future ages, every human being who breathes the air of this State, shall enjoy the privileges of a freeman." Like some members of New York's slaveholding elite after the war, Morris may have imagined abolition as a gift to his state over time, a token not of radical egalitarianism but rather of sober moral stewardship.

Just as Jefferson's more vociferous language on the slave trade was excised from the Declaration of Independence, even a moderate antislavery gesture was not destined to find its way into the New York constitution in 1777. Over the next two days, after stripping the abolition clause of its expansive language regarding a religious mandate for universal freedom, the gathering endorsed by wide margins the principle of a future gradual abolition. Yet, for reasons that the convention record leaves unclear, the delegates did not have the stomach to include this antislavery language in the final document. Likely, this choice reflected a concern, similar to Morris's, that the current conditions in New York were already dramatically unsettled without adding abolitionism to the mix. Indeed, the new constitution affirmed all laws passed by the legislature prior to the outbreak of hostilities in 1775, which included, implicitly, the law of slavery. Thus, to the regret of Morris and his friend John Jay, there would be no gradual abolition language incorporated into the state constitution of New York, no explicit linkage of white and black freedom.[30]

While New York failed to initiate gradual abolition through its constitution, two neighbors with far fewer slaves, Vermont and Pennsylvania, accomplished just that in the midst of the war. In 1777, the same year that New York state declined to act against slavery, its three northeastern counties, which comprised the disputed Vermont territory, banned slavery in its new constitution. No male Vermonter would be bound "as a servant, slave or apprentice" after twenty-one, no female after eighteen. Unlike states supporting gradual abolition schemes, Vermont did not confine emancipation only to the offspring of current slaves. Its abolition proviso was consistent with the radical alternative that Vermont offered to neighboring New York. Besides defying New York's attempts to prevent separation, Vermont also enfranchised all adult male citizens, whereas New York merely revised property-holding requirements established during the colonial era. Vermont would continue to offer a radical alternative to New York during the 1780s, granting freedom and citizenship to any slaves brought into its territory.[31]

In contrast to Vermont's more immediate constitutional approach, Pennsylvania passed a gradual emancipation statute in 1780. The law granted freedom to children born of slave mothers after March 1, 1780, but obligated those children until age twenty-eight to serve their masters. Unlike breakaway Vermont, where slavery had barely existed before 1777, African American bondage in Pennsylvania had substantial roots. By 1780, there were almost seven thousand slaves in Pennsylvania. The highest concentration was in Philadelphia, where slaves comprised approximately 8 percent of the total population during the third quarter of the eighteenth century.

Pennsylvania's abolition law would prove to be a significant precedent, inviting comparisons with New York at the time and in retrospect. Private decisions about manumission, especially by Quakers, formed the leading, albeit uneven, edge of antislavery activity in Friends-founded Pennsylvania. Ideological support spread beyond the Quaker community, with leading revolutionary propagandists Tom Paine and Benjamin Rush authoring antislavery pamphlets in the 1770s. By then, the slave population in Pennsylvania was in precipitous decline. The dwindling slave trade failed to compensate for high slave death rates, and slaves increasingly ran away, with the war providing more opportunities.

As practicing Quakers had withdrawn from office holding during the colonial era, their objections to slavery were ultimately enacted by non-Quakers. An initial 1778 bill envisioned a significantly shorter period of mandatory service for the technically free children of slave mothers. The final bill passed Pennsylvania's unicameral legislature by more than a two-to-one margin, mixing high-minded universalist language with an extremely gradual approach to emancipation. More committed abolitionists, including Quakers, understood that in the long run securing and enforcing even the modest terms of this precedent-setting law would require significant effort. In time, these antislavery Pennsylvanians would attempt to extend their influence to their more reluctant neighbors in New York.[32]

In the shorter run, the practical implications of Pennsylvania and Vermont's actions against slavery, as well as New York's inaction—were very much contingent on battlefield events. The Revolution itself may have had to occur first in the hearts and minds of men, but to have any meaning for the political confederation or for slavery, the actions of ordinary people—slaves, soldiers, and generals—would be crucial. As war swept across the new nation, comprised almost entirely of states still committed at one level or another to slavery, African Americans and whites would continue to calculate what, if any, basis there would be for black freedom.

IV.

Like white revolutionaries, slaves did not confine the expression of their grievances to mere petitions. Indeed, New York slaves stamped on the independence movement their own interpretation of highly fluid events, adapting long-standing methods of resistance to the military conflict dividing colonial masters.[33] While many white patriots temporized, African Americans expressed their hostility to bondage in unmistakable terms. British officials in turn exploited for their own purposes the real and potential breaches between masters and slaves; for example, freeborn black Long Islander Benjamin Whitecuff was hanged by patriots for spying on behalf of the Crown.[34]

Even before the outbreak of war, let alone the declaration of American independence, unsettled revolutionary circumstances enlivened the possibility of organized, violent reprisals of black slaves against their white masters. In 1775, word arrived in New York City of menacing plots in slave-rich Ulster and Queens Counties. In March, an Ulster County slaveholder reported a conversation between two African Americans regarding plans to set fire to several houses and then attack the fleeing victims. Authorities jailed several blacks in this scheme designed for "the Recovery of their Freedom." Less detailed news also arrived from Queens about a "Conspiracy . . . to destroy the white People," with "most of the Slaves for many Miles" allegedly involved. Later in 1775 the town of Newburgh in Orange County passed additional ordinances regulating the movements of African Americans, as did the city of Albany in 1776.[35]

Wartime encouraged certain types of slave resistance and created hardships for masters which underscored the tenuousness of master-slave attachments. Overall, opportunities for running away in New York and New Jersey increased during the war. In 1777, for example, slaves on the Van Cortlandt manor in Westchester County plotted to escape when British forces returned to the area. Meanwhile, the absence of male heads of households may have undermined authority on some white farms; Mary Clinton reported to her absent husband, Gen. James Clinton, that she had to call on neighbors in order to compel her slave to harvest the hay in September 1778. When slaves did remain faithful to their Whig owners, economic hardship might lead to their sale, hiring out, or, for the elderly, manumission to reduce household expenses. Frederick Jay of Westchester County reported to his brother John that the family struggled to maintain their slaves in the midst of the hardships imposed by the war, even after reducing their household through a combination of manumission, renting out, and sales.[36]

The British occupation of New York City and its environs made it an even more attractive destination for runaways than it had been before the war. The city drew slaves because of the possibility that the British might free them there and because British lines created a barrier to pursuit by patriot masters. Even so, New York's *Royal Gazette* continued to advertise rewards for runaways, such as the one for Savinah, who, along with a nineteen-month-old son, was purported to be "lurking about this City."[37]

Militarized conditions, especially when African Americans fought on behalf of the British, provided the most dramatic instances of ideologically charged slave resistance. Black soldiers on the loyalist side hoped not only to secure their freedom but also to strike a blow against their former masters. British commander-in-chief Sir Henry Clinton confirmed this belief by offering "full security" to all African Americans entering British lines. Black efforts on behalf of the British increased pressure to deliver freedom to fleeing slaves. The British employed black irregulars in the "Neutral Zone" surrounding New York City to carry on guerilla warfare. Incursions into nearby Monmouth County, New Jersey, at times targeting old masters and neighborhoods, demonstrated black loyalists' rejection of their pasts.[38] Whether serving in the British army or not, African Americans protecting British lines seized the opportunity to socialize freely in streets and taverns, to organize balls, and to identify themselves by first and last name. Thus, as one recent historian has noted, "a British proclamation rang out more loudly than the Declaration of Independence" for African Americans in and around New York.[39]

Patriot whites in New York, after hesitating initially and without embracing any broader problack agenda, made their own attempt to enlist black manpower. In 1781, New York's state government tried to fill out two regiments by offering white owners a bounty for volunteering their slaves for service. The law promised that the state would cover the cost of provisioning those slaves during the war and would manumit them at its end. Regardless of Whig efforts, however, serving the British remained more attractive to slaves. Such service, unlike patriot enlistment, did not depend entirely on the consent of individual masters. Most blacks behind Tory lines did not actually carry arms against their former masters, but their labor aided British efforts, as did the work of blacks still enslaved to loyalists.[40]

New York's experience represented one aspect of complications stemming from the presence of slaves in various theaters of the Revolutionary

War. Word of Lord Dunmore's decree offering freedom to Virginia slaves enlisting in the British cause reached slaves in New York and New Jersey, inspiring loyalist sympathies among them. Indeed, throughout America, thousands of blacks sought to achieve independence for themselves by reaching Tory lines and joining the pro-British fight. To counter this developing African American–British alliance, all the new states but South Carolina and Georgia eventually enrolled some blacks in the patriot cause. Among the most prominent proponents of employing black soldiers was New Yorker Alexander Hamilton, who had secured a position as an aide-de-camp to George Washington.[41]

The prospect of peace did little to ease tensions over slavery generated by the war between masters and slaves, or between victorious colonists and vanquished British. When the mother country surrendered the fight at Yorktown, many African Americans pursued a last chance for freedom. They crowded into British-occupied New York City during the negotiation of a final peace settlement. Blacks, most from the South, acted under British assurances for their safety. Americans' fears that they would lose the human property gathering in New York prompted diplomats to secure a preliminary promise that "his Britannic Majesty shall, with all convenient Speed, & without causing any Destruction or carrying away any Negroes, or other Property of the American Inhabitants withdraw all his Armies Garrisons and Fleets" from the new nation's territory. The manner in which the British implemented— or failed to implement—this provision of the peace aroused the lasting anger of New Yorkers, complicating future arguments for gradual abolition.[42]

Liberal British procedures determined black eligibility for evacuation to Nova Scotia, allowing three thousand men, women, and children to seize the opportunity for a new life beyond the grasp of American whites. The British considered as legitimate refugees all blacks who had congregated behind British lines for a year or more. To be sure, many white loyalist refugees retained ownership of their slaves. Indeed, loyalist masters preparing to leave Manhattan for Europe sometimes put their slaves up for sale, prompting their slaves to actually flee New York City rather than be acquired by new masters. The final year of British occupation witnessed spikes in newspaper ads for slave sales and notices concerning runaways.[43] Nonetheless, British commander Guy Carlton made no secret of his intention to assist African Americans in avoiding reenslavement, and authorities gave unprecedented credit to the testimony of blacks claiming their freedom. Americans never accepted the official British determinations that ships leaving New York for Nova Scotia contained no property "belonging to the Citizens of the United

States of America." Moreover, British promises to remunerate aggrieved white slaveholders for their loss foundered for years because of British claims that Americans had violated other aspects of the peace treaty.[44]

By the time the British completed the evacuation of New York in November 1783, they had assisted African Americans from almost every former colony. The largest portion, more than one-seventh of the total, came from New York. For black New Yorkers, as for other American blacks, escaping to Canada represented the crowning collective achievement of more than a century of resistance. As their own former masters believed themselves to have done in the Revolution, the evacuees cast away their chains.[45]

v.

The war-torn 1775–83 period was a paradoxical capstone to the long history of slavery in colonial New York. For the most fortunate slaves, the war conferred freedom. The Revolution also provided an enlarged sense of where resistance could lead for the thousands of blacks enslaved in New York, including Sam, whose Poughkeepsie master Nathan Bailey placed an advertisement in 1784 expressing the concern that his twenty-one-year-old slave would attempt to reach Nova Scotia. Clearly, slaves would not easily forget the insecurity of their masters and their own attempts to exploit that insecurity.[46]

During the war, expediency and opportunism encouraged the British and, sometimes, white patriots to put into action the principle of black freedom which had gained currency during the Revolutionary era. Yet New York and the national government had declined to enact lasting antislavery measures. Moreover, despite wartime disruption, the practice of slavery in New York continued largely unabated.[47]

Some New Yorkers, however, seized on their neighbor's antislavery measures as a reason to push for reform in their own state. In September 1780, John Jay wrote from overseas to his New York associate Egbert Benson that they would do well to imitate Pennsylvania's recently passed gradual abolition law. Commented the future president of the New York Manumission Society, "Till America comes into this measure, her prayers to Heaven for liberty will be impious." In response to a Connecticut court that granted freedom to a slave who had served in the Continental Army, a New York City newspaper suggested that "negroes in similar situations in this state (and there are not a few) may be encouraged to apply in similar manner for that liberty to which they are entitled as a reward for their spirit and courage."[48]

Passionate adversaries of slavery drew dramatic conclusions from the

Revolution. Antislavery pamphleteer and Calvinist minister Samuel Hopkins sought to dispel the notion that God's reward of American independence signaled divine acceptance of slavery. Rather, according to Hopkins, the apparent steps taken toward abolition in over half the states maintained God's allegiance, an allegiance which the legal resumption of the slave trade placed at serious risk. Reflecting on the British conflict in the *New-York Journal,* an anonymous essayist threatened the Lord's wrath on a nation that during wartime enlisted divine aid by banning the slave trade, only to go back on its word once danger seemingly had passed. Reworking Jeremiah 34:8–21, the writer held the whole of "North-America" responsible for this sin.[49] Such protests revealed the galvanizing effects of the American Revolution on the sensibilities of some groups of whites and blacks, but it also laid bare the harsher fact that in New York slavery stubbornly remained in place.

The demographic map of slavery in New York illustrates that the fight for independence—as a war and an ideological movement—did not remove slavery from New York. The British evacuation in 1783 certainly contributed to the absolute drop of approximately one thousand in the state's black population from the 1770s to the 1780s. The decline occurred primarily in Westchester County and New York City, as well as the Long Island counties of Queens and Suffolk, areas subject to British occupation and harassment. By contrast, slave populations in the rest of the state increased by more than 2,500 between 1771 and 1786. New Yorkers still enslaved over eighteen thousand people in 1786. These numbers suggest that the war-era disruptions increased the movement of slaves throughout New York. Some slaves permanently escaped behind British lines, and others were freed because of military service or confiscation from Tories, but perhaps as many or more were sold or relocated to areas of the state remote from freedom. Moreover, the slave population began to climb again in the late 1780s, so that the first U.S. census showed a 1790 New York state slave population of over 21,000, in addition to over 4,500 free blacks. In certain areas, such as southern Orange County, along the New Jersey–New York border and New York City, the slave population rose throughout the 1790s.[50]

After the war new demographic trends seemed to signal support for antislavery measures. The proportion and number of free African Americans rose, most notably in New York City during the 1790s, so that by 1800 more free than enslaved blacks lived there. Wartime disruptions, successful escapes, and at least a few manumissions made black freedom more common than it had been during the colonial period. Although more than 80 percent of blacks in the state remained slaves in 1790, free friends and relatives offered encouragement and, in time, enhanced the cultural resources upon which all blacks might draw. Meanwhile, the rapid growth of the white population led to a drop in the percentage of enslaved New Yorkers. From a prewar proportion of almost 12 percent of the total, slaves comprised approximately 6.3 percent and African Americans as a whole 7.6 percent of New York's population by 1790.[51]

Nonetheless, the fundamental continuity of the New York slave regime prevailed throughout the eighteenth century. The geographical pattern of slaveholding in New York did not radically change, perpetuating intimately experienced personal deprivation, economic exploitation, cultural accommodations, and overt acts of resistance across the varied landscape of early-national New York. The largest number of African Americans inhabited Manhattan, and Albany, Queens, Ulster, and Dutchess Counties. The largest African American presence as a percentage of the population concentrated in and around New York City, especially in Kings, Richmond, and Queens Counties. In these areas, between 20 to 33 percent of white households held slaves. Slavery, as these numbers indicate, would not collapse from economic changes or demographic trends alone. The Revolution itself, moreover, did not alter the master-slave relationship in a positive manner. As of 1783, the legal disabilities of slaves, the social authority of masters, and the threat of sale southward all continued to circumscribe the lives of African American New Yorkers.[52]

VI.

Crèvecoeur, New York slaveholder and erstwhile American, tapped deeply into the emerging American view of itself. In his guise as itinerant agrarian observer, the Frenchman traced the immigrant's trajectory toward citizenship in terms that evoked the metaphor of political slavery that so animated the revolution. Thus, a white newcomer to America could expect to move "from a servant to the rank of a master; from being the slave of some despotic prince, to become a free man, invested with lands, to which every municipal blessing is annexed! . . . he forgets that mechanism of subordination, that servility of disposition which poverty had taught him." Moreover, such new men would seize an active role in shaping public and private life. Crèvecoeur wrote, "As citizens it is easy to imagine, that they will carefully read the newspapers, enter into every political disquisition, freely blame or censure governors and others."[53]

The prolonged revolutionary crisis helped ensure that slavery would be a subject of much disquisition in the ensuing decades. As Jefferson's famously deleted assault on George III for perpetuating the slave trade indicated, it was less clear who would be censured. At the very least, the nation's highest ideals had run ahead of the will, or even the desire, to make major revisions in law and social practice. John Jay worried that slavery marked the nation as "impious." Certainly, as long as most new states declined to administer plans for some sort of abolition, the Revolution remained incomplete. Yet even the most cautious challenges to slavery then underway inevitably forced some examination of the quasi-racial categories that Crèvecoeur attached to his reflections on America's new citizens.

The reconstruction of New York and the United States had only just begun in 1783. Having been won with widespread, although far from unanimous, popular support, independence had transformed the context in which New Yorkers conducted their political lives and constructed their political debates. New York's government now operated free of imperial oversight. As a result, the conditions of early-national politics encouraged a wider public to register their opinions on a host of questions which emerged in the new state and the new nation.

During the 1780s and 1790s, the engaged political public that Crèvecoeur had begun to imagine would join slaveholders, slaves, and Quakers in debates about political values, economic aspirations, and slavery itself in ways that forced the future of African American bondage onto the public agenda. Together with the colonial, social, and legal legacy of slavery, the ideas and events that animated the revolutionary conflict created the fluid context in which future arguments over gradual abolition would take place.

II

IDENTITIES

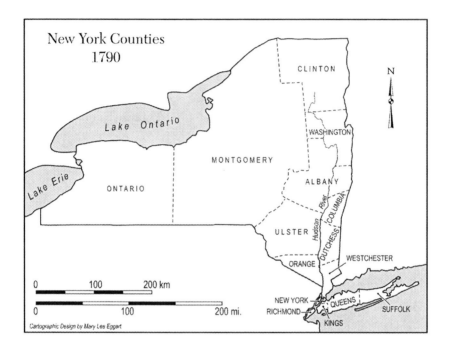

New York Counties 1790

CLINTON

Lake Ontario

Lake Erie

MONTGOMERY

ONTARIO

WASHINGTON

ALBANY

Hudson River

COLUMBIA

ULSTER

DUTCHESS

ORANGE

WESTCHESTER

N

NEW YORK

QUEENS

RICHMOND

SUFFOLK

KINGS

0   100   200 km

0   100   200 mi.

Cartographic Design by Mary Lee Eggart

3

1785

The Road Not Taken

In March 1784, New York City's Common Council passed "A Law Regulating Negro and Mulatto Slaves," which required slaves to carry lanterns at night, banned gaming, required daytime burial of deceased slaves, and prohibited the "disorderly" riding of horses. Violators of all but the daytime burial provision could suffer a public flogging, unless their masters paid a fine. The next month the *New-York Journal* published a letter from Pennsylvania ridiculing the racial distinctions drawn by the regulations. The Pennsylvanian wondered whether "it would not wound the feelings of a parent so severely, to have its child's skull broke by the hoofs of a freeman's horse, as by those of a" slave. The writer marveled that "intelligent citizens, surrounded by the full blaze of liberty . . . [would] dream of such intollerant" practices as those that slavery produced. The correspondent even foresaw that someday there would emerge a standard of justice treating blacks and whites equally.[1]

The city ordinance and the letter from Pennsylvania were indicative of the countervailing pressures weighing on masters and political leaders as the state of New York emerged from the Revolutionary War. The nearly nineteen thousand African Americans remaining in bondage represented a significant amount of property and labor power, a source of wealth but also of potentially ongoing disruption for white New Yorkers. Imposing order upon slaves would require resolve and coercion by whites. Slaves themselves were unlikely to forget the freedom that some African Americans had seized during the conflict or their masters' recent vulnerability.[2]

Meanwhile, challenges mounted to the long-term commitment of white New Yorkers to slavery. Although egalitarian wartime rhetoric had failed to liberate New York's slaves, nearby states' actions to begin dismantling slavery bore the impress of revolutionary logic. In 1784, the legislatures of Rhode Island and Connecticut joined Pennsylvania in instituting gradual emancipation schemes. That same year the Pennsylvania Abolition Society (PAS) reorganized itself; antislavery advocates in New York's neighbor to the south sought to enforce the broadest possible interpretation of their state's abolition law. The letter to the *New-York Journal* portended a brisk cross-border commerce in antislavery principles and plans.

The effort to import other states' gradual emancipation procedures in the years immediately following the final British departure from New York revealed the political weaknesses and strengths of its slave system. If the actions of New York's legislators in 1785 can be taken as an indication of wider public attitudes, then gradual emancipation enjoyed broad but shallow support. A Pennsylvania and southern New England–style gradual abolition law failed in 1785 amid deep-seated concerns about the relationship between race and freedom. Despite the pronounced gradualism of such laws, in the aftermath of the Revolutionary War, these schemes appeared to some to have threateningly egalitarian implications. The political complications of upsetting New York's long-established, racially defined social order in the name of libertarian principles thus proved insurmountable for the time being.

I.

As victorious patriots sought to reassert their control over New York City after the British evacuation, so too did white leaders seek to reassert authority over the city's two thousand slaves. The ambiguity introduced into master-slave relations by wartime resistance and pro-fugitive British policies threatened a social order already frayed by the disruption of war and occupation. Aside from regulating slave behavior, the Common Council passed ordinances encouraging Sabbath observance, monitoring the arrival of "strangers" to the city, fire prevention, and local commerce.[3]

The reimposition of social order was harmful to the 9 percent of city residents who were black.[4] Municipal regulation of slaves had three interrelated goals: to ensure renewed public calm, to limit dangers stemming from slave autonomy, and to hold masters accountable for their slaves' transgressions. The city's ordinance monitoring Sabbath observance explicitly applied to slaves, while additionally limiting slave gatherings to three people on Sundays and enjoining slaves from recreation as well as work. A slave's violation of the general provisions of the law could lead to a brief stay in prison; violation of the slave-specific provisions triggered a public whipping unless the master was willing to pay a fine. The Common Council also governed slave participation in the commercial economy, prohibiting "any negro or other slave" from selling items outside officially sanctioned city markets.[5]

Much like the colonial-era law of slavery, which remained in effect throughout the state, the city's postrevolution laws rested on the presumption that African Americans should be treated as criminal suspects to be carefully monitored. Indeed, the Common Council sought to develop a ward-by-ward accounting of "the Names Ages & Places of Abode of every Negro & Molatto

. . . Distinguishing, if they are Slaves," to whom they belonged, and if free, the basis of their claim to freedom.[6] African Americans in peacetime were not to be allowed to take advantage of the ambiguities in legal status that had provided cover for the British evacuation of so many blacks.

At least some New Yorkers, however, were open to liberating alternatives to the strict enforcement of social discipline. A correspondent to New York City's *Packet,* identified only as "C——," proposed that an intermediate alternative to punitive restrictions on slaves might lead to freedom and even political integration. The author offered a five-point plan for ordering slave life. The proposal called for slaves under the age of twenty-one to be granted freedom but to be held as indentured servants while they acquired training in literacy and numeracy. Slaves over twenty-one were to receive two days off a week in which they could earn money toward the purchase of freedom. "The government" would set a single price for all adult slaves, with the slave and the "public treasury" sharing equally the cost of buying freedom. Former slaves, under this plan, could even gain access to major tools of citizenship "such as serving on a jury and holding public office" after suitably lengthy waiting periods and certification of fitness.[7]

The plan embraced working and civic participation as the cornerstones of freedom in the new republic. The proposal also envisioned government as a gatekeeper, subsidizing slave opportunity and passing judgment on black qualifications for citizenship.[8] Like existing laws, this proposal assumed the need to monitor blacks in some fashion. But in contrast to the city's Sabbath law, which sought to shackle slaves in leisure as they were shackled in labor, the plan anticipated that slaves would take advantage of the possibilities of wage work. Still, the design had a far-fetched quality and was unlikely to appeal to those who viewed slave autonomy as a threat to social peace.

For their part, African American New Yorkers faced more vexing and immediate threats to whatever peace they might already enjoy under current conditions, as well as to their future freedom. Kidnappers could turn free blacks into bondspeople and take them anywhere in the Americas where there was a demand for slave labor. According to a November 1784 *New-York Journal* account, man-stealers "forc[ed]" a group of free blacks "on board a vessel in this harbour, destined either for Charleston, or the Bay of Honduras." Even though city authorities intervened in this instance, local law supported the notion of black subordination, identifying slaves by race and classifying their ordinary actions as subject to punishment.[9] At least with regard to black inhabitants, municipal authorities prioritized order over liberty.

II.

A broad, albeit conservative, vision of future black liberty nonetheless enjoyed considerable support in the immediate aftermath of the war. At the session that opened in January 1785, the state legislature appeared poised to enact gradual abolition, after having given only brief attention to the matter the year before.[10] The initial 1785 proposal received a warm reception in both houses. The bill's core purpose was to grant freedom for "any Negro, Mulatto, Indian, Mustee, or . . . any person of any other description whatsoever, commonly reputed and deemed a slave" born in New York subsequent to the enactment of the bill. These free people, however, were to serve their mothers' masters as if indentured, until the age of twenty-five for males and twenty-two for females.[11] This service requirement was less stringent than Pennsylvania's 1780 law, which extended the indenture for all slaves until age twenty-eight, and Connecticut's 1784 law, which imposed service until age twenty-five, but did not go as far as Rhode Island, where males served until twenty-one and females until eighteen.[12]

The idea of freeing all men and women currently held in slavery, instead of their future offspring, received almost no support from New York's legislators. New York City's maverick young representative Aaron Burr suggested granting freedom to all slaves in the state. This idea did not receive serious backing. Not only was Burr's proposal voted down thirty-three to thirteen, but several of those supporting the motion were actually staunch opponents of abolition who presumably cast their votes in mockery of what they viewed as the wrong-headedness of any form of emancipation.[13]

In contrast to the lack of support for immediatism, many representatives hoped that if New York did approve a gradual abolition bill, that the age of actual freedom would be set to extract almost as many years of labor as Pennsylvania's law called for. By mere two-vote majorities, the assembly staved off motions by proslavery representative Comfort Sands of New York City to raise the effective age of manumission to twenty-eight for men and twenty-five for women.[14]

The legislative journals did not record actual debates stating the particular appeal of gradualism to New York's political representatives, but they were likely animated by the same mix of politically egalitarian and socially conservative ideas expressed in the neighboring states upon whose laws New York's legislature modeled its 1785 bill. The text of Pennsylvania's 1780 Gradual Abolition Act appeared in a New York City newspaper several days before legislators formally began to take up the subject. That law included an expansive preamble, which stated that the "blessings" of liberty fought for in conflict with Britain ought to be shared with the new state's black slaves, with outworn prejudices set aside. The actual terms of Pennsylvania's emancipation law revealed that "extend[ing] a portion of that freedom to others, which hath been extended to us," in practice meant freeing only the unborn after they had served their masters for many years. Connecticut's Levi Hart explained in a 1775 essay that this version of liberation was necessary because slaveholders should not be deprived of their property rights and slaves were allegedly unready for the rigors of free life.[15]

To proslavery legislators, neither the conservative pragmatism of gradual emancipation nor the high-minded ideals offered in support of it had much appeal. As these men introduced the issues of race and citizenship into the legislative debate, support even for the broad principle of abolition wavered. Amendments to the core bill linked emancipation to the political and social order that might emerge to replace slavery. Attempts to curtail the rights of free blacks ultimately proved to be the bill's undoing, exposing in the process the influence of slaveholding interests and the racialized views of Revolutionary-era citizenship. The social order which the Common Council sought to restore to New York City, in other words, appealed to many legislators as much as the model of antislavery reform undertaken by neighboring states.

The bill that the assembly sent to the senate contained proposals exposing race and citizenship to careful scrutiny. The upper house asked the lower house to retract three provisions. The first stated "that no negro, mulatto or mustee whatsoever, shall hold or exercise any office or place of trust, nor shall be admitted a witness or juror in any case civil or criminal against any citizen or white person whatsoever." A court, however, could specifically certify an individual freed under the gradual abolition plan as fit for testimony. By a single vote, the assembly agreed to abandon this amendment, which sharply distinguished between white citizens and racially suspect others in judicial matters.[16]

Two other racially stigmatizing amendments garnered more support. By a comfortable three-to-two ratio, the lower house clung to language that "no negro, mulatto or mustee, shall have a legal vote in any case whatsoever." Proslavery representatives from Ulster, Kings, and Richmond Counties retained enough allies and picked up additional ones from Albany, Westchester County, and elsewhere to forge a solid majority opposed to extending the franchise across the color line. The assembly refused to rescind a third amendment, imposing a one-hundred-pound fine on each party to any marriage between a white person and a person of African descent. This antimiscegenation amendment carried a smaller majority than the franchise prohibition, suggesting that assemblymen were more concerned with political rather than social engineering.[17] In any case, only a minority of representatives committed themselves to a modicum of racial equality or citizens' fundamental right to the franchise.

When the senate again challenged the lower house on the remaining two amendments, representatives jettisoned the antimiscegenation amendment but clung to the franchise restriction.[18] Drawing a line at the ballot box proved more critical than drawing a line at the bedroom. The strongest opponents of gradual abolition, who supported almost all measures that would hollow out any victory gradual abolition might enjoy, found themselves supported by their ostensibly more moderate colleagues. A majority of the assembly perceived that at the inner sanctum of the republican temple lay the franchise, and there blacks must not tread. With the political exclusion in place, gradual abolition moved within a single step of becoming law.

The Council of Revision, however, vetoed the bill because of the racially coded version of citizenship it would institute. In an extraordinary veto message, the council—composed of Governor George Clinton, head of the court of chancery Robert R. Livingston, and justice of the supreme court John Sloss Hobart—laid out precisely why gradual abolition could not take place on the assembly's terms. The council objected to barring blacks from serving on the state legislature and the right to vote for the state legislature. They found the bill internally contradictory, having "placed the children that shall be born of slaves in the rank of citizens" in some respects but not in others.[19]

The council identified the franchise as the keystone of the political order established during the American Revolution and complained that race was a clumsy tool "and one not to be found anywhere in the state constitution" for securing it. Under the 1777 state constitution, property requirements were lowered for state assembly elections from the colonial standard but raised for state senate and gubernatorial elections. They were enshrined, along with gender, age, and residency, as the legitimate means of determining voter eligibility. Since any free adult male in theory could acquire the funds necessary to attain a freehold or rent property of sufficient value, the council viewed voting rights as a universal right (for males) rather than a limited aristocratic privilege.[20]

Thus, the council forecast trouble if New York implemented the bill's program. A "class of disfranchised and discontented citizens, who at some future period, may be both numerous and wealthy" could arise to jeopardize political stability. Race would serve as a markedly unreliable and unrepresentative indicator of citizenship, creating "the foundation of an aristocracy of the most dangerous . . . kind." The council offered demographic projections to support this argument: seventeen generations hence, "every man will have the blood of many more than 200,000 ancestors running in his veins, and that if any of these should have been coloured, his posterity will by the operation of this law be disfranchised." By the council's reckoning, "if only one thousandth part of the black inhabitants now in the State, should intermarry with the white, their posterity will amount to so many millions, that it will be difficult to suppose a fiftieth part of the people born within this State" would be eligible to vote. Franchise rights, "which our excellent constitution intended to secure to every free inhabitant of the State," would instead be manipulated by self-serving leaders. Indeed, the process by which "the Legislature may arbitrarily dispose of the dearest rights of their constituents" had already begun, as the final paragraph of the veto message noted that innocent "black, mulatto and mustee citizens" now eligible to vote would be stripped "of this essential privilege."[21]

The council's estimate of the intermarriage rate, deliberately conservative, underscored its understanding of race as a dubious distinction that threatened basic political principles. Legislators showed concern for the aftermath of abolition in their deliberations by inserting language about education and by attempting to regulate black access to the courts. In response, the council offered a thoughtful consideration of the relationship between abolition, race, and representative government, one which confirmed that political citizenship was central to the meaning of freedom.

Unfortunately, because abolition begged questions about citizenship, proslavery tactics were particularly effective in blunting this initial drive for gradual emancipation. Although the senate carried an override of the council's veto, the assembly fell a few votes short of the necessary two-thirds majority. In one sense, the defeat of the gradual abolition bill represented a clever tactical victory for abolition's opponents, who created "a bad bill" that forced the council to veto it.[22] But such parliamentary maneuvering was effective because of the specific ideas and fears about race emerging from the consideration of the gradual abolition bill. Proslavery legislators refused to ignore the details of gradual abolition, helping those with less clear views to define what they did not want, foremost of which was black equality at the ballot box.

The failed override vote in the assembly revealed how limited New York's commitment to black citizenship was in 1785. Those representatives who voted to sustain the council's veto did not do so out of opposition to disenfranchisement or disdain for racism. Indeed, representatives who during the course of numerous roll calls had cast votes in favor of restricting black rights as witnesses, spouses, and voters also chose to sustain the veto, thus killing gradual abolition under any circumstance. The override vote on March 26 was twenty-three to seventeen, whereas earlier in the process, majorities of thirty-six to ten and thirty-six to eleven had shown themselves at least somewhat favorably disposed toward the broad concept of gradual abolition. Slavery's defenders had gained allies by raising awareness of specific concerns, enabling them to kill even a gradual abolition that incorporated those concerns.

Supporters of slavery had picked off enough sympathizers to carry the day. Two early procedural votes on gradual abolition yielded one or more proslavery votes in less than two-thirds of the counties. By contrast, in the final override vote, at least one representative from nine of twelve counties voted against gradual abolition; in eleven of twelve counties at least one person voted to retain the antimiscegenation clause. In every county at least one legislator voted to hold onto the franchise ban. With the representatives from Ulster, Kings, and Richmond Counties voting proslavery positions in most instances, this shift elsewhere in the state made a difference, exposing the tenuousness of the commitment to antislavery. As a result, the whole gradual abolition enterprise was defeated.

The clear lack of consensus on matters of race and citizenship, however, did not prevent the 1785 legislature from enacting a ban on importation of slaves into the state. The ban, by trying to reduce slavery to local rather than national or international dimensions, marked a first step toward gradual abolition. The prohibition against importing slaves for sale applied to domestic and foreign commerce, authorized suits carrying a substantial fine, and brought freedom to slaves illegally brought into New York.[23]

Legislators also defined more precisely the conditions under which masters could manumit their own slaves. These new rules had ambiguous implications. A master or his heirs could manumit a slave without having to pay an indemnity to local officials. This provision eliminated an impediment to manumission. Nevertheless, the law accounted for long-expressed antimanumission rationalizations regarding the suspected financial burden that former slaves would represent to local governments. Owners had to have local authorities certify that the slave was less than fifty years of age and prepared to take care of himself or herself before manumission could go forward. The same safeguards applied to manumissions by wills of deceased masters, ensuring that elderly and otherwise improvident slaves did not wind up in the public's care.[24]

The New York legislature's initial postwar effort to determine slavery's legal status revealed that any consideration of emancipation implicated issues of race and citizenship. Moreover, while slaveholders believed that state-induced emancipation might impose unacceptable costs on them, the state, in authorizing individual manumissions, indicated its fears about the cost that private emancipations might impose on the public. Only restricting sale of slaves imported into the state seemed to be a relatively easy burden for the body politic to bear. The legislature's extended consideration of gradual emancipation indicated that slavery in New York, as elsewhere, stood on a shaky foundation. Yet, with its relatively large slave population and its colonial and Revolutionary-era experiences with slave restiveness, the New York legislature found itself incapable of imitating its neighbors and attacking domestic slavery in direct, albeit gradual, fashion. Failure to pass a gradual abolition law notwithstanding, 1785 would turn out to be a high-water mark for legislative support for gradual abolition, not to be approached again until the mid-1790s. Race, citizenship, public finance, and political priorities would combine to thwart mounting public denunciations of slavery until the very end of the eighteenth century.

III.

Even as the legislature took steps to discourage the slave trade and permit private manumission under prescribed conditions, public commentary reflected the intense passions stimulated by the central issue of emancipation itself. Antislavery and proslavery correspondents alike acknowledged that race and citizenship were the active fault lines upon which the legislature had attempted to build the unstable edifice of gradual emancipation. Depending on one's perspective, the collapse of gradual abolition therefore expressed gutless vacillation or clear-sighted recognition.

A New York city newspaper contributor identified as Tiberius Gracchus took the occasion of gradual emancipation's consideration before the New York legislature to launch a broad-based assault on the contradictory manner in which the new nation had implemented its stated principles of citizenship. Appropriately, the original Tiberius Gracchus was a Roman noble who as a tribune cultivated a popular following and whose ambitious legislative program for agrarian reform, prompted in part by concerns about slavery, was at one point thwarted by a veto. The New York Gracchus quoted the language of universal equality from the Declaration of Independence, as well as declarations of equal rights from Massachusetts and Pennsylvania, to demonstrate that America had fallen woefully short of its own professions. New

York in particular practiced "inconsistencies," including color-coded slavery. As Gracchus put the problem: "All men have an *unalienable* right to liberty. But persons of a black colour are evidently *no men*."[25]

Such citizenship-oriented antislavery sentiments provoked a fierce reaction. The following week "American" attacked Gracchus, whose "Roman like ideas of liberty" would be destroyed by racial egalitarianism. American proclaimed that neither social nor political mingling of the races could be permitted in New York: "the shame we should most inevitably incur from a mixture of complexion, and their [blacks] participating in government" would be intolerable. The polemicist imagined "seated in our Senate and Assembly, General Quacco here, Col. Mingo there." The writer also invoked painful memories from the Revolutionary War, in which blacks "fought against us by whole regiments," conjuring up a renewed unholy alliance of loyalist Quakers and African Americans. Racial equality, according to American, would lead in time to racial murder.[26] The writer thus sought to limit his nation's republic to whites, contrasting his allegedly realistic analysis of the contemporary American republic with fanciful ideas of a Roman one.

The failed 1785 gradual abolition bill provoked even more stunningly polarized reactions. "A Letter from Cuffee to the Printer" and "A Serious Address to the Whig Slave Holders, in the State of New York" appeared on the same page of the March 31, 1785, *New-York Packet,* responding to the state government's actions. The "Letter from Cuffee," offered a crude satire of black pidgin speech to illustrate the inappropriateness of black citizenship and to gloat over the failed veto override. Cuffee informed "Mista Pinta" of his ambition to be "Legislaterman" and make *"two turd."*

Philanthropos in the "Serious Address," by contrast, lambasted "the great joy, rejoicing and exultation of all slave-mongers" provoked by the defeat of the gradual emancipation law. Indeed, Philanthropos suggested that making policy on the basis of skin color might arouse divine retribution, asking "are you so case hardened with impudence, as that you dare to erect your impious crest towards your just and merciful Creator, and tell him that black skins, woolly pates, [and] flat noses . . . have no right to freedom[?]" Legislative scheming was almost as contemptible to Philanthropos. The subversion of the abolition bill through the inclusion of language intended to "frustrate the design of emancipation" betokened the "wickedness" of proslavery legislators. Indeed, voters could not trust "a slave-monger to represent them" because such a person would enslave whites too if expedient. Thus, Philanthropos imagined that New Yorkers operated in such a perilous moral climate that the political chains they lately burst might soon be refashioned.[27]

With the exception of the satirical "Letter from Cuffee," the responses published in the *New-York Packet* to the 1785 legislative contest over gradual abolition drew on familiar revolutionary metaphors of liberty and enslavement. Yet even the crude racist satire shared a sense of urgency with the earnest responses of American, Gracchus, and Philanthropos. New York and the new nation, each pseudonymous writer indicated, stood at a crossroads between recently won independence and a future that might or might not validate the principles of self-government upon which the war had been fought. The proslavery American and the antislavery Philanthropos shared a belief that permanent release from the metaphorical slavery of the past was contingent on the wise policies of the present. A false move—toward hypocrisy for defenders of abolition, toward foolhardy inclusiveness for abolition's critics— might render future iterations of the nation's crucial principles meaningless. Race and citizenship were thus core issues in determining slavery's future in New York and New York's future in the American republican experiment.

The 1785 defeat of gradual abolition and the half-measures taken against slavery confirmed it as an issue that would continue to press for the attention of politically alert and active New Yorkers. Revolutionary ideas about liberty and equality, along with the actions of nearby northern states, provided the impetus for New York's legislature to consider gradual abolition. But broad transatlantic organizational and ideological forces as well as local efforts would ensure slavery's continuing place in New York's public discourse, even, or especially, in the wake of abolition's defeat.

4

Containing Slavery

The Manumission Society and the Law, 1785–92

In the spring of 1792, the New York Manumission Society (NYMS) assessed the difficulties of combating slavery. In much of the state, according to the standing committee of this New York City organization, black people "have been obliged to submit in silence to their severe fate merely because they were friendless and unprotected and because their oppressors were powerful and strong." The situation, however, was far from hopeless. The report suggested how public opinion might operate to the slave's advantage in a moral marketplace. Each new convert to the views of the society would add to "the influence of benevolent opinions, operating to render property in Slaves precarious, and the traffic in them disrespectable." The public's antislavery views would have the effect of "lowering" slave "values," thereby eliminating "the objection by which so many have been induced to oppose their emancipation."[1] By challenging the moral economy of slavery the society hoped to depress the institution's actual economy, revitalizing the prospect of gradual abolition.

When New York's legislature failed to enact a gradual abolition law in 1785, the public debate over slavery in the state had scarcely commenced. The NYMS itself held its first meeting only a month before the legislature took up the subject of gradual abolition. By its second meeting, the society had signed up an impressive 202 supporters. By its third meeting, however, the society found itself dealing with the aftermath of gradual emancipation's defeat.[2] The second state antislavery society in the nation thus quickly found itself in a much different position than its predecessor. The Pennsylvania Abolition Society focused upon the enforcement of the provisions of their state's gradual abolition law, seeking their broadest construction in order to extend freedom to as many African Americans as possible.[3] By contrast, shadowing the NYMS at every step was the need to foster support for a state-enforced, institutionalized system of emancipation. Otherwise, the private manumissions that the society encouraged were likely to have little effect.

Fundamentally moderate in its tactics and aims, the NYMS during its early years spearheaded a multifaceted campaign to weaken the legal and social foundations of slavery. The organization encouraged the state legislature to revisit gradual abolition but, absent a definitive victory, urged lawmakers to sever domestic slavery in New York from the broader American and transatlantic slave-trading systems. Over time, this containment strategy would provide manumission society members, like their Pennsylvania brethren, the leverage to effect individual manumissions and provide rudimentary protection to the state's free blacks. Meanwhile, limiting the ability of the state's slaveholders to traffic in human property served as a prelude to future assaults on slavery. The NYMS also actively pursued a program of education and social supervision for the city's black population, hoping to advance the individual status of African Americans and to broaden public approval of the battle for black freedom.

Underlying much of its activity was the presumption that what the public thought about slavery and what public officials could do about it were fundamentally intertwined. Although not as strident as the more famous abolitionist campaigns of the antebellum era, the NYMS sought to operate in, rather than outside, the public eye. While subsequent generations have found appalling the organization's accommodation of slaveholding members, the NYMS unapologetically embraced gradualism as a principle worth fighting for and one consistent with its vision of social change. The NYMS also operated under the paradoxical assumptions that elite stewardship offered the best way to promote racially egalitarian attitudes. Contradictions in tow, the NYMS helped to define the terms of the abolition debate from the mid-1780s to the end of the century.[4]

I.

In terms of membership and its program, the NYMS fused the Quaker antislavery tradition with Revolutionary-era politics and ideology. The large Quaker presence in the NYMS—perhaps half its membership, including twelve of the original eighteen members—clearly influenced its program.[5] The society's preoccupation with education, moral regulation, and antislavery itself had precedents in the practices of the New York Friends Yearly Meeting. Similarly, the Quaker program of meetings with individual slaveholders to convince them to release their slaves also would be adapted by the NYMS standing committee.[6]

Although in his wealth and prominent connections merchant John Murray Jr. may not have been typical of the New York Friends, his career and ethos helped exemplify the NYMS's fusing of sectarian and broader reform values. Born into a wealthy New York Quaker family with London connections, Murray was educated in Philadelphia and England. After his early business ventures profited, Murray, still in his twenties, began to devote himself to philanthropy. In 1785, he became a founding member of the NYMS.

He served the organization faithfully, holding the position of treasurer until his death in 1819 and actively participating in the formation and operation of New York City's African Free School.

For Murray, as for other members of the society, the religious and social obligation to service extended to a number of other causes. He was an active supporter of initiatives such as penal reform and missions to the state's Indian population. An opponent of capital punishment, he advocated and later served as a commissioner for the state's penitentiary system. A loyal Quaker and an active public citizen, Murray in some ways embodied the ethos of genteel social stewards who dominated reform causes prior to the Jacksonian era. He moved easily within religious, philanthropic, and government circles while maintaining his distance from partisan politics.[7]

Non-Quakers in the society included some of New York's most prominent political and professional elite. John Jay, who by 1785 had already served as architect of the state's constitution, leading member of the Continental Congress, and a key U.S. diplomat, was the society's first president. Alexander Hamilton also joined Jay, his future Federalist comrade, in the NYMS, as did judge and New York City mayor James Duane, and Revolutionary-era patriot leaders such as Alexander McDougall and Melancton Smith. Historian David Brion Davis's survey of leading NYMS members found a high proportion of merchants, bankers, lawyers, and other professionals, leading him to comment that "abolition societies were . . . one of the municipal meeting grounds of men of wealth, influence, and political power."[8]

Jay exemplified the moderate, gradualist caste of the NYMS. Before, during, and after his service as president of the society, this wealthy and well-connected lawyer and patriot leader was also a slaveholder. Indeed, his father's slave Brash had been transported to Madeira after confessing to a role in the "Negro Plot" against New York City in 1741. While Quaker opponents of slavery visited their coreligionists to personally renounce their ties to slavery, Jay actually bought slaves with the stated intention of freeing them after they had worked off the value of their purchase price. Jay nonetheless asserted his prerogative to discipline slaves and even to sell those who met his displeasure. His statements on slavery in the 1780s varied depending on his audience: sometimes he denounced slavery with great moral clarity; at other times, he counseled patience. To Pennsylvania abolitionist Benjamin Rush, just prior to the veto the 1785 emancipation bill, Jay expressed his "wish to see all unjust and all unnecessary discriminations everywhere abolished, and that the time may soon come when all our inhabitants of every colour and denomination shall be free and equal partakers of our political liberty." A few months later, having fully absorbed the defeat of the 1785 emancipation bill, Jay admitted with some resignation, "All the best men can do is, to persevere in doing their duty . . . leave the consequences to Him who made it their duty; being neither elated by success . . . nor discouraged by disappointments however frequent and mortifying."[9] Jay identified slavery as an immoral institution, but a combination of self-interest, realism, and patience guided his personal and public actions.[10]

New York's leading abolitionists believed that gradualism and their own social leadership were not only legitimate but positively desirable. Society, they thought, should be reformed in their image and under their direction. Hence, they sought "lawful ways and means to enable" slaves "to Share equally with us, in . . . civil and religious Liberty."[11] Rather than chastise their slaveholding members, the society supported a private program of gradual emancipation. Unlike official New York Quaker intentions to unilaterally divest themselves of slave labor, the secular NYMS offered only mild inducement for members to effect their own private manumissions. And the slaveholding membership of the society, at least at its founding, was no small group. Historian Shane White calculated that over half of the signatories to the 1786 petition to the legislature, including society president Jay, owned slaves as of the 1790 census. Indeed, the disproportionately elite society membership owned on average 2.9 slaves in 1790, which is especially striking given that the average slaveholder in New York City in 1790 owned only two slaves.[12]

Indicative of their faith in their own good intentions, the society's rules were in some respects more generous to masters than were the gradual abolition programs proposed in New York and adopted in nearby states. The blow to NYMS slave owners was to be cushioned through delay. Members were to free any slaves under twenty-eight by the time those slaves reached age thirty-five; slaves between the ages of twenty-eight and thirty-eight were to be manumitted within seven years. The pattern for gradual abolition laws, by contrast, was to set the terminal age for mandatory service in the twenties or even late teens. In any event, members were not to sell their slaves without securing a promise for future manumission.[13] Overall, the NYMS sought a process rather than a singular, decisive act to realize broader ends. Private manumission, which the organization encouraged for its members and at large, and a public program of gradual emancipation, were two such means to that end.

Despite the influence and connections of its members, the NYMS understood from the start that no aspect of its program could be achieved simply at its behest. Certainly, it could not afford to operate as a mere extension of the Quaker community. Broad segments of the political elite and the public at large—segments not primarily made up of Quakers—had to be reached and their antislavery convictions sharpened. Indeed, as discussed in chapter 5, Quakers were a target for proslavery scorn. Thus, the society's alliance of Quaker and non-Quaker leadership was critical to any success it hoped to enjoy.[14]

The NYMS envisioned its project in terms of pragmatic incrementalism and moral idealism. Chastened by the undoing of the gradual abolition bill, which was due to deep-seated concerns about the racial and political implications of emancipation, and disposed to support gradualism itself, the NYMS assumed that the road to "compleat Freedom" would be a long one. The August 1785 minutes reflected the broad challenge before the new organization. Society members believed that "a great number of Persons are violently opposed to the Emancipation of their Slaves"; nonetheless, they reasoned that "the good Example set by others, of more Enlarged and liberal Principles, and the face of true Religion, will, in time, dispel the mist which Prejudice, self Interest and long habit have raised. . . ."[15]

II.

The advocates of abolition in New York were not simply gradualists; they were also internationalists. Their first president, John Jay, had already made his mark on the world stage as a leading diplomat during the Revolutionary War and as one of the principle negotiators of the Peace of Paris. Quaker antislavery, for its part, was almost by definition an international movement. British and American Friends communicated and coordinated their abolitionist principles via the same transatlantic networks that sustained and transmitted Quaker religious principles and commercial operations.[16] The nonsectarian New York Manumission Society similarly wished to cultivate an international network. At its second meeting, the NYMS declared British abolitionists Granville Sharp and Thomas Clarkson, as well as Revolutionary War hero Marquis de Lafayette, honorary members. In addition, it distributed Clarkson's exposé of the slave trade and corresponded with French and British antislavery societies.[17]

Antislavery discourse in the newspapers mirrored the perception of New York abolitionists that the problem of slavery in their state belonged in a broad, international context. By identifying itself with British allies the NYMS risked being accused of Tory leanings; nevertheless, it was readily apparent to newspaper readers that American affairs, including slavery, remained very much part of a British-dominated Atlantic world. Indeed, New York's newspapers tracked antislavery activity near and far, recording the widening abhorrence of the transatlantic slave trade. Slavery remained an ongoing practice in the state, in the nation, in the hemisphere, and in the transatlantic culture in which New Yorkers participated. Commentaries against slavery might operate in one or more of these circles, but, at least implicitly, the arguments put forth encompassed all of them. The cruelty of the slave trade and a championing of basic human rights comprised the major themes of attacks on slavery.[18]

Consideration of slavery in multiple contexts helped to maintain its place on the public agenda and to validate the emerging NYMS strategy of containment, which aimed at limiting the trade of slaves in and out of New York as part of a first step toward gradual abolition. Significantly, the rejection of the 1785 gradual abolition law preceded, and perhaps intensified, much of the printed antislavery discourse in New York. In the years immediately following emancipation's defeat, newspapers carried denunciations of slavery and commentary on the slave trade's ills.[19] Ground inadequately prepared in 1785 was subsequently fertilized with stinging critiques of slavery.

The broadest published denunciations asserted the incompatibility of a commitment to Lockean natural rights with the maintenance of bondage. Critics confronted the possibility that racial difference might invalidate claims based on natural law and the "universal morality" allegedly enshrined in the new nation's founding principles. David Cooper's *A Letter from °°°°°°°°, in London, to his Friend in America,* published in New York in 1784, denied any moral refuge to slaveholders, no matter how they obtained their slaves. "Your avarice is the torch of treachery and civil war, which desolates the shores of Africa, and shakes destruction on half the majestic species of man!"[20] In February 1785, as the New York legislature was crafting the ill-fated gradual abolition bill, an imaginary "Paradoxical Prophecy, wrote in the year 1691," predicted that some day "men who have opposed the tyrant of Britain, on the mighty waters, shall forge chains for the natives of Negroland, because their noses are flat." A year later, in an address "To the Inhabitants of the State of New York," Humanitas juxtaposed the universal language of the Declaration of Independence with the perpetuation of slavery, commenting, "This is such a stain upon our national character, that though my greatest boast is that I am an American . . . yet the reflection that so many of my fellow creatures are treated in such an unjust manner, checks my pride. . . ."[21]

Confronting slavery thus became a matter of national honor, according to some early New York polemicists.

Slavery assaulted the most fundamental principles of human society, according to a writer known as the American Spectator. When this essayist in 1786 directed the attention of his series on public morals to slavery, the "inconsistency" he denounced related to deeper concerns than the ideals of the new nation. Picking up on secular and religious strands of antislavery rhetoric, the Spectator wrote that "natural law doth not authorize barbarity," nor did the golden rule. Nevertheless, suffering mightily in slavery became the fate "of our fellow creatures." While awaiting what the writer saw as a necessarily gradual abolition, American slaves promptly should receive "the blessings of christianity."[22]

Critics often built the case against slavery through brutal descriptions of contemporary reality rather than on the basis of philosophical principles. The objections of French masters in the West Indies to a law limiting punishment to fifty lashes indicated the callousness of West Indian slavery. A vivid description of the muzzle used to prevent field slaves from eating West Indian sugar cane while working their masters' plantations indicated a cruelty far more shocking. Indeed, after a clinical explanation of the muzzle's mechanics, the author of the piece issued a direct challenge to apologists: "Let the planters come forward and contradict this; let them show to the world that they are misrepresented; let them prove the contrary." Meanwhile, the story of a South Carolina man desperate to drown himself after being sold away from his wife and children made clear enough that the malignity of slavery occurred on the American mainland as well.[23]

Familiarity with the slave regimes of the American South and the West Indies gave rise during the 1780s to surprising moments in which newspapers defended the slaves' right to vengeance. The *New-York Packet* reprinted a description by Hector St. John de Crèvecoeur, who would shortly join the New York Manumission Society and who allegedly had encountered a tortured American plantation slave. The bondsman was "suspended in a cage," birds pecking at him as he was on his way to death. Prefacing this account was a polemic defense of the slave, who was being punished for murder, speculating about the "injuries" which could have "provoked" him to kill: "In a case like this. . . . those who originally bought him, or those who detained him in slavery, are rather accountable for his life, and the life of the overseer."[24]

New York newspapers more than once during the 1780s offered a forum for open sympathy toward violent attacks by West Indian slaves. A correspondent, reflecting on "barbarous murders" that had taken place in some of the islands, commented that "the greatest philanthropist will not afford even a pitying sigh for those, who have been, or may be plundered, tormented, and even massacred by the avenging hands of their purchased slaves." Indeed, such actions were an expression of "LIBERTY [which] is inherent."[25]

The horrors of the slave trade proved that bondage furnished a rotten foundation for society. Critics shocked readers with a report of the atrocity of a captain ordering a ship's doctor to kill six slaves for gratuitous "anatomical" investigations, menaced readers with the image of "the ghosts of those unhappy victims, torn from the arms of tender affectionate" families, or persuaded them with statistical information about the many thousands of Africans annually perishing while adjusting to life in the West Indies. In August 1787, the editor of the *Packet* seemed to be speaking for and to New Yorkers through the comment "that one rational being should be claimed by another as his absolute property" is so "repugnant to all the principles of humanity, at least to a majority of the citizens of America, that the slave-trade can never be censured too freely." This unattributed insert in the New York news column continued, "The advocates for slavery, indeed, are chiefly those who are mediately or immediately blessed by interest to defend it; or who, by residence, where slavery exists, have lost those honest tender feelings, that prompt us to do as we would be done by."[26] In a state where the practice continued, such remarks and examples of slavery's horrors were poignantly relevant.

Stories about places as close by as Connecticut and as far away as Cuba reinforced the notion that if New York lived in the midst of a world marked by slavery, that world was also experimenting with change. Rhode Island's banning of the slave trade won positive attention in two New York City newspapers, despite the usual depiction of that state as a radical pariah. Virginia and New Jersey also received favorable notice for their laws banning further slave imports. Such actions implicitly confirmed the wisdom of New York's own recent prohibition on importation. Newspapers also monitored measures taken beyond the bounds of the United States. One paper suggested that a partial emancipation scheme in Cuba "may afford lessons of the soundest policy at the present moment."[27]

British indignation provided provocative material for New York newspapers. The upsurge in anti-slave-trade agitation in the former mother country helped frame the debate over slavery in New York.[28] That it did so stemmed partly from the nature of eighteenth-century newspapers. Even after independence, Americans perceived Britain as near the center of the political universe and at the center of English-language culture. New York editors assembled information from around the globe on dense sheets of newsprint.

Comments about slavery, whether directed at New Yorkers or the British Parliament, formed part of an ongoing conversation. By the same token, slavery on the American mainland existed in the same interpretive space as slavery in the British West Indian colonies.[29] International institutional ties and elite Anglo-American antislavery correspondence encouraged interest in the mother country and her remaining colonies; so too did Quaker networks. But newspapers provided the most dramatic, publicly influential forum connecting New York with Great Britain.

The British delivered a series of rebukes to the slave trade. The *New-York Packet* and *New-York Magazine* each published an extensive excerpt from Thomas Clarkson's 1785 "Essay on the Slavery and Commerce of the Human Species."[30] The *Federal Herald* (Lansingburgh, New York) excerpted the published memoirs of an English former slave-ship captain who became a clergyman. After a horrifying description of conditions on board, the penitent Reverend Dr. Newton stated, "Yet perhaps, they would wish to spend the remainder of their days on ship board, could they know before-hand, the nature of the servitude which awaits them on shore. . . ." New York newspapers also published the texts of various petitions submitted to Parliament against the slave trade. The borough of Bridgewater conveyed to the House of Commons, and to readers of a New York newspaper, "a just abhorrence of a system of oppression, which no prospect of private gain, no consideration of public advantage, no plea of political expediency, can sufficiently justify or excuse." Such items drummed home slavery's pernicious nature, exposing New Yorkers to the broad range of British opposition.[31]

News from Britain sometimes reminded Americans that while they were monitoring developments in the former mother country, observers in the mother country took note of American activity. In May 1787, praise for the work of the New York Manumission Society found its way back to the United States from London and into the pages of Poughkeepsie's *Country Journal*. Voices from each side of the Atlantic thus validated one another.[32]

The incorporation of British opinion into American debates underscores that opposition to the slave trade and opposition to slavery shared an agenda in New York. The attempt to pass gradual abolition provided the occasion for attacking the slave trade as well. Criticism of this commerce comprised a key element in the larger assault on slavery's foundation during the 1780s. In the broadest context of American slavery in the decades after the Revolution, attacks on the slave trade may have masked the difficulty of unseating slavery itself. But in New York, assaults on the slave trade provided a vehicle for the ongoing battle against domestic bondage. On neither subject was there a shortage of commentary. Denunciations of slavery and the slave trade blended, functioning in a mutually supportive fashion. Thus, the news that Rhode Island had passed a ban on the African slave trade prompted an expression of hope in the *New-York Journal* that this law would serve as a "worthy example [to] be followed by those in power, to the total abolition of every species of slavery." [33]

Worse conditions elsewhere did not lend respectability to slavery at home. A commentary in the *New-York Journal* sandwiched a condemnation of slavery in the South between the notation that many states had initiated abolition societies and the closing remark, *"How little is that mind which feels not for another's woes."* Northern audiences, implied the *Journal,* ought to engage the issue of slavery. Similarly, Rhode Island Congregationalist theologian Samuel Hopkins's 1776 pamphlet *A Dialogue Concerning the Slavery of the Africans,* reissued in New York by the NYMS in 1785, proclaimed that whatever regional comparisons of slave regimes were drawn, all were "answerable for the whole." [34]

III.

Antislavery writings published in New York bolstered the tactical priorities of the NYMS and its broad, self-identified humanitarian responsibility for black New Yorkers. Denunciations of the slave trade comported with NYMS efforts during the 1780s to contain New York slavery by curtailing the sale of slaves into and out of the state. Attacks on other aspects of slavery underscored the diverse cruelties of the system and legitimated organized efforts to generate support for gradual abolition and, in the meantime, to provide legal assistance to free blacks who found their freedom threatened. The cultivation of sentimental sympathy toward blacks, explored at greater length in chapter 6, legitimized organized opposition to slavery, as evidence of the slaves' suffering humanity made their exclusion from a republican polity at, the very least, problematic. Slavery's cruelty might seem to manifest itself most dramatically far beyond New York's borders, but reformers were committed to attacking the institution, at least around its margins, closer to home. Indeed, the federal constitution, discussed in chapter 5, in some sense, seemed to make local action the only viable option.

Thus, the cause for which the NYMS labored may have been international, but members of the organization recognized that their own role was local and sometimes even technical. The NYMS sought to extend at least some immediate protection to free and enslaved blacks whose status remained uncertain in the wake of the Revolutionary War. One lingering problem stemmed from the seizure of Tory property. Through such seizures, the state of New York had come to possess slaves formerly owned by loyalists, many of whom were likely sold to new masters. In 1786, the legislature amended "An Act for the speedy Sale of the confiscated and forfeited Estates" to include a clause manumitting all slaves still held by state officials as the result of such seizures.[35]

The NYMS leapt at the opportunity presented by the state-mandated manumission. For more than two years after the passage of the law regarding confiscated loyalist slaves, the society worked to effect the liberation of individual black New Yorkers entitled to freedom but still held in bondage. The society also sought an official copy of the law in hopes that they could place it in one or more newspapers so that masters illegally holding blacks as slaves could "not plead Ignorance." Nonetheless, the problem of confiscated slaves illegally held in bondage persisted, prompting the society in 1788 to appoint a committee, which included Jay and Hamilton, to explore what further means were available to free the former slaves of loyalists.[36]

A broader imperative identified by the society during the 1780s was severing New York's ties to slave trading and containing slavery within the boundaries of the state. Legal exportation of slaves southward ensured that any gradual abolition or upsurge in manumissions would come too late for many unfortunate individuals. Thus, in 1786 opponents of slavery launched a campaign against the exportation of slaves out of New York. As part of its lobbying effort, the NYMS submitted to the legislature a petition bearing more than 130 names, including members of some of the state's most prominent families. One of the signatories was the publisher of the *New-York Packet*, Samuel Loudon, who printed the petition in his newspaper. The memorial bemoaned "the additional miseries" imposed on New York slaves by being shipped to the Caribbean and to the South, a practice which inevitably shattered families. According to the petition, the relatively "tolerable and easy" conditions of New York slavery magnified the immorality of exporting slaves.[37] Whether the petition overstated regional differences in slavery, the distinction strengthened arguments for moving New York's own legal code in an antislavery direction.[38]

The society's commitment to private manumission and the protection of free blacks made combating slave exportation a practical and moral imperative. As long as exportation of slaves remained legal, kidnappers had sufficient cover under which to carry free blacks into slave markets south of New York. A personal letter excerpted in a Manhattan newspaper reported the case of George Morris, a free black from New York City "offered by a public sale to the highest bidder." "I am persuaded," wrote the correspondent from

Charleston, "that many are kidnapped, brought from New-York and sold, and I could wish some mode might be adopted to prevent and deter people from pursuing so villainous a practice." Three days later, "Benevolus" reported on the same illicit connection, drawing attention to a ship anchored in New York but headed for Charleston with "a considerable number of negroes." This situation created the scene of "distressed objects . . . ringing their hands, and praying to their relentless proprietors that they might be permitted to remain in New-York."[39]

Essays published in New York newspapers elaborated upon the NYMS's commitment to containment. A writer calling himself Philanthropos disputed, on practical and moral grounds, the efficacy of ridding New York of slavery by shipping slaves out of state. Many rural slaveholders, Philanthropos argued, would never give up their slaves, so allowing slave export simply exposed their human property to "diabolical purposes." More importantly, the slaves already exposed to "cruelty, injustice, and horrid oppression" did not deserve the even worse fate of exportation. New York City's free black population had proven remarkably law-abiding, noted Philanthropos, and did not need the threat of exportation to menace them into better behavior.[40]

Public protest against kidnapping and attempts to sway the legislature to intervene were part of a coordinated effort by the NYMS. The excerpted letter written from Charleston likely was placed into the hands of the *Packet's* publisher by the NYMS, as society president John Jay had been its original recipient. The NYMS plans to lobby the state legislature in early 1786 for greater protections against shipping New York blacks into southern slavery included distributing to legislators copies of Hopkins's *Dialogue Concerning the Slavery of the Africans,* which the society itself had previously reprinted.[41]

IV.

The New York Manumission Society's goal of outlawing the commercial exportation of slaves from the state, which would legally separate New York's slave system from that of the rest of the nation, was finally achieved in 1788. After floundering in 1786 and 1787, the export ban was incorporated into an omnibus slave law passed in 1788. The new law made it illegal for "any person" to "purchase or buy" or act "as factor or agent to another, [to] take or receive any slave with intent to remove, export, or carry such slave from this State . . . to be sold. . . ."

Even this anti-export provision represented a partial victory for the NYMS. Achieving an export ban had been more difficult and more important than curbing imports because in theory it more directly breached the property rights of New York slaveholders. Regulating slave export meant limiting the right of a property owner to dispose of his property and, in the case of human property, also limiting the owner's discretion over discipline. Significantly, however, the provision enforced the one-hundred-pound fine not on slave owners themselves but on middle men—purchasers, "factor[s]and agent[s]." Slaveholders thus remained protected from the full impact of the law, as the provision neither enjoined them from nor punished them for selling a slave for export. The export ban, although a significant achievement, was also indicative of continued slaveholder power.[42]

The legal closing of the border to slave imports and exports had two effects in New York. Any future reform would be a less drastic step because the state had begun to sever its connection to the broader slave society. Moreover, the ban on cross-border slave trading opened up a new avenue for slaves and their allies to resist the institution in New York. When slaveholders transgressed such laws, individual African Americans could use the legal system to their advantage.[43] Indeed, the state created a clear incentive for the NYMS to represent slaves in enforcing the law. Successful plaintiffs and the state were to split the fine imposed on slaveholders who were found to be illegally importing African Americans, with the slaves gaining freedom.

Yet the inclusion of a prohibition against slave exportation in a law supporting slavery's existence also revealed the precarious state of the antislavery campaign in the years after 1785. The 1788 "act concerning Slaves" accepted lifelong, inherited African American bondage as a legal and, implicitly, social norm. The statute confirmed the long-established legal principle that Christian baptism did not change a slave's status. New York law continued to carry penalties against anyone assisting runaway slaves, continued to limit the rights of slaves to engage in commerce, and continued to prohibit slaves from "strik[ing]" whites. In addition, the law touched upon issues that had recently concerned the legislature, such as state-mandated procedures for voluntary manumissions and the highly restricted use of slave testimony.[44]

Despite the mixed messages of the new statute, the legal sealing of New York's borders to the slave trade from the inside and the outside encouraged the NYMS to view the 1788 slave code in a positive light. The society's minutes record the view that the import ban "has *much* the same Effect as a Prohibition, and will prevent the Increase of Slavery amongst us." An intermediate victory of this kind signified the possible turning of the public's attitude against slavery. In the wake of New York's new slave law, the Manumission Society noted with pride that "the minds of Men are becoming daily more enlightened, and that a Liberality of sentiment begins to prevail, which will admit the Claims of Africans to a rank among the rational Beings and to the natural Rights of Mankind."[45] In practical legal terms and in the battle for public opinion, the society believed the law approached the essential goal of gradual abolition.

Subsequent legislative rebuffs revealed that society members indulged in excessive optimism. In the aftermath of the 1788 affirmation of slavery itself, the urgency of gradual abolition faded rather than gained momentum. Slaveholders, who made up a significant portion of the legislature, asserted their considerable political power to blunt additional initiatives against slavery and to protect and even extend their prerogatives.

An attempt in 1790 to further advance New York antislavery goals through the legal code got swept away in a countervailing effort to tighten the laws governing slavery. On January 20, Matthew Clarkson—representative from New York County and a member of the NYMS who later served as its president—introduced a gradual abolition bill to the state assembly. As had been proposed in 1785, the new bill stipulated that all people born of slave mothers after a specified date would be eligible for freedom upon reaching a particular age. The matter stalled in an evenly divided assembly. A Quaker petition, which complained that ships outfitted in New York participated in the African slave trade, also failed to arouse legislative action.[46]

Encouraged by the feeble support for antislavery initiatives, defenders of slavery reopened the issue of exporting slaves out of the state. A motion was put to the lower house which would allow for export as an appropriate form of punishment "for certain misdemeanors" with consent of a local justice of the peace. Cornelius Schoonmaker, owner of twelve slaves and part of the proslavery Ulster County delegation, then moved for the elimination altogether of the export ban. This provocative motion lost by a mere three votes. Clarkson's counterattempt to forbid exportation as a means of punishment for slaves lost overwhelmingly, forty-eight to ten, failing to carry a single county's complete delegation.[47] Later, a senate bill, which the lower house reluctantly approved, placed discretion for the use of "transportation" in the hands of the courts actually trying and convicting slaves of crimes. Masters still had the final decision to send their unruly slaves out of state but could do so only if the court first deemed that their crimes deserved such a punishment. Somewhat paradoxically, the senate inserted an amendment that potentially liberalized the manumission law by giving masters recourse to an appeal if the local overseers of the poor would not certify a slave as self-sufficient enough for freedom. Overall, however, the containment policy established in 1788 had not led quickly to further major reform. Instead, a serious leak opened.[48]

New York's elected representatives had grown measurably less receptive toward gradual abolition between 1785 and 1790, especially after 1788. Whereas in 1785 gradual abolition had gotten a lengthy and nuanced consideration, winning endorsement in principle if not final passage, the very idea was preempted in 1790.[49] The six lower-house roll-call votes involving gradual abolition and slave exportation illustrate how tenuous legislative support for the antislavery cause had become. The staunch antislavery representatives, who voted a liberal position all six times, included just eight people, with another eight people voting the antislavery position five of six times. In comparison, proslavery positions enjoyed stronger support, garnering thirteen six-time supporters, and another eight five-time adherents. While proslavery representatives did not reverse the modest legislative gains of 1788, sufficient backing for a major breakthrough on abolition did not exist.

Not surprisingly, slavery continued to draw strong support from major slaveholding counties such as Kings, the county with the highest percentage of African Americans, and Ulster County, where over 10 percent of the population was black in 1790. Albany County, where the state's largest black population comprised a relatively small percentage of the total population, also contributed to the proslavery vote. Most, if not all, of the representatives from these counties, owned slaves as of 1790.[50] Slave-owning delegates from Orange County, which contained neither a large number nor high percentage of slaves, also voted in defense of slavery. Montgomery ranked twelfth among New York counties in percentage and number of blacks, but its six-man delegation, which included at least three slaveholders, provided solid proslavery support.

Some delegations demonstrated their antislavery commitment. Washington and Clinton Counties in northeastern New York contained few blacks. Their delegation was the only one in the entire 1790 assembly without a single slave owner and, perhaps not surprisingly, provided a quarter of the most consistent antislavery votes. Even though New York City contained large numbers and a relatively high percentage of slaves and even though its delegation included slaveholders, the city supplied another 25 percent of the steady antislavery votes. The presence of the Manumission Society, along with the unusually large proportion of free blacks among the total African American population, shaped a unique perspective on the dangers of export-

ing blacks southward and the benefits of gradual abolition. In an urban setting, the alternative to slave labor also probably seemed more palatable than
in rural areas, where slaves provided crucial agricultural labor.

However, simple connections between slavery and local demographic
conditions—or even individual ownership of slaves—cannot be drawn.
Slave owners tended, but not uniformly, to oppose all antislavery legislation.
Yet even a conservative estimate reveals that almost half of the delegates to
the state assembly owned at least one slave, and thus slaveholders were in a
strong position to defend their interests. New York's franchise rules, which
restricted voting to propertied men, and the tendency to elect men of significant property to office, ensured that, at least within the legislature, slaveholding as of 1790 was not a marginalized minority interest. Put another
way, New York's 1777 constitution intended to protect property-holding interests—and, with regard to slavery, effectively did so.

That the legislature supported export bans and private manumission suggests that the primary interest of New York's slaveholders was safeguarding the human labor assets they already possessed rather than trading slaves
across state lines. Of those legislators who can be definitively identified in the
1790 federal census as slaveholders, almost as many voted to maintain the
export ban as voted to eliminate it. Had slave owners voted as a block, this
measure would have passed the lower house.

Most slaveholding representatives wished to retain their flexibility and
control over slave discipline. Thus, slaveholding assemblymen overwhelmingly favored allowing masters to export slaves for disciplinary purposes, traditionally one of the most punitive weapons in a master's arsenal. Slaveholding representatives, however, were divided over whether to oppose a senate
amendment potentially giving masters slightly more latitude over private
manumission decisions, some presumably supporting the masters' prerogative to reward a loyal slave or dump an unproductive one, while others opposed anything that might make manumission more common.[51] As of 1790,
such judgments were being worked out in a complex legal environment: New
York's slave system was partially limited to the state's boundaries, yet slavery
remained protected within those boundaries.

Reformers hoping to win support for gradual emancipation faced powerful opponents who had experienced and often benefited from New York's
deep slaveholding tradition. Building and sustaining antislavery sentiment
and bringing the weight of antislavery public opinion to bear on political
decision making remained difficult. If, in the short-term, the Manumission

Society could not dislodge the legislative power of slaveholders, the society and New Yorkers who shared its antislavery views, could seek to move public opinion over the long term.

V.

Even as the New York Manumission Society sought to prompt the state legislature to action, the organization undertook a project meant to educate African Americans and whites about the efficacy of black freedom. By establishing a model school for New York City's black children, white opponents of slavery attempted an empirical demonstration of the fundamental equality of blacks and whites. The African Free School became an assertion of egalitarian faith, abolitionist symbolism, and the cultural authority of white philanthropists.[52] The school was also indicative of the society's assumption that achieving full emancipation would require a sustained commitment of resources.

Abolitionists understood that they remained suspect in the eyes of many of their white fellow citizens. In January 1790, an unidentified NYMS member sought to publicly "justify" the organization's mission of fighting the slave trade and "promot[ing] a gradual abolition." The advocate acknowledged himself "no stranger to the ungenerous sentiments which some have expressed, that promoting the emancipation of negroes is attended with injury." Some whites believed "that when liberated, and acting for themselves," blacks "do not conduct so well as they did in a state of slavery, but in many instances contract vicious habits and lead disorderly lives." His own sentiments led the writer simultaneously to claim that the society could not itself be blamed for the vices of blacks, that slavery had produced conditions inhibiting self-sufficient virtue, and that "an equal number of whites in similar circumstances" exhibited comparable faults. For its part, the society sought to combat "the loose and immoral behaviour of divers negro families."[53]

The efforts of the NYMS to manage black life in the city took two forms. Society members visited with people in the free black community to exhort more circumspect conduct, and they sought to educate black children, slave and free, imparting skills and manners. Each of these practices in part reflected the Quaker roots of many of the society's members. The Friends Yearly Meeting, like the NYMS, expressed a desire that Quakers educate black servants on the verge of freedom. The New York Friends' practice of exercising moral oversight of potentially wayward members—including the visitation of those unwilling to free their slaves—also had echoes in NYMS plans to visit the black community.[54] The society's goals went beyond an internal sense of moral duty: the NYMS wished white New Yorkers to perceive blacks as worthy recipients of assistance and ultimately freedom. This project would help the society to persuade state lawmakers to ameliorate and abolish slavery. Local magistrates also might be more likely to rule favorably in cases where the freedom of particular individuals was in dispute. Masters might even manumit their slaves more readily if they could be persuaded to accept blacks' capacity to handle freedom responsibly.[55]

The NYMS attempted to convince blacks of the advantage of conforming to white-defined appropriate behavior.[56] At the society's fifth meeting, in August 1785, the standing committee received the charge of monitoring the moral character and work ethic of free blacks. Several months later, the society broached the idea of a school for African American children. Education, the antislavery reformers reasoned, would thwart the development of future behavior reflecting badly on African Americans. After establishing a committee to solicit subscriptions for the school's benefit, the NYMS announced its plan to the general public.[57]

A 1787 outline for the school emphasized mechanisms for selecting and controlling students. The society intended to target for enrollment free blacks between five and fourteen years of age, with "Preference . . . to those . . . Families which are most regular and orderly in their Deportment. . . ." Approval for admission depended upon a visit by the school's governing committee to a prospective student's family. The NYMS desired a posture of quiet obedience from children while in school and in the street back and forth. Following the rules was a key to success, with expulsion an available disciplinary option. If operated properly, the school would "redound to the Honor of the Society and prove singularly beneficial to the Community at Large."[58]

The Manumission Society believed that it faced a great challenge and a great opportunity in refashioning black intellects and morals. Success, reformers imagined, would have an impact on popular thought. Although acknowledging the power of slavery to create "minds . . . so depressed as to be scarcely capable of exulted sentiments," reformers simultaneously regretted that "the unhappy Subjects of it are too often considered as a Race of Beings of inferior Rank in the order of Creation. . . ." By exposing blacks to positive white models and formally educating them, the African Free School had the opportunity to undermine white "Prejudice" and black "Vice."[59]

By the school committee's early estimates, the program functioned effectively from the outset. With nearly forty children "regular in their Attendance," reported the trustees in August 1788, "the progress of the Scholars in Learning and Behaviours . . . have surpassed . . . Expectations." [60] The society continued to record positive observations, sometimes indicating that the school and its students were every bit as good as white schools and white students. Even "prejudiced" persons could not correlate skin color to "orderly behaviour" or "Genius" in the face of such an example. The education of New York's black children, the society felt, had a bright future. [61]

The Manumission Society's assumptions about black education reflected broader suppositions about the virtuous role of education in republican society. Although endorsing a hierarchy of virtue based on knowledge and training, this educational argument had antiracist, or at least nonracist, implications. Publicly announcing plans for the school, the society wrote, "When it is considered that a good education in early life lays a foundation for usefulness in society; and that . . . society" had denied blacks access to it, support should be forthcoming "to carry into execution a plan so consistent with the feelings of humanity, the dictates of christianity, and the principles of sound policy." Just a few months prior to this solicitation, "A Plain Dealer" had expressed comparable sentiments in an essay, "On Education." The writer presumed that "the minds of all men are equal," that the talents of nations, as well as persons, are malleable, and that perceived racial differences really stemmed from differing access to "knowledge." White Americans should draw the proper lessons from their success: "Neither a white skin, or European blood, would have raised this country to its present estimation in the world, without the education and manners our ancestors brought . . . and transmitted to their posterity." [62] The spread of education thus represented one of the new nation's great accomplishments. An editorial observed that "The members of a republic are mutual guards upon each other's conduct," whereas monarchies maintain "*ignorance*" and "*slavish insensibility.*" [63] Commentators saw education as counteracting the worst social ills that might threaten to undermine civil society. [64]

The Manumission Society's commitment to an education program was also an expression of broader environmentalist views held by many opponents of slavery during the late-eighteenth century. According to this line of reasoning, whites' perception of black inferiority could be attributed to the conditions blacks labored under. Shortcomings did not indicate inherent differences permanently barring blacks from full New York or American citizenship. Altered surroundings and expectations would produce African American cultural characteristics and achievements commensurate with those of free whites, whose own virtues and intellects were benefiting from the new nation's republican environment.[65]

The NYMS sought tight control over those to whom it offered help and thus over the laboratory that would prove its environmentalist point. An NYMS committee report wrote explicitly of "Patronage" powers, including the admission of children to school, which could be "withheld" upon discovery of inappropriate behavior by free blacks. When patronage was withheld in a particular case, the society wished that "some mode of informing others of it could be devised; that a Stigma might be fixed upon" the violator "and others . . . thereby deterred" in order "to impress their minds with Sentiments of Respect for the Society." Posting such information at school was viewed as one possible means of doing so.[66] Clearly, then, moral uplift and education represented to the society a means of social control as well as a strategy for combating racism and strengthening long-term abolitionist goals.[67]

The manner in which the NYMS conceived its strategic vision and its relationship to African Americans curiously mirrored the legal approach to slaves adopted by nonabolitionist New York City and state authorities. To New York City's Common Council, as discussed in chapter 3, black violations threatened white control over the peace of the city; for NYMS leaders, black violations threatened their ability to shape the debate over slavery in New York. Common Council regulations of black activity applied most explicitly to the enslaved, with clear implications to free blacks. Manumission Society regulations were mostly pursued with regard to the free but had clear implications for the prospects of the enslaved. City authorities wielded the threat of harsh physical discipline, whereas the antislavery advocates sought to coerce through ostracism by denying support and protection. In some ways, the NYMS picked up where the city left off, urging upon those no longer suffering the direct controls of slavery the need to place restrictions on themselves.[68]

The willingness of the NYMS to accommodate slaveholding members—and of slaveholding members to accommodate continued ownership of their fellow human beings to their broader emancipationist vision—mirrored the state legislature's simultaneous restrictions upon and endorsement of slavery, with uninspiring results for the abolitionist agenda. Thus, during the 1790 legislative session that went so poorly for abolitionists, the discussion tilted away from liberty and toward discipline. Previous debates over quarantining slavery in New York by banning imports and exports transformed into a discussion over the means by which sale outside the state could still be employed to punish law-breaking slaves. The slaveholding interest in maintaining power and authority remained strong in state law and the Manumission Society.

A desire for control and a willingness to accommodate slaveholders notwithstanding, the New York Manumission Society was committed to undermining, not advancing, the future of rights to human property. The Free School and supervision of the free black community were but one part of a broader strategy to undermine support for slavery and to assist individual slaves and former slaves. That effort had enjoyed some limited success by 1792. Reforms in the state's slave code marked a critical first step toward curtailing the absolute property rights of masters. Such restrictions not only set a precedent for further antislavery legislation but also provided slaves and their allies with a new weapon against the institution. Yet such laws were no substitute for a gradual emancipation law, of which the prospects seemed to have slowly dimmed after the initial success in 1785. Slaveholders certainly had not surrendered, and public support for gradual abolition was tenuous.

Slavery's opponents very much hoped to remain attuned to the sensibilities of New York's increasingly politicized public and refused to concede the broadest antislavery principles that animated their cause. A May 14, 1792, standing committee assessment of the NYMS affirmed a commitment to "widely disseminating *truth*" as a means of building their "influence." Earlier that same May, a *New-York Journal* correspondent was even more specific and direct, challenging the argument that the rights of "private property" protected slaveholders from legislative intervention. Government officials, after all, could tax property in certain circumstances. Thus, "how much more have they a right to say in defence of liberty, that every person shall equally enjoy the right of liberty, which is but their own." The polemic went farther in its application of principle, demanding, "Let things speak—they will speak—and actions louder than words. To say I fought for liberty, and hold slaves, is a contradiction that actions cannot say amen to, but most openly declare SELF, *not* LIBERTY."[69]

To assess why antislavery advocates continued to believe that the public might respond favorably to legal and rhetorical attacks on slavery—and to appreciate the obstacles to executing even a gradualist agenda—requires looking well beyond direct criticisms of bondage and the operations of the New York's legislature and the Manumission Society. As the next three chapters detail, the discourse of freedom and slavery shaped and was shaped by debates about political economy, national political ambitions, and regional identities. Indeed, New York—as the last major state to consider the ratification of the U.S. Constitution, as the temporary capital of the nation, and as a site of enormous economic ambition—was well situated to absorb debates about slavery into a broad range of vibrant discussions. Moreover, any consideration of American identity, citizenship, or slavery in New York necessarily entailed constructing new visions of race and challenging existing constructions.

Thus, for political and ideological reasons, the discourse on slavery in New York leaped the narrow bounds of policy making and elite moral advocacy. This was no accident. Opponents and proponents of slavery ensured that the discourse of antislavery worked itself into multiple contexts as they attempted to advance a variety of agendas. As a result, from at least the late 1780s, the subject of racially defined human bondage became inescapable, even as antislavery goals proved largely elusive until the very end of the eighteenth century.

5

Pirates, Sugar, Debtors, and Federalists
The Paradoxes of Antislavery Political Economy

Neglecting commerce and abusing slaves could bring a society to ruin. In the spring of 1786, "Americanus" sought to impress on New Yorkers these lessons from ancient history. "The method in which the Spartans treated their slaves, formed the strongest proof of the pernicious influence of their government," wrote the pseudonymous essayist in the *New-York Journal.* Americanus also lamented, "The rights of mankind, gratitude, and self-interest, were all equally neglected by them in their treatment of slaves." Moreover, the folly of Lycurgus the lawgiver extended beyond slavery to the entire Spartan political economy. The law maintained an artificial conformity of conditions among citizens, rather than giving free play either to their "industry" or to the "natural" pursuit of "happiness." Thus, slavery produced an internal threat to safety, while the larger system restricting consumption left Sparta unprepared to handle the wealth it inevitably acquired. Republican citizens—ancient or modern—were better off mastering commerce than mastering men.[1]

In the wake of independence, many New Yorkers projected for their state and nation a future of trade, growth, development, and economic autonomy. As the parable of ancient Sparta suggested, slavery fit uneasily within this project. Opponents of slavery and proponents of rapid economic expansion—who were sometimes the same people—constructed slavery as undermining the legitimacy of consumption, wealth, and power in New York's growth-oriented political economy.[2] Slavery, at home and abroad, appeared as a practical roadblock and a symbolic converse of this political and economic vision, deterring free trade and confining the potential of free labor.[3]

Slavery's critics thus inserted the issue into a wide variety of debates and discourses that otherwise seemingly had little to do with domestic slavery. A willingness by New York newspapers and activists to funnel arguments from outsiders, especially Pennsylvanians, showed that antislavery in the postrevolutionary North relied on a network of determined advocates capable of acting with ideological dexterity. Many of the arguments regarding slavery during the late 1780s—which swirled around such issues as debt imprisonment, sugar production, Algerian piracy, and the powers of the national government—paid little heed to the technicalities of gradual abolition. Rather, criticism of slavery focused on New York's projected position in the national political order and the Atlantic trading system. Opponents of slavery thus sought to build a case against slavery that matched the tenor of the times.

As vulnerable as slavery was to attacks based on analysis of and analogies to political economy, such an emphasis, until the mid-1790s, also created difficulties for the campaign against slavery. Successful practical applications of antislavery political economy were hard to come by. The debate over the ratification of the U.S. Constitution temporarily trumped all other discussions of political economy, with avatars of growth and development ultimately outflanking their Anti-Federalist rivals. As a matter of perceived tactical necessity and nationalistic priorities, Federalist opponents of slavery in New York by their silence on slavery and by their open complicity in the compromises built into the Constitution seemed to concede that slavery complemented rather than detracted from America's economic and political ambitions.

The years 1788 to 1790 thus brought an additional series of potentially debilitating compromises to state and national antislavery interests. As discussed in chapter 4, in February 1788 New York's state legislature recodified slavery with some concessions to growing opposition within the state. That summer, after overcoming significant dissent, New York ratified a proslavery federal constitution. Subsequent debates in the first federal congress, which met in New York City through 1790, further revealed how difficult it was to apply arguments based on morality or political economy, particularly when acting on the national political stage.

Even so, political expediency and federal politics did not prevent slavery's critics from continuing to highlight a perceived incompatibility between slavery and contemporary visions of economic growth as well as emerging republican social values. Regardless of the constitutional compromise on slavery, New Yorkers pursued their own regional and, sometimes, national campaign against slavery in which indirect critiques harmonized with emerging notions of citizenship, economic ambition, and social order. The antislavery case continued to forge a broad avenue into the state's public discourse, which, combined with shifting perceptions of race, created an ideological context in which white New Yorkers might come to regard gradual abolition itself as plausible, desirable, and necessary. The scope and diversity of antislavery arguments ensured that the case against slavery in New York remained dynamic and politically relevant into the 1790s.

I.

Attaching the language of slavery to specific social problems created opportunities for evaluating African American enslavement in New York and elsewhere. Capital punishment and other forms of public discipline provide examples in which slavery bubbled to the surface as a means of determining relative cruelty. Bondage served as more than a rhetorically charged metaphor in such discussions; it helped measure the relative presence of justice amid postwar attempts to ensure stability. Comparisons to perpetual enslavement helped to evaluate whether capital punishment and debt imprisonment were acceptable social discipline. Conversely, discussion of criminal punishment encouraged New York newspaper readers to contemplate where, if anywhere, slavery fit into a social order still marked by certain forms of enforced hierarchy. Some commentators implied that slavery—like hierarchy—still had its place in a revolutionary society.

Both sides of the capital punishment debate drew on the concept of slavery for justification. In the fall and winter of 1788–89 the *New-York Packet* featured an exchange on the death penalty in which the participants disparaged slavery.[4] The first commentator invoked the enslavement of Africans to advance the argument that neither biblical nor social precedent could justify an immoral practice. The writer suggested with irony that if the Bible commanded the execution of murderers it might also be necessary "to sell every Guinea Captain to our West-Indian planters" as punishment for the slave trade. However awkwardly, this author connected an immoral labor system and an immoral form of punishment.[5]

The pro-execution rejoinder argued that capital punishment enforced a divinely sanctioned system of social ranking, while slavery lay just beyond the pale of acceptability. The example of slavery helped clarify proper and improper ways of maintaining order. The essayist argued that more, not less, bondage would result from an abolition of the death penalty. Fewer executions would embolden potential murderers; more crimes would be committed if they were punishable by permanent slavery rather than death. Although viewing slavery itself as a wrong, this writer saw it as "only a partial abuse of a good and lawful thing," by which he meant the "necessity of . . . the relation of master and servant." Thus, from slavery, this author built a bridge between the subjects of social discipline and social hierarchy. Even if chattel bondage itself did not fit into this vision of class, the concept of slavery contributed to the argument for social ranking.[6]

Discussion of criminal punishment rehearsed the long-standing philosophical notion of slavery as a substitute for death and as a form of criminal justice.[7] In the 1780s, these associations were vivid and immediate rather than abstract. Not only did New Yorkers debate whether to make criminal punishment less violent during this era, but they also knew that African Americans were subject to this ultimate form of retribution, as well as to judicially sanctioned corporal abuse. West Indian executions were described in gory detail. Bloody retribution took place in New York, New Jersey, and the American South as well. Meanwhile, the alternatives to capital punishment for criminals in general remained some form of forced captivity or labor.[8] Capital punishment thus helped to keep the subject of slavery before the reading public. In the 1790s, social reformers pushed for substantive reforms of both practices.[9] The relationship between capital punishment and slavery stimulated reflections about the nature of justice, even though no consensus was reached.

II.

The punishment of debtors also occasioned commentary in which slavery's alleged leniency illustrated debt imprisonment's severity. Imprisoning debtors and enslaving African laborers shared characteristics of coerced subordination, according to two writers for the *Packet*. One essayist prefaced remarks on debtor imprisonment by noting that the international effort to curb the slave trade had borne some fruit in New York with a legislated ban on the further import of slaves into the state.[10] Expressing a hope that slavery would soon disappear, the writer abruptly pivoted: "Would to God a slavery and oppression in many instances more cruel than negro slavery, could also be done away, or the horrors of it mitigated, and brought to be more consonant to the principles of religion, and . . . natural liberty. . . ." The imprisoned debtor lacked basic opportunities "seldom denied to the race of blacks" and became "civilly dead." Another essayist cast the comparison of slavery and debt imprisonment in less antagonistic terms, saying both practices "involve the whole period of" the victim's "life in one black night of substantial misery."[11] These writers intentionally raised the stakes of their arguments by invoking slavery, not simply in the abstract but as a concrete form of racial oppression.

A newspaper essay reprinted from Britain integrated proslavery arguments into an analysis of debt imprisonment. The fifth installment of "The Tradesman" series turned to the issue of African slavery in the West Indies to drive home the necessity of reform. Abolitionists, the commentator claimed, should recognize that the African in the island colonies suffered less material deprivation, enjoyed "infinitely more freedom," and answered to fewer mas-

ters than the British debtor. These arguments appealed to proslavery parlia-
mentarians. West Indian slavery at least had national economic necessity and
productivity on its side. Debt imprisonment, by contrast, produced neither
the alleged benefits of paternalistically granted privileges nor the advantages
of wealth-generating labor. Antislavery advocates would "rip up established
branches of commerce . . . risque a revolution, and convulse the universe"
for "the stranger."[12] This essayist, like some New York readers, prioritized
national commercial development in the analysis of a political problem.

Constructing the new commercial order prompted significant debate over
humanitarian and commercial reform.[13] Between 1786 and 1791, New York's
legislature revised its statutes on insolvency and debtor imprisonment no
fewer than eight times. Although the bulk of the considerable commentary
on the wrongs of debt imprisonment did not mention slavery, the two issues
echoed allied themes of unwarranted suffering, tyranny, and dependence.[14]
Capital punishment, slavery, and debt imprisonment raised questions about
the trade-offs between civil and actual death. Evaluating such trade-offs had
become critical to defining social order in a new era. Whether the civilly
dead had any role to play in a commercially and politically vibrant society
was now very much open to question.

III.

Stories of American sailors kidnapped on the high seas by Algerian pirates
and held as slaves provided a platform for directly denouncing domestic slavery in New York's newspapers. Such stories also exposed the vulnerability of
the nation's commerce in ways that created opportunities and challenges for
the relationship between slavery and the requirements of a vibrant American political economy. Antislavery advocates purposefully capitalized on the
parallels between their cause and specific public preoccupations. Slavery's
opponents insisted on American slavery's special connections to particular
struggles for justice and national sovereignty. Thus, the nation's shaky international standing and New York's economic potential occasioned the fortuitous blending of antislavery tactics and humanitarian ideas.

A story emerged in the mid-1780s which simultaneously spoke of the
literal slavery of individual Americans and the more figurative slavery of the
nation. Under the auspices of the Dey of Algiers and the Moroccan em-
peror, approximately 150 captured Americans between 1784 and 1796 were
subjected to slavery on the other side of the Atlantic Ocean. For some, the
outcry over Algerian enslavement suggested the opportunity to publicly
question African slavery in America. For others, the new nation's inability to

prevent the enslavement of its people epitomized its extreme vulnerability. In either case, the concept of slavery fostered debate over America's identity.[15] Antislavery advocates seized upon the nation's self-righteous grievances about Mediterranean slavery to draw attention to the evils of African bondage in America. The essayist "Humanus" remarked on the absurdity of shedding tears for white slaves torn from their families and not for black slaves torn from theirs. Humanus asked if any difference existed between American slaveholders and "the disciples of Mahomet?"—a rhetorical question answered by a harrowing description of a slave market in Charleston, South Carolina.[16]

A Pennsylvania reprint appearing in a Poughkeepsie newspaper used even more condemnatory tones to force readers to contemplate the moral implications of Algerian piracy and American slavery. The writer noted that America's own "worship" of "LIBERTY" and "FREEDOM," did not comport with the existence of slavery, nor did the nation's dismay over Algerian assaults. The writer pushed further: "They perhaps, are only retaliating for the cruelties which *we christians* exercise towards their unfortunate brethren the Africans—(Algiers is in Africa) but we are without excuse." In the light of the suffering that Americans inflicted on Africans, the essayist urged slaveholders and legislators to act resolutely to free their black slaves. A Poughkeepsie editor the following year published the Pennsylvania Abolition Society's earnest proclamation that assisting Americans held captive in Algeria fell within the organization's antislavery mandate, thus underscoring the moral equivalency between white and black enslavement.[17]

Expression of moral equivalency between different forms of slavery was, for some, a bitter irony. A 1787 dispatch printed in the *New-York Packet* on sailors from Philadelphia held captive in Algiers denounced the continued outfitting of slave ships in Boston and Philadelphia: "The equipment of vessels, in your own ports, by your own subjects, for the open and avowed purpose of enslaving their fellow men, bears ample proof of your sanction and approbation! and the stigma will be fixed on you as a people and not on the individuals who are immediately engaged in the business for pecuniary motives." One illicit form of commerce was no better than another, and, according to this correspondent, there was no such thing as innocent American bystanders to the malign traffic.[18]

The debate over the U.S. Constitution's ratification magnified the significance of Algerian slavery, seemingly dislodging the subject of any connection to American slavery in order to place the Algerian saga in the midst of a story about the nation's broadest ambitions. In David Humphreys's "A

Poem on the Future Glory of the United States," which appeared in the *Albany Journal* in late winter 1788, national self-image and commercial aspirations coalesced. The poem employed the conflict with Algiers to construct an elaborate drama of national redemption based on these themes.[19] After describing the promise of domestic development and commercial greatness, Humphreys asked readers to contemplate "the shrinking slave, th' uplifted lash, / The frowning butcher and the red'ning gash" characteristic of American imprisonment. The poet excoriated European powers for making deals with "Afric's lords" whose "dark limbs" wear the Asian finery given to them as bribes for safe passage. The poem offered solace through an imagined naval battle in which the Americans triumphantly "free" not only enslaved prisoners but also all mankind. The closing couplet enjoined the American audience to look to the future: "Unbar the gates of commerce for their race, / And build the gen'ral peace on freedom's broadest base!"

Humphreys's poem, by bringing together themes of slavery, race war, and national, commercial triumph, illustrated how much more serious than lost cargo was America's conflict with the corsairs. Humphreys, a man who had won George Washington's trust as a soldier and who, as a diplomat, was involved in negotiations with the Barbary powers, constructed a narrative of national triumph that could only be achieved by overcoming tremendous national adversity.[20] Thus, in his poem, as in the later work of playwright Susanna Rowson, national slavery and personal slavery became almost one, the metaphor of enslavement blending with anxieties over white Americans in chains. Moreover, continuous assaults on a free nation's commerce compromised its dignity. If commerce represented the engine of international freedom, as so many English and American writers believed, then confrontation with foreign slavery became essential to the advancement of unfettered trade.[21] Humphreys in essence Americanized the themes of English antislavery poet William Cowper, whose "Charity" (1781) linked international commerce to human advancement and freedom for black slaves. In Humphreys's poem, the links to black freedom were at best implicit, leaving it to antislavery advocates to make the connection explicit.[22]

Nationalism aside, opponents of slavery continued into the 1790s to invoke Algerian enslavement in order to make their case and punctuate their rhetoric. Before and after the United States reached a diplomatic accord with Algiers and captive American sailors finally returned home, antislavery advocates used the image of Barbary piracy to hound their opponents.[23] Algerian piracy thus kept the evils of enslavement before the public in a fashion at once poignantly specific and broadly evocative of the nation's political and economic preoccupations.

IV.

As Americans contemplated a new federal system to protect and nourish the nation's worldly ambitions, debt, disorder, and weakness spawned a set of conflicting narratives about slavery's place in the future political order. The travail of Algerian harassment of American shipping represented the kind of national failure that the new constitution would correct. According to one speaker in late 1787: "You are not in a condition to resist the most contemptible enemy. What is there to prevent an Algerine Pirate from landing on your coast, and carrying your citizens to slavery?"[24] But a few months earlier, one writer drew a more abrupt, direct connection between slavery and the nation's political ills. In the midst of an essay on Shays's rebellion of agrarian Massachusetts debtors—an event that lent urgency to plans to draft a new federal constitution—appeared the stunning demand: "[D]iscountenance your SLAVE-TRADE!" for "the arm of freedom and the voice of humanity will ever *revolt* and *rebel* against it!" Clearly, slavery could infiltrate New York's political discourse during the 1780s and 1790s even at the most improbable moments, alternately highlighting America's weakness or its moral shame.[25]

The debate over the U.S. Constitution's ratification tested—with mixed results—the proposition that New York should answer for the ongoing national problem of slavery. Yet just as New York legislators lacked the political will during the late 1780s to gradually abolish slavery, Federalist proponents of the national charter almost entirely subordinated their antislavery views to the cause of ratification. Instead, Federalists championed the Constitution as a potential bulwark of political and economic freedom. The banners of growth, order, and national greatness, which opponents of slavery sometimes waved, were planted in the Federalist camp. To secure ratification, Federalists preferred not to address the slavery issue directly.[26] Indeed, the New York Manumission Society (NYMS), which included leading Federalists, in August 1787 aborted a plan to memorialize the Constitutional Convention on the subject of slavery.[27] Thus, while the debate over the Constitution provided another avenue for denouncing slavery to the New York public, it also demonstrated the difficulties and compromises still confronting the antislavery cause.

Although never mentioning slavery by name, its framers riddled the Constitution with allusions to the institution. In most instances in which slaveholding southern interests sought language favoring racial bondage—on subjects such as representation, the slave trade, and fugitives—the Constitutional Convention acceded to one degree or another. Slavery clearly ranked as a low priority among the many ills that America's leading political intellects sought to cure during the summer of 1787.[28]

Gouverneur Morris's response was indicative of the dilemma of antislavery Federalists and their ultimate acquiescence to slaveholding interests in the writing of the Constitution. Although representing Pennsylvania at the 1787 Constitutional Convention, Morris was a native New Yorker. As a delegate to that state's constitutional convention a decade before, this son of one of New York's largest slaveholders had attempted unsuccessfully to insert abolitionist language in the state's new charter. Morris's dislike of slavery and his commitment to a strong national government conflicted in Philadelphia. He vigorously denounced concessions made to southern slaveholding states. Yet he not only signed the new national Constitution, he employed his noted skills as a draftsman to polish the language of the final document.[29] Morris's even more prominent New York associates, Alexander Hamilton and John Jay, both founding members of the Manumission Society, championed the proposed Constitution during the ensuing New York ratification debate.

The last major state to approve the new charter of union, New Yorkers were exposed to a full range of arguments about the new system of governance through essays written by and for New Yorkers, as well as those circulating from other states. Americans did not have to read between the lines to understand the rhetorical and metaphorical significance of slavery to the proposed Constitution. The ratification debate provided new impetus for invoking the symbol of political enslavement. If, for Federalists, the travail of Algerian enslavement represented the kind of national failure that the new Constitution would correct, opponents might imagine that the federal system itself would demand from the people the obedience of slaves. Remarks by Maryland's Luther Martin, printed in the *New-York Journal,* highlighted the imbalance between small and large states in the House of Representatives, invoking the traditional political slavery metaphor. Small states, he argued, "would be as absolutely slaves as any negro is to his masters. . . . whenever their master pleased he might draw them so tight as to gall them to the bone." Defenders of the Constitution, on the other hand, could counter skeptically, "who are these people that are about to enslave us?"—"our countrymen, our brethren, chosen from among us."[30]

Federalists would have to parry not only insinuations about metaphorical slavery but also attacks on the Constitution's handling of actual bondage.

Anti-Federalists seized the moral high ground when addressing slavery's role in the controversial document. Article I of the Constitution prohibited Congress from passing a ban against slave importation until 1808. This clause became the target of righteous indignation. A "Countryman from Dutchess County," whose actual identity remains uncertain, assailed this protection of the slave trade from a variety of angles. It contradicted Federalist pretensions to "universal Benevolence" and made a mockery of the ideals of the American Revolution, as well as the Christian religion. While this country was "entailing endless Servitude on Millions of the human Race, and their unborn Posterity," seemingly less liberty-minded nations in Europe had, claimed the Countryman, taken steps against the trade.[31]

Anti-Federalists demanded the framers account for the use of slavery in the calculation of representatives to the national legislature. The clause of the Constitution counting each slave as three-fifths of a person when determining the size of the states' congressional delegations appeared to pervert the very meaning of representation. The ancient tradition of self-government had long established that free males who had reached an appropriate age had the right to participate in politics. New York's own constitution recognized that the concept of representation was an extension of this principle. The U.S. Constitution dramatically abandoned it. Through an interregional compromise, the South gained an extra advantage with logic as absurd as if "horses" and "oxen" were "represented." Adding further insult, the Constitution contained a domestic insurrection clause that might require northerners to help crush the revolts of the slave trade's victims.[32]

Opponents of the Constitution argued that the document's concessions proved that the Federalists could not be trusted. Obfuscating language that never expressly mentioned slavery insinuated the institution into the plan of government. The Countryman from Dutchess County suggested that some men at the Constitutional Convention had been duped by those hostile to popular liberty. The sinister intent of the framers was to use the nation itself as "Cloaks . . . to cover their Wickedness." Said the "Centinel" of the slave-trade clause, "The words are dark and ambiguous; such as no plain man of common sense would have used. . . ." The three-fifths clause suffered from the same suspicious debility. "What a strange and unnecessary accumulation of words," "Brutus" wrote in the *New-York Journal*, "are here used to conceal from the public eye" that slaves would be represented in the federal scheme.

"Cincinnatus" offered an even more conspiratorial reading. The Constitution renounced the authority to amend the slave trade protection until

1808, which to Cincinnatus indicated that the federal government intended to expand its authority in other unnamed ways. The framers' underhanded approach to the indefensible institution of slavery added weight to the charge that the people should not trust the new plan of government and those who designed it.[33] New York's own proslavery legislators had faced a similar charge of evil-minded manipulation after the defeat of a gradual abolition bill in 1785.[34]

Although proponents of the Constitution addressed the slavery question in terms that also resonated with the perspectives of white New Yorkers, it was the Virginian Madison and not New Yorkers Hamilton and Jay who took up the onerous task in the Federalist Papers of apologizing for the document's proslavery tilt. Federalists offered a mix of legalistic rationalizations and sanguine assurances to protect their credibility and neutralize this delicate problem. Defenders of the Constitution noted that the Articles of Confederation had not even contemplated an end to the slave trade. Thus, the possibility of ending this commerce two decades hence, and in the interim permitting a ten-dollar tax on each slave imported, represented progress. Besides, as the Madison-authored essay Federalist 42 noted, the individual states were well on their way to shutting off the African slave trade. Madison's "Publius" failed to note that the Constitution did not require the federal government to do anything about slavery, even in 1808.[35]

With regard to the three-fifths clause, Madison, in Federalist 54, urged readers to respect the rights of individual states to define citizenship. The South allegedly had made a concession. Other states could exclude individuals from the franchise while fully counting them toward population totals for the purposes of federal representation. Attempting to broaden the appeal of his apology for slavery, Madison, writing as Publius, noted, "Government is instituted no less for protection of the property, than of the persons of individuals." New Yorkers, the essay continued, could relate to the importance of constitutional protections of property. In their own state charter, a higher property requirement for casting ballots in state senate elections made that body "the guardian of property" rights. Thus, Madison cleverly sought to create a community of interest between New Yorkers and southerners on the grounds of political common sense, citizenship, and property rights.[36]

Publius's defense of the insurrection clause made common cause with New Yorkers in a provocative fashion. Federalist 43's explanation drew attention to "an unhappy species of population abounding in some of the States, who during the calm of regular government are sunk below the level of men"; during "tempestuous scenes of civil violence" such people "may emerge into the human character, and give a superiority of strength to any party with which they may associate themselves." This reference to slave rebellion would have resonated with many white New Yorkers, who in 1788 could remember the ties between slaves and the British during the Revolutionary War. Given bitter Anti-Federalist criticism and the emerging antislavery tone of New York political discourse, such an allusion made more sense than an attempt to ally the South and New York as fellow slave territories. Madison thus executed a strategy, at various moments evasive, persuasive, and subtle, to blunt the righteous indignation of Anti-Federalists in the debate over ratification in New York.[37]

When trumpeting the economic benefits of interregional unity, Madison's principle pro-Constitution colleague, Hamilton, directly declared the document's virtues; the NYMS member preferred not even to acknowledge the slavery issue in his discussion of the economic advantages of an enhanced union. Hamilton's Publius, in Federalist No. 11, proclaimed, "The importance of the Union, in a commercial light, is one of those points, about which there is least room to entertain an opinion. . . ." Hamilton celebrated a united America's potential greatness in transatlantic trading as well as mutually beneficial internal trade: "An unrestrained intercourse between the States themselves will advance the trade of each . . . not only for the supply of reciprocal wants at home, but for exportation to foreign markets." He concluded his essay on commerce, "Let the thirteen States, bound together in a strict and indissoluble union, concur in erecting one great American system. . . ."[38] Hamilton did not need to—and perhaps did not want to—add that internal and international trade in the newly invigorated union would be fueled by the products of slavery. Nor, unless pressed, did he wish to acknowledge the compromises reached with slaveholding states to secure centralized political authority. For him and other northern Federalists who looked toward eventual abolition in their region, slavery's malign influence on economic development and public morals was at that moment more safely ignored than addressed. The sources of Federalist optimism about a nation united in commerce were hardly obscure. Optimistic reports of the potential of southern cotton and unbridled enthusiasm for the future of cotton manufacturing in the north provided reason for the public to view the South in a less jaundiced light and to back off from antislavery ideals.[39]

As the ratification debate proceeded, leading New York proponents of gradual abolition did not adopt a unified response to the Constitution, further limiting any damage that slavery might have done to ratification's prospects. Even Quakers seemed to offer tentative support for the new charter.[40]

Symbolizing the debilitating split in antislavery ranks, Melancton Smith, also an NYMS member, and Hamilton debated the three-fifths clause at New York's ratifying convention. Smith attacked the concession to southern interests. "He could not see any rule by which slaves are to be included in the ratio of representation . . . it was absurd to give that power to a man who could not exercise it. . . . The very operation of it was to give certain privileges to those people who were so wicked as to keep slaves." Smith conceded that the compromise, "though utterly repugnant to his feelings," probably was necessary to secure southern support of the compact. It was the compact itself that Smith rejected.

Hamilton, who was the only New York delegate to the Philadelphia convention who signed the final document, attempted to defend the proposed system for apportioning federal representation by shifting the question from moral to practical grounds. He viewed the vast southern slave population as an "unfortunate situation" that had to be accommodated. That "accommodation," moreover, would serve the entire nation's economic interest in securing profits from trade in southern "staples." Like Madison in Federalist 54, Hamilton emphasized that the formula flowed from conventional political wisdom that representation should reflect and protect property-holding rights. The "laws of nature" understood slaves to be "persons" but insofar as slaves were taxed as property, Hamilton asserted, southerners should receive a compensating increase in their representation. In a contest between higher law and practical calculations, Hamilton awarded the victory to the practical logic of politics. Unless one accepted Smith's broader assertion that the allegedly high ratio of voters to representatives would place citizens under the will of their federal lawmakers, transforming ordinary people into slaves, Hamilton's calculations of political right and wrong on slavery were perhaps sufficient to blunt Smith's attack on the three-fifths clause itself.[41]

In New York, as elsewhere, federal union did not seem worth sacrificing to concerns over slavery, especially when slavery represented but one issue in the broad and spirited contest over ratification.[42] Indeed, the rights of "freemen," not slaves, proved the most fruitful avenue for mollifying the concerns of Anti-Federalists. Thus, the Bill of Rights extended the meaning of citizenship for already largely enfranchised white men.[43] The potential citizenship of blacks, enslaved or free, was left, at least for the moment, to the devices of the states. Such a move, ironically, comported with anti-Federalist opposition to centralized federal power.[44] In the end, the vision of a unified, vigorous commercial nation largely vanquished Anti-Federalist objections, including those relating to slavery.[45]

The ultimate acceptance of the U.S. Constitution in New York, however, cannot be read as an endorsement of slavery. The antislavery perspective of some Anti-Federalists forced Federalists on the defensive, at least regarding this one point. New Yorkers were exposed in yet another way to the problems that slavery raised about citizenship and national identity. As discussions of Algerian enslavement, domestic sugar production, and criminal reform also demonstrated during this era, they continued to face issues surrounding political economy and social stability.[46] The Constitution could resolve these challenges no more decisively than it could remove the problem of slavery from the political landscape. Ubiquitous and persistently relevant, slavery's entry into the political discourse of national and state life remained unavoidable. Indeed, the consolidation of the republic achieved through ratification of the Constitution subsequently magnified slavery as a national issue of immediate interest to New Yorkers.[47]

v.

While ratification of the Constitution confirmed slavery's national future as well as a variety of commercial ambitions, growth through the development of internal resources and territorial expansion provided new ways to imagine a robust New York economy explicitly divorced from slave labor.[48] Although the much anticipated prospects of domestic maple sugar proved illusory, the campaign to promote New York sugar illustrated the public's continued taste for antislavery ideology. With a vast, undeveloped hinterland climatically suited to maple sugar production, New York state was to be one of the prime locations for this new source of national wealth.[49] Maple sugar dramatized the intertwining of slavery with American attempts at self-definition and economic self-determination. As with discussions of Algerian captivity and debtor imprisonment, sugar allowed New Yorkers to view the moral implications of slavery in relation to the broader goals of economic growth, national self-interest, and a positive American self-image.

Maple sugar advocates trumpeted the product's quality and its ability to improve America's balance of payments, as well as its moral utility. A November 1788 Albany newspaper item, reprinted from Philadelphia, noted the large amount of money spent on West Indian sugar, suggested that Americans produce their own with maple syrup, and offered recipes for maple molasses, beer, wine, and vinegar.[50] Another reprinted Philadelphia report in 1789 held similarly high hopes with an added moralistic dimension: "immense sums of money will be saved to our country, and what is more, our country freed from guilt of encouraging the detestable traffic in human creatures."[51]

Supporters of domestic sugar production hailed the interconnectedness of moral responsibility and commerce. In the best case, economic self-interest and moral scruples would go hand in hand. In any case, national economic goals would be served. A letter written to New York City's *Daily Advertiser* advocated boycotting sugar made by slaves, in part as a token of moral earnestness. The writer also promoted the maple tree, a source of sugar and salvation which happened to be "boundless" in America. He calculated that America might "save" close to $1.5 million each year. Moreover, the United States could launch its own sugar exports, thus slashing the profits of West Indian slaveholders.[52]

Maple sugar offered the possibility of sweetness and profit without guilt or danger. The potential boon attracted the attention of prominent New York politicians and civic leaders. The state government expressed support for the cultivation of maple sugar. In Albany, money was secured to disseminate literature and to sponsor a contest designed to stimulate production. Unlike antislavery circles spreading optimistic projections about maple sugar, such local explorations focused more narrowly on economic benefits. Still, the New York City newspaper that printed the Albany contest announcement felt compelled to follow it with a pointed reference: "Why should we risk the poison and filth of the West-India negroes in our sugar and molasses, when we can have the pure juice of the maple for nothing?"[53] Although not advancing a vision of social justice, such a statement nonetheless underscored the relationship between slavery and sugar production in the Americas.

The leading New York figure in the elusive campaign for sugar-fueled independence was William Cooper, a tremendously ambitious frontier Federalist politician who also enjoyed close ties to prominent Pennsylvania Quaker businessmen. In the mid-1780s, Cooper, himself a lapsed Quaker and moderately successful New Jersey speculator and merchant, projected his social, economic, and political ambitions onto the heavily forested lands surrounding New York's Lake Ostego. With the help of his lawyer, Alexander Hamilton, Cooper secured a large land patent on the frontier. He then eagerly began selling parcels of land to settlers for commercial development. Fusing his ambition with the desire of his Pennsylvania patrons to do good in the world, he heavily promoted a plan to tap into the state's vast wealth of sugar-producing maple trees. Cooper thus served as a conduit for helping to channel Pennsylvania-inspired antislavery idealism into the arena of New York elite, Federalist-directed frontier economic growth.[54]

Would-be frontier grandee Cooper linked the maple tree to a positive vision of socioeconomic development. He likened maple sugar to the bur-

ied treasure of Latin American mines but worried that hasty and ill-con-
sidered action by American farmer-pioneers would squander this resource.
Perhaps three million New York maple trees suffered destruction each year.
Yet he believed that "a full supply" of sugar "may be manufactured within the
boundaries of this state, for the consumption" of the nation.

Slavery provided a public foil for Cooper's version of the west. He described for the Agricultural Society of the State of New-York a system of
maple sugar sharecropping. Landlords would provide tools and land "to be
settled by families," as well as "transportation" to market, thus creating a
system of debt and credit "ensur[ing] profit to landholders." Maple sugar did
not require "the lash of cruelty on our fellow creatures," just tree preservation and economic incentive.[55]

Advocates of maple sugar indulged in imagining virtuous economic development. Maple sugar, according to its promoters, had the unusual merit of
generating wealth without requiring a large amount of effort. Individual and
national advantage could be gained by harnessing an idle resource, unused
time, and untapped household labor. An optimistic essayist remarked, "it is
plain, that a farmer . . . could raise nothing on his farm with less labor, and
nothing from which he would derive more emolument, than the sugar maple
tree." Another writer celebrated the "buxom health and voluntary labor" of
"girls" in gathering and processing maple sap in contrast with the dismal
West Indian "scene" of "the famished mother on the parched mountain with
her child tied to her back."[56]

Maple sugar advocates thus helped to introduce into public dialogue
the notion that certain types of labor harmonized better than others with
the standards of a just and economically healthy society. They indicated
free labor's superiority to slave labor. Indeed, the labor to produce maple
sugar was almost literally free, at least as far as male heads of household and
landowners were concerned. As much as a positive work ethic, maple sugar
cultivation demonstrated the benefits of household prerogative, speculative
landownership, and nature's well-managed bounty.[57]

As William Cooper's personal practices suggest, the future promise of
sugar hardly erased the current reality of slaveholding in New York. Like the
members of the New York elite he emulated, the ambitious developer maintained slaves as personal servants in his impressive frontier home. There,
slaves served not only his family but also his desire for tokens of his affluence
and gentility.[58]

The issues raised by sugar were much broader than the personal inconsistencies of Cooper and others like him. American sugar consumption it-

self made the commodity an appealing symbol and a difficult challenge for antislavery efforts. America's identity as a country in which even people of humble social status lived prosperously rested in part on widespread sugar consumption. Sugar was a ubiquitous part of daily life, bound up with slavery and other issues of equality.[59] Indeed, the choice of sweeteners for the American table cut remarkably close to the core ethical issues of eighteenth-century capitalist development. Bernard Mandeville's 1714 parable *The Fable of the Bees* had touted to European intellectuals the social benefits of the unrestrained commercial pursuit of luxury. While Mandeville's model of self-serving economy ensured marked inequality, greater wealth and productivity were deemed the more-than-sufficient social dividend. But did men have to be used like bees to produce such dividends?

"A Fable for Sugar Eaters," appearing in a 1792 *New-York Magazine,* offered a more particularized, literalized version of Mandeville's capitalist conundrum. The updated fable presented a conversation between a bee and an African plantation slave in the West Indies. The slave recalled the relative ease of subsistence in Africa as compared with the fatal cruelty of Caribbean field work. The bee, noting the joyous, natural process of making honey, wondered at the white preference for the black man's labor over that of the insect's. Although in other contexts the beehive metaphor was employed to legitimate a variety of conflicting institutions and ideals, this particular parable offered a stark choice. The exploitation of bees, mere insects even when anthropomorphized for literary effect, belonged in an entirely different category than the systematic abuse of real human beings. Consumption, no less than production, thus entailed moral decisions even as the mighty river of commerce swept onward.[60]

Solutions to the sugar conundrum, moreover, betrayed the fantastic quality that often typified conversations about race during the early national period.[61] The sugar fantasy, like that of ending slavery through mass resettlement, could retrace the steps of the slave trade back to Africa, thus linking the two projects. New York newspapers carried suggestions for shifting sugar cultivation to African soil. Free-labor African sugar would eliminate the need for slavery and the slave trade, and might even carry the added bonus of developing new markets for American and European trade.[62] In racially oriented colonization fantasies and sugar fantasies, Americans thus imagined a straightforward solution, involving minimal sacrifice on their part, which would remove black people and slavery.[63]

The effort to fight slavery through economic development represented a historical irony that was not mentioned by earnest maple sugar promoters. Colonial New York City's tremendous growth as a port during the early eighteenth century resulted from expanding opportunities to provision West Indian sugar islands. Some merchants themselves entered the slave trade, and the colony's population of black slaves expanded accordingly.[64] The new antislavery entrepreneurial ethos of maple sugar production offered the prospect of moral self-congratulation rather than sobering backward glances to New York's previous economic expansion.

For all its fantastic qualities and unanswered questions, discussion of alternative sugar production signaled slavery's continued relevance to New York's sense of itself and its place in the Atlantic commercial order. Rather than divert attention away from racial bondage, sugar, like Algerian piracy and domestic legal reform, highlighted servitude's uneasy relationship with the state's economic ambitions and moral identity. Slavery helped to define the outer boundary of cruelty for domestic legal reformers. Algerian piracy prevented the international free trade central to commercial development. And the importation of slave-produced sugar prevented trade from being an authentic exercise in freedom. Political realities such as a union with southern slaveholders who insisted that the Constitution protect their most productive assets did not stifle efforts to promote an antislavery version of moral equilibrium within the American political economy. Indeed, the earnest discussion in New York's newspapers of maple sugar's economic and moral potential illustrated how readily antislavery ideas could gain a hearing in a political environment preoccupied with many other matters.

VI.

At the same time that the virtues of maple sugar were being promoted, New York and Pennsylvania abolitionists pressed their case in the arenas of national politics and international commerce. In February 1790 three distinct petitions to Congress arrived in New York City, the nation's temporary capital, broaching the subject of regulating U.S. participation in the slave trade. The congressional response to these petitions briefly made New York City the center of a national antislavery debate.

One memorial was forwarded by the Yearly Meeting of Pennsylvania, New Jersey, Delaware, western Maryland, and Virginia; another arrived from the Pennsylvania Abolition Society bearing the signature of its president, Benjamin Franklin; and a third came from Quakers in New York and western New England. Although all the memorials were operating in the shadow of the Constitution's protection of the international slave trade until 1808, the two Pennsylvania petitions spoke in lofty rhetoric to advance a broad antislavery vision. The Pennsylvania Abolition Society openly favored the general goal of emancipation, hoping that Congress would "step to the very verge of the power vested in you for discouraging every species of traffic in the persons of our fellow men." The New York Friends' more specific and limited appeal was as much a response to local political conditions as an expression of high moral principle. The New York Friends and the Manumission Society had petitioned the state government to crack down on those participating in the slave trade in violation of the spirit of New York's laws. According to the congressional petition, the lack of uniformity among the states allowed "avaricious men" in New York to continue participating in the inhumane commerce on behalf of non–New Yorkers. When the Friends had sought redress from New York's own legislature, that body claimed that the U.S. Constitution put the matter in the hands of the federal government. The New York Quakers thus sought U.S. congressional help to maintain the policy of legal containment, which in theory separated slavery in New York from slavery elsewhere.[65]

Despite limits to what Congress itself could do and despite the modesty of the New York petition compared to the two Pennsylvania memorials, the possibility of federal regulation of slavery touched off a broad-based attack on Quakers and other northern emancipationists. Southern congressmen responded with lengthy diatribes that advanced three interlocking themes: the economic and racial necessity of American slavery as practiced in the South, the impracticability of a national policy of emancipation regardless of northern beliefs and measures against the institution, and the illegitimacy of the Quakers as petitioners to the U.S. government. Coverage in New York City's *Daily Advertiser* and other newspapers thus gave public prominence to a full defense of slavery itself.[66]

Congressional remarks justifying slavery appealed to American prejudices. Southerners lectured on the natural inequality of Africans, with the cruelties of bondage in Africa itself represented as much worse than the happy life of the southern slave. Yet, invoking Thomas Jefferson's *Notes on the State of Virginia,* proslavery southern speakers claimed that African Americans had to be treated as a people apart, lest miscegenation degrade white America's racial stock.[67] These and other broad points bolstered specific claims about the Constitution's protection of slavery, the inextricability of slavery from southern life, and the inviolable rights of property.

On the national stage, southerners, led by South Carolina congressman William Loughton Smith, felt compelled to debunk northern self-congratulation over the potential effectiveness of gradual abolition. Northerners were accused of wishing to close off the slave trade so that they might sell their own economically unnecessary slave population to southern buyers. Moreover, the whole notion of gradual emancipation, predicated on granting freedom to the children of current slaves, would fail. Slave mothers would simply impart the bad habits of slavery to their children. Worse still, in the southern view, gradual abolition and an end to the slave trade would lead inexorably to racial amalgamation. In his proslavery assault, Congressman Smith also questioned the notion "that public opinion was against slavery." A few Pennsylvanians and Quakers hardly constituted a "whole continent." One region could not "dictate to Congress" another region's interest. Smith even wisecracked that despite objections to certain elements in the northern population, southerners did not ask Congress "to exterminate the Quakers."[68]

Ostracizing Quakers from public discourse was a central priority of the proslavery counterattack. Southern speeches repeatedly disparaged Friends. The petitions did not stem from "any real necessity which existed . . . but to gratify . . . the theoretical speculations on humanity, of a society of Quakers." It was not slaves but Quaker pacifists who undermined the nation's military security. The most damning point to which these assailants returned was the sect's lack of devotion to America. The bloody shirt of Quaker loyalism during the conflict with the British acquired added power from the fact that the mother country also had used former slaves against the breakaway colonies. Bringing the indictment of the Quakers full circle, congressional assailants charged that wartime loyalism made the Friends "supporters of the most abject slavery . . . a slavery attempted on their countrymen from the disgraceful yoke of foreigners." Proslavery congressmen turned Revolutionary slavery rhetoric to their own advantage by seeking to sever the link between the metaphor and the reality of bondage. In the process, they exposed the vulnerability of an abolition movement associated too tightly with Quakers. Although Quaker energy was crucial to the gradual abolition cause in New York and elsewhere, identifying the cause with Quakers undermined its effectiveness.[69]

Excerpts published in the *Daily Advertiser,* which devoted significant space to the 1790 congressional debate, gave comparatively little space to the remarks of northern congressmen friendly to the Quaker and antislavery perspective.[70] But other readers of the New York daily took up the banner of antislavery, even as the paper printed paragraph after paragraph of proslavery oratory. The most spirited defense of emancipationist Quakers came from "Rusticus," who penned an essay published in four parts. Rusticus responded directly to a number of the proslavery congressional arguments:

"One is almost tempted to conclude from the observations of those amongst us who find it their interest to support slavery, that virtue and truth are mere terms, signifying nothing; that self interest is the sole directing principle of men; still, I hope, for the honor of human nature that these orators do not speak the language of their hearts." Men might adapt logic to any cause. But, taking a common position that the next chapter analyzes in detail, the heart's language produced the highest truth. This truth compelled an understanding of black slavery as an assault on humanity which slaveholder resisted only through a "most unnatural insensibility."

Of course, one did not have to rely on the heart alone, as logic and evidence also impugned slavery's defenders. Thus, Rusticus regarded claims of southern slavery's mildness, black inferiority, and the ancient world's pro-slavery precedents as misleading falsehoods. In the final installment, Rusticus accused proslavery speakers of defaming Quakers in order to divert attention from the real problem at hand before concluding with a devastating analysis of the South's attachment to the slave trade. Southern planters, whom Rusticus labeled "Obdurate tyrants," preferred to purchase and brutally exploit two African slaves for the price of one free, efficient worker. Political economy without moral economy was thus of limited value. Indeed, from Rusticus's perspective, the more modest proposals of the petitioners did not go far enough in combating human anguish: "on whatever side we turn, the sufferings of these poor slaves, are innumerable, nor can they be mitigated by any other means, than that of gradual emancipation after the inhuman traffic is totally prohibited."[71]

The debate stimulated comparisons, some more serious than others. As a further rebuttal to southern arguments, the *Daily Advertiser* printed an essay suggesting that black slavery in the United States was comparable to Russian serfdom. Serfdom was less harsh, the essay noted, than slavery, but was nonetheless an indefensible, exploitative institution, demanding gradual reform that would ultimately vest degraded peasants with full property rights, to the benefit of Russian civilization. "X.Y.," by contrast, submitted a half-serious parody of northern views of southern slavery and perhaps of the entire debate itself. Taking a jab at Manumission Society–style monitoring of free black households, X.Y. appraised the conditions of southern slave life, concluding, "With all their weight of poverty . . . it is nevertheless pleasing to observe that these people are left undisturbed in their huts, and were never yet to my knowledge pestered with committees of white men appointed to visit their families, inspect into their conduct, and report plans for regulating the same."[72] Puncturing the pretensions of reformers, the writer suggested that the problem of slavery was not serious enough to require so much rancor, let alone active intervention.

The tepid response of the congressional committee actually handling the petitioners' substantive proposals affirmed the Constitution's protection of the slave trade and essentially preserved the status quo. The committee declined any authority over emancipation and the treatment of slaves living in various states, but it did subtly imply a potentially expanded jurisdiction over slavery after 1807. The committee, in addition, suggested that congressional authority could be used to limit American participation in the foreign slave trade and conditions aboard U.S.-owned slave ships. Yet no action, was called for or taken.[73] As had been the case with the U.S. Constitution, the demands of the southern political economy overwhelmed moral scruples about slavery when it came time to actually set policy.

The ferocious response of southern congressmen demonstrated that the national ideological climate regarding slavery was very different from the local one. Congress's inaction on the substance of petitions also indicated that the campaign against slavery in the North was far more easily prosecuted on a state-by-state basis than on a national scale and that the concessions to slaveholding interests embedded in the U.S. Constitution were not to be tampered with. Antislavery political economy notwithstanding, southern congressman closely identified the slave trade with the broader principle of free trade.

Moreover, with the congressional debate exposing sharply diverging regional perspectives on slavery, New Yorkers evinced some recognition of southern interests in 1790. Congress moved from New York to Philadelphia after that year's session, while awaiting the preparation of a permanent capital on the Potomac. A *Daily Advertiser* commentary warned southern congressmen against "think[ing] they gain a point by obtaining a more southern position"; these men "forget that Quaker politics predominate in Philadelphia, and that once fixed there they will always there remain."[74] The capital could move southward, but the institution of slavery itself remained in New York, and with that long-lived institution the ongoing, multifaceted debate about slavery's future—a subject of great significance for many besides the southern planters and Pennsylvania Friends who faced off in 1790.

In the final publication of his long and distinguished career, Benjamin Franklin addressed the vexed political and moral economy of slavery. Writing under the pseudonym Historicus, the dying Franklin responded to the proslavery orations of Congressman James Jackson of Georgia during the 1790 petition debate. Franklin pretended to unearth a document from seventeenth-century Algiers on the trade in European Christian slaves.

Franklin's article, published in New York City, Philadelphia, and elsewhere, rehearsed satirically many of the standard justifications for slavery. The Algerian courtier could not imagine who would do the work if not Christian slaves; without them the economy would surely collapse. If freed, these Christian slaves would tax society; if colonized elsewhere they wouldn't work on their own behalf. Franklin's Algerian courtier soothed his royal patron's conscience by noting that Christians were treated no better than slaves in their European homes, but at least in Algiers they would be exposed to Islam. Muslims who objected to this slavery were, moreover, only seeking to feel good about themselves. In a contest between *"problematical"* antislavery morality and the clear "interest of this state" in the slave trade, the proslavery position necessarily prevailed.[75]

Like antislavery writers before him who drew attention to the ironies of Algerian captivity and like advocates of maple sugar, proponents of debt imprisonment reform, and those who debated the Constitution, Franklin highlighted a set of choices posed by slavery that were economic as well as moral. Who did the work and produced the wealth of the new nation and to what end? These questions preoccupied many Americans—including New Yorkers—in the late 1780s and early 1790s.

When emphasizing local and regional growth, emerging visions of economic development and social order in New York marginalized slavery. When New York's future was placed in the wider frame of national union, the power of antislavery political economy dissipated. A Federalist like William Cooper, when serving his own ambition and his Quaker investors, could more openly embrace a postslavery political economy than could Alexander Hamilton when serving his ambition to forge a commercially powerful, centrally governed nation.

The constructive imagination of a New York without slavery, and the place of former slaves in that imagined New York, was still an ongoing process at the beginning of the 1790s, subject to political considerations beyond the morality of slavery itself. Opponents of slavery proved themselves skillful at inserting the problem into a variety of political discourses in New York. Issues of national concern—including Algerian piracy, constitutional ratification, and the international slave trade—provided a forum in which critiques of slavery from Pennsylvania and New York City received a thorough airing in New York state. Along with frequent reports of antislavery activity in Britain, these critiques formed a substantial antislavery discourse. Yet the actual translation of arguments into antislavery victories at times proved as difficult as replacing West Indian sugar cane with New York maple trees.

Franklin's imaginative, ironic voicing of the antislavery argument perhaps betrayed a surfeit of deathbed hopefulness. The Historicus essay pressed against racist assumptions that would not so readily give way. White Americans were less likely than Franklin hoped to regard European Christians as analogous to black slaves, or the work of Christianizing heathens as analogous to enlightening Christians with Islam. Nonetheless, Franklin, the great emblem of hardworking, ascendant, self-made America, gestured toward a practical, effective means of addressing the tremendous problem posed by racialized thinking about slavery and abolition. For, as chapter 6 details, racial identity, imaginative projection, satire, and the voicing of others were as fundamental to the debate over slavery's status in the north as formal essays on economic development and national union. Put another way, the status of former slaves—of "black" people—if emancipation did come to pass was a central element of the debate over gradual abolition in New York. To work out answers to questions about race, New Yorkers relied heavily, like the creator of *Poor Richard's Almanac,* on satire, aphorisms, and the assumption of imaginary personas.

6

Race, Citizenship, Sentiment, and
the Construction of an Antislavery Public Sphere

"CATO MUNGO, who lately arrived into this city from the United States of America, where he has been kept in slavery for upwards of twenty years, has given us a long and melancholy account of the treatment of the poor African in that land of cruelty," read the opening line of an excerpt from the imaginary "Gazette of Guinea." This curious parody, printed in a 1795 edition of *Mott and Hurtin's New-York Weekly Chronicle*, provided a multilayered satire of public discourse regarding racial bondage. Conferring the name Cato Mungo on the African returnee made him the bearer of two names—one evoking Rome, the other evoking Africa—used to signal black characters in newspaper poems and anecdotes. The heading "AFRICAN INTELLIGENCE" placed above the "Gazette of Guinea" by-line was a racially motivated pun. Africans did not produce such "intelligence" as a newspaper, which was presumably a reflection on their backwardness.[1]

Paradoxically, this item was also an assertion of African intelligence, an issue central to an emerging discourse on the nature of racial difference in late-eighteenth-century America. By imagining what such an African newspaper would report in standard English prose—that American slavery unnaturally degraded its victims and divided them from their families—this submission also attacked American slavery. The "Gazette of Guinea" announced that Mungo's full story would soon be printed "in a pamphlet . . . [so] that the people here may be informed of the miserable state of their brethren, who have been so unfortunate as to fall into the hands of the Americans." The piece turned the tables on the United States' racially myopic view of justice at a time when newspapers decried the enslavement of white American sailors on Africa's Barbary coast. An item that incorporated elements of racially disparaging humor actually extended a form of sympathy in a forum where New Yorkers debated the contours and details of public life. Thus, this curious item in the *Weekly Chronicle* had done Benjamin Franklin's Historicus satire one better by enlisting an imagined black African slave, rather than an imaginary Algerian enslaver, to critique slavery.

I.

Throughout the 1780s and 1790s, New York newspapers employed the voices of Africans, usually fictive and enslaved, to develop arguments about the nature of citizenship in post–Revolutionary War America. Editors represented black voices in poetry and prose, in soliloquy and dialogue. Language from the mouths of black speakers could convey the irreducible nobility of the captive, the essential ignorance of the servile, or gradations in between.[2] How African and African American voices were rendered provided race-laden commentary on the suitability of slavery and the proper dimensions of the public sphere.[3]

New Yorkers grappled with the relationship between race and citizenship as they considered gradual abolition. Newspaper portrayals of black voices revealed some of the perceived implications of abolition. Such portrayals also displayed the proslavery and antislavery tactics deployed to persuade the public. Sometimes published black voices articulated standard, or elevated, English speech; at other times, words tumbled forth in a dialect fraught with nonstandard pronunciations and misspellings. Editors and correspondents also used black voices to critique slavery directly. Whatever the degree of explicit political content in an individual rendering, the context and varied potential associations were political in nature.[4]

Through these voices, some real but most imagined, New Yorkers discussed the possibility of African American citizenship. In a region moving irresolutely toward a slaveless democracy, the prospect of black freedom stimulated consideration of African American access to public discourse and exercise of the franchise. Constructing the black voice in newspapers thus became an exercise in evaluating such qualities as intellect and moral character.[5] This discourse emerged when ideological conceptions of race were at best partially articulated and in pronounced tension with republican egalitarianism. Thus, this earlier discourse was distinct from the succeeding nineteenth-century working-class and immigrant embrace of black minstrelsy as a way to reinforce "whiteness."[6]

The method and terms of the debate over black citizenship grew out of larger patterns of thought on late-eighteenth-century public rhetoric. The post-Revolution expansion of published material, such as newspapers aimed at a broad public audience, encouraged a definition of discourse that hinged as much on the printed as the spoken word. One of the crucial advantages of print was its pretense of capturing spoken words. Publishers reproduced these words for repeated consumption by a public not present to hear the original utterance. Print, which depended on the reader's literacy, could enforce rules of discursive style in ways that could stigmatize some and elevate others. Each individual listener might judge whether another person spoke English intelligibly or intelligently.

Newspapers provided cues to readers which indicated that a correspondent or character exhibited a command of language appropriate to full participation in public discourse. Syntax became a public symbol of the person constructing it. Phonetic spellings that betrayed an accent and a lack of knowledge of more accepted spellings and pronunciations degraded a speaker among the imagined community of readers. An essay reprinted in 1783 in an Albany paper proclaimed, "Among the sympathies that unite men, there is scarcely any so powerful as a sameness of language."[7] An imagined public, culturally anglicized, could reach its own conclusions as to whether an author-character exhibited the "sameness" worthy of sympathy. On this basis, a reading public also could debate who might occupy a meaningful place in the political deliberations that printed organs like newspapers were intended to facilitate.[8]

Rhetoric during this era gravitated toward a form of self-presentation meant to reveal the qualities of the person behind it. A person's eloquence should move an audience to give its assent. The speaker or author earned respect not so much by stirring up unregulated, diffuse fervor but by making manifest a truth that touched an emotional chord in the audience. The feeling created by individual performance then could connect private emotion to broad claims on the public about rights and justice. The African voice in print sought to deny or to establish such claims through the manipulation of linguistic formats and reader emotions.[9]

Speech could make the man, or even the race. Thomas Jefferson's insistence on the authenticity of Mingo Indian chief John Logan's moving oration on the murder of his family complemented the contention in *Notes on the State of Virginia* that Native Americans possessed an admirable gravity comparable to that of whites. Jefferson refused to accord similar praise for people of African descent. Indeed, Jefferson alleged that their blackness rendered their feelings invisible to sensitive observers, making negroes untrustworthy and perhaps incapable of the sublime. Readers, prompted by various manipulations of the African voice in print, confronted such racial questions, not in terms of quasi-scientific racial speculation or direct perceptions of the speakers' pigmentation, but rather in terms of the ongoing effort to define the polity.[10]

II.

African Americans publicly claimed their own voice in a manner consistent with their view of black equality, never allowing themselves to become merely elements of white fiction. Indeed, African Americans from New York and elsewhere participated in and helped to establish the substantive and stylistic debate over the character of black voices in a society undergoing rapid transformation. Calls for respect and even equal citizenship emanating from diverse locales in the Afro-Atlantic world made their way into the pages of New York's newspapers as well as appearing as free-standing publications. The act of producing such documents denied the assumption that the public sphere belonged to whites or that the black voice was solely a tool orchestrated by whites.[11] Moreover, petitions by free blacks, black literary productions, and black accounts of revolutionary events mitigated against the extremes of mocking, dialect-driven anecdotes and carefully wrought, tragic poetry.

At the same time, historical circumstance, existing political inequality, and white control over the printing press guided the voices of actual black speakers toward moderation in style of expression and substantive demand. Appeals aimed at stirring sympathetic emotion were not limited to the poet's corner of the newspaper. As the end of this chapter shows, even a revolutionary of the stature of Toussaint L'Ouverture could be made, through the reproduction of his words and retelling of his deeds in New York's newspapers, to play the part of a deferential pragmatist. To be sure, a black version of the black voice appeared in print on only a handful of occasions. But its existence nonetheless verified what literary products suggested and racist humor attempted to deny—the interracial potential of the post-Revolution public sphere.[12]

The African American effort to define a written voice began in New York prior to the early national period and encompassed written material besides newspapers. Jupiter Hammon, later identified as "America's first Negro poet," set a precedent for subsequent, more political black voicings. Hammon himself spent his life as property of the Lloyd family of Queens County, Long Island. Hammon and his masters spent much of the Revolutionary War in Connecticut, to avoid loyalist harassment in New York. His disciplined poetic creation acted as a metaphor for simultaneously finding a voice and following the Lord. Hammon's 1782 "Dialogue" between "The Kind Master and the Dutiful Student" ended with the servant instructing the master on the precedence of spiritual duties, even in times of military and political upheaval. Wrote Hammon:

Dear Master now it is a time,
A time of great distress;
We'll follow after things divine,
And pray for happiness.

On earth Hammon followed his master into exile during the war, but it was the heavenly master who owner and bondsman alike were to follow. The servant, by reminding the master of their mutual obligation of spiritual service to God, established his equality and his spiritual "authority."[13]

This authority may be more poignant and profound than most literary historians have indicated. Two years prior to the appearance of this poetic dialogue, Hammon's master Joseph Lloyd had taken his own life, utterly dejected over news of apparent patriot military reversals in the south. Thus, Hammon's spiritual cautions belong in not only a generalized, abstract, revolutionary context but also a specific personal, revolutionary context and make his religious conviction far more than a deferred salve for the slave's earthly woes. The desire to exercise spiritual leadership complemented, even necessitated, his literary authorship, while personal observation confirmed for him the dangers of investing too much of oneself in the events of this world.[14]

The itinerant minister and early-nineteenth-century spiritual memoirist John Jea offers revealing grounds for comparison. Jea grew up a slave during the era when the aging Hammon wrote his poetry and prose. Jea recalled the earthly torments of blighted crops and property-destroying storms visited upon his cruel master by a disapproving God, and he remembered discovering his own salvation by turning to the "language of" his "heart," which lead him to a version of Christianity free from the hypocrisy of those he served.[15] While Hammon hinted that the war was in some sense a punishment and disclosed in verse inconsistencies between the master's actions and words, his condition, temperament, and experience led him to emphasize a spiritual way out for all believers, even if it was too late for Joseph Lloyd.

Moral superiority to a deceased master notwithstanding, Hammon, writing in the late eighteenth century, sensed that he occupied a precarious discursive position as a slave, a black, and a writer. His writing revealed a man who was less defiant and more idealistic than many of his fictional counterparts in the late eighteenth century, let alone his successor Jea. Hammon's prose wavered between assertions of black slaves' spiritual equality with their white masters and cautions against blacks resisting too forthrightly the bonds of servitude.[16] In his 1787 *Address to the Negroes in the State of New-York,* Hammon explicitly urged slaves to "obey" their masters "cheerfully, and freely," while "mak[ing] religion the great business of your lives." Although acknowledging earthly freedom as good, the black man ought to focus on slavery and freedom in God's eternal kingdom after death, for "If we should ever get to Heaven, we shall find nobody to reproach us for being black, or for being slaves."[17] Hammon thus voiced the same themes of freedom-in-death and fundamental human equality invoked by various imaginary black characters in the antislavery literature of the period.

Hammon's response to Phillis Wheatley, the celebrated black poet from Boston, submerged the act of black self-voicing, as Wheatley herself sometimes did, in the larger context of spiritual freedom that enslavement in Africa and transportation to America allegedly allowed. Thus, Hammon's 1778 poem, comprised of twenty-one rhyming four-line stanzas, traced the contours of Wheatley's life as a movement from Africa to heaven. Hammon sought to subordinate Wheatley's literary activities to her spiritual purposes. He nonetheless subtly acknowledged that it was poetry that permitted the communication of the Christian bond they shared:

> While thousands muse with earthly toys;
> And range about the street,
> Dear Phillis, seek for heaven's joys,
> Where we do hope to meet.

In following a godly rather than an earthly muse, the two black writers shared not only the same earthly origin but the prospect of a common eternal fate.[18]

Hammon was not the only New Yorker who found significance in Wheatley's work, though subsequent responses offered a more secular reading of the her accomplishment. A 1784 newspaper "Address to the Legislature" of New York referred to Wheatley to verify the author's assertion that "the few [blacks], alas the very few, who possess their rights, [are] greatly sensible of the blessing." The 1796 poem "On reading the Poems of Phillis Wheatley, the African Poetess," in *New-York Magazine,* portrayed black talent as emerging from the "shade" of degradation to the light of freedom. Giving a more terrestrial narrative of progress than Hammon offered, the anonymous author associated literature with liberty.[19]

Wheatley and Hammon, moreover, were forerunners of another famous literary narrator of the black journey to uplift and equality. *The Interesting Narrative of the Life of Olaudah Equiano,* the 1791 New York edition of which was the first published in America, told a story of progress toward enlightenment, spiritual and temporal. Equiano's autobiography mixed Hammon-like themes of Christian salvation with an eloquently polite but insistent urging of black ability, black equality, and black rights.[20]

The petitioning of white authorities offered other African Americans an opportunity to voice a more direct claim for equality in the political sphere. The few such appeals that made their way into New York newspapers offered a deferential tone similar to Hammon's while sometimes voicing the heightened emotion of literary antislavery. In 1786, a New York City newspaper reprinted the 1783 petition of an aged Massachusetts slave whose loyalist owner had fled during the war, leaving her destitute. Belinda's words prefigured and perhaps inspired the types of heart-wrenching images enshrined in antislavery newspaper poetry. This aged supplicant wrote vividly of her cruel removal from Africa. After Belinda's arrival in America, "she learned to catch the ideas, marked by the sounds of language, only to know that her doom was slavery, from which death alone was to emancipate her." At the end of her days, all she asked for was the means to ensure her and her daughter's "comfort over the short and downward path of their lives." The voicing of her story thus functioned as consolation rather than liberation.

A statement of black grievance less drenched in pathos appeared in the same newspaper two years later. The petition to the Massachusetts general court addressed a pressing problem afflicting northern blacks—the kidnapping and sale southward into slavery of "free citizens." This illicit practice reproduced on the western side of the Atlantic the slave trade's appalling pattern of family break-up. But the memorial also carefully argued that key principles of citizenship were at stake. "What then are our lives and liberties worth, if they may be taken away in such a cruel and unjust manner as this?" By forcing black men to remain land bound, the threat of kidnapping, moreover, deprived "good seamen" of the opportunity to obtain "a handsome livelihood for themselves and theirs." Thus, the pursuit of equal citizenship had distinct but related political and economic facets. These petitioners assumed the stance and employed the method of freemen to make a case that rested not solely on emotion but also pragmatic principle.[21]

III.

The contrast between the published poetry and petitions of real African Americans and the more prevalent derisive voicing of imagined black speakers could be jarringly stark—conveying an entirely different meaning. Indeed, the dialect in which New York's newspapers presented much African American speech in the mid-to-late 1780s rendered the enslaved class as largely incapable of serious political discourse. The stumbling manner of expression accorded blacks in these lampoons nonetheless conveyed a variety of political messages. Some items mocked black mental capacity. At times, alleged black voices emerged from specific political or social controversies. Seemingly feeble black voices could also be used to mock the pretensions of whites and even the racial prerogatives of slavery—without insisting that blacks receive an equal voice in the political discourse. In general, however, the printed rendering of black dialect served to enforce a distinction between the clear voice of the public sphere and the garbled voice of those destined for something less, often far less, than full citizenship.[22] These renderings emphatically sought to close any openings for legal emancipation, social equality, or spiritual parity encouraged by the Revolution.

The appropriation of the black voice to belittle the prospect of black citizenship could be venomously direct and political. As discussed in chapter 3, the 1785 gradual abolition bill was defeated because the state legislature failed to muster enough support to override the Council of Revision's veto. This event inspired racist gloating in the pages of one New York City newspaper.

"A LETTER from CUFFEE," appearing in the aftermath of the assembly's March 1785 vote, imagined the disappointment of a black man through language meant to underscore the absurdity of any move toward expanding the rights of New York's African American population. The letter began, "DE Legislaterman no makee de poo nega free las Sataday, because dey no makee *two turd.* . . ." Despite the defeat and this vague articulation of the legislative process, the black man's aspirations for equal citizenship remained undimmed: "Me wante be freeman, Legislaterman too; Pompey too; Cato too; ebery nega an him wife too . . . den you will alway habbe *two-turds* for makee boon law." By leaving readers with the image of stereotyped black slaves—Pompey and Cato along with Cuffee—providing the swing votes in legislative deliberation, this proslavery submission mocked the notion of black citizenship. "Two turds" would be the most likely product of such citizenship. Moreover, the burlesqued correspondent was portrayed as so misguided that he unwittingly transgressed clear gender norms by imagining that black wives would join their husbands at the polls. This crude satire warned that even the mild step of gradual abolition would stimulate inappropriate black political aspirations.[23]

More typically, racist insinuations emerged in response to situations in which blacks appeared to breach the unspoken color line that defined the public sphere and the informal arrangements of public life. Revolutionary-era social upheaval along with the prospect of gradual abolition may have heightened sensitivity to black public displays. The bemused observations of racially mixed promenading on the Bowery printed in an August 1785 edition of the *New-York Journal* provoked a hostile response. "Landaff Freeman" wrote "Massa Pinter," wondering whether such an item should appear in print, in the process openly mocking the entire concept of African American literacy. "A BE hangd if it is not a badest ting in a world to learn us *black men* to read and rite and to spell—Kefe why, ders our black negar Dick, dat must still be kripling an riting ven he mout better be kleening e nives and forks," began the letter. The submission went on to offer a farcical explanation of the origins of the previous week's account of the Bowery. The underlying point was that such reports had no place in the newspaper. White uneasiness with hints of relative black equality in casual public life thus prompted contradictory assertions on the printed page. Landaff Freeman's ineloquence urged that the black public voice be stifled.[24]

African American preaching of Christianity to mixed audiences aroused scorn, including comments comparing white and black language. The literary and spiritual territory claimed by Hammon thus was sharply contested in the street and in print. Two New York City newspapers disagreed about the ability and the value of a black preacher named Harry who came to the city in 1786. The *Packet* praised his mission of religious awakening as well as his skill. Despite his illiteracy, "his language and connection is by no means contemptible," the report declared. A *Journal* correspondent greeted this same man with dismay and concern. The paper wondered how New Yorkers, who had access to ministers of "profound erudition," could find appealing such "praying at the corners of the street," and asked "whether a *declaimer* ought to be countenanced amongst us?" In disagreeing on the merits of this particular preacher, as well as with revivalistic Christian expression, each paper staked out its positions on this black preacher with reference to linguistic presentation and educational attainment.[25]

Sometimes alleged African American ineloquence could be used to underscore that black participation in meaningful political discourse could only occur in a political economy turned dangerously on its head. A purported debate published in October 1786 over Rhode Island's radical monetary policies cultivated white status anxiety by pitting a merchant's slave named Dick against an artisan's slave named Cuff, each speaking in dialect. Dick informed Cuff that the temporary circulation of paper money provided merchants like his master cover to gather hard currency in anticipation of a return to that standard: "Den," explained Dick, "you Masser children be poor as dog, eatte no meat, worke all day, bad poor negro, aha!" Dick elaborated on this vision, "I breve Missers ride in coach . . . keap white servant run after him, I drive him boy, cheigh!" Cuff, in contrast, offered hope that "every one keep he place," if the state maintained the paper money regime honestly. Far in advance of nineteenth-century imaginary voicings of "whiteness"-anxiety, the dialogue implied that well-heeled whites might tolerate or even promote black advances at the expense of working whites. In New York, where Rhode Island's renegade fiscal policy was held in some disrepute, the blackface exposé likely also would have been read as evidence of how infuriatingly simple was the folly of paper money finances. If Dick and Cuff figured it out, so might anybody who gave the matter a little thought. Neither Dick's cynicism nor Cuff's naïveté constituted a celebration of the possibilities of African American citizenship. Ultimately, the dialogue's conceit depended upon white imprudence rather than black uplift.[26]

Pretending to unmask anonymous essayists as actually being African Americans, or drawing attention to black participation in a partisan cause, was another technique for deriding political opponents. A convoluted 1788 letter war in the Poughkeepsie newspaper regarding an election in Dutchess County reached its nadir in crude sexual humor revolving around the racial identity of "Ezekiah," renamed "Cudjoe" by another writer. A local wit further lowered the exchange by writing under the name Pompey Blackamoor. In this clownish letter, the writer expressed his concern that "yu woodnt print poor negros ritin, but wen I red dat pece in yure disse wekes papur, sined with sich a dammony long name, me growd very much curraged; me thot if yu print sich a pece as dat, you wood print mine tu." Thus trivialized, the letter war subsided.[27]

If blacks could not serve usefully as citizen-speakers, then the urgency of passing gradual abolition into law diminished. The belittling of the African American dialect, whether done in an attempt to shore up the racial boundaries of the public sphere or to score some other political point, contributed to a negative view of black intellectual ability. Although not necessarily constituting endorsements of slavery, stories purporting to examine African American English ratcheted up the burden of proof that slavery's opponents would have to meet.

Even when African Americans appeared to measure up to the standard of Anglo-American linguistic ability, whites degraded them for it. A French traveler touring the United States in 1788 encountered a black child prodigy in Newport, Rhode Island, recalling, "People amused themselves by getting him to perform spontaneously. . . . This seemed to me a cruel and thoughtless sort of diversion." Whites in the United States, the Frenchman observed, "must renounce" their scornful attitude "if they wish to be consistent." This white American predilection for inconsistency manifested itself well in a 1787 letter written to the *New-York Journal.* As an example of the correspondent's claim that "knowledge" was often confused with a strong "memory," the correspondent cited "a negro who cannot read, and yet can deliver an extempore rhapsody, that will captivate weak minds, and give not offence, even to the ears of intelligent men." Skepticism and cruelty posed an ongoing challenge to establishing a viable black voice for emancipatory equality.[28]

IV.

Newspapers employed stereotyped black dialect in more paradoxical fashion to produce ostensibly comical anecdotes about African American encounters with one another and with whites. Such anecdotes, which appeared throughout the 1780s and 1790s, were grouped toward the back of the newspaper as light counterpoints to the regular news and advertising copy. Anecdotal humor, concerning a wide variety of ethnic groups, was a common feature. The context, the language, and the themes of these anecdotes imparted political significance to even the simplest jokes.[29]

A few anecdotes employed African American dialect to criticize directly slavery and slaveholders. "A Modern Anecdote," placed prominently in both a New York City and Poughkeepsie newspaper in November 1788, rendered a slave named Caesar momentarily triumphant against a white justice of the peace. Caesar won his case by making a persuasive analogy between the slave trade and theft. He stated, "Well den . . . here be Tom's massa—hold him fast, constable—he buy Tom as I buy de piccaninny knife and de piccaninny cork-screw. He knew very wel *poor Tom* be tolen from his old fadder and mudder; de knife and de cork-screw have neider." That an uneducated slave could make such a successful argument about the vagaries of slavery illustrated the institution's injustice. Another story printed that month showed Cato, who declined his dying master's offer that someday the slave might receive burial in the white family's crypt, thus further mocking the master-class mentality: "but suppose, massa, we should be both buried in one vault, and the devil come looking for massa in the dark, he might take away poor negar in mistake, and that would be neither honor nor profit for Cato."[30]

Even when not striving for comic effect, an anecdote deriding slavery still distinguished its slave actors with stereotypical names and dialect. The story of a black soldier named Sambo's stoic endurance of having his leg amputated—"Well, come massa, take um off, and say no more about um"—at the Revolutionary War siege of Yorktown brought the observation, "Had he been a Roman, instead of an African, how would he have been celebrated!" Blacks could be marked for heroism rather than servility, but they were marked nonetheless. Indeed, the same issue carried an anecdote about a South Carolina officer, who, after losing two legs in combat, urged his son to fight on. Given that a 1781 New York law conferred freedom and, by extension, citizenship, on slaves carrying arms in the patriot cause, corrosive distinctions made through dialect took on added poignancy.[31]

African Americans served as tools to expose the worst excesses of white public life. Scenes of blacks dueling, discussing theology, and dressing in the latest fashions—replete with broken words, bad grammar, and intellectual incomprehension—made the point to white audiences that they behaved almost as foolishly as their putative inferiors. A would-be black theologian's pathetic analogy gave rise to the authorial comment, "This is a permanent caution to us, not to dispute about matters we do not understand. . . ." If blacks should know their place, so too should whites. Given the intensifying rivalry in New York between elitist-minded Federalists and populist Republicans during the 1790s, it is perhaps appropriate that such items appeared in Federalist-leaning newspapers.[32]

The mocking of whites in these anecdotes rarely elevated blacks; rather, their allegedly inferior elocution simply exposed the overinflated egos of white counterparts. This technique did not imply an increased respect for African Americans or even necessarily accord blacks a role in combating slavery. The black slave "Quash" managed to best a New Jersey minister's attempt to distinguish between his own mental labor and the black's physical labor by fooling the preacher with a riddle. But the clever black man, identified at the outset of the vignette as "by no means fond of working," displayed limited virtue at best.[33] A purported news story in a 1798 edition of the Federalist *Albany Centinel* reproduced the alleged comments of an African slave-trading king, "Why you no catchee dat Wilbafoce? why you no bringee to Pepel? I soon do um—I soon makee know why he poil trade."[34] The grand-scale venality of the African king, expressed in language similar to that of the illiterate American slaves of anecdote, denied blacks a role as agents in their own freedom while trumpeting the nobility of their white advocates.

Whether to evoke amusement or contempt, the black voice reproduced in newspapers tended to draw racial lines in order to distinguish the marginalized from the white mainstream. Even if some black characters displayed a modicum of cleverness, the humor for the white reader lay largely in see-

ing in print the black speakers' misuse of language. The comedy also sometimes hinged on guilelessness, sometimes bordering on stupidity. Closer to
the contemptuous end of the spectrum was a story that found its way into a
Federalist newspaper. Cato has a shrewish wife called "Citoyenne Phillis,"
her moniker designed to mock French, black, and Jeffersonian Republican
pretensions about equality. Phillis attempts to stave off a beating by implor-
ing, "O pray now, Cato, do let us live in lub and unicorn, so as we us'd to do."[35]

The partisan implications of some anecdotes, which are further discussed
at the end of this chapter and subsequently, were not so much systematic as
symptomatic of the popular availability of pseudo-black voices designed to
amuse some white readers while reinforcing their sense of superiority. The
well-circulated poem "True African Whit" played silliness for laughs. While
on his death bed "Old Cato" heard his friends "Cuff and Caesar, Pomp and
Plato" discussing his pallbearers. Cato objected strenuously to plans to include Scipio in the burial party:

> "Scip rascal—tell about me lies;
> And got me whip'd" . . .
> "Mind me," cries Cato, "if dat cur—
> Dat Scip, comes bearer—I won't stir."[36]

The rapidity with which blacks in northern cities shed slave-era names,
classical and African, as slavery slowly crumbled confirms that blacks would
have seen little of themselves in various anecdotal characters. The names
Cato, Cuffee, and Caesar, condescendingly affixed by masters to their slaves,
were rapidly giving way to Anglo-Saxon names in the north's port cities, where
a free black population had begun to emerge as a result of manumission and
immigration from the countryside as well as from the West Indies. Although
New York City's free blacks often lived in the homes of white employers
rather than with other blacks, the nascent free black community was starting
to define independent economic and social identities. Free blacks worked as
artisans and vendors, as well as domestic servants and dock laborers. By the
mid-1790s, the city's free blacks began to exert increased control over their
religious lives as well, forming a burial society that would be the precursor
of an independent church. Although in tension with the reality and the prospect of black freedom, particularly in the cities, identifying black speakers
as such was simultaneously a racial marker, a continuing manifestation of
customary rural humor, and a way of reinforcing fraying stereotypes.[37]

Significantly, pseudo–African American speech in New York's newspapers was comparable to other forms of ethnic baiting in the late eighteenth

century. Accents, as conveyed by unusual spellings, were a means of deriding Jews, Irish, Indians, Dutch, and Germans in print. The lack of English-
language competence helped emphasize purported Irish stupidity, Dutch
boorishness, and Jewish venality. The occasional drunken Indian managed
in pidgin English to question the efficacy of Anglo-American blue laws; this
did little to advance the claim of universal ethnic equality. The public sphere
accepted certain voices and shunned others by coding degrees of articulate-
ness through the rendering of difference in print. Performed on the printed
page rather than in blackface on a stage, anecdotal humor defined membership in the community of citizen-speakers that was not articulated solely on
white-black lines. Nonetheless, race was one of the critical lines that such
voicings maintained.[38]

Although the political implications of the specifically black-voice anecdote at times subverted a defense of racial slavery, that possibility came at
the price of implicitly undermining viable black participation in ordinary
public discourse. More topical uses of black dialect suggested that African
Americans at best only partially understood the political world that debated
their status. This ascription of black ignorance did not make African Americans any less a subject of political debate. Far from it. The fictive African
American voice was rendered in print so as to evaluate, critique, and, some
hoped, contain it.

V.

Other parts of the newspaper imagined the words of Africans in a manner
that allowed the black voice to contend for respect in the public sphere.
Poetic and prose compositions offered to newspaper readers a black voice
that not only openly questioned the premises of slavery but did so in a deliberately rigorous literary voice. Newspaper poetry, in particular, offered
rhythms, rhymes, and imagery that drove home the themes of unjustifiable
suffering and fundamental human equality. Instead of playing the anecdote's
fool, however wise, these alternatively imagined black speakers donned the
mantle of world-weary, yet defiant victims. This stance served as a counterweight to prevalent racial stereotypes. It also extended the reach and
adapted some of the themes that black writers like Hammon, Wheatley, and
Belinda deployed.[39]

Maligned by historians for its maudlin sentimentality, literary antislavery writing requires reconsideration. This style of antislavery rhetoric has
been dismissed as serving the psychological needs of white reformers more
than the interests of black slaves, or as simply diverting attention and energy
away from more central problems. Winthrop D. Jordan wrote that this genre

represented "a retreat from rational engagement with the ethical problem posed by Negro slavery." Another potential critique is that these pseudo-black voices merely provided another set of white renderings to an already white-monopolized discourse. Consciously or unconsciously, according to this line of thinking, the white public would deduce that such renderings did not necessitate an acceptance of black equality. They might even reinforce prejudice.[40]

Such evaluations of a genre with roots wide and deep in the Anglo-American poetic tradition do not stand up to scrutiny.[41] Indeed, recent scholarship has emphasized that sentiment played a crucial role in cementing national identity during the early republican period. Looking specifically at slavery, the literary scholar Philip Gould even argues that exposing the evils of the slave trade to a sentimental critique was directly related to Anglo-American attempts to place trade and commercial expansion on a moral foundation.[42]

A close examination of the poetry in New York newspapers, particularly poetry imaginatively creating black speakers and actors, reveals how this literature engaged questions of slavery's morality within the specific political context of the debate over domestic abolition. Indeed, such literary efforts addressed prevalent concerns about race and citizenship—concerns that made abolition a particularly difficult step in this northern slave state. Given the provocatively hostile manner in which defenders of slavery rendered the black voice, it was imperative that such alternative imaginings of that voice deliver rebuke. Dramatized sentimentality may have over-enthusiastically cast black slaves in the role of helpless victims. Yet this literature, often produced by anonymous authors or people whose authorship went uncredited in the New York press, invested characters with the virtues of spirit and intelligence of voice. Reticence would have damaged the cause of abolition far more than rhetorical excesses or mixed motives. When black characters in these literary creations did not speak as citizens, they nonetheless endowed themselves with qualities requisite to citizenship—including humanity, equality, and a command over language. Indeed, they possessed the critical ability to move and persuade.[43]

New Yorkers, and Americans generally, found the appeal to emotional identification effective in enlisting support for victims of unjustified suffering, people such as debt prisoners and the poor. Formal domestic bondage represented but one of several unfortunate circumstances in which the loss of freedom stimulated sympathetic rhetoric. "The Prison," published in two New York City newspapers, began,

O WELCOME, Debtor! —In these walls
Thy cares, and loves, and joys forego:
Approach—a Brother Debtor calls—
And join the Family of Woe.

The next stanza imagined the debtor's wife, burdened with her "weeping babes," observing her suffering husband, formerly the family's source of support. "The Dying Prostitute. An Elegy" imagined a degraded woman speaking on her own behalf, "Spurn not my fainting body from your door, / Here, let me rest my weary weeping head." Such victims, alone in the world, unable to protect or be protected by loved ones, sought to claim sympathy in words that figuratively elevated them above the abjectness of their suffering. In addition to pleading their case directly in letters written home, white American sailors held in Algerian slavery inspired emotional descriptions of the plight of men separated from their homes and families. The themes and the literary techniques applied in these situations were also much in evidence in literary efforts that imagined black Africans' appeals.[44]

The format of this literature mitigated somewhat the stereotyped images of black speakers conjured elsewhere in the newspapers. Poems written in the voices of suffering slaves or family members left behind to grieve in Africa guided readers through regular rhythms and rhyme schemes. Imagining the black voice in composed English-language poetry helped connect slavery's victims sympathetically to the reader, who might give voice to his feelings in similar tones. The slave Cuff blended dreams of Africa and nightmares of America in a poem reprinted in 1787 in Poughkeepsie's *Country Journal.* He imagined reuniting with his wife, who assured him

Each lonely scene shall thee restore
For thee the tear is duly shed,
Be lov'd till life can charm no more,
And mourn'd till Pity's self be dead.

Fittingly the poem ended with Cuff waking to discover "my tears upon the rock," against which he lay—the rock of slavery.[45]

Metaphors, straightforward rhyme schemes, and iambic lines of six, eight, or ten syllables may not seem impressive in the grand scheme of literary accomplishment. But such poetic conventions, especially given the contrast to the dialects mockingly attached elsewhere to African American voices, made a statement about how to evaluate the slaves' claim to freedom. Slaves conceivably could speak in a fashion equal to white victims of oppression or wounded lovers. In conveying universally accessible motives, they exercised the control of language that would be expected of them as citizens. Thus, they claimed a place within white discourse.[46]

The rejection of stumbling pronunciation was implicit in the language of these literary offerings, although one author made a more direct attempt to challenge assumptions about speech. An English poem written in response to Isaac Bickerstaffe's 1768 play *The Padlock* and published in the *Albany Journal* explicitly rejected in its first lines the black voice of parody. The poem, appearing under the heading "Mungo Speaks," began:

> "T'ank you my Massas! have you laugh your fill?"—
> Then let me speak, nor take the freedom ill.
> E'en from my tongue some heartfelt truths may fall,
> And outrag'd nature claims the care of all.

The poem went on to assert for the speaker the rights of other Britons. As part of this claim, the poet nodded toward Shakespeare's Shylock and his plea of human sameness. Thus, Mungo proclaims, "Alike my body food and sleep sustains; / Alike our wants, our pleasures, and our pains."[47]

The poem is revealing of the complex history of black voicings in Anglo-American and transatlantic racially inflected parody and New York antislavery sentiment. Bickerstaffe's play was an adaptation of a novella by the great sixteenth-century Spanish novelist Miguel de Cervantes. *The Padlock* and *El Celoso Extremeno* tell of a jealous older man who goes to great lengths to ensure the faithfulness of a younger woman against possible suitors. Both include a black servant who is unwittingly induced to aid in the thwarting of the jealous fiancé. Bickerstaffe transformed Cervantes's black eunuch Luis into Mungo, whose broken dialect, as well as his love of music and liquor, contributed to the comedy's amusements. Mungo's weakness for song and drink also provide an opening for Leander, an enterprising suitor, to visit the beautiful Leonora, who is held captive in her own home. *The Padlock* was performed with some regularity in the New York City theater during the 1780s and 1790s. Indeed, the comic Mungo character, played by Lewis Hallam, one of the leading figures of the city's stage during the period, was a show-stealer.[48]

The poem "Mungo Speaks," imported from England to Albany, repudiated the play's comic slights and the stereotypes that it helped to inculcate.

Intriguingly, the poem may have been almost as old as the play itself and may often have accompanied performances of it. Whether Albany readers were aware of the genealogy of Mungo's antiracist rejoinder, the casting off of entrenched literary assumptions, ingrained through colloquial anecdotes, would have been apparent just the same. Moreover, taken together the play and poem demonstrate the entwined relationship between sentimental embrace and humorous put-down in Anglo-American racialized discourse. At least in this instance, one was literally a response to the other.[49]

A decade after "Mungo Speaks" appeared in Albany, New York City's Republican *Time Piece* published a narrative poem in two installments, "Quashy; or, The Coal Black Maid," which openly reversed the roles of eloquent whiteness and brutish blackness. Quashy was portrayed as beautiful and intelligent; "from her lips such melting accents broke." In this melodrama set amid a West Indian uprising, Quashy seeks her freedom in accordance with a colonial emancipation decree, approaching her dissolute mistress only to find "Reason to passion is oppos'd in vain."[50] Neither African names nor skin color prevented the imaginative assertion of freedom's cause. Indeed, inverting prejudicial expectations lent force to this rhetoric.

Granting imagined slave characters a voice that echoed popular white sensibilities reinforced a core message of such literary efforts—racial equality. These imagined Africans used the language of English poets, expressing themselves with a formality proper for public consumption. They also addressed directly the underlying problem with slavery and the slave trade. If Africans were the equals of white men, then the magnitude of slavery's crime increased exponentially. English poet William Cowper's widely circulated, "The Negroe's Complaint," originally printed in an English antislavery pamphlet and almost immediately picked up in 1788 by a Poughkeepsie newspaper chided,

> Fleecy locks and black complexion,
> Cannot forfeit nature's claim;
> Skins may differ, but affection
> Dwells in black and white the same

and concluded, "Prove that you have human feelings / Ere you proudly question ours!" "A Negro's Hymn," printed in 1795 in a New York City newspaper, directed its plea for freedom heavenward, based upon the premise of human equality:

> O THOU! who dost with equal eye
> All human kind survey,
> And mad'st all nations of the earth
> From the same mass of clay.[51]

Such expressions of fundamental human identity amid creation's variety explicitly stated what the poetic voice of antislavery sentiment implied as a whole: the justice of black and white conditions should be judged by the same criteria.[52]

Because the authors of these poems believed that arousing the feelings of human fellowship made the best argument against slavery, imagined African speakers repeatedly invoked the theme of familial love torn asunder. "The African Slave's Soliloquy" recalled the violent assault that placed the speaker on his path across the Atlantic: "I see my parents, hear my children cry, / And in the flaming cottage see them die." A poem reprinted in New York in 1788 and again in 1798 sought to conjure up the feeling of a family's anguish. A girl abducted onto a slave ship pleaded on behalf of her brother cast into the hold:

> Take me white-men for your own;
> Spare! oh spare my darling brother!
> He's my mother's only son.

The impassability of the Atlantic for the American slave—"seas roll between us which ne'er can be cross'd"—emblematized the familial heartbreak of slavery in several poems.[53]

The sentimentality of such appeals attacked slavery by shortening the perceived distance between black experience and white emotion. A 1786 submission to the *New-York Packet*'s "Poet's Corner" included a prefatory note making its goals and methods explicit. The poet wished to "paint so naturally the feeling of a distressed African, that I hope they will not fail to move with pity and compassion. . . ." This "call[ing] forth [of] a sympathetic tear" was no mere gesture; for the author "blush[ed] at human nature" when those "whose boast is the freedom of this western world, decline . . . friendly aid in diffusing the blessing to his brethren." For the opponents of slavery, as for other Americans, truth registered affectively on the speaker and the audience.[54]

Conveying miseries also could prompt the reader's emotional response through a more plain-spoken African voice. British abolitionist Thomas Clarkson, excerpted in the *Packet*, sought to lend power to his own words by describing the slave trade through the eyes of an African guide. Instead of using poetic rhythms or figures of speech, Clarkson's African spoke with reportorial "precision" in order to authenticate personal traumas stemming from the slave trade. The informant detailed the descent into slavery of several people assembled on the African coast. Later, Clarkson's European narrator commented on another group of slaves: "Here we indulged our imagination; we thought we beheld in one of them a father; in another a husband, and in another a son; each of whom was forced from his various and tender connections, and without even the opportunity of bidding them adieu."[55] In prose and poetry, antislavery writers encouraged readers to reconstruct the emotional universe of the enslaved.

In a handful of instances, black rebellion provided a striking context in which to imagine the legitimacy of the African American voice. These fictionalized renditions of a real phenomenon of servile insurrection wedded words and deeds more tightly than the laments over the slave trade, as rising up against white masters represented a confidence in black rights which went beyond the request for sympathetic identification. In New York, the memory of black loyalism during the Revolutionary War remained fresh, while the West Indian slave uprisings of the 1790s enjoyed more than a passing presence in the newspaper discourse. Nonetheless, the poetic words of black rebels could emphasize the same themes of family breakup and the artificiality of color found in soliloquies of men and women mournfully gazing across the Atlantic. In "On the Death of an AFRICAN SLAVE. *Condemned for Rebellion in Jamaica*, 1762," the speaker asserts at the outset, "In freedom's cause I bared my breast" but directs these and subsequent words to his wife, imagining death as a return to a better life in Africa.[56]

The voice of rebellion might also be imagined in more militant terms, such as an Obi chant, rewritten by English abolitionist William Shepherd, which emphasized violent reprisal. An "Address of an Indian Chief, to a party of Slaves, previous to the midnight Massacre of their inhuman Masters" mixed expressions of justified "revenge," human equality, heroism, and freedom-in-death in twenty lines of rhyming couplets. Although they are perhaps reckless in their attempts to gain freedom, the enslaved offer a persuasive account of their motives in these poems.[57]

Literary episodes of suicide sought to elicit sentimental responses in a manner perhaps less threatening to white readers than stories of rebellion. Through suicide black actors directed rebellious tendencies inward. Heightening emotional impact, black characters followed words of resistance or suffering with a deliberate act of self-destruction. An African mother who watched her children sailing away to slavery hurled herself into the ocean. Another speaker concluded his reflections from a slave-ship with the words,

> To-morrow the white-man in vain,
> Shall proudly account me his slave;
> My shackles I'll plunge in the main,
> And rush to the realms of the brave.

Most disturbing, an excerpt from a play, *The Negro Slave*, published in a New York City newspaper, offered a mother's explanation for killing her three-day-old child. She horrifically explains that "Maternal love" guided her action, stimulated by the beating she received from an overseer shortly after the child's birth. Of her pregnancy, she explained, "We are used worse than dogs in the same situation, for they are spared and left a home; but the negro woman must work till she rolls in the sand with the pains of child birth." Such story lines not only threatened whites less but underscored black victimization.[58]

Scenes of suicide also imparted to the slaves a Roman nobility, a useful ploy in a society attracted to the lore of ancient republicanism. Jefferson, in his *Notes on the State of Virginia*, whose first sanctioned publication appeared in London in 1787, castigated American blacks for allegedly failing to live up to the inspired record of intellectual achievement established by Roman slaves. In the literary imagination of some whites, blacks nonetheless could eloquently express the spirit of ultimate self-denial. As if to answer Jefferson's charge in an elliptical transatlantic conversation, the English reformer Hannah More's *Slavery, a Poem* appeared in New York the following year, explicitly linking a slave's suicide to the characteristic of "pride" which "in Rome is deify'd." Literary suicides figuratively rectified the mocking bestowal of classical names on American slaves by having the slaves embrace classical virtues.[59]

One of the most striking uses of the black voice to evoke noble self-sacrifice and to attack slavery came in the form of an upstate New York slave's overheard prose soliloquy, submitted to Lansingburgh's *Federal Herald*. The white scribe, T.W. from Schenectady, insisted on the private speech's "authenticity." T.W. neither loaded this 1788 work with tell-tale malapropism and mispronunciations nor sanctified it with poetry; he conceded that "the language may perhaps vary a trifle," but "the sentiments are entirely" the slave's. A truthful accounting of the slave's case, in other words, argued for presenting him as a rhetorical equal to any white polemicist.

This reflective New York slave's hardships resemble those of bondspeople elsewhere, with perhaps only the politics of the situation differing slightly. The slave, as many of his poetic fellow victims, suffers the indignities of familial destruction at the hands of the Atlantic slave trade. But the present reality of slavery equally concerns him: at the end of the day, "I must return to the house of a severe master, a haughty and disdainful mistress, and insolent, abusive children," he complains. Those slaves with families in America suffer the "piercing" yet inevitable "anguish" of seeing children sold off as slaves to someone else. Neither American "principles" nor American politics seemed to afford the appropriate relief, according to this piece published in the wake of the ratification of the U.S. Constitution and New York's recodification of slavery. The speaker imagines that former slaves might claim some portion of western land as their own to settle, but "No such prospect is opening to view." Indeed, the New York legislature, remarks the slave, had failed to act against slavery, flouting the spirit of American independence, as well as "the laws of God, and human reason." The story concludes with the white listener intervening to prevent the elderly slave from drowning himself in the Mohawk River. The white reporter then records parting remarks, which display "a sensibility that surprised me." The slave deftly manipulates Genesis 18, in which Abraham pleads with God to spare the evil cities of Sodom and Gomorrah to save a handful of innocents: "for the sake of one honest white man, one who can feel for the anguish of his species, I will endeavor a little longer to" save "a being that is thought contemptible in this life by their oppressors; but one whom the God of the just may not think so."[60] Too modest to call the Lord's wrath on the state or nation, the enslaved speaker, by sparing himself, reduces the burden of New York's guilt by one life.

T.W.'s narrative underscores the symbolic power and rhetorical potential of enlisting African American voices on their own behalf in the ongoing debate over race, slavery, and citizenship. The submission stands out among examples of literary antislavery in late-eighteenth-century newspapers in terms of its length, style, and singular focus on New York slavery. Nonetheless, it is emblematic of how white opponents of slavery inserted into political discourse a black voice that staked, stylistically and substantively, a claim to the attributes of citizenship. As a result of such efforts, arguments about abolition necessarily became arguments about equality.

The context of literary attempts to imagine African American voices is vital to understanding their value. Newspapers, as conveyors of political discourse and cultural standards, were in the process of carving a central place in New York's public sphere during the late eighteenth century. Perceived racial difference translated into print helped to establish the contours of that public sphere. Sentimental poetry seeking to adapt African speakers for newspapers contrasted sharply with anecdotal humor in which the joke derived from black ignorance or the flaws of black dialect. Literary efforts, with their emphasis on suffering and severed familial ties, placed slaves on the same stage as white victims of the day, whether Algerian captives or debt prisoners. Moreover, all these examples use a sentimental idiom to critique how human cruelty could become a corrupt form of commerce.[61]

The sympathetic white voicing of blacks carried a price. In some cases, white writers may have overplayed their hand by creating a formulaic noble victim. One of the damaging suppositions of the genre was that blacks required whites to construct a voice for them because they lacked an appropriate voice of their own. As the English poet Hannah More explained, "For thou was't born where never gentle Muse / On Valour's grave the flow'rs of Genius strews."[62]

Yet the cause of antislavery certainly would not have been better served by poetic silence. In the racist anecdote and dialect parody, the champions of equality found an insidious opponent requiring a response. The resulting literary efforts constructed characters whose words, in style and substance, declared the fundamental equality of the races. The emphasis on families torn apart by the slave trade and the assertion that blacks and whites shared a claim on the rights of man were crucial to the debate over slavery in New York. The imagined poetic black soliloquy may, in some sense, have placed the African voice above the political fray. This, however, was an improvement on the barely literate version of the black voice rendered by overtly racist defenders of slavery. Thus, creative literary approaches to antislavery usefully challenged white sensibilities about a racially integrated public sphere.

VI.

However problematic voicing African Americans through sentiment-inflected poetry may have been, blacks themselves helped to create the form and contributed to its legitimacy as a strategy of rhetorical antislavery. In 1796, William Hamilton, who went on in the nineteenth century to became one of the leading organizers of black institutions in New York City, quoted Cowper's "Negro's Complaint" directly in a letter to Governor John Jay. Hamilton effectively blended sentiment with informed political criticism, informing Jay, "I cannot help shedding a silent tear at the miserable misfortunes Providence hath brought upon" fellow blacks who remained in slavery. Yet like T.W.'s imagined slave, Hamilton did not shy from naming the specific political hypocrisy that created such a state of affairs: "how falsely and contradictory do the Americans speak [of] . . . a land of liberty and equality . . . when almost every part of it abounds with slavery and oppression." Likening those who purchased slaves to "thieves," Hamilton further documented his indignation with two passages from Cowper's poem, including this critique of racism:

> Deem our nation brutes no longer
> Till some reason they can find
> Worthy of regard and stronger
> Than the colour of our kind.

For Hamilton, the misidentification of the black nation as "Brutes" directly called into question America's identity as a "free nation."[63]

For Hamilton, sympathy was the platform upon which a demand for action might be mounted and claims about the nation's identity made. His reading of black-voiced sentimental poetry within the context of the ongoing emancipation debate encouraged political engagement, not meekness. Thus, he petitioned Jay, one of the most prominent political figures in the nation, for a fundamental solution to the problems engendered by slavery. At the end of his 1796 letter to the governor, Hamilton plainly stated his purpose: "The intent of my writing to you was this: to know whether there can be no measures taken for the recovery of the objects of pity?" Going well beyond pity, perhaps even crossing the line of deference, Hamilton proclaimed, "Is it not time that negroes should be free? Is it not time that the robbery should cease?"[64]

Hamilton's letter integrating antislavery poetry with prose polemic highlights that black and white writers developed the language of literary and sentimental antislavery in dialogue with one another.[65] Poetic voicings of black equality came from black and white sources and could be called upon by both blacks and whites. In quoting English poetry and posing questions in his letter to Governor Jay, Hamilton, moreover, attempted to enter into a cross-race, cross-class dialogue with the former president of the New York Manumission Society, hoping to cement a community of moral sentiment and to stimulate action.

By the time Hamilton addressed Jay, St. Domingue had been roiling for several years, mocking the notion of black slave acceptance of the status quo and perhaps fueling Hamilton's impatience. The era's transcendent figure of black rebellion, Toussaint L'Ouverture became a powerful voice of responsible black citizenship in the pages of New York's newspapers, in the process extending the dialogue on race and freedom. Through the reproduction of his words, as well as the recounting of his personal qualities and deeds, the West Indian revolutionary acquired the attributes of a fully autonomous character in a fashion unachieved by racist parodies or poetic newspaper soliloquies during the years preceding gradual abolition. Treated with admiration, albeit mixed with some distrust and occasional condescension, L'Ouverture was given the opportunity by New York publishers to demonstrate the political capabilities of a freeman. In New York state, where slavery had not reached depths of degradation comparable to the French sugar colonies and where black freedom in the 1790s seemed unlikely to result from violence, this figure made manifest the racially integrated nature of the public sphere.

Toussaint L'Ouverture's emergence during the mid-to-late 1790s as the central figure in the St. Domingue slave revolution had a major impact on New Yorkers' perceptions of the Caribbean rebellion.[66] The strength and competence of this black slave-turned-general, along with the ambiguous course he pursued, challenged conventional racial interpretations of events. A leader of rebellious slaves received recognition as a force for order. Reports lauded L'Ouverture's ability to command a large military force. Two New York City newspapers carried brief translations of his military orders in easily comprehended English prose. The return of the island to cultivation also appeared to correlate with the rise of the black general.[67]

Most dramatically, L'Ouverture was allowed to take credit—in words presented as his own—for protecting whites from bloody racial reprisals. In Albany and New York City Federalist newspapers, a first-person exchange accompanied news of the black general's refusal to be manipulated by the French commissioner Sonthonax. The Frenchman sought L'Ouverture's sanction for independence from France and the slaughter of St. Domingue's white population.

L'Ouverture self-consciously produced his report in "the form of dialogue" to bring his audience, originally French, into the contest of wills between a slave-become-military commander and the prodigal French official. He hoped to convey "not only the meaning of the propositions that were made to me, but even the same expressions, the same words." Thus, L'Ouverture sought mastery over the political crisis and its language. The question of who might serve as the voice of the former slaves of the colony was fundamental to the conflict between the two men. Sonthonax, in defending himself, asserted, "It is not for myself that I speak; it is for you, it is for the blacks"; and later, "we [meaning he and L'Ouverture] shall be the masters

. . . I will direct you." L'Ouverture steadfastly resisted such blandishments. The general, in spurning the commissioner concerning independence, imagined that the French would conclude that "the colonists were right to assert, that the blacks were not worthy of enjoying liberty." With regard to the liquidation of the whites, L'Ouverture grasped the personal and racial implications: "if there was one white assassinated here, I should be responsible." The black man maintained the upper hand over the white man, rhetorically and politically. A perhaps surprising by-product of his skillful maneuvering was that in accounts circulating in New York, L'Ouverture's role was solidified as a force for order and he was seen as largely in control of his own and his island's affairs.[68]

The tantalizing ambiguity of L'Ouverture's goals added to the power of his public persona. In the spring and summer of 1799, as American hopes of scoring a commercial and diplomatic victory in St. Domingue intensified, so too did uneasy speculation over the general's plans. Talk surfaced of his "*deep game*" or his "strange game" with the Americans, British, and French regarding his plans for independence, commerce, and alliance. Still, the combination of Toussaint's prominence and American commercial aspirations mitigated against, at least in New York, a hostile lashing out.[69] The novelty of his exercising such authority, bolstered by his demonstrated skill at speaking on his own behalf, made L'Ouverture into a singular character in the newspaper literature evaluating slavery. Skeptics of abolition and black participation in the public discourse of New York could not be vanquished by such a figure alone. But black resistance, temperate yet steadfast, had gained a public voice commensurate with the epochal goal of black freedom.

VII.

Attempts to mock or disparage the possibility of the black voice participating in a reasoned printed discourse stood in tension with sympathetic imaginings of the black voice—usually expressed through tight control of poetic form. This literary antislavery writing, despite being more common, did not annihilate the voice of actual black actors. Real and imagined creations participated in the same idiom, operating under similar assumptions about literary format and emotional impact. Literary antislavery, cast in the moderate language of sentiment, thus advanced the cause of black freedom and black participation in the public sphere.

It is important to note that black voicings did not line-up neatly along partisan lines—Federalists championing sentimental equality, Republicans embracing racial disdain. Indeed, the pro-Republican *Time Piece* published several examples of antislavery literature, while Federalists, as discussed above, were not above mocking Republican pretensions by comparing them to black social pretensions. Consistent with the Adams administration's inclination to establish a working relationship with Toussaint L'Ouverture, the general's impressive dialogues were featured in the Federalist press. Yet during this same period—when many Federalists were voting for gradual abolition in the state legislature—party newspapers reported that a group of Republicans on Long Island, "including several African brethren," constructed a liberty pole, which Federalists and local officials removed. According to this report: "Cudjoe, Cuffe, and other associates, wisely abandoned . . . [the] idol to its fate." Here the race-baiting associated with Republicans in early nineteenth-century New York was practiced ably by Federalists. Such racial slurs sometimes served the Federalist's narrower political purposes and indicated that a deep ambivalence over black citizenship crossed party lines.[70]

Nonetheless, the varied, often positive, voicing of blacks represented a critical front in a larger battle. The battle could not be settled at the level of cultural prejudice but necessarily engaged it as well as the more liberal ideological sentiments of the time. African Americans, white reformers, and white politicians realized that freedom and citizenship rested on how New Yorkers defined the public sphere in relation to race. Whites and blacks shaped their rhetorical—and thus their political—strategies accordingly. In the face of racial scorn, fictive and actual black voices made a strong case that African Americans could occupy a legitimate place in public discourse. With the possibility of black citizenship very much on the minds of New York legislators, antislavery activists, and the public at large, anecdotes, poems, and prose helped to shape the political and ideological landscape. Blacks spoke, if not yet as citizens then at least as people possessing the qualities of equals. The victory of gradual abolition in New York, depended in no small part on the contested nature of the African American voice. In 1785, gradual abolition foundered over whether free blacks should be eligible to vote. When the New York legislature finally passed gradual abolition in 1799, it notably did not place political disabilities on free blacks.[71]

The prospect of a racially integrated public sphere did not win unambiguous approval. Indeed, the prejudices reinforced through such language lingered into the next century when the intellectual architecture of racial ideology was more firmly in place, the partisan dynamics of sectional rivalry were more thoroughly institutionalized, and the anxieties of working-class whites more fully exposed.[72] Late-eighteenth-century literary presentations blunted attempts to peremptorily dismiss the black public voice as absurd.

Apologists for slavery and negrophobes wished to correlate black identity with a voice that, by design, uneasily translated into the written word, but resistance to racial slavery also required and received a public voice. Antislavery gained that voice during the course of the 1780s and 1790s, helping to shape a debate that irrepressibly emerged wherever partisan tempers flared.

7

Slavery and the Politics of Upheaval
The 1790s

"Men have not thus a right to trifle with truth, and with social confidence and happiness," lectured Noah Webster in 1797. Unscrupulous parties would have the public believe that urban America's destructive encounter with yellow fever had its origins in Africa. They wished to sabotage the development of an African free-labor cotton colony, which might signal the end of the transatlantic slave trade, a projection of antislavery political economy akin to earlier hopes for maple sugar. Webster, a Federalist editor and publisher with powerful sponsors and broad nationalist ambitions, had taken a moment of his lengthy disquisition on the domestic origin of disease outbreak to castigate slavery's apologists, indicating that their falsehoods poisoned public dialogue itself.[1]

Webster refused to accept yellow fever as a permanent feature of life, at best kept at bay, just as he, a member of the New York Manumission Society (NYMS), refused elsewhere to accept slavery as a natural facet of economic life. Humans, he made clear, constructed their own living environments for good or ill.[2] Urging officials to enact appropriate urban public-health practices, Webster provided a glimpse of the American public sphere's highest aspirations: "a free inquiry, after combating innumerable prejudices and mountains of obstacles, will prevail and correct the errors of other nations."[3] During the 1790s, New Yorkers—whose political inquiries were increasingly as fractious as they were free—continued to ascend toward the summit of gradual abolition, drawing on the errors of other parts of the nation to correct their own missteps. As they worked through a tangled thicket of regional resentments and partisan competition, the state's writers and politicians increasingly perceived the wrongs of bondage as amenable to political resolution.

Continuing to consider slavery's place in their own state, New Yorkers evaluated themselves in terms of a national contrast between north and south. The process by which politically engaged New Yorkers worked out their relationship to slavery and section was, however, a slow and uneven one. In the 1780s, New Yorkers failed to traverse the distance between denunciation of metaphorical political enslavement to the British Empire and abolition of actual slavery in their midst. In the first half of the 1790s, New York Republicans even attempted to make political hay out of the alleged antislavery leanings of their Federalist opponents. By contrast, regional differences stimulated morally charged or contemptuous rhetoric, in which the south's vulnerability served as an irresistible target, especially for Webster's fellow Federalists. As the decade moved forward, white New Yorkers of both parties distinguished between their position as a northern state and the needs and threats faced by southern states. National perspective helped New Yorkers focus attention on their own regional identity and interests in ways that further undermined slavery's domestic political cover.[4] Despite and because of the atmosphere of partisan upheaval, the century's end witnessed bipartisan support for the gradual abolition of slavery in New York. Amid bruising partisan-inflected rhetorical battles for political hegemony, relatively few Federalists or Republicans in New York found themselves holding a political stake in saving slavery.

I.

Racial discourse and partisan competition converged in New York's 1792 gubernatorial election. The George Clinton–John Jay contest was a harbinger of the rancorous political environment of the 1790s and a product of a long history of competition for political authority in the state. Clinton supporters found in slavery a tempting tactical weapon, the use of which may have affected the outcome of this extremely close battle for political supremacy in New York. It was perhaps the first time, but certainly not the last, that partisanship and the debate over slavery intersected in the state's newspapers during this turbulent decade.

New York politicians and printers were instrumental to the partisan polarization of national public debate.[5] Indeed, by the mid-1790s, partisanship in New York, as elsewhere in the new nation, would be fueled by a growing number of newspapers founded in part to advance the ambitions of contending Federalist and Republican factions. New Republican journals such as the *Time Piece* and the New York City *Argus* joined established Republican-leaning papers to participate in the increasingly intense political debates sparked by the Jay Treaty and the apparent Federalist hegemony in national and state politics. Meanwhile, Noah Webster's *American Minerva*, which also published the *Spectator* as a twice-weekly edition, received financial backing from leading Federalists John Jay, Alexander Hamilton, and

Rufus King to help ensure a dependable and articulate Federalist presence in New York City. On the frontier, Federalist developer and erstwhile maple-sugar booster William Cooper, who sought to control the social and political tone of his would-be domain, sponsored Cooperstown's *Ostego Herald*.[6]

The need of Whigs of all class and ideological orientations to cooperate during the Revolutionary War and the carefully crafted compromises of the state's wartime constitution never fully eclipsed the fractious nature of political life in New York nor obscured deep divisions in its society. The great landed families such as the Van Rensselaers, Van Cortlandts, and Schuylers supported the patriot cause but often were deeply suspicious of a democratizing tide that threatened to undermine their political, social, and economic power. The hotly contested debate over the ratification of the U.S. Constitution stoked existing political rivalries, even though Anti-Federalists ultimately accepted the legitimacy of the new national charter. Postratification partisanship in New York was further fueled by the ascendancy of Federalist New Yorkers in the first Washington administration, especially Secretary of the Treasury Alexander Hamilton and U.S. Supreme Court chief justice John Jay. Conservative nationalist standard-bearers like Hamilton and Jay, who had familial ties to mercantile and landed elites, never reconciled themselves to the rule of popular governor George Clinton in their home state.[7]

Clinton's governorship of New York extended back to the Revolutionary War. During the fight over ratification of the U.S. Constitution, he became a leading Anti-Federalist, eager to protect the state's power from an encroaching national government. In the 1790s, he served as a central figure in a New York–based partisan Republican faction. Placing the respected and influential John Jay before the New York electorate represented an opportunity for Clinton's detractors to unseat their powerful rival.[8]

Jay's gubernatorial candidacy not only jeopardized Clinton's political dominance in New York, it also threatened to install the former NYMS president at the head of a government that still sanctioned racial bondage. In 1792, however, being identified with black emancipation could prove hazardous, especially for a candidate also vulnerable to being labeled an elitist not properly attached to the common voters' interests.

As political jockeying got underway in 1792, revealing discussions on race and antislavery appeared in the Republican-leaning *New-York Journal*, offering a more rigorous-sounding, less artful version of the era's anecdotal and poetic discourse. This exchange echoed the conflict between those endorsing Jefferson's suspicions regarding fundamental racial differences versus the environmentalist assumptions favored by abolitionists. A letter written under the pseudonym Africanus offered to bring scientific insight to acrimony over the morality of the slave trade and domestic slavery. Africanus claimed, "The first and greatest point to prove, is, that they [blacks] are an inferior tribe," which analysis of their telltale "physiognomy" and a historical record of underachievement purported to demonstrate. This argument brought an indignant response from "Americanus," who found such reasoning "palpably ludicrous." Americanus submitted that Africans, like much of the world's population, suffered from cultural deprivations and other "contingencies" that prevented the full realization of their God-given potential as humans, including "sentimental refinement."[9]

In the same issue in which Americanus attacked racism, however, antislavery activism itself came under assault. The *Journal* reprinted an item from London largely blaming the slave revolution in St. Domingue on antislavery leader William Wilberforce's "wild visions respecting the emancipation of the negroes." The speeches of this otherwise conservative member of Parliament, claimed the extract, were "so many exhortations to the blacks to destroy the whites."[10]

"A Queens County Farmer" expressed racial and class anxieties of a more local nature in a March letter to the *Journal*. The farmer complained of mounting economic grievances afflicting hardworking rural folk. In addition to currency manipulators and untrustworthy city types, white farmers found themselves afflicted by their slaves' allegedly faithless service and their propensity to run away.[11] While hardly an endorsement of the benefits of slavery, this letter, like the Africanus-Americanus debate and the denunciation of Wilberforce, suggested something of the ambivalence New Yorkers felt about race, class, and slavery as they decided which gubernatorial candidate best represented their values and interests.

Clinton's backers seized on Jay's opposition to slavery as a means of undermining his formidable candidacy. An associate complained to Jay, "As your opponents cannot or dare not impeach your integrity and ability, necessity obliges them to descend to the lowest subterfuges," namely, to overstate Jay's role in the NYMS and the extremity of his antislavery stance. Contemporary observers warned of potential difficulties for Jay in Ulster County on the Hudson River, where slaveholding was particularly widespread. Residents of Columbia County, although less dependent on slave labor, also reportedly expressed concern over Jay's disposition toward slavery.[12]

At least one Jay supporter sought to counter damaging public perceptions by turning the tables on the Clintonians. "A.B.," in a letter appearing in the *New-York Journal*, defended Jay against charges that he wished for "an absolute manumission of the slaves" and was hopelessly "aristocratic" in his views. Noting the Manumission Society's gradualism, its attempts to enforce the state's slave-trade ban, and its educational program for black children, A.B. used Jay's antislavery principles to deny the charge of political elitism. If Jay were aristocratic, wondered the writer, "how happens it that he should be also considered as a man anxious to abolish the only distinction of ranks, which now subsists among us?"[13]

An ambiguously crafted dialogue published in the city's *Journal* but set in Ulster County placed Jay's antislavery leanings directly within the context of his alleged social biases. The discussion between two farmers about electioneering in their neighborhood cast neither the Jayites nor the Clintonians in a good light. Farmer David chides farmer Abraham for getting caught up in the organizing techniques of Jay's elite supporters. "You know," says David, Jay "is for making the negroes free . . . that they may mix their blood with white people's blood, and so make the whole country bastards and out-laws, or else confuse our representation in the assembly." Abraham explains, to the contrary, that masters would be better off without "negroes [who] were generally thieves, idiots and squanderers." Abraham, moreover, accepts the alleged Jayite belief "that great folks, who puzzle their heads so much about our liberty, ought certainly to live better in the world than we farmers, who . . . ought to work our farms ourselves. . . ."

This creative piece of political analysis aired fears and assumptions on both sides of the slavery debate, although its expression of alleged Federalist condescension may have tipped the balance toward the Republican camp. Similarly, in terms of abolition itself, the message was intentionally ambiguous but Republican leaning. Emancipation might serve as a first step to freeing whites from contact with blacks or it might dilute white racial purity and political power. In any event, politicians who spoke about black liberty had to be watched carefully.[14]

Clinton's disputed victory in the closely contested election may have reflected in some measure the impact of the slavery issue. That was the expectation of one observer, who wrote to Alexander Hamilton prior to the vote that the situation was "Very *Tight*. Mr. Jays [*sic*] being one of the Emancipation Committee opperates much against him."[15] At the most immediate level, Clinton owed his election to the disallowance of the ballots from Ostego County, where William Cooper had worked hard to deliver the vote for Jay. Putting procedural problems aside, it is noteworthy that five of the six counties with the highest proportion of blacks in the population polled in Clinton's favor; the governor achieved over 64 percent of the vote in four of these counties. Yeoman farmers, who comprised Clinton's core constituency, may have defined their material requirements and political affiliations with reference to the black slaves in their midst. Such slaves ranked below them on the rural social hierarchy and provided labor useful to their own and their communities' well-being.[16] The only county with a relatively high percentage of blacks which Jay carried was New York County, where one of the closest contests in the state took place among Manhattan's unusually urban constituency. That it was the home of the Manumission Society also helped. Jay scored more impressive victories in counties with lower percentages of slaves, where his association with antislavery activity presumably posed far less of a threat.

The election of 1792 suggested that slavery remained a charged issue, suitable for partisan contrivance. The floundering of gradual abolition in the New York Assembly in 1790 and the consistently staunch antislavery voting patterns of certain county delegations, such as Ulster's, indicated the possible political advantages of tagging Jay with an antislavery label. Presumably realizing this problem, Jay supporters sought to diffuse the slavery issue by suggesting that Clinton himself was as strongly antislavery as their candidate.[17] Nonetheless, Jay seemed to bear more of the political burden of being identified with antislavery views, in part because of his prominence and in part because he did not generally play the role of the populist.

As it turned out, New Yorkers would overcome their reservations about Jay's aristocratic reputation more easily than their ambivalence about slavery. The Federalists once again put forward Jay as their nominee in 1795, while Clinton decided against running for reelection. With additional prestige accruing to Jay as the U.S. representative dispatched by President Washington to forestall further conflict with Britain, and bolstered by the Federalist desire to avenge their controversial defeat in 1792, Jay swept to victory by a 6 percentage-point margin. Renewed attempts to paint Jay as an elitist did not mobilize enough new voters to overcome increased Jay turnout in strongholds such as New York City, his home county of Westchester, and Cooper's Ostego County.[18] Yet not long after Jay won the governor's office in 1795, the treaty he negotiated with Britain the year before set off a tumult of protest, at least some of it concerning his seemingly cavalier disregard for the interest of slaveholders.

II.

The debate over the ratification of the Jay Treaty brought the issue of slavery into a contest involving national pride and the role of the citizenry in making national policy. The attacks on the treaty's handling of slavery at first revealed the potent hostility that even indirect emancipationist policies aroused, not just in the South but in New York itself. Yet the Federalist-backed treaty's triumph in the face of intense partisan attack ultimately may have eased the path toward gradual abolition, exorcising the memory of the British evacuation of American slaves at the end of the Revolutionary War. By the time the Jay Treaty debate subsided, this nagging ghost ceased to hamper subsequent prospects for gradual abolition.

Slavery contributed only slightly to the impetus for dispatching New York native John Jay, then serving as chief justice of the U.S. Supreme Court, to negotiate a treaty with Britain. During the mid-1790s, resentments festered on both sides of the Atlantic over unimplemented aspects of the 1783 Paris treaty that ended the Revolutionary War. This animosity combined with new grievances to threaten the peace between Britain and her former colonies. British harassment of American shipping, impressment of American sailors into the British navy, and denial of access to West Indian ports added to old complaints, such as the continued occupation of forts in western territories officially belonging to the United States, as well as Britain's refusal to compensate masters for the slaves who fled with British troops in 1783.

Hamiltonians in the federal government sought to head off further conflict internationally and domestically. The ongoing war between Britain and revolutionary France had encouraged Britain to interfere with America's Atlantic trading vessels, while contributing to an increasingly confrontational American political climate. Hamilton and his allies believed that commercial peace with England would counter the aspirations of the rival Jeffersonian faction, which preferred that America cast its lot with France. Proponents also thought a British accord would provide stability for the Hamiltonian economic program, which relied on a brisk and friendly Anglo-American trading relationship and gave an institutionalized form to the prevalent desire for dynamic national economic growth. Hence, the document that Jay negotiated settled for evacuation of British posts on U.S.-owned western territory, some openings for American trade in British West Indian and East Indian ports, and compensation procedures for unlawful confiscations on the high seas.

The failure of the Jay Treaty to extract compensation from the British for American slaves carried off at the end of the Revolutionary War sparked controversy. The original British actions, some Americans continued to claim, violated the diplomatic terms that officially ended the struggle for national independence. Such criticisms of the 1794 treaty were part of many Americans' perception that Jay had wrestled only minor concessions and failed to win sufficient respect from the nation's former rulers. Indeed, as opponents of the treaty complained, a host of British abuses in the northwest territories and the harassment of neutral American vessels would continue to go unpunished.[19]

Reflecting slavery's contested status in mid-decade New York, some Republicans calculated that vocal support for slaveholders remained a viable political stance. In New York City's *Argus*, a mainstay of Republican opinion, Robert R. Livingston complained about the failure to obtain compensation for slaves. Writing as "Cato," Livingston, the patroon scion, head of the state chancery court, and Republican convert, did not recognize the irony of his additional indignation over British violations of the "personal liberty" of American sailors impressed into the British navy. "Decius," also writing in the *Argus*, critiqued the treaty, listing "negroes wantonly stolen—ships most wickedly plundered—and a great extent of territory wrongfully detained" as serious U.S. grievances improperly addressed. This writer recounted the final months of the British occupation of New York City, quoting Jefferson's analysis that British behavior "was a *direct, unequivocal,* and *avowed* violation" of the peace of 1783. "All America believed Mr. Jay was sent to demand justice . . . for this palpable sacrifice," Decius declared. He then calculated the British owed Americans $1.25 million on this score.[20]

In Republican complaints over the carrying off of American slaves, as well as the impressment of American sailors, lie parallels to the issue of Algerian captivity, which so starkly exposed America's inability to control its own commercial destiny on the high seas. Yet such parallels also exposed the weakness of the Republican argument with regard to compensation for evacuated slaves. For, with regard to their former slaves, it was the Americans who were in effect making ransom demands. Federalists thus had the opportunity to deliver a strong counterpunch in response to initial blows from Republican polemicists. Political, economic, and moral logic could be brought to bear on the side of treaty ratification.[21]

Hamilton, writing in the *Argus* under the pseudonym Camillus, defended the treaty, including the absence of slave compensation. He offered a combination of complicated legalistic reasoning and moral principle to make his case. As a general matter, Hamilton wished to persuade readers that even if the United States did not win every point in this negotiation with the British, it did not make sense to risk war over an essentially positive agreement.[22]

With regard to slave compensation, Hamilton attempted to deconstruct the original 1783 treaty provisions so as to prove that Britain did have a case for denying payment for evacuated slaves. He suggested that in wartime combatants had the right to seize each other's property.

Switching gears, Camillus's "Defence" considered the moral implications of the negotiations in 1783 and 1794 for the human beings categorized as slaves. "In the interpretation of Treaties things *odious* and *immoral* are not to be presumed," Hamilton lectured. To return to bondage these black people, "who had been induced to quit their Masters in the faith of Official proclamations promising them liberty . . . is as *odious* and *immoral* a thing as can be conceived." British officials in New York had no choice, and neither did subsequent diplomats: "The general interests of humanity conspire with the obligations which Great Britain had contracted towards the Negroes to repel this construction of the Treaty if another can be found." Hamilton implicitly attacked slavery and suggested that black slaves had recognizable contractual claims that superseded white American claims. Given the choice between a clear moral imperative and ambiguous treaty language, Camillus indicated that a moral interpretation of the treaty should take precedence.[23]

The Republican response to Camillus employed close argumentation, ridicule, and moral evasiveness. A defense of British actions that violated the plain language of the Treaty of Paris confirmed defenders of the new accord as apologists for a hostile foreign interest. "Cinna" accused Camillus of "sophistry" for regarding slaves as ordinary chattel and as human beings in virtually the same breath. The real moral transgression occurred "in alluring" the slaves "away" and turning "them against their masters." Cinna wondered "if such promises were really made . . . between his Britannic majesty and the swarthy domestics of America, why" had British negotiators not openly made this point at the time? More caustically, he asked, "Does Camillus imagine that the interests of these Africans lay nearer the heart of their gracious monarch" than those of white Americans?[24]

Taking the antislavery high ground, regardless of Republican incredulity, served Hamilton's immediate purpose of seeing the treaty ratified, as well as his long-term opposition to slavery in New York. With more than adequate arguments against slavery in his favor, accepting even this one Republican objection made little sense. At the time of the evacuation, and certainly in the years thereafter, Hamilton probably was glad to have seen a few more slaves disappear from New York. Accepting the principle, as well as the monetary figures, of his opponents in this instance would have set a difficult precedent in future arguments over government-subsidized manumission. It is worth noting that Hamilton displayed considerable consistency in his private and public handling of the evacuation issue. "The Defence No. III" stated publicly the analysis of the matter that he presented directly to President Washington. Indeed, Hamilton for years had soft-pedaled the significance of the alleged British transgression against American slave owners.[25] With his moral principles, his economic and diplomatic ambitions, and his tactics comfortably in line with one another, Hamilton held firm against Republican attempts to make common cause between slaveholder interests and opposition to the Jay Treaty.

Over the course of the protracted political struggle occasioned by Jay's mission, Federalists wielded the issue of slavery for their own rhetorical purposes. The broader controversy over an accord with Britain swallowed up lingering resentment over the compensation issue. Advocates of the treaty secured Senate ratification and increasing public approval. Public support was crucial because the Republicans in the House of Representatives sought to block the treaty by refusing to grant the money that would implement it. Federalists accented their bitterness during the long, hard fight to secure the treaty by lashing out against southern Republicans. Some northern Federalists even criticized the basis of southern political power by drawing attention to the additional representatives the South received from the three-fifths clause of the Constitution. Breaking up the nation on regional lines even became imaginable; the new northern government "shall not admit of Negro representatives," jabbed one commentator in the *Ostego Herald*.[26]

The Jay Treaty episode complicates the standard view of the American Revolution as a catalyst for antislavery and northern abolition. Old resentments over the racial conduct of the war remained strong, particularly when the case could be made that ordinary—in other words, white—citizens were the victims of a new treaty foisted on them against their interests and desires. Such resentment, however, did not prevent a Federalist critique of slavery's moral underpinnings. Perhaps Camillus had even persuaded a few more New Yorkers of slavery's essential evil. By convincing an initially hostile American public of the treaty's merits, the Federalists achieved a major victory. The vigorous battles over public opinion also established a precedent for the young nation, whose emerging political parties would increasingly use the press to present their cases and rally their supporters.[27]

More immediately, the treaty's lack of compensation for departed American slaves, and the debate it encouraged, helped to nudge New York past an obstacle to gradual abolition. Had a gradual abolition law already been in place by the 1790s, demands for compensation from Britain might have rung hollow. But in the summer of 1795, harangues against the treaty's failure to secure compensation could still be directed toward a state that protected perpetual slavery; compensating its slave owners for gradual emancipation would cause confusion and consternation. As Federalists in the mid-1790s fashioned a victory in the Jay Treaty controversy, lingering anger over the 1783 evacuation became, after more than a decade, a moot point in New York.[28] The arduous task of legislating gradual abolition was about to begin anew with one less encumbrance from recent history. Indeed, Jay's election as governor and the successful counteroffensive mounted to ratify Jay's Treaty demonstrated that opponents of slavery could hold their own politically and rhetorically in the mid-1790s.

III.

During the decade in which New York's white citizens waged increasingly partisan rhetorical battles over treaty ratification and electoral office, a civil war raged in the French Caribbean sugar colony of St. Domingue. The rebellion threw masters and slaves, creoles and colonials, whites, mulattoes, and blacks into a violent struggle fueled as much by the horrors of racial bondage as by the liberating ideology of the French Revolution.[29] The St. Domingue revolution lent special urgency to all American discussions of slavery occurring in the 1790s. This ongoing insurrection ensured that New Yorkers and their countrymen would have before them a vivid series of images of the potential consequences of abolition, antislavery, and regional division.

The Haitian revolution, besides providing alternative ways to portray African American voices and actors, as discussed at the end of the previous chapter, raised a number of policy questions that stimulated New Yorkers to rethink their relationship to other slave states and to slavery itself. During the 1790s, the partisan press showed increasing flexibility in recording the positive aspects of the racial revolution in the Caribbean. Discussion of St. Domingue and its impact on various parts of the United States helped New Yorkers to calibrate their own attitudes toward race and freedom, as well as toward their fellow countrymen. In the South, the slave uprising alarmed white southerners, prompting them to look for ways to quarantine themselves and their slaves from the revolutionary "contagion." By contrast, New York's changing, surprisingly positive, public perception of black freedom in the Caribbean paralleled the renewed and ultimately effective effort to pass a gradual abolition law.[30]

Initially, New York's newspapers recorded America's hostile reaction to this slave-society variation on the French Revolution. The press in the early

1790s expressed fear and anger over disruptive free mulattoes and, later, enslaved blacks claiming revolutionary rights. Most Americans at first felt optimistic about the French Revolution and may have viewed events in Caribbean as a dangerous diversion from the white European struggle for liberty. Perhaps, too, Americans recognized their own revolution in a racially inverted form and recoiled.[31] Events in St. Domingue may have prompted white Americans, including New Yorkers, to recall with discomfort or distaste the rebelliousness of their own slaves during America's war for independence and liberty. Whatever the case, some early accounts encouraged an image of chaotic racial furor. One report noted, "Every white man who appears in the country is destroyed, and a great number of white women and children are detained by the blacks as servants, and treated with the utmost brutality." The very first edition of the *Catskill Packet* in 1792 savored the details of white vengeance amid the ongoing racial melee. A letter written in Jamaica recounted the execution of two alleged murderers "broken on the wheel. . . . the mulatto expired on receiving the third stroke upon the breast, his legs and arms being first broke in two places."[32]

In the second half of the 1790s, a greater moderation crept into New York's public discussion of St. Domingue, signifying an increased flexibility with regard to race and black freedom. The protracted and politically complex nature of ongoing events in the Caribbean worked against identifying heroes and villains by race, especially as many Americans soured on the bloody course of the Revolution in France. French commissioners Sonthonax and Polverel could bear as much or more of the blame for "fomenting the animosities" in the civil war as parties of color. The political jockeying of individual actors took on greater importance, dampening the effects of atrocity mongering and racial stereotypes.[33] As discussed in chapter 6, Toussaint L'Ouverture's portrayal as a compelling force for order overturned the conventional racial expectations of white readers; his was presented literally as a voice of control and relative moderation.

A reevaluation—in poetry and prose—of the entire St. Domingue revolution took place in some quarters. A 1794 poem printed in New York City's Republican *Columbian Gazetteer* mournfully recalled the early days of violence in St. Domingue, where

> Impell'd by sanguine rage, by vengeance sir'd,
> With deadly haste the sable myriads rush'd;
> Beneath their steps *humanity* was crush'd;
> Reluctant from their presence *hope* retir'd.

Three years later the Republican *Time Piece,* a paper under the direction of leading Jeffersonian publicist Philip Freneau, offered poetic portrayals that assessed the situation in a different light. One pseudonymous poet acknowledged the tragedy that traveled in the wake of violent revolt—"And here humanity lets fall a tear / That innocence with guilt the doom must bear"—but hinted,

> Yet had the owners of this fair domain
> Gently relax'd the ever galling chain—
> Had acts of kindness cheer'd the dreadful doom
> And some faint hope of freedom ting'd the gloom[,]

the French colony might have taken a different path.[34]

Such rethinking went well beyond sentiment-inflected artistry. St. Domingue economic redevelopment and U.S. national self-interest shaped the fluid response to slave rebellion. Thus, French republicans suggested to Pennsylvania abolitionists that Americans help the tumultuous colony to develop a successful postemancipation economy and society.[35] Because L'Ouverture's own agenda led him to battle at various times British and French forces, as well as to negotiate with both, Republicans and Federalists could find reason to praise him. Particularly in the late 1790s, when British-sponsored independence for St. Domingue seemed possible, a commercial relationship appeared alluring to Federalists.[36]

Coverage of the West Indian revolution in New York's newspapers also exposed widening regional divisions. Early in the decade New Yorkers may have shared the fears of their southern neighbors about the threat posed to racial order by the events in St. Domingue, especially after an arson episode in Albany which lead to the hanging of three black alleged co-conspirators.[37] During the latter portion of the decade, however, the more intense fears of the southern states helped to underscore for New Yorkers the difference between their relationship to slavery and that of the South. In New York state, the St. Domingue threat registered implicitly in the background.[38] But in South Carolina French blacks actually were seized, tried, and executed for planning to burn down Charleston. One New York City paper prefaced its report of the Charleston episode with the remark, "The existence of *slavery* in a republic such as that of the United States, must always be productive of similar acts."[39]

The South was most obviously the target of a generalized threat to the United States. At one extreme, a dispatch from South Carolina carried a palpable sense of immediacy and alarm all its own, reading in part: "remove your wives far from the Infernal Fraternal embrace, or you may prove witnesses of their violation and expiring agonies. . . ." More typical newspaper items recorded the South's special vulnerability, with varying degrees of sympathy and self-righteousness.[40] Congressional debate in 1799 over U.S. policy toward the French West Indies made clear that the security of the South was of paramount concern, but its reliance on racial slavery could become fair game for regional and partisan sarcasm. A remark carried in the Federalist *Albany Centinel* wondered if southern Republicans "wish to introduce into their own plantations that happy freedom of burning and throat cutting, which has so long existed in the French colonies?"[41]

The St. Domingue revolution clarified in the 1790s some of the regional paradoxes which race had posed for the nation in the 1780s. The slavery-related clauses in the U.S. Constitution included congressional authority to require the states to defend one another against domestic uprisings.[42] Northern states thus might resent but could not ignore the threat posed to the south by the example of St. Domingue. The commercial ambitions of New Yorkers and others encouraged by the prospect of a St. Domingue under independent black leadership made the South's sensitivity frustrating. The quest for abolition and equality in St. Domingue thus posed challenges for American commerce and race relations which exposed regional differences.[43] As they contemplated calls for gradual abolition in their own state, white New Yorkers could measure their good fortune in having the chance to deliberate peacefully about how to rid themselves of the manifest problems of race and freedom. These same issues, New Yorkers knew, destroyed French plantation owners and made southern whites tremble in fear.

Significantly, for some in New York City, the consequences of events in the Caribbean could be seen right on their own streets, perhaps further prompting the impulse to draw regional contrasts. As historian Shane White records, significant numbers of white refugees from France's war-torn colony emigrated to New York during the 1790s—with their slaves in tow. These newcomers added to New York City's slave population, while directly exposing native New Yorkers to the diverse nature of New World slave systems. New Yorkers, white and black, could observe the brands the black West Indian migrants bore on their skin. In 1795, a disgusted correspondent to the *Argus* reported the beating of a female slave by her French master—an incident that exposed the general evils of slavery and the distinction between accepted norms of discipline in New York as compared to those in more southern climes.[44]

IV.

A willingness, especially in the Federalist press, to inflame regional resentment by encouraging negative impressions of southern racial bondage eroded support for slavery. Despite a reluctance to initiate gradual abolition, images of the South helped New Yorkers to shape an identity that separated them from the South and from slavery. Newspapers, because of their politicized character and because they drew news from other regions, provided an ideal forum for making and interpreting regional distinctions. Stories of black resistance put sectional differences, even if they were overdrawn, in particularly strong relief.[45]

At its worst, southern slavery produced horrors that cast blacks and whites in a harsh light. A letter from Savannah indignantly reported the abandonment to certain death of two hundred slaves aboard a sinking ship bound for Georgia. A polemic against decadent American public life called attention to Georgia's "making a bonfire of its laws and records," citing, "a negro murderer taken and flung alive into a fire by his pursuers without a form of law," and a separate instance in which the murder of a black slave brought a mere fine.[46]

Newspaper accounts suggested to New York's readers that southern slaves produced a more alarming threat than northern slaves. Southern slave resistance often appeared to have a menacingly collective quality to it. Criminal gangs of southern blacks from time to time made their appearance in the New York papers during the 1790s. Whether prompted by incendiaries from St. Domingue, local Quakers, or other causes, groups of "restive" blacks worried southern authorities. Security provided a complex challenge in cities like Baltimore and Charleston, as well as on plantations. Congressional consideration of the president's authority to call out militia from the states raised questions about whether applying the familiar three-fifths formula to bolster southern quotas would aid or detract from it. Putting more whites under arms might draw too many of them away "from home," leaving the remaining whites "exposed."[47] New Yorkers experienced concerns of a much lesser magnitude in their own world, despite the perseverance of slavery.

Sometimes black discontent erupted into brutal murder. At least three New York newspapers carried accounts of a Georgia plantation uprising by recently imported slaves. One version alleged that "they appeared to be happy and content, never receiving hard language or blows from their master." Nonetheless, they killed two white men, including their master, and had the "design . . . to murder all" before a loyal slave summoned help. In the white counterattack, three rebels "were shot dead, in the act of resistance." Once caught, the ringleader was "committed to the flames." [48] Murder made attractive copy for eighteenth-century editors, with southern slavery providing a reliable source of such stories. [49]

A tale of the violent effects of manumission promises gone askew carried ambiguous implications but perhaps more direct relevance for a northern audience. Slaves, it seemed, might commit murder under the mistaken notion that they could activate the manumission provisions in their masters' wills. As recorded in a gruesome and didactic 1797 piece printed in Albany, Cooperstown, and New York City, a Maryland slave woman poisoned three of her masters' children. Incorporated in the report was the comment, "Let this serve as a solemn warning to those who are disposed to testamentary liberation of their slaves!" [50]

Another possible response of the northern reader to this shocking story would be to consider the value of an orderly process of abolition, where rules applied uniformly to a whole class of slaves yet to be born. William Dunlap, a Manumission Society member and early-national-era promoter of American arts and letter, critiqued calls for immediate emancipation in the South by some of his fellow abolitionists. Dunlap imagined such a measure would produce "devestation, misery & murder." On the other hand, Dunlap presumed that George Washington was "gradually preparing the minds of his slaves for emancipation . . . giving liberty to them as he finds them fitted to receive it, that is capable of using it for their own advantage & benefit of those around them." The prudence and security that Dunlap admired in Washington provided the ideological rationale for the gradualism supported by emancipationists and contemplated by legislators in New York itself. [51]

Significantly, stories surfaced of black criminal resistance in the North, including New York, which were comparable to the Maryland poisoning story. This northern news, however, did not carry the additional baggage of harsh regional assessment nor generate the same level of fear. New York newspapers recorded attacks on masters in the North as sudden, almost insane, spasms of rage perpetrated by individual slaves. [52] In 1797, the punishment of a black man in Georgia convicted of robbery contrasted sharply with that administered to an Ulster County, New York slave who attempted murder. Whites displayed the black Georgian's amputated head above his grave. The New Yorker, who unsuccessfully tried to stab and bludgeon his mistress, received thirty-nine lashes, brutal to be sure, but measured on a different scale of judicial terrorism than the Georgia case. As long as slavery persisted, New

Yorkers faced problems of resistance and discipline. But they could appreciate the more limited danger they faced compared with what confronted their southern countrymen.[53]

Commentary addressing an outbreak of local and national urban arson favored measured pragmatism over panic. The *Herald* focused inwardly on prevention, taking to task a cumbersome city government structure. Despite "incendiaries" in their midst, New Yorkers could obviate further difficulties through administrative reforms, including expanded law enforcement. As Webster's *Spectator* would shortly argue with regard to yellow fever, the *Herald* emphasized the efficacy of temperate public management rather than impulsive, ideologically presumptive expedients such as vigilantism or quarantine. Similarly, the Federalist *Albany Chronicle* considered possible culprits for the east coast fire epidemic, including "combinations among" blacks in the South "for punishing the citizens that hold them in slavery." The *Chronicle*, however, dismissed the idea of organized conspiracy. To the degree that slaves participated, they did so for the covert pleasure of creating a public nuisance. Albany's own experience in 1793 revealed those responsible to be "only two or three idle, giddy and profligate slaves" who just wanted "to see a great fire, and to laugh at the people while engaged in its extinguishment," an analysis that was patronizing rather than fearful.[54]

Whatever the similarities in northern and southern black resistance, newspaper coverage suggested that New Yorkers did not perceive the threat in the same fashion. Northerners had the luxury of waving a dismissive hand toward black restiveness in their own midst. Meanwhile, northerners could point a judgmental finger at the South for exposing themselves to grave racial dangers.[55]

V.

The Alien and Sedition Acts of 1798 tangled the web of partisanship, regional identity, and slavery in New York on the eve of the gradual abolition law. The Federalist-inspired congressional legislation created an explosive political situation nationally, superheating public rhetoric and galvanizing the emerging Republican press even as some Republicans were harassed under its terms.[56] In New York, these laws also further exposed the effectiveness of regionally and racially charged rhetoric in seeking partisan advantage in New York. As with the Jay Treaty and St. Domingue, the Alien Act debate demonstrated the powerful paradoxes that questions about slavery introduced into New York's public discourse. Unlike during the Jay Treaty debate, Republicans and Federalists found reasons to distance themselves from southern proslavery positions as they had in discussions of St. Domingue. If regional posturing did not directly undermine slavery in New York, it nonetheless further demonstrated the weakening foundation of support for slavery in this northern crucible of racial and partisan politics.

The Alien and Sedition Acts touched off one of the U.S. Constitution's first major crises. The Federalists attempted, through these infamously heavy-handed laws, to punish their Republican adversaries—through the Alien Act by curtailing the rights of radical republican immigrants, and through the Sedition Act by silencing dissent against the federal government. Combined, these acts offered a stringent redefinition of access to citizenship while limiting the scope of the public sphere in which citizens might express themselves.[57]

The issue of slavery became relevant to partisan debate because of the Republican suggestion that the new legislation governing aliens violated Article I, Section 9, of the Constitution. The aversion of the Constitution's authors to the explicit mention of slavery left open the wording of this section on the international slave trade: "The Migration or Importation of such Persons as any of the States shall think proper to admit, shall not be prohibited by Congress. . . ." This clause barred Congress from banning the slave trade before 1808. Its language, however, left the door open for Republicans to claim as unconstitutional any regulation of immigration, including the new Federalist legislation.

Slavery caught the Federalists in a historical contradiction as they defended the Alien Act. A decade earlier, northern proponents of the proposed constitution had downplayed the significant concessions made to slavery and took some solace in the document's lack of explicit references to slavery. Now latter-day Federalists found themselves proclaiming firmly that the Constitution had taken a clear stance to protect slavery—and, in the clause in question, only slavery.[58]

Meanwhile, Republicans manipulated to their own advantage interpretations of the constitutional concession to the slave trade. Edward Livingston, a Republican congressman from New York, looked at the Constitution's language from two perspectives in a 1798 speech. He denied that the migration clause applied to slaves alone; he claimed that southern delegates had wanted the clause to protect the slave trade while "middle states" allegedly wished to protect the flow of immigrants. He then poked fun at the Federalists' more narrow interpretation, mockingly stating that special authority granted to the president would mandate that he deport all slaves because they were aliens and "dangerous to the peace and safety of the United States." Several months later, in the New York Assembly, Republicans sought approval of language confirming their immigration-oriented interpretation of the 1808 clause. Federalists narrowly managed to reject this effort while successfully disavowing the Alien and Sedition Acts.[59]

Internal division in New York did not discourage—and may have encouraged—northern suspicions of the South in the midst of this controversy. Albany's Federalist *Centinel* published a commentary grouping *"sedition-mongers"* in New York with their Republican brethren in Virginia as people driving the nation toward disintegration along regional lines. A few weeks earlier the same paper carried a reprint severely mocking purveyors of principle from Virginia, where slaves "are bought, sold, and bartered like beasts." This commentator wondered how "the legislators of this State of Slaves talk about their attachment to the Constitution, and their anxiety to preserve the *liberty* of their fellow men?"[60]

As willing as Federalists were to link Republicans to southern racial hypocrisy, they also attacked Republicans for practicing too much racial equality when contemplating political matters closer to home. A contemptuous report appeared in the Federalist press of a "Sedition Pole" surreptitiously set up in Queens County by "about a dozen jacobins, including several African brethren." After describing how local government officials and Federalists dismantled the offensive symbol, the item sardonically noted, "Cudjo, Cuffe, and other associates, wisely abandoned their idol to its fate." Scorn of black citizenship offered a reliable means to discredit a political opponent, even at a moment when New York itself stood on the verge of passing a gradual abolition act. Ambivalence about the possibility of black citizenship and the nature of the black public voice was thus put at the service of political opportunism.[61]

The cynical manipulation of racist rhetoric notwithstanding, national political rivalries encouraged polemics painting southern life in harsh tones. The *Albany Centinel* reprinted a regional self-critique from Virginia, which portrayed the abuses of plantation slavery and denounced republican hypocrisy. The piece contrasted the domestic harmony of "the industrious farmer" of Pennsylvania with the slave-state master unable to enjoy his own lazy "luxury" because of the "anger" he feels at the "incompetency" of "lash"-driven slave labor. The New York Federalist newspaper presumably identified with the virtuous Pennsylvanian more than the venal Virginian.[62]

In early 1799, as the state's legislature readied to pass a gradual abolition bill, northerners bitterly scorned southern slavery. New York City's *Daily*

Advertiser reprinted the jeering of a Boston paper regarding the Virginia Resolutions: "Poor Virginia! how art thou fallen! In case of an Insurrection of her lacerated Blacks how would she call on the States she seems about to desert!" In the midst of controversy over the Alien and Sedition Acts as well as pending bankruptcy legislation, the same paper published a reminder to its readers that the opponents of Federalism were self-serving, debt-ridden slaveholding Virginia aristocrats.[63]

Federalists and Republicans displayed the ability to deflect the issue of slavery southward, if possible putting their opponents in a difficult position. Federalists tried to associate slavery with the South to discredit Republicans of all regions. Northern Republicans associated institution with the South to dissociate themselves from the taint of slavery and to make Federalists uncomfortable. Livingston's call on Federalists to follow their alleged principles and end southern slavery was meant to be ironic as well as embarrassing. But before the climate created by the Alien and Sedition Laws precipitated the demise of the *Time Piece*, this Republican paper had published earnest criticisms of Federalist icon George Washington for holding slaves.[64] Such criticisms were indicative of a post–Jay Treaty Republican press increasingly at ease with publishing antislavery material.

While historian Alfred Young was no doubt correct that emerging Republican antislavery reflected a "new egalitarianism," it also helped to deflect an association of the New York party with southern slavery.[65] The Alien and Sedition laws backfired; as a result a Republican opposition press spread rather than dissipated.[66] Yet southern ties notwithstanding, a burgeoning Republican press would not be, at least in New York, a redoubt of proslavery positions, indicative of an emerging consensus on slavery and regional identity.

Political disputes such as those over the Jay Treaty and the Alien Act emerged in national and state political discourse to help New Yorkers see themselves in relation to their southern countrymen. Not all northerners were comfortable with partisan and regional jousting, viewing slavery as a national problem. Threats of southern slave rebellion served, some hoped, to drive the regions together, thus checking southern democratic radicalism.[67] Printed descriptions of the murders of southern whites by blacks surely provoked intraracial sympathy in white readers. But a desire for interregional harmony and recognition of racial danger was not the same as a perception of shared experience. By the late 1790s, legalized slavery failed to offer a strong source of common identity between New Yorkers and southerners. New Yorkers largely viewed slavery as a southern institution that caused problems for the nation and fomented a variety of potential partisan embarrassments. Thus, discussions of race and slavery in New York's burgeoning fleet of newspapers helped promote what one historian recently argued was the tendency of the early national press to simultaneously promote local and national identities, "parallel imagined communities" in which an "internal 'other'" helped define the American political self.[68] For New Yorkers in the late 1790s, internal "otherness" did not have a fixed definition based solely upon race, party, or region, but rather was an unstable mix of all three elements.

Holding slavery at arms length in partisan discourse helped to move New York closer to abolition. The Alien and Sedition Act debates, like the other examples discussed in this chapter, must be judged for their indirect rather than their direct impact on slavery in New York. Clearly, the subject of slavery acquired additional intensity during the final decade of the eighteenth century. Public discussions begun in the 1780s on the relationship between slavery and American national identity—such as those regarding maple sugar, Algerian captivity, the U.S. Constitution, and the morality of slavery itself—set the stage for specific partisan debates over issues of state and national importance, such as the Jay Treaty and Federalist domestic security measures. Such debates cumulatively created a new context in which gradual abolition legislation would be considered.

The marginalization of rhetoric sympathetic to slavery occurred only gradually and never with complete success. The 1792 gubernatorial race and the 1795 debate over the Jay Treaty revealed that protecting the interests of slaveholders still had political appeal in New York. In the wake of the Jay Treaty dispute in the mid-1790s, when proslavery polemics were overwhelmed by other arguments in favor of the treaty, national political conflicts encouraged New Yorkers to assess their state's relationship to various regions of the country largely in terms of slavery. Divisions between *us* and *them* could be drawn according to the difference between the North's and the South's attachment to slavery as much as by the racial distinctions between black and white, or partisan divisions between Federalists and Republicans. Meanwhile, information and ideology circulating through New York from the U.S. South and the West Indies served to bolster northern regional identity and even pride, as southern slavery gathered particularly negative associations. By contrast, the black voice, even the rebellious one of Toussaint L'Ouverture, could be imagined as sympathetic, citizenlike, or morally heroic. These tendencies, in combination with the political and rhetorical tactics of slavery's opponents across the racial spectrum, rendered slavery more problematic than it had been in New York since the years immediately following the Revolutionary War. In the midst of such dynamic public discussions, gradual abolition returned to the state legislative agenda. When it did, a transformed political geography opened the way to success for antislavery activists committed to bringing New York into the fold of an abolitionizing North.

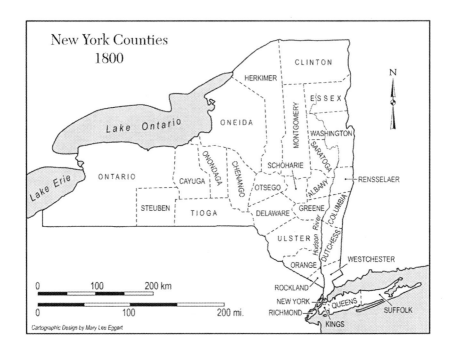

8

Ambiguous Victory
Gradual Abolition Becomes Law

On March 29, 1799, the New York Council of Revision informed the state assembly of its approval of "An Act for the gradual abolition of Slavery." All children born to New York slave mothers after July 4 of that year would be free, with the requirement that males serve until age twenty-eight and females until age twenty-five. After more than 170 years, racial slavery did not abruptly end in New York, but 1799 nonetheless marked a permanent break from the state's slave past.

The political, ideological, and social ground from which plans for gradual emancipation sprung was much more extensively tilled by 1799 than it had been in 1785, when the gradual abolition bill failed to bear fruit. The combined actions of African Americans and white reformers during the 1790s further undermined the viability of New York slavery and was essential to forging the ambiguous achievement of gradual abolition. Blacks contested the institution and pushed the New York Manumission Society (NYMS) to enforce laws limiting slaveholders' freedom of action. Thus, black resistance fortified the strategy of containment launched in the 1780s. Meanwhile, the NYMS drew additional strength from participation in a national antislavery organization, and from the fact that gradual abolition had taken hold in every northern state except New Jersey.

Inevitably, passing a gradual abolition law required subjecting debates about slavery to the give and take of legislative politics, with all its competing interests, compromises, and distractions. A building desire to distinguish between justifiable and unjustifiable forms of public coercion and dependence helped ensure that slavery would remain on the state's legislative agenda until its fate was resolved. A sustained discourse impugning slavery on moral, economic, and political grounds, along with a sympathetic literary sensibility, set the antislavery agenda for over a decade. This agenda was at least partially reflected in the provisions of the final law.

Ultimately, a variety of political calculations determined the timing and nature of the outcome. The contrasting needs of various regions of the state proved especially important in determining the fate and character of gradual abolition. The shrinking slaveholding interest in the state legislature no longer could make common cause with other legislators regarding legal stigmas for free blacks and the direct compensation of former slaveholders. Interracial citizenship did not pose a significant threat in newer counties with few slaves, while potentially diversionary proposals for financing compensation to slaveholders offered these regions only the opportunity to pay higher taxes.[1]

To the very end, however, significant obstacles existed to even moderate emancipationism. To enact a gradual abolition program during the late 1790s entailed surmounting economically oriented reservations about black freedom and interracial citizenship. Free future citizens not only might participate in politics; they also would have to provide for themselves and their families. The prospect of exchanging coercive slavery for dependence on public assistance threatened to deny African Americans the economic vitality necessary to fortify their standing as citizens.[2] Considerable anxiety, much of it redounding to the benefit of abolition's opponents, helped delay passage of gradual abolition until the end of the 1790s and limited the law's scope.

In 1799 the commencement of gradual abolition waited no longer. Yet its presumptive beneficiaries, black New Yorkers, often had to wait years for freedom, under conditions partly of the state's and partly of their master's choosing. Thus, the final stages of the debate over gradual abolition in New York produced a distinctive milestone that bore the marks of fierce, prolonged contestation. As New Yorkers passed this milestone, blacks and whites, abolitionists and racial obstructionists, took a new course at the dawn of a new century.

I.

The New York Manumission Society acted with continued vigor, buoyed by participation in a national organization and the cultural optimism of new members committed to sustaining the campaign against slavery. Organized abolitionists in New York, as well as the new Convention of Delegates from the Abolition Societies Established in Different Parts of the United States (ACPAS) emphasized the prospect of black citizenship based on environmentalist assumptions about race, as well as the necessity of maintaining order in the free black community.[3] Accordingly, abolitionists in the 1790s continued to invest their hopes in cultivating a free black clientele and white public opinion, all the while recognizing that state legislators were the ultimate arbiters of antislavery's progress.

The presence of men like Elihu Hubbard Smith and William Dunlap in the NYMS of the 1790s indicated the widening appeal of the cause, at least to men of a certain class and disposition. In the mid-1790s, these close friends were relatively young men with broad ambitions. Smith, still in his twenties, was a medical doctor and a published poet who associated through the Friendly Club with men of similar literary ambitions, such as Dunlap and the novelist Charles Brockden Brown. Dunlap, who was born in 1766, was just coming into his own as one of New York's and the young nation's leading playwrights. He imagined that he was participating in America's emergence on the world cultural stage, at the same time that the country also took its place on the political and economic stage. Noah Webster, another cultural entrepreneur in the prime of life who traveled in the same circles, joined the NYMS in 1794. Also fitting this mold was Friendly Club member, active NYMS participant, and future business leader William Woolsey.[4]

Dunlap and Smith's acceptance of gradualism and cautious counsels about the readiness of blacks for freedom indicated their paternalistic assumptions. Yet their participation on the board of the African Free School also bespoke their belief in the educability of African Americans, which paralleled their faith in American literary arts and self-improvement. As Smith indicated in a 1798 speech, given only months before his premature death in a yellow fever outbreak, he had a thorough contempt for those whites who would obstruct the progress of black emancipation in order to protect their narrow ends and misplaced prejudices. Dunlap, despite his defense of gradualism, personally embraced a more direct course of black freedom. He recalled in an 1834 memoir that upon his father's death in the mid-1790s, he freed his father's slaves, "retaining some as hired servants."

Dunlap's plays and his lifelong advocacy of the arts sought to balance the competing claims of past paternal authority with the more democratic possibilities of the future. A deist, he believed in the guiding, though not overbearing, hand of established authority. Whatever his attraction to abolitionism, his involvement, like Smith's, in this cause, suggests that the society's membership had not calcified along its dominant Quaker-merchant elite axis, nor was its appeal reducible to conventional Christian moralisms.

Though by no means a popular, let alone a mass organization, the society provided an attractive humanitarian outlet for cultural optimists and cultural nationalists, men like Dunlap and Webster, who sought to unshackle the new nation's potential greatness. Such men took up the optimistic banner of nationalist economic ambition that fueled a variety of public critiques of slavery: the maple-sugar boosterim of William Cooper, who imagined a resource that could simultaneously advance the moral and political economy; the denunciations of Algerian enslavement and debt imprisonment; even the Federalist refusal to let lingering demands for compensation for British-evacuated slaves impede the progress of a sound commercial treaty.

With regard to abolition, the 1790s Manumission Society approach was firm, forward-looking, yet temperate. Like its sister organization in Pennsylvania, the NYMS sought to operate within existing rules of slavery while seeking to change those rules.[5] Smith summarized the society's task as "disseminat[ing] the knowledge" of their work "far and wide, to the young as well as the old, to the enslaved as well as to the free . . . to act . . . with zeal but with prudence."[6]

Participating in the ACPAS reinforced such an approach, while also underscoring that the battle for gradual abolition in New York was interconnected with similar activities in states as different as Pennsylvania and Virginia. The convention encouraged its constituent state organizations to think systematically about their activities and goals.[7]

During its formative years, the American Convention accentuated the theme of citizenship—white and black—in mapping out its antislavery strategy. An address published after the 1794 inaugural convention invoked the "ties of citizenship" among Americans. The address also voiced the link between dependence and citizenship in classic antislavery fashion, asserting, "An unlimited power over the time, labour, and posterity of our fellow-creatures, necessarily unfits men for discharging the public and private duties of citizens of a republic." Slaveholders, as despots dependent on the slaves they dominated, compromised their own capacity for citizenship regardless of the material rewards slavery afforded them.[8] Elsewhere, the convention suggested that laws gradually abolishing slavery would serve as a necessary catalyst for the extension of rights, privileges, and social obligations to freed blacks.[9]

Samuel Miller, a New York City Presbyterian minister who gave a NYMS-sponsored address in 1797 amplified the convention's rhetoric of emerging black citizenship. He declared: "Say not that they [blacks] . . . can never be made honest and industrious members of the community. . . . Make them freemen; and they will soon be found to have the manners, the character, and the virtues of freemen." This understanding of the economic and political aspects of citizenship helped to illustrate the sharp distinction between the expectations facing free people and slaves. The high standards of public morality associated with citizenship extended to self-sustaining labor.[10]

Underlying this argument was the environmentalist logic that characterized not only much of this era's speculations on race but also the cultural nationalism of NYMS members like Dunlap and Webster. Miller's projection of the capacity of blacks for citizenship, like the ACPAS's denunciation of slaveholding citizens, rested on the assumption that human institutions rather than inherent, inborn qualities shaped a person's behavior. Such environmentalism was also of a piece with the sentimentalized literary voicings of African Americans in newspaper poetry and prose. If any characteristic was inborn in slavery's victims, it was the human desire and capacity for freedom.[11]

At the same time, national and state opponents of slavery also stressed that blacks bore the heavy burden of demonstrating their fitness for freedom. Free blacks were to validate the environmentalist assumptions of their white patrons, whose impulse to regulate would-be black clients showed that confidence in environmentalism was real, though not unwavering. "The noblest and most arduous task which we have to perform," according to the American Convention, was not to sway white legislators but to raise the moral and intellectual level of degraded slaves. Smith presented his environmental assumptions more optimistically, affirming that blacks, "like all men else, are creatures of education, of example, of circumstance, of external impressions." Organized proponents thus acted on their paternalistic instincts and their desire to demonstrate to the public their intention to channel and restrain the activities of blacks, girded by a belief in the power of positive educational environments.[12]

In New York City, the African Free School remained a tool for asserting to blacks and the general public the carefully controlled nature of the NYMS's enterprise. The society attempted to gather members of the free black community at the school to communicate the American Convention's moral lectures, which advocated churchgoing, literacy, skills, families, temperance, and public restraint.[13] Appeals for financial support of the school provided an opportunity for advertising the benefits of the Manumission Society's goals and methods. An announcement in *New-York Magazine* noted the "very good progress" of the school's students toward becoming "safe and useful members in religious and civil Society." Another newspaper used the occasion of a successful "public examination" of the school's students to censure racist proslavery views and note the potential of blacks for citizenship.[14] The NYMS, meanwhile, received public funds to help finance the school. Such support reflected some measure of wider acceptance of the cause of black education. It also signaled that the NYMS's guarded approach could be effective in governmental circles.[15]

The NYMS's concern with black orderliness shaded into inflexibility. In 1796, the standing committee of the NYMS encouraged a group of free blacks who wished to form an "association" for policing "every species of vice among" their peers. But in 1797 a committee of blacks sought "advice" from the society on their desire to establish and secure a site for "a Religious Society." A seven-man committee of the NYMS, however, found it "not expedient for the Society to patronize or encourage the formation of any Religious Society whatever." The society preferred quiescence to organized black autonomy, even when dutifully expressed.[16]

The nascent free-black community's religious initiative was not so easily stifled; the African Americans sought help not permission. In 1795 free blacks successfully obtained funds from the municipal government to build a church and burial ground. Meanwhile, Peter Williams Sr. had begun conducting services for his fellow black congregants of the John Street Methodist Church, who had been confined to segregated pews in the biracial congregation. Within the black community, the cultural and social winds clearly had begun to shift.[17]

Besides threatening white authority, black autonomy troubled white reformers on public relations grounds. In the late 1790s, white opponents of slavery believed the nation's cantankerous political climate demanded heightened vigilance regarding their own public actions, as well as the actions of blacks. In 1798, citing "the situation of public affairs," perhaps meaning increased partisan and regional invective or ongoing racial upheaval in the Caribbean, the American Convention suggested the need for "caution." The American Convention attached particular urgency to "submission" on the part of slaves. As Elihu Smith had suggested in his oration to the NYMS earlier that year, antislavery men wished to navigate tricky public currents with white hands on the tiller.[18]

A disposition toward caution and control and a commitment to gradualism did not mean that antislavery whites wished to indefinitely postpone emancipation. The American Convention regarded the ultimate eradication of racial bondage as its goal. The convention sometimes even viewed abolition as not far distant. In its second address to the constituent state societies, the organization plainly expressed its "principal design" as "the universal emancipation of the wretched Africans who are yet in bondage."[19] A modicum of racial integration might even facilitate abolitionist goals. New York's delegation reported to the convention on small-scale instances of integrated education, suggesting that providing tuition for blacks to attend white schools offered a viable method of education in rural areas.[20]

New York Manumission Society members also expressed their desire for abolition, offering varying opinions on timing and on how much influence slave owners should be allowed to exercise over the terms of that gradualism. Rev. Miller, despite stressing moderation and gradualism, insisted, "The time . . . is not far distant, when there shall be no slavery to lament. . . ." Smith, in his NYMS address the following year excoriated legislators for their inaction, although he offered only vague assurances of progress toward eventual black equality. Dunlap, who was a member of the NYMS standing committee and delegate to the American Convention, expressed in a private letter a more conservative mind-set. He contrasted his utilitarian views on emancipation to some of the more extreme views expressed at the 1797 convention. Dunlap doubted whether "the greatest portion of happiness" would result from an immediate emancipation that disregarded the likely hostile reaction of slaveholders.[21]

Antislavery advocates recognized that statutory reform represented the key to securing gradual abolition, with the influence of the public at large a means to that end. The convention urged participants to work to alter the laws in which slavery was rooted by interceding with legislatures and courts. The convention understood the limited power of antislavery organizations, however, communicating to the state societies in 1796 to persevere, "Although you cannot controul Legislatures; and though, when you plead the cause of humanity, they will not, at all times, listen to you. . . ." Accordingly, cultivating public opinion became that much more important: "You can do much, by directing your efforts to the conviction of individuals--by diffusing proper publications amongst them, and by presenting the evils of slavery in various forms to their minds."[22]

Not patient for public opinion to trickle down, Elihu Smith expressed his own frustration with lawmakers in his 1798 NYMS address. He proclaimed, "You, yes you, Legislators of America, you are the real upholders of slavery!" The accusation applied specifically to New York as well: "You, yes, you, Legislators of this Commonwealth, you foster and protect it here! . . . It is you who are deaf to the demands of justice, the sighs of humanity, the representations of policy, the calls of interest. . . ." Smith sought to shame lawmakers in New York and elsewhere by claiming they forsook the clear "remedy" to curry favor with slaveholders. It mattered not to Smith whether slaveholders represented "a small, or even a considerable part" of the body politic—every serious consideration of morality and "policy" dictated some form of abolition.[23]

II.

New York slaves indicated their impatience with the law and the hopes of white antislavery men through resistance. Remarkably, during the 1790s, some of these acts of black resistance even bridged, however tentatively and however temporarily, the divide between blacks and white abolitionists. Indeed, African Americans prompted the NYMS, despite the organization's preference for black placidity, to combat slavery directly by seeking enforcement of laws protecting certain types of freedom claims.

During the 1790s, running away, an age-old tool of slave resistance, presented the distinct possibility of living free. Numbers of runaways spiked, putting stress on New York's slave system. According to historian Shane White's survey of runaway advertisements in and around New York City from 1771–1805, fugitives were mostly young adult males traveling on their own. The vast majority of runaway slaves likely intended to escape permanently. Some runaways, however, sought to maintain social ties with distant friends and relatives or even hoped to gain negotiating leverage within the confines of their circumscribed existences. The growth of New York City's black population, over half of it comprised of free people by late in the decade, made it an appealing destination for slaves seeking to elude masters and mask their earlier identities. Over a third of the advertisements listing a likely destination for runaways listed New York City. There, runaways, especially those with marketable skills, might find employment and the protective shelter of a substantial black community. Other New York slaves sought their freedom in Philadelphia or in New England, where gradual abolition was well underway by the 1790s.

Runaways likely knew that the ground upon which New York slavery rested was shifting. News of successful black resistance in the West Indies would not have been hard to come by in the port city of New York, especially given the presence of significant numbers of blacks brought there with their French refugee masters. Similarly, many blacks were surely aware of legislative challenges to slavery in New York and elsewhere, even when these attempts fell short. The rising expectation of future freedom was as likely to stimulate restiveness as patience.[24]

Running away gave expression to individual aspirations while imposing a collective price on the slaveholding society. Although departing the home of one's master was prompted by individual and collective motives, running away constituted an effective form of resistance in part because it raised the costs of slaveholding. Not only did masters lose the labor of runaways, but they also paid for advertising and retrieval. Runaway advertising provided a steady source of income to newspaper editors in the eighteenth century. The pages upon which they published antislavery polemics and sentimental poetry were in part paid for by masters seeking their slaves and others hoping to sell theirs.[25]

The continued advertisement of slaves in New York newspapers rankled slavery's critics. One correspondent prefaced remarks submitted to the *Poughkeepsie Journal* in 1795 by noting the complicity between newspapers and slave sellers. The anonymous writer sought acceptance of his antislavery contribution on the principle of editorial balance, "As (contrary to thy wishes, I hope) the paper is obliged to be the channel through which those unfeeling mortals dare advertise their fellow beings for sale . . . and when done, withhold their names and hide behind 'Enquire of the Printer. . . .'"[26]

The NYMS sought a more direct approach to getting newspapers out of the slavery business. In June 1795, the society convened a three-person committee of Willet Seaman, George W. Woolsey, and William Dunlap to solicit New York City printers to cease advertising slave sales and runaway slave announcements. The following February, the committee indicated that newspaper publishers "had shown themselves favorably disposed . . . but were desirous that some general engagement might be entered into, by all, at the same time." Only one printer seemed willing to take the initiative to cease publishing slavery ads. A year later the still-optimistic committee reported no concrete results to their peers. In the financially risky newspaper business, the call by the printers to act together or not at all against slave advertisements was likely fatal to the initiative's prospects for success.[27]

The Manumission Society's opposition to advertisements complemented slave resistance at one level, yet at another level attempted to downplay its significance. Eliminating slavery-related advertising would handicap two pillars of the institution—commerce and enforcement. The runaway advertisement, in New York as in all other times and places in the history of American slavery, offered a mechanism for surveillance, capture, and control.[28] A ban on slave advertising thus would lessen the scope of the institution in an analogous fashion to the New York laws passed in the 1780s against the import and export of slaves.

Likely of equal significance to white reformers, the antiadvertisement strategy was consistent with NYMS emphasis on shaping public beliefs about slaves and slavery. A printers' boycott on slave advertisements would have been a blow to the institution's legitimacy. Slave advertising served as an ongoing retort to all manner of antislavery polemics. Announcements of sales and runaways continually communicated the so-called chattel principle, representing the slave as "a person with a price" rather than "a man and a brother" or potential citizen. Removing the chattel principle from public view thus would constitute a victory for antislavery principles.[29]

A ban on slave advertising would, from the perspective of the Manumission Society, remove another problematic image from public view—the image of the slave as a rebel openly contesting law and authority.[30] New York runaways projected an image of restiveness and confrontational autonomy at a time when the NYMS believed that just the opposite view of blacks would advance their cause. Thus, the society must have been all the more disappointed that New York City printers conducted business as usual in their advertising sections.

Ambivalence about runaways and black agency notwithstanding, slave resistance offered white antislavery activists irresistible opportunities to confront the existing regime. When African Americans questioned their status under the actual law of slavery, resistant blacks and reform-minded whites worked together toward shared goals. In particular, the laws passed in the 1780s making it illegal to sell slaves into or out of New York state provided a weapon for containing slavery which matched the goals of individual blacks to the disposition and skills of the society's membership.[31] One of the most important functions of the NYMS's standing committee was to ensure that those entitled to freedom by law actually received or maintained their freedom. Blacks who claimed liberty on statutory principles thus provided the society with the chance to enforce state law.[32]

A running battle developed between slaveholders, who sought to preserve and profit from slavery, and the standing committee, which sought to keep New York slavery closed from the inside and from the outside. Masters kept the regional slave system alive by carrying or selling slaves across state lines, or even international boundaries, into New York.[33] Sometimes slaves passing by this route into New York were sold one or more times, every sale obscuring the original violation and allowing illegal enslavement to masquerade as a normal transaction in a still-legal system of domestic slavery. The standing committee sought to trace such transactions to their origins; turning up a violation in the state's slave-import ban automatically freed the slave in question.[34]

Rather than seeking constitutional precedents and interpretations that might invalidate the right to own slaves, a strategy pursued by some slaves in New England, the committee tried to gain freedom for individual slaves within the context of existing statutory law.[35] Into the 1790s, the standing committee still found itself coming to the defense of blacks entitled to freedom as the former property of Revolutionary-era loyalists. In 1794, Cato, Massa, and their daughter, once part of a confiscated loyalist estate, sought the committee's help on these grounds. Other duplicities countered by the standing committee included indentures unilaterally extended to life servitude, refusal to recognize previously arranged manumissions, and the sale of slaves out of state in contravention of New York's containment policy.[36]

The standing committee largely relied on aggrieved African Americans to report their predicaments, along with any facts that might be useful in pursuing justice. Who knew better than an individual slave such as Thomas Dawdle in 1796 that he had been transported from New Jersey to New York City seven years earlier, sold, and then promised that he would have to work five and half years more, only to find himself "still detain[ed]"? William Harmon was born free in Delaware, brought to New York by Nathaniel Coldman, and then sold to George Copeland. Similarly, slave William Burdon indicated that his wife Phillis had changed masters three times since entering New York via New Jersey. In the abstract, advocates of gradual abolition continued to fear "the consequences of making the slaves know the *extent* of their rights." But as a practical matter in New York, African American knowledge of those rights abetted the struggle for abolition.[37]

Blacks disputed their own status because they understood the new legal terrain upon which slavery operated and knew the facts of their individual cases. Word had disseminated to portions of New York City's black community that they had potential white allies who could help blacks use the law to their advantage. Although not persuading the standing committee or the courts of the merits of every claim, African Americans used New York's legal system, striking a blow against slavery.

Having secured institutional allies in the form of the standing committee, slaves gave scope to their own expansive thinking on the problem of race. A small but suggestive subset of freedom cases handled by the committee involved the ancestry of individual slaves. People held as black slaves who could trace their lineage to free Indian mothers and grandmothers discovered the opportunity to contest their status on the basis of race. More rarely, as in the case of Molly Sears of Newburgh, New York, who won her freedom with the standing committee's help in April 1794, free white maternity served a similar purpose.[38] Although the mere assertion of Indian or white ancestry could not of itself win freedom, an individual slave's own rendering of the family tree supplied a crucial starting point.

Making a case for Indian lineage could be complex. In February 1798, Richard Hallett, a free black, reported that his wife Catherine had an Indian grandmother. Nonetheless, Robert Furman held her and her four children in slavery on Long Island. Two women substantiated that Catherine's grandmother was indeed an Indian; Ann Field, according to the standing committee's records, claimed the grandmother "had every appearance of a

Squaw." Representatives of the NYMS negotiated and recorded the terms of Catherine's manumission, to be granted within a year. Three of the children would gain their freedom at specified ages, and Furman sold the fourth, an infant, to her father Richard Hallett for one dollar. The imprecision of racial categories made this type of claim particularly effective.[39]

The number of successful freedom claims handled by the standing committee was modest. The Manumission Society reported to the ACPAS in May 1797 that from January 1796 forward, ninety blacks had contacted them, with thirty-six obtaining their freedom, and forty cases either in suit or "under consideration." In June 1800, the NYMS reported handling another seventy-four since 1798, twenty-five ending in freedom and the majority as yet unresolved. The society also indicated that individual members gained freedom for additional people "by their personal interference."[40]

Mere numbers, however, cannot record the meaning of freedom to those slaves who challenged their masters, nor the effect such challenges had on slavery in New York. The Manumission Society itself understood the individual urgency of freedom, even as it continued to advocate gradualism as a far better policy than immediate abolition. As Rev. Samuel Miller pointed out, even though local circumstances for slaves might be better in New York than in the South, freedom was its own reward, the significance of which could not be reduced to material conditions alone.[41] The standing committee offered slaves new ways to resist which further magnified the impact of more traditional resistance.

Moreover, the enforcement of New York's laws limiting the scope of slavery sent a signal that slave owners had to tread carefully. The threat of suit, and the collection of real damages in some cases, raised the potential cost of maintaining slavery in a way that supplemented the structural cost of runaways. At least in the vicinity of New York City, blacks had some recourse against masters who failed to honor wills, manumissions, and indentures. The standing committee's tactical alliance with African Americans adds substance to the claim that blacks actively negotiated their own freedom during slavery's final years. Indeed, such negotiations began before New York changed the terrain dramatically by legislating gradual abolition.[42]

As the New York Manumission Society's name suggests, encouraging and securing private acts of emancipation were another critical part of the white reformers program. Prior to 1800, results of this effort were mixed at best. Historians have noted only a small increase in private manumissions during the final decade of the eighteenth century. Indeed, the growth of New York City's slave population by almost five hundred from 1790 to 1800 outstripped manumissions. This continued growth of urban slavery, however, was partially offset by the increase in the free black population in some of the neighboring counties.

In any case, for either antislavery legislation or private manumissions to have a long-term effect, freed people had to remain free. The low rate of private manumission made preserving black freedom all the more crucial. However, the combination of manumission, legal action, and running away ultimately was insufficient to eliminate slavery in New York—even if such actions had been far more common.[43] As NYMS members themselves understood, containment of slavery legally and geographically meant nothing if lawmakers did not take further steps toward abolition.

III.

By November 1795, the opponents of slavery in New York had decided to renew their commitment to seeking gradual abolition legislation. The previous January, the American Convention had called for state manumission societies to use "every method in your power which can promise any success" to alter state laws protecting slavery. At a special meeting in November, the NYMS formed a committee to plan a petition to the legislature, hoping to accumulate the signatures of "as many of the respectable citizens of this State" as possible.[44]

At the state assembly's session in January 1796, Representative James Watson of New York City moved to bring a gradual abolition bill before the lower house. Watson was closely tied to recently elected governor John Jay, himself a man of long-standing antislavery views, and may have acted at Jay's behest. The Federalist governor, according to a later account by his abolitionist son William, believed that his direct intervention would inspire antagonism on partisan grounds. Such a judgment may have been reasonable given the firestorm over the Jay Treaty and the recent rhetorical standoff with Republicans on the lingering issue of British slave confiscations.[45]

The assembly responded cautiously. The abolition of slavery became linked with the possibility of compensating slave owners for taking away their property. The assembly also proceeded on the principle that the benefits of any abolition plan would not accrue to men and women presently in bondage but rather to their children. The concept of compensation to owners to be deprived of a full lifetime of service won approval by a one-vote majority. Deferral to a five-man committee of the entire subject of gradual abolition effectively ended its chances for the 1796 session, with compensation having gained a tentative endorsement.[46]

Proponents of gradual abolition clearly were not sure what mix of principle and strategy to pursue. Thus, compensation confused legislators sufficiently to derail the broader question of emancipation. Watson, who initially brought gradual abolition to the floor, voted in favor of compensation, as did twelve other supporters of gradual abolition. By contrast, a group of fifteen legislators committed to abolition voted against compensation. Those who opposed abolition outright were also split on whether to support compensation.[47] The rise of compensation as an important issue exposed the diversity of legislative opinion on how much slaveholder interests should be accounted for in the event of a gradual abolition. It also undermined expeditious legislative consideration of abolition itself.

On the other hand, the question fueled wider public debate over gradual abolition. An unsigned commentary in New York City's *Herald* reviewed the compensation issue. The writer focused on whether slaveholders could claim property rights in people unborn and, by the same token, whether the state could regulate slaveholder's access to property that had not yet come into existence. The state legally could set limits on the holdings of corporations, in effect barring corporate bodies from "*acquiring* a particular species of property, even the interest of their own capital, when the public good requires it." Thus, the paper implied that the state had no obligation to compensate slaveholders and had a right to manumit slave children under conditions of the state's choosing, treating this as a matter of political prerogative and moral economy.[48]

Manumission Society speakers viewed compensation with moral skepticism, while conceding that as a practical matter it might be necessary. Samuel Miller, in a 1797 address, insisted that the individual human rights of slaves should have priority over the property rights of slave owners, citing the Declaration of Independence as the appropriate guide. Elihu Smith tempered his strong principles with realism. He suggested that slave owners had extracted more than their fair share of labor already and, if anything, deserved a much rougher divine "recompence." Yet he also conceded that slave owners' property rights would not likely be ignored, whatever the merits of the situation.[49]

The legislature's handling of gradual abolition in 1796 inspired partisan scorn from both conservative and populist perspectives. Another piece in the Federalist-leaning *New York Herald*—one of three on February 10—blasted the handling of gradual abolition, excoriating some legislators for prioritizing parochial attachments to bondage when slavery was in fact a matter "of *general* concern." The paper also wondered, "Who would believe" that a democrat "should assert, in the legislature that *slavery* is so interwoven into our political system, that it cannot be eradicated? This is extraordinary doctrine in a republican government."[50]

Provincial political advantage also could provoke condemnation of compensation. In William Cooper's Ostego County, political deference began to fray at middecade, as better-educated lawyers began to contest the quasi-aristocratic patronage power that Cooper had established on the frontier. Jedidiah Peck, a former Cooper protégé, stepped into the new scramble for political power with a vigorous populism into which he folded antislavery views. Peck assailed Ostego County assemblyman Jacob Morris's candidacy for the state senate. As part of a broader antielitist, antiparty attack, Peck denounced Morris's vote in favor of compensation. Morris, who had been elected the previous year as an anti-Cooper candidate, defended himself, first by noting the "self created" political ambitions of his rival and then by pointing out the merits of his own votes. Morris claimed his support of compensation stemmed from his "sacred regard to the property of the Citizens."

Peck painted Morris as serving elite interests at the expense—in terms of money and power—of more ordinary citizens. Taxpayers, his critique implied, should not have to subsidize a slaveholding minority. In Peck's remarks, compensation, not the abolition of slavery, represented a dangerous extension of state power. Although Peck failed to unseat Morris in an election about local, regional, and personal rivalries, his use of antislavery rhetoric indicates how politically portable opposition to slavery had become by the mid-1790s. The issue did not tip the contest, but he had annunciated a frontier view of compensation and slavery which would in time undermine the ability of slaveholders to stave off a gradual abolition law.[51]

Even as state legislators wrestled inconclusively with gradual abolition, other white New Yorkers debated the moral implications of different paths to emancipation.[52] In late May 1797 the Republican *Time Piece* touched off a broadly focused literary battle in New York City when it published remarks by English radical Edward Rushton. The poet, who as a sailor on a slave-trading voyage contracted a disease that made him blind, wrote a letter assailing George Washington for continuing to hold slaves. His letter to Washington, reprinted in the *Time Piece,* directly assailed the just-retired president as "more culpable than the callous-hearted planter" because "you persevere in a system which your conscience tells you to be wrong." Included in Rushton's indictment was the Revolutionary War hero's lack of support for northern abolition.[53]

The ensuing poetic debate explored the policy implications of the sentiment engendered by much of the black-voiced poetry of the period. The contest juxtaposed an almost indefinite gradualism to the moral certitude of slavery's evil. Coming to Washington's defense, a poem by "Matilda" weighed the relative merits of gradual and immediate abolition. Matilda raised the specter of race war and French-style revolutionary chaos to discredit Rushton's assault. In a subsequent poem entitled *"On the necessity of a* gradual *abolition of Slavery,"* Matilda advised against "bow[ing] the mind to sympathy's controul." She opposed emotional and rational responses to the dilemma of slavery:

> But while the guilt and avarice of our fires,
> Indignant rage or pity soft inspires,
> Let us by reason's rules the ill redress,
> And from our pure intentions hope success.

Attempts to unduly speed matters along through an "excess of virtue," Matilda suggested, "often leads to crime." Anthony Benezet, the pioneering Pennsylvania Quaker abolitionist, served as a model of patient reform, cultivating black minds and bringing closer days of racial harmony. Matilda thus endorsed incremental reform with abolition as its distant end. Moreover, Matilda questioned whether readers should be governed by emotion-driven moral aspirations rather than practical considerations.[54]

Matilda's deference to slavery and defense of Washington encountered sharp criticism that embraced rather than cautioned against emotional identification. "The Slave," in his initial response, conjured images of the slave trade and southern slavery rather than revolutionary violence. The Slave directly praised sympathy itself: "Hail to the man, whose feeling heart / Can bear in others woes a part," having earlier in this poem informed Matilda that if she had experienced the physical and emotional pain of enslavement, she ". . . then dissolv'd in sympathy / . . . wouldst deplore the SLAVE with me." In another poem, the Slave indicated the policy implications of his argument, striking down Matilda's case for gradualism by noting that even those pursuing the legacy of Benezet by petitioning Congress regarding slavery received "abuse" from slaveholding interests. The author argued that each generation could postpone abolition indefinitely by insisting, like Matilda, that the time was not yet right for freedom. Curiously, the Slave exempted from the general condemnation New York, where, the poet implied, sympathy already structured the slave's experience. In the North "scarce the slave his bondage knows," in part because of the climate. Meanwhile, the northern slave, in the poet's view,

shares the harvest which he rears;
Well fed and cloth'd he tills the soil,
Sure that reward attends his toil.

Whether this reward would include freedom, the author did not say. The Slave's remarks on New York's allegedly more bearable bondage perhaps represented an implicit acceptance that gradual abolition might be legitimate in this northern state.[55]

Other responses to Matilda took less compromising stances. Concluded one poem,

No distinction of *fair* or of *black* or of *brown*,
Can consistent with liberty be;
No distinction but virtue and vice will she own
As the WHOLE HUMAN RACE SHOULD BE FREE.

Sarapering lectured Matilda, "Morals change not with time or with place."[56]

Despite the sharpness of the exchange, all participants in this poetic debate conducted in the Republican *Time Piece* at the very least paid lip service in favor of some form of abolition. The exchange further revealed the polemic and political value of verse, while expressly taking up the contributions and limitations of sentiment in debating emancipation policy. As legislative events unfolded, sympathy would be tempered by practical-minded caution and self-interest, in keeping with the poetic briefs of Matilda and the Slave.

Of equal significance, no true proslavery voice leapt to the fore in this debate. Assailing George Washington from the left on the issue of slavery was a far cry from Republican attacks against the Jay Treaty just two years before for failing to secure compensation from Britain for fugitive slaves. In this new debate, compensation was not even an issue; indeed, most of the contributions refused to accept apologies for gradual abolition. Interestingly, it was Webster's Federalist-oriented *Minerva*, observing the *Time Piece* exchange, that defended Washington and, by implication, gradualism. The Rushton-inspired poetic dialogue thus signaled growing approval across party lines for taking action against slavery, even though, through 1797, legislators themselves avoided decisive action.[57]

IV.

In the 1798 state assembly session, new political circumstances, shifting policy priorities, and public opinion brought gradual abolition much closer to passage. As the question reached a crossroads, emancipation became more explicitly associated with public finance and poor relief than race and political participation. All these issues had potential value to opponents of abolition seeking to derail its passage, but the economic questions raised in the late 1790s proved to be a less daunting obstacle than questions about the racial makeup of the polity had been in the mid-1780s.[58] As momentum for a gradual abolition law grew, proslavery legislators were forced to consider how to soften the blow to slaveholders if and when emancipation came to pass.

The size and composition of the state assembly now worked against those who wished to protect slavery and slaveholder interests. In 1796 the reapportionment and expansion of the assembly, a measure urged by westerners, gained approval in the state government, which Federalists controlled. The new formula placed more power in the hands of antislavery representatives. Frontier-county delegations increased in number and size.[59] Meanwhile, New York City's delegation had become the largest in the assembly, with thirteen representatives. This group, which had voted reliably against slavery since 1790, became even more consistently antislavery. Constituting approximately 12 percent of the lower house, city representatives alone could muster almost a quarter of a majority on any given question.

The new electoral math left slaveholder power stagnant. In a legislative chamber where at any one time about eighty-five to ninety-five representatives cast votes on slavery questions, defenders of slavery, based in Albany, Queens, and Ulster Counties, could count at best on thirty-five votes—only about ten more than they started with in 1796 when the lower house was considerably smaller. Proponents of slavery thus found themselves with proportionally fewer allies to help them place additional restrictions on abolition. Such qualifying language in the past had proved effective in short-circuiting gradual abolition in the legislature.

Votes on packaging gradual abolition with compensation to slaveholders began to follow a consistent pattern. In 1796, the principle of compensation had received approval with a total of thirty-two votes. In 1798, Dutchess County assemblyman William B. Verplanck's proposal to add a compensation clause to the gradual abolition bill before the lower house in 1798 again received thirty-two votes, but fifty-eight opposing representatives brought compensation to overwhelming defeat. Unlike in 1796, every New York City representative present voted against compensation. But it was the overwhelming unpopularity of compensation in the northern and western parts of the state that ensured its thorough defeat. In these counties, some of which had not even existed in 1790, compensation lost twenty-nine to four.[60]

Representatives from northern and western counties had a particular incentive to oppose compensation. Any form of state funding amounted to a transfer of wealth from their counties to eastern counties, where the vast majority of slaveholders resided. Another motion would have made the state financially responsible for any former slave gaining freedom who then became a pauper in need of public support. Almost as large a proportion (twenty-five to eight) of northern and western county representatives contributed to the defeat of this proposal as had voted against compensation. Keeping any proposed gradual-abolition legislation free of such encumbering clauses, moreover, increased the likelihood of overall passage by limiting difficult choices for those who favored gradual abolition but disliked the way slaveholding interests shaped the actual bill. In any case, by the end of the 1798 session, compensation was vanquished.[61]

The enactment of a gradual abolition law nevertheless remained illusory in 1798. Despite the lower house's hard work—it had taken twelve separate roll-call votes to get a finished bill out of the assembly—the senate declined to take up the matter. It was late in the session. Members of that body may not have worked out fully their own thoughts about compensation. State senators also represented not counties but four districts, each of which contained significant areas of slaveholding. This situation, along with the fact that senators were chosen by a smaller, wealthier portion of the electorate, may help explain the upper house's conservatism in 1797 and 1798 regarding gradual abolition.[62]

The 1798 session also demonstrated the growing emphasis on abolition's financial and public welfare implications. Prior to defeating a proposal to make the state responsible for free black paupers, the assembly considered a motion to impose on free blacks between the ages of twenty-five and fifty in every New York town a special tax "to be appropriated for the support of the free black poor" in each jurisdiction. In some respects, this proposition evoked the racially exclusive amendments regarding black franchise and jury service that helped doom gradual abolition in 1785. The 1798 amendment, however, lost fifty-nine to twenty-five, receiving solid backing almost nowhere in the state.[63] Yet the spirit of the proposal, in its anticipation of a growth in the state's poor black population and assumption of collective public responsibility, indicated a shift in public policy focus which helped to shape the passage of gradual abolition. The economic dimensions of freedom and citizenship had become more central to gradual abolition since the 1780s, when political participation had provided the principle sticking point to emancipation.

Part of the emphasis on economic implications was the prospect that gradual abolition might be imminent. Based on assembly voting patterns in 1798, slavery's defenders must have understood that some form of gradual aboli-

tion soon would pass; these legislators thus had to seek the best monetary arrangement they could. In 1798 and 1799, legislators revealed their increased
preoccupation with the relationship abolition might have to poverty in the
state and to nettlesome questions of public finance. Would-be liberators, as
well as apologists for slaveholding, perceived future freed people as potential
paupers as much or more than as voters, jurors, and legislators. Given that
voting eligibility was based on property-holding, these two issues bore some
relation to each other. By definition, adult male paupers in early national
New York were nonvoters. Perhaps this changing emphasis in perceptions of
emancipation's implications made gradual abolition a less threatening prospect than it had been in the 1780s.[64] In any case, the ground upon which the
legislative battle over gradual abolition took place had shifted.

v.

The potential economic impact of abolition resonated with broader trends in
1790s discussions of social reform and citizenship. These discussions in turn
reflected long-term changes in economy and society that were underway in
the 1790s. Economic and social life in New York increasingly was characterized by voluntary commercial relationships. Although it would take decades
to fully work out this process, the calculation of self-interest and physical
mobility were replacing ascriptive hierarchy and lengthy leases on land and
labor. Those who imagined themselves as moral and social stewards of this
society could not ignore the effects of these transitions on public finance and
private poverty—old problems in need of new solutions.[65]

In seeking to serve the less fortunate as well as to maintain their legitimacy, reformers at least implicitly grappled with the proper means of measuring citizenship in a republican society. The right to participate in electoral
politics was the most obvious but not the only pillar of citizenship. Another
crucial indicator of citizenship status in late-eighteenth-century New York
was access to the ability to earn a living, to maintain oneself and one's family without sinking into dependence. Racial slavery, of course, deprived its
victims of both.[66] Whether emancipation would remove these barriers remained an unresolved but vital issue.

Individuals and organizations during the 1790s publicly insisted on the
virtues and social usefulness of caring for the poor, a class many black people
soon might join. The charitable impulse, sometimes expressed in poetry and
exhortations, found its realization in such New York City projects as immigrant
aid, a public dispensary and hospital, an organization to assist debt prisoners,
and of course, the NYMS. In addition, governmental or quasi-governmental

institutions like the almshouse and the new state prison sought in one way or another to protect the unfortunate and correct improvident behavior.[67]

A sense of financial limits and ambivalence about the poor conflicted with a desire to assist those living on the margins of citizenship, including slaves. New Yorkers, especially those in New York City, found that the needs of the poor tested the capacity of authorities and charitable institutions to care for them. The problem appeared to stem from inadequate charitable means and abuses of good will. A piece in New York City's *Weekly Chronicle* praised the foundling hospital's decision not to allow parents to simply dump unwanted children, "for what can have a more manifest tendency to suppress that dissoluteness amongst the common people, than the consideration of being obliged to support their offspring, or suffer imprisonment?"[68]

The simultaneous preoccupation with the opportunity to offer succor to the poor and the costs of doing so was rooted in the dramatic economic growth of New York City in the 1790s. The 1792 financial panic notwithstanding, the city found itself enjoying the fruits of European warfare, as well as its own superb harbor. As commerce accelerated in this neutral port, which was also linked to an expanding upstate hinterland, the merchant class and the general population exploded. New York became a center of the new nation's banking facilities, while further down the economic pyramid, some artisans became entrepreneurs employing an expanding class of wage laborers.

In the midst of this economic transformation, urban poverty increased dramatically. Exposed to the ups and downs of business as busy seasons alternated with slow ones, poor workers lost ground relative to their increasingly wealthy neighbors and employers. The gap was exacerbated as formally autonomous craftsman became day laborers. As a result, the need for city services to the poor raced ahead of facilities and financial resources. By the mid-1790s, the almshouse budget had more than doubled from the previous decade. Immigrants and native-born poor overwhelmed the capacity of the old almshouse and the new one built in 1797. Civic and cultural leaders, often drawn from similar social circles if not always the same political parties, understood that their aspirations to lead a great city made up of responsible, economically energetic citizens required effective management of the city's wealth and its poverty. Education, healthcare, and poor relief were thus cornerstones of civic health.[69]

The institution of slavery and the prospect of abolition posed distinct challenges for the administration of charity and maintenance of the poor, especially in New York City. The almshouse readily processed some free black and mulatto youths for apprenticeship. But the arrival of other black people at the almshouse necessitated the determination of their status. Almshouse board members wished to recover the full cost of care for sick and indigent slaves who came under their auspices—such as New York City merchant William Constable's "black man Adam, [who] lies in the Almshouse, with frosted feet"—but for whom legal liability lay elsewhere. Unfortunately, whites like Constable might deny actual ownership of the slaves in question. Almshouse officials had to expend additional effort if an indigent black came from another jurisdiction. Frustrated, the board declared in its May 29, 1797, minutes "that taking boarders into the Almshouse on pay, is not agreeable to the design of the institution, especially such boarders, as appear to be Slaves." The almshouse did not wish to rent its relief services to masters who did not look after their own slaves. Thus, the directors no longer would "recommend persons who are in a state of slavery to the magistrates of the City, as proper objects of the Almshouse."[70]

Apparently unsatisfied with unilateral action, a New York City petition launched in early 1798 to the state legislature complained of the "burthen" placed on the almshouse. One aspect of this problem, according to the petitioners, was abuse of the legal ban on buying slaves outside the state for the purpose of settling them in New York. Despite the law, according to the petition, citizens brought slaves from Nova Scotia, the West Indies, and other American states, indenturing them and then manumitting them after they became no longer useful. "Incapable of helping themselves," these smuggled humans were left for the public to support.[71] Whether New York City's almshouse lacked the means, or simply the desire, to support certain categories of poor blacks, slavery created additional duties that its directors found irritating and expensive. Thus, these violations of the revised slave code, designed to isolate New York slavery, caused complications for public welfare at a time when the problem of poverty attracted significant attention. Further modifications to slave law would have to account for stresses on the provision of poor relief. Yet concerns over relief finances were expressed within the context of the desire to care for society's distressed and to limit legal arrangements that compelled some individuals to remain in situations of coerced dependence, such as slavery and imprisonment for debt.

How New York polemicists and politicians continued to find debt imprisonment problematic sheds further light on the slavery issue. As discussed in chapter 5, slavery and debt prompted similar anxieties about dependency and inefficiency. During the 1790s, scores of essays and comments condemning the practice appeared in publications of a variety of political orientations. Sentimental descriptions, like contemporaneous portrayals of slavery, evoked suffering victims and afflicted families.[72] Arguments against debt imprisonment stressed the unnecessary exposure of those experiencing economic misfortune to the vices of true criminals, the terrible conditions of prisons, the economic counterproductivity of current debtor-creditor law, and the uncivilized nature of the practice in a nation of republican ideals. The creditor had no right to exercise tyrannical power over the life of the debtor. Advancement as a society required sorting out real criminals from the victims of circumstance and subordinating one man's exclusive power over another to publicly determined standards of justice. New Yorkers, members of a society of sovereign citizens, wished to distinguish themselves through their laws and practices from those they had grown into the habit of defining themselves against, whether Old World tyrants, Barbary pirates, or southern slaveholders. And yet, anti-imprisonment commentaries reminded readers, even Turks and American Indians might legitimately look down upon this practice from morally superior ground.[73]

Similarly, the problem of supporting slavery and slaves posed an ongoing ideological and practical problem in the late 1790s. The ideological costs were high, as unfree labor and coerced confinement appeared antithetical to emerging principles and practices in New York. Yet, as the almshouse directors learned on a case-by-case basis, managing the transition from slavery to freedom created legal ambiguities and imposed unwanted costs. Meanwhile, other charitable institutions had learned to be cautious about managing their budgets and husbanding their generosity with regard to their mostly white clientele.

While the costs of a markedly gradual emancipation could be spread out over time and various jurisdictions, the means of doing so was something political representatives throughout the state felt compelled to consider. Freed people, it seemed, were likely to be both citizens and wards of the state, with all the potential contradictions and skepticism toward free African Americans that the latter status implied.[74] Yet it would be a mistake to isolate the consideration of the charitable impulse to black emancipation in order to conclude that gradual abolition solely reflected a desire to enact into law condescending assumptions in order to hamstring black citizenship. A swirl of mixed goals and messages surrounded the political economy of 1790s reform: doing good meant addressing embarrassing social anachronisms, extending the sympathetic boundaries of the public sphere, and accounting for financial resources. Both prejudice and experience with public relief indicated that emancipation would have some concrete public cost. At the far end of the discourse over such matters lay the give and take of the legislature, the republican laboratory for the proverbial "art of the possible," where the only working model for abolition on the table was a gradual one.

VI.

In January 1799, New York's legislature appeared ready to address their state's most glaring inequities. The unfinished business of emancipation, as well as debtor imprisonment, returned to the political agenda. The resulting abolition legislation very much reflected a reform impulse that incorporated postindependence experiences with poor relief and the desire to limit the liability of whites for the consequences of slavery and abolition.

As in 1798, much of the legislature's focus on gradual abolition centered on who would bear the financial responsibility for prospective freed people. That children and masters would absorb much of the cost—to the benefit of their masters—was by now well established.[75] Thus, the first enacting clause implementing gradual abolition adhered to the formula of proposing a date after which all children subsequently "born of a slave" would be free. The obligation to serve their mother's master until a certain age would be determined by the legislature when the bill moved closer to passage. The general design met little resistance, passing sixty-eight to twenty-three.[76] The initial working majority for gradual abolition had thus expanded since 1798 by over ten votes.

Determining how much flexibility to build into the system of gradual abolition proved to be a major challenge bearing on public finance. The proposed second enacting clause would permit masters to renounce their rights to slave children within one year of their birth. These children were to become the wards of their local jurisdictions, which would bind them out. Antiabolition representative John I. Van Rensselaer of Rensselaer County moved to make support for these abandoned children the expressed financial responsibility of the state government. This motion passed by six votes, the support of traditionally proslavery counties like Queens and Ulster supplemented by split delegations elsewhere in the state, including the support of nine of eleven New York City representatives. Predictably, new frontier and northern counties opposed state funding by a margin of about two-and-a-half to one. Perhaps fearing that such state funding might erode support for gradual abolition, the next day the lower house reversed itself, antislavery representatives this time overwhelming proslavery representatives fifty-six to twenty-eight in a vote not to permit voluntary abandonment. A motion to make the state financially responsible for supporting black paupers whose freedom could be traced to the gradual abolition act received more support but not enough to carry the assembly. Proslavery interests had failed to undermine support for gradual abolition.[77]

Having lost the larger battle, defenders of slaveholding interests sought to prolong service by these freed children. A motion to set the male age for freedom at thirty lost by a substantial margin. Mandatory service for the children of slaves would last until the age of twenty-eight for males and twenty-five for females.[78] The age differential apparently reflected expectations about the peak productive years of males and females. The difference also may have reflected a desire, on the one hand, to minimize liability for the cost of supporting mothers distracted by their need to care for unproductive children, and, on the other hand, an assumption about the alleged social dangers of autonomous, unsupervised black males.[79]

The senate recrafted the abolition bill in a manner fraught with irony. The upper house overcame its initial reservations about the gradual abolition bill by reinserting state support for abandoned slave children.[80] Before giving final approval to the bill, the senate decided to liberalize the rules governing private manumissions. To do so, an odd coalition of opponents and proponents of gradual abolition managed to defeat another group of supporters of gradual abolition.

Most senate defenders of slavery favored liberal manumission policy without restrictions on the freeing of elderly or otherwise dependent slaves. So, too, did about half of the twenty-four senators who ultimately signed on to the new gradual abolition bill favoring unrestricted manumission. But most of the original senate supporters of gradual abolition voted against liberalizing manumission rules. Liberalized manumission thereby passed over the opposition of, arguably, the most committed group of antislavery senators. Faced with defeat, the defenders of slavery sought to maximize their options. The bill thus held out the prospect of accelerating manumission while allowing masters maximum flexibility to reduce the cost of slaveholding during its waning years. Such adaptability apparently made some proabolition politicians nervous. Slaveholding interests were as responsible as any group for advancing the long-held cause of slavery's opponents, to encourage private citizens to manumit their slaves of their own free will. At any rate, the assembly expeditiously approved the senate's modifications of the bill, as did the Council of Revision, thus making gradual abolition the law of New York state, set to take effect after July 4, 1799.[81]

Support for "An Act for the gradual abolition of Slavery" followed well-established regional patterns and reflected the bipartisan support that antislavery positions had begun to attract in the late 1790s. Diehard proslavery delegates in Ulster and Queens Counties only attracted scattered support elsewhere. Supporters of gradual abolition in Albany, Orange, Westchester, and Dutchess Counties joined representatives from New York City and the newer northern and western counties to provide gradual abolition its comfortable margin of victory in the lower house. The voting patterns of newer northern and western counties for abolition, moreover, indicated that William Cooper's otherwise erstwhile vision of a maple-sugar producing, free-labor, antislavery future was not entirely off the mark. For the most part, neither slaves, slaveholding aspirations, nor politicians willing to protect slavery traveled westward onto the New York frontier.

Equally telling, gradual abolition passed with almost two-to-one support of Republican and Federalist assemblymen (using that session's vote on the pro-Republican Virginia and Kentucky Resolutions as a guide to party identification). As chapter 7 illustrated, slavery was more than once an issue drawn into the vortex of party politics in New York. Only a few years before, Republicans tried to make political hay out of compensation for slaves departing with the British. No longer did they do so. Unlike such national issues as the Alien and Sedition Acts or foreign policy toward Britain and France, attitudes toward slavery's future in New York proved to be a more local and personal matter. Federalists and Republicans could and did reason their ways to support or oppose gradual abolition while passionately disagreeing with one another on a host of other principles.[82]

A race-inflected practicality nonetheless characterized the final outcome. The senate and the assembly had demonstrated serious concern regarding the costs, funding, and implications of abolition for poor relief. Of the six clauses comprising the gradual abolition law passed on March 29, 1799, the final four reflected such considerations.

The law created a special obligation for the state to cover the costs of children abandoned by their masters. These abandoned children were to be incorporated into local poor relief through each town's or city's overseers of the poor at state expense. The law thus represented a compromise between the long-standing New York policy of making each town responsible for its own poor and the unusual circumstance of the statewide creation of a new class of people in transition to freedom from slavery. The law attempted to eliminate the types of ambiguities that had plagued the New York City almshouse. Masters had to register each newborn child of a slave mother after July 4. The responsibility of each household or town for its own poor was fortified. Registration also served organized antislavery's traditional goal to record manumissions. This worked to the advantage of free blacks as well, who remained vulnerable to kidnapping and transportation south. The state also set precise limits—$3.50 a month—on the level of support for abandoned children, while additionally obligating masters to cover the cost of the first year of every such child.[83]

The new law served several competing groups.[84] It protected localities with large concentrations of slaves by offering state funding for abandoned children, thus spreading the cost of gradual abolition throughout the state. The law also safeguarded New York City, where there was some concern that Manhattan had become a magnet for destitute former slaves, by specifying that regardless of the funding source, local overseers of the poor remained responsible for processing children born in their own jurisdictions.[85] Western and northern counties with few slaves may have had greater obligations for the costs of gradual abolition than they might have wished, but their strong opposition to directly compensating slave owners or expanding state obligations to all free blacks foreclosed an even less palatable option.

For black New Yorkers, the paradox of gradual abolition stemmed from the diverging implications for black citizenship contained within the statute. The gradual emancipation law implicitly recognized political citizenship, imposing no suffrage or jury restrictions on free blacks. The economic aspects of their prospective citizenship, by contrast, were undermined.[86] The willingness to forego political limitations was not accidental but emerged from a decade or more of public debates. Since 1785, when political restrictions had proved gradual abolition's undoing, slavery had undergone a barrage of rhetorical assaults, on its own merits and in conjunction with increasingly bitter regional and partisan disputes. Stripping African Americans of the political rights of citizens would have proved controversial and impolitic for New York Federalists and Republicans in 1799. Opponents of slavery had brought the battle into the public sphere, linking the institution negatively with unbearable cruelty, high-seas piracy, and a vulnerable, self-serving South, while linking antislavery with elevated sympathy, economic advancement, educational environmentalism, and even justifiable resistance. Meanwhile, a small but significant number of blacks had prodded white reformers and the legal system to endorse their freedom on an individualized basis. Rhetoric and activism not only kept slavery on the state's political agenda, it also helped keep explicitly racist measures out of the final gradual abolition formula.

Despite the political opening for free blacks under the gradual abolition law, a combination of racialist social observations and shifting policy priorities worked against the practical realization of full citizenship. Along with state funding for abandoned children, gradualism created hurdles to the construction of equality. Many white leaders, including those in the NYMS, operated on the assumption that once free, blacks would not support themselves adequately and would drain public resources.[87] Accordingly, blacks also could not be expected to take care of their own potentially indigent. The terms of gradual abolition may have reinforced this concept of black dependence by creating a probationary period during which the children of slaves remained under the charge of white masters well into adulthood.

In some, though not in all, ways New York's new law mirrored laws passed in New England a decade-and-a-half earlier. New York imposed an even more stringent period of service for the freeborn children of slaves than did Connecticut and Rhode Island (although under Pennsylvania's pioneering law, the age of actual freedom was twenty-eight for men and women). Strikingly, New England's laws, even more than New York's, took away with one hand the freedom granted with the other. Children of slaves in Connecticut and Rhode Island had to rely exclusively for support on their masters. The New York law, by contrast, did establish the potential for a set of contract-like relationships to govern the children of some slaves—those officially renounced by their mother's masters before the children reached the age of one. These children would then be bound out for service under the auspices of the local overseers of the poor. Rhode Island had originally instituted such a system, only to repeal it two years later. More important than such technicalities, however, was that all such laws instituted a system of African American–bound service that lasted well into adulthood.[88]

New York's law, like those in other northern states, also indirectly compromised black political citizenship. As all these northern states had freehold requirements for voting, bound servitude had the effect of undermining the sort of independent property accumulation necessary to reach the bar of full and active citizenship in postrevolutionary America. Such laws thus created a framework for racial inequality that subsequent generations of whites could impose, should they so choose, through a combination of laws and social practice.[89]

Presumptions of future black dependency also reflected the realistic expectation that whites would deny African Americans access to the opportunities and economic roles that most whites enjoyed.[90] In addition, the law took into account the potential unscrupulousness of white masters by requiring the registration of children born to their slaves and requiring masters to support unregistered but subsequently abandoned children. The New York City almshouse experience indicated that some masters could be expected to try to manipulate the poor relief system. Almshouse records indicate that some blacks, like a growing number of whites, required public poor relief and that in some cases this could be handled routinely, but that the ambiguous status of blacks during any transition from slavery to freedom would lead to confusion and abuse. Even if masters were the source of the problem, this only underscored the legacy of disadvantage and inequality that blacks carried into freedom.[91]

Organized white opponents of slavery helped create this gradual but suspect version of African American freedom. The American Convention emphasized citizenship, including political rights, as the ideal toward which it strove. A belief in equal rights and equal treatment had always been major motifs in antislavery arguments put forward in New York. Moreover, the NYMS envisioned remedial measures to overcome the problem of conditioned inequality and, especially when pushed, sought to restore freedom to individual African Americans. Yet the disposition, prevalent among reformers, to supervise blacks as needy people fueled the assumption that under gradual abolition blacks would operate at an economic and social disadvantage. Indeed, the organized abolitionists' obsession with good behavior and fears about public perceptions of indolent blacks betrayed a lack of faith in black abilities which was virulently shared by lawmakers at large.[92]

Abolition created a conundrum, and gradualism a conundrum within a conundrum, which abolitionists only partly appreciated. As abolitionist literature quoted at the beginning of the chapter indicated, some whites anticipated that freedom's blessings would quickly allow individual African Americans to take their place as equals in society. Yet almost no whites imagined, let alone advocated, mass, publicly mandated manumission. Gradualism coupled with private manumissions, or, for that matter, immediate abolition, was likely to create a new burden on the public relief system in an era when caring for the poor was deemed an important, albeit not always welcome, response to changing economic conditions. Without any better ideas as to how to manage that burden and with a political and perhaps racial predisposition to take into account the interests of slaveholders and the continued existence of slavery, no one proposed breaking with the formula that left the children of slaves in the hands of their mothers' masters. Thus, gradualism endorsed the deepest contradictions of racial environmentalism. The degraded environment of slavery would be perpetuated as the first technically free generation of black New Yorkers came of age.[93]

White New Yorkers' increasing concern with the economic aspects of citizenship thus was double-edged. Slavery could be viewed from yet another angle as a problematic institution. But a focus on economic vulnerability also highlighted the considerable delicacy of the prospect of liberating slaves. Upon return to the legislative agenda in 1796, gradual abolition required four years to resolve. These four years produced a slow form of gradualism which granted masters great flexibility without giving them everything—especially direct compensation—for which they might have hoped.

Various scholars have claimed that the gradual abolition law constituted a plan indirectly to compensate slaveholders. Masters could officially abandon slave children and then volunteer to bind them from the overseers of the poor at the state's expense. This ruse did take place, but it is not at all clear that the law was designed for that purpose. Elaborate calculations by economic historians have shown that the kind of gradualism envisioned in New York's law, preserving owners' rights to the offspring of slaves well into adulthood, constituted a *de facto* compensation scheme in which the slaves themselves paid the price. Historians also have calculated that the ages selected promised owners a reasonable return on their investment in the raising of these children during their early years.[94]

More immediate priorities than indirectly compensating masters, however, had as much or more to do with the shaping of the legislation. Orderly administration of aid to the poor and assuaging local fears of expanding an ambiguously defined population of poor people considerably influenced legislative policy. Given fears of abuses against institutions of charitable relief, it seems likely that the lawmakers would have tried to prevent slaveholder abuse of the law had they anticipated it. Once detected, the state did not long tolerate this abuse, dismantling state funding for abandoned freed children without discarding gradual abolition itself. In 1802, Republican governor George Clinton lectured the assembly on the need for fiscal discipline, including state financial support for the freeborn children of slaves officially abandoned in infancy by their mothers' masters. The legislature reduced state payments to local overseers of the poor to a maximum two dollars per month, only covering the expenses of children under the age of five.[95] Two years later the state eliminated any further recourse by masters or overseers of the poor to state-financed abandonment of young black children.[96]

New Jersey's experience with gradual abolition showed New York's influence and repeated the pattern of slaveholder exploitation of an abandonment clause leading to the repeal of that practice. In 1804, New Jersey's legislature dramatically reversed a previously staunch opposition to gradual abolition; subsequent to Independence Day 1804 the children of slave mothers would be free but males would be obligated to serve their mothers' masters until the age of twenty-five and females until age twenty-one. An abandonment clause like New York's permitted masters to free infant children and then have them bound to their former masters by local poor officials in exchange for cash payments from the state. By the next year, under pressure from constituents, the New Jersey legislature again followed New York's lead and eliminated any future use of this very expensive state program. Flanked by Pennsylvania, long committed to gradual emancipation, and New York, New Jersey finally joined its neighbors.[97]

The establishment of the ages at which individual blacks would be released from servitude, first in New York and then in New Jersey, reflected precedent more than carefully calibrated calculation. The general idea of setting the age of freedom in the midtwenties had been around from at least 1785 in New York, following Pennsylvania, Connecticut, and Rhode Island. Given their druthers, some slaveholders would have selected older ages for freedom, as high as thirty-five for males.[98] Moreover, slaveholders and defenders of their interests in the legislature clearly thought of compensation more in terms of monetary grants than extended service. As late as 1796, considerable support existed for monetary compensation, and the possibility remained alive into 1798.

In any case, the very nature of gradual abolition ensured that masters received compensating benefits. The law accommodated the interests of slaveholders at the expense of slaves, whose interests received only partial consideration in the actual shaping of the legislation. The law preserved flexibility for masters, who could retain rights to service for a considerable amount of time. Moreover, the act's second clause promised masters the right to sell or will the service of these nominally free people before they came of age. Gradualism emerged from a context in which finances and ideology, racism and antislavery interacted to shape the final outcome. It was to the advantage of whites besides slaveholders to consider their financial interests as part of the process of evaluating gradual abolition.[99]

New York lawmakers, moreover, regarded gradualism as an appealing solution to problems besides slavery. In the same session during which emancipation finally passed, the legislature contemplated a similar formula for solving the ongoing problem of debtor imprisonment. The 1799 assembly entertained a bill to abolish debtor imprisonment for contracts arrived at after an unspecified cutoff date. Republican Aaron Burr, also a consistent foe of slavery, moved to set that date at July 4, 1799, the same date incorporated into the gradual abolition of slavery. This initial attraction to July 4 for both abolitions cast them each in the light of a major break from a no longer acceptable regime. In point of practice, setting up a cutoff date ensured that neither plan operated retroactively—in deference, no doubt, to property holders and their political clout.[100] The senate rejected the abolition of debt imprisonment, instead passing another debt imprisonment reform bill, without abolishing the practice itself.[101] Thus, like the abolition of slavery, the abolition of debt imprisonment proceeded gradually through the accretion of reforms.

The absence of more forthright action did not preclude New Yorkers from perceiving slavery and debt imprisonment in moral terms that recommended strong action against these long-standing practices. Neither issue would have gone before the legislature repeatedly over the years absent moral hectoring in polemic, literary, and organized forms.[102] That a moral principle was at stake, however, did not stop the intervention of regional or personal interests from shaping the final outcome. It could hardly have been otherwise given the financial implications of the abolition of slavery and debtor imprisonment. Attempts to decriminalize glaring forms of dependence, touched on ideology and interest.[103] The context for doing something to end slavery was shaped by discourse that prized sentiment and championed certain visions of a just political economy, without producing a sentimental law or one that meted out anything but a rough version of justice.

Nevertheless, reform in the late 1790s emerged from a context in which officials and the public sought to distinguish between types of coercion. They did so in order to more clearly elaborate coercion's function and establish a morally defensible, economically serviceable regional identity. Ideology as expressed in the public discourse set the agenda through which political officials shaped the law. In 1797 one critic of imprisoning debtors remarked, "The innocent should be legally distinguished from the guilty. The punishment of the guilty should be desined [*sic*] and limited by law—and the innocent should not suffer at all.—These things are not well ordered in our country. —The laws are deficient and ought to be amended."[104] The gradual abolition of slavery attempted to make up for just such a deficiency.

VII.

For all its shortcomings and compromises, the passage of the gradual abolition law marked a critical departure in the long history of New York slavery. The extended battle to delegitimize racial bondage legally had been won. A slaveless society and economy in the northern United States had received powerful endorsement. The gradualism of slavery's abolition owed as much to the failure to pass such a law in 1777, 1785, or at any time prior to the turn of the century as to the terms of the law that finally did pass in 1799. Abolition would have proceeded even more gradually if New York lawmakers had waited another five, ten, or fifteen years, and would have taken longer still had they waited for slaveholders themselves to agree.[105] Instead, slavery unraveled quickly after 1799, as blacks and white opponents of slavery gained new weapons to fight their battle across a transformed landscape.[106]

Prior to 1799, New Yorkers had granted few openings for a more rapid approach to abolition. A motion for immediate abolition served as a mere ploy for proslavery representatives in 1785, with little chance of serious consideration. A constitutional or judicial version of abolition might have provided a more realistic alternative to the elongated, cautious legislative process of gradual abolition. Precedent existed in New England for the judicial invalidation of slavery, although even the discovery that a state constitution disallowed slavery might entail a slow, rather than immediate abolition.[107]

Reflecting years later on the 1799 legislative session, Erastus Root, representative from Delaware County, offered a telling variation on the theme of constitutional emancipation. He recounted his attempt at that time to limit the period of service for the children of slaves to age eighteen for females and twenty-one for males. Referring to white children similarly bound out for service, Root recalled, "I urged the propriety of putting the children of slaves upon the same footing as children of freemen—that they were so already, both by the Constitution of this state and by Divine Law." According to Root, "The declaration of Independence was made the preamble to the Constitution of this State, and of course part and parcel thereof . . . and thereby became law, and of as much binding force as any part of that [i]nstrument." Such constitutional high-mindedness, even in the cause of rendering gradual abolition a little less gradual and a little more fair, fell on deaf ears. Slavery had survived too long and remained too strong in New York to be swept away by a clean application of revolutionary principle.[108] In a variety of direct, indirect, and conflicting ways, the currents of public discourse influenced but did not control slavery's fate. In New York, only the give and take of the political process could synthesize competing interests and ideas to abolish slavery within a generation. On a moral level, we cannot excuse compromisers by pointing to positive subsequent events that they themselves did not foresee. Yet no one, not whites, and certainly not blacks, viewed the 1799 law as an end unto itself. Slavery's opponents, white and black, knew that much work remained to be done.[109]

Antislavery advocates themselves put the passage of a gradual abolition law into reasonable perspective. The New York Manumission Society's report to the June 1800 American Convention commented on educational programs, legal interventions on behalf of free blacks, and the appalling shipment of blacks from New York through southern ports into West Indian slavery. Toward the end, the report noted briefly that New York had passed a gradual abolition law for "this populous and extensive state," followed by the observation: "We cannot perhaps terminate our report more properly, than by a reflection on the means by which, under Divine permission, have appeared to be thus far useful, in freeing the oppressed, and enlightening the minds of the ignorant." The report concluded with the image of "our living in a community in which, within a time, not far distant, nor difficult to estimate—Domestic Slavery will be unknown, and where the blessings of civil and religious liberty will be equally extended to all." [110] New York entered the new century with an entirely new relationship to slavery and bright prospects for its eradication. As little as slaves themselves appeared to be taken into consideration by the actual "Act for the gradual abolition of Slavery," that law would make a tremendous difference to black New Yorkers and to the state, region, and nation in which they lived.

III

REFLECTIONS

9

Freedom, Slavery, Memory, and Modernity, 1800–27

The light with which Providence has been pleased to enlighten the minds of men, as it regards moral or religious truths, is gradual—as was the commencement of the abolition of slavery.

    —THOMAS EDDY TO J. GRISCOM, July 8, 1818

If this practice of ancient times be almost sunk in oblivion, does not circumstance encourage us to hope that the enslaving of black men may hereafter be forgotten: and should we not forbear to make our constitution a record thereof?

    —RUFUS KING, speaking at the New York State Constitutional
    Convention, October 20, 1821

THE AFRICANS ARE RESTORED! No more shall the accursed name of slave be attached to us—no more shall *negro* and *slave* be synonimous [*sic*]. . . . This day has the state of New-York regenerated herself—this day has she been cleansed of a most foul, poisonous and damnable stain. I stand amazed at the quiet, yet rapid progress the principles of liberty have made.

    —WILLIAM HAMILTON, Emancipation Address, New York, July 4, 1827

Emancipation reached its summit on July 4, 1827. In compliance with a law passed ten years before, Independence Day brought freedom to those men and women still legally enslaved. From Rochester to Albany, from Cooperstown to Manhattan, African Americans celebrated something more vital than a national anniversary in July 1827—they celebrated the end of racial bondage in the state of New York.[1]

Commemorative speeches expressed thanks for past exertions, as well as hope that a people fully free would in time demonstrate its complete equality. William Hamilton, in an address at the African Zion Church in New York City, dramatically apostrophized the goddess Liberty: "thou hast by the powerful charm of reason, deprived the monster of his strength—he dies, he sinks to rise no more." A speech delivered in Rochester's Public Square devoted itself to moral strictures, issuing the call for "INDUSTRY, PRUDENCE, and ECONOMY." Meanwhile, blacks in faraway Fredericksburg, Virginia, as well as nearby New Haven, Connecticut, gathered to celebrate New York slavery's death, confirming the national magnitude of the achievement.[2]

Between the original gradual abolition statute in 1799 and the implementation of its final abolition act in 1827 New Yorkers participated in not only a number of political, legal, and constitutional battles but also a contest over historical memory. Memory and policy became inextricably intertwined during debates over the relationship between emancipation, race, and citizenship in the new century. What role had slavery played in New York's colonial and revolutionary past? What had lawmakers intended to do in 1799? Was history itself best remembered or forgotten? Black and white New Yorkers, Federalists and Republicans, democrats and elitists, egalitarians and racists did not reach consensus about the meaning of the past. Indeed, the paradoxical settlement of slavery's legacy in the state during the first three decades of the nineteenth century reflected the disparate answers that various New Yorkers gave to these questions.[3]

As New Yorkers grappled over memory, they forged a path toward what one scholar has called "racial modernity" in the antebellum North.[4] For those whites anxious to separate democratization from racial equality, the foundations of the emerging white republic required the least amount of historicized reflection. Race replaced slavery as a marker of inferiority to be acknowledged and enforced. True to the spirit of Jefferson, the past, including the still unfolding history of abolition, did not entail the present or the future, though it might serve as a reminder that blacks were a "degraded" people.[5]

For white philanthropists, the link between the racial past and the racial future was considerably more ambiguous than it was for the advocates of white men's democracy. Some whites continued to believe that the cruelties of slavery and the promise of abolition created obligations between whites and blacks. But how far these obligations extended was uncertain and growing more so as the ability of elite white antislavery reformers to impose their authority over either black clients or white political rivals continued to atrophy.

In the midst of increasing racial antagonism, exclusion, and harassment, African American New Yorkers asserted in varying ways the continuing significance of a historical trajectory from slavery to freedom to equality. African Americans recognized the consequences of emancipation for black life and political culture as profound, the need to mark its milestones as compelling, and the struggle against slavery and racism as ongoing. Remembering history even as they continued to make it, New Yorkers in the early nineteenth century established the contours of the antebellum debates over race, slavery, and political power which helped to define New York's connection to the nation from the 1830s through the Civil War.[6]

I.

Coming eight-and-a-half years after New York's gradual abolition law, the U.S. withdrawal from the international slave trade on January 1, 1808, prompted memories of the movement for gradual abolition as well as hopes for further progress. The debate over domestic slavery in New York from the beginning had been embedded in a national and transatlantic discourse. In the postindependence period, opposition to the international slave trade encouraged the broader emancipationist hopes of slavery's opponents, while provoking proslavery barbs from southerners already digging in their heels against abolitionists. At the same time, literary renderings of the African experience of enslavement had contributed steadily to domestic antislavery rhetoric. Moreover, before successfully tackling the issue of domestic slavery, opponents of slavery in New York had acted to limit the import and export of slaves from the state. Speeches commemorating the termination of U.S. participation in the international slave trade drew on all these eighteenth-century discursive legacies.

At the time of the international slave trade's official demise in the United States, leaders of the emerging free black community in New York City were already busily building bridges between the past and the future. Disabling the transatlantic engine of slavery and serving the daily needs of the slave trade's sons and daughters in New York were regarded as related accomplishments. In the earliest years after the passage of the gradual abolition law, leading black spokesman assumed the interracial nature of these reform projects. Black community organizations forged identities in reference to a predominantly white discourse, while simultaneously asserting the particular identity of the black community through these same organizations.

African American churches offered one valuable forum for marking events of historic significance to black New Yorkers. The existence of such churches indicated the emergence of a community embracing a separate identity within the framework of religious and social acculturation. As in Philadelphia, New York's black religious leaders grew impatient with discrimination in white churches. They sought to establish institutions that were under black direction and were more open to black worship-style preferences.[7]

The very naming of "African" churches and other associations was a reminder of the slave trade and its geographical and cultural ties. Yet as historian Patrick Rael has argued, the term *African*, chosen by the free black

communities' self-selected, relatively acculturated stewards, did not necessarily signal the maintenance of substantive ties to African culture, which
had grown attenuated for some. Rather, community leaders sought to "claim
a legitimate national affiliation." The *African* moniker served as an assertion
to a wider public that blacks had an ethnic identity no different and no less
worthy than the connection of white citizens to their national origins. Especially prior to the rise of white efforts to colonize American free blacks in
Africa, the term *African* offered a distinction and forged a historical connection without overemphasizing fundamental difference.[8] It also highlighted
the transatlantic nature of the antislavery narrative for black New Yorkers.

Peter Williams's January 1, 1808, address to the New York City's African Methodist Episcopal Zion Church marking the end of U.S. participation
in the Atlantic slave trade, evoked two sets of historical memories. First,
Williams, whose father Peter Williams Sr. helped found New York's African
Methodist Episcopal Zion Church in 1796, discussed the depredations of the
African slave trade. Second, he sought to pay tribute to the efforts of white
activists and philanthropists who put an end to this evil. Williams spoke of
greed-driven European powers seducing Africans into the slave trade "by a
dazzling display of European finery" and ravaging the continent as a result.
This situation continued until the intervention of the American Revolution's
egalitarian principles inspired an appropriate response to the archetypal
"bleeding African," who "lift[ed] his fetter, [and] exclaimed, 'am I not a man
and a brother.'"[9]

Williams then offered a glowing description of the abolition societies,
which, "on the pure basis of philanthropy," lobbied, published, educated,
and "became the vigilant guardians of all our reinstated joys." As Williams
described the effort of abolitionists: "Books were disseminated, and discourses delivered, wherein every argument was employed . . . and numerous
instances related, calculated to awaken sentiments of compassion." This emphasis on the emotional strategy of abolition and its memory evoked the literary antislavery of the 1780s and 1790s. Moreover, by recalling the Quaker
origins of the antislavery movement and invoking the British antislavery slo-
gan, Williams offered a cosmopolitan rather than a narrowly national view of
the historic moment. He remembered the history of slavery and emancipation as a battle between good and evil, in which whites played the primary
role. Blacks, in turn, inherited the role of preserving this narrative and, by
adopting "a steady and upright deportment," advancing it. Tellingly, the published version of Williams's address to a black audience included a certification of his authorship by white figures of authority, among them Manumission Society stalwart John Murray Jr. Rather than criticize the cautiousness

and paternalism of white reformers, Williams praised the tangible results his white allies had helped to produce.[10]

The following year, Henry Sipkins, like Williams, gestured broadly toward the Atlantic world and Africa rather than casting his remarks in a narrowly American idiom. Sipkins noted that "the exiles of our race are emerging from the depths of forlorn slavery" and looked forward to a time "when the Africans shall be reinstated in their former joys—when the exulting shouts of Princes, embracing their long lost oppressed subjects, shall reverberate on our ears. . . ." Although much previous antislavery discourse also offered an international orientation, Williams and Sipkins did not merely walk in lock step with late-eighteenth-century discussions, which often linked economic growth with the growth of freedom. Both men recalled commerce as a force of oppression, a means of beguiling and exploiting rather than liberating black people. For these two speakers, it was "disinterested" disregard for tangible rewards that functioned as a force for humanitarian liberation among early white abolitionists and which, presumably, would guide their own efforts in this new era.[11] Thus, even in recalling the largely white discourse of eighteenth-century abolitionism, Sipkins and Williams reconfigured that discourse to emphasize their own values.

Joseph Sidney's 1809 commemoration of the slave trade's abolition embraced the American context of free black life and emphasized active black participation in the secular affairs of their country. Sidney delivered his address to fellow members of the Wilberforce Philanthropic Association, named for British antislavery's great parliamentary champion William Wilberforce. This society was one of a number of self-help and mutual-aid societies formed by free blacks in the early nineteenth century. The group's name was perhaps less a symbol of internationalism than of the intermeshing of past deeds and present accomplishments, white and black, in New York black life.[12]

In seeking to place the anniversary in perspective, Sidney told his audience that he would not dwell on the well-known and universally acknowledged evils of the African slave trade. Imagining that the ban presaged "the total abolition of slavery in America," Sidney drew his audience's attention to what he viewed as the happy history of gradual abolition. To the New England states went the initial credit for this profound reform, with imitators in New York and the middle states following suit. Sidney spent the bulk of his remarks addressing his fellow African Americans as citizens engaged in the ongoing struggles of partisan political life. As a prelude to his celebration of the Federalist party and denigration of the Jeffersonian Republicans, Sidney noted, "Freedom has broken down that wall of separation, which formerly distinguished our rights and duties, from those of the white inhabitants. Our rights and duties have, of course, assimilated to theirs." Thus, in urging his African American audience to vote, he was pushing them to embrace their political assimilation and to claim the Federalist party's heroes as their own. Sidney's partisan address in effect denied the Jeffersonians any credit they might claim for executing the very anti-slave-trade law that Sidney ostensibly was celebrating. Led by the slaveholding Jefferson, southern democracy was manifestly not the black man's democracy. The Federalist party of Washington, who freed his slaves in his will, was, in Sidney's view, the freedman's proper home. Before closing his comments with praise for God, Sidney urged his audience to focus its memories and its "gratitude" on the New York Manumission Society, "whose kind interference has greatly ameliorated our condition. . . . Long may they all be remembered."[13]

Sidney's speech was at once conservative and progressive. Defending gradualism and embracing patrons in the elitist Federalist Party, Sidney's vision might seem cautious or deferential. He sentimentalized the memory of slavery and abolition through his recollection of the Manumission Society's "labours of love," but overall his speech was aggressively political and implicitly optimistic about the future place of blacks in New York public life. Sidney boldly lashed out at the ascendant Republican Party and openly affirmed his Federalist affiliation, visualizing a political world inhabited by citizens, black and white, freely and legitimately forming allegiances in a competitive, partisan political public sphere. He offered his fellow leaders in the cause of black philanthropy the image of a black community still distinct but not isolated, functioning in a republic whose commerce would be reinvigorated by a return to Federalist leadership.[14]

Although his partisan hopes for a Federalist restoration went unrealized, Sidney's remarks reflected the emerging possibilities for black life and liberty during the early years of gradual abolition. He was unquestionably correct that the passage of the state's original gradual abolition law stimulated new conditions for African Americans to test the boundaries of their potential freedom, collectively and individually. Despite the graduated schedule of emancipation, the 1799 abolition law altered the dynamic between white masters and their black servants. As slavery's legal extinction in New York became likely, slaves sought concessions from their owners. To secure compensation, slaveholders accepted requests by bondspeople for sale to different masters. Manumissions increased in the new century, in part as slaveholders sought to encourage loyal service at least for a few additional years. New arrangements among masters and between slaves and masters were far from ideal. John Peter de Lancey of Mamaroneck several times purchased slaves on condition that he would free them after several years of loyal service. Such de facto slave rentals were hardly humanitarian: a woman named Betty faced an extra year of service for each child she bore during her final period of enslavement; and should a man named Jack Purdy, purchased for a terminal period of five years, have suffered disability "when he is on his own business or pleasure or in consequence thereof he shall make up all such Time he may be absent . . . and also serve so long Time as will pay for his board and Doctor's bill." Not surprisingly, even with increased leeway for negotiation as to whom and how they would serve, some slaves refused to delay their freedom, running away instead; masters, still valuing black labor, continued to offer significant rewards for their capture and return.[15]

While evidence of black slaves pushing white masters to grant them freedom in advance of the legal requirement is anecdotal, the rapid decline of the slave population in the early nineteenth century is clear. There were ten thousand fewer black New Yorkers held as slaves for life in 1820 than there had been in 1800. In New York City, between 1800 and 1810, the slave population decreased by more than one thousand, while the number of free blacks increased by more than four thousand. On Long Island and in the Mid-Hudson Valley, the ratio of free blacks to enslaved rapidly escalated between 1800 and 1810 and again in the succeeding decade. By 1810, three-quarters of the African Americans living in Suffolk and Queens Counties were counted as free. By 1820, over 80 percent of blacks in Suffolk, Queens, and Westchester Counties were nominally free, and over 95 percent in New York City. New York was not the same state in terms of race relations after the passage of the 1799 abolition law and liberal manumission rules. Slavery had suffered a blow far greater than the legal language of careful gradualism implied.[16]

Freedom, moreover, provided opportunities for economic initiative, particularly in urban settings, not readily available amid full-blown slavery. Free blacks in New York City who established households independent from whites pursued a number of artisanal endeavors. African Americans also engaged in street peddling, most notably as oystermen. Black managers controlled the chimney-sweeping business.[17] In the context of this growing free black population, Sidney's vision of civic and political engagement was not unfounded. In the early decades of the nineteenth century, black economic initiative helped provide the impetus for making claims on government. Both material strength and political access were critical building blocks of citizenship. Black chimney-sweep managers asserted the right to petition the Common Council in 1816, 1817, and 1818. They sought, with some initial success, revisions of the rules governing their business.[18]

New York City blacks found that local government cooperation was useful, even essential, to maintaining community institutions. The African Methodist Episcopal Zion Church requested and received from the city a watchman to prevent disruptions outside its Sunday service. Black citizens also thanked the city for providing officers to keep the peace as they celebrated the U.S. withdrawal from the international slave trade, offering council members tickets to attend the church oration marking the occasion. For its part, the church responded to the city's public-health demand that it cease interring the dead beneath the church itself by successfully requesting that the city provide a burial lot. Thus, blacks approached white authorities as citizens with legitimate claims for public support and assistance against those hostile to their interests.[19]

A free black, with the help of the judiciary process, might even circumvent the authority of whites claiming to provide protection. An 1817 lawsuit on Long Island brought into conflict a twenty-six-year-old former slave and the executors of his master's will. The deceased Ichabod Brush provided for the freedom of James Williams, a West Indian by birth, and granted him a substantial payment, distributed, "at the discretion of my Executors." Williams claimed that the defendants never honored his requests for the money, which he now wanted in order to return to his West Indian home. In reply, the executors argued that they had looked out for "the best interest of the complaintant [*sic*]," who they said was an alcoholic incapable of managing his own finances. Moreover, they asserted that if Williams went back to the West Indies he would be made a slave. The court ruled in favor of the black man, awarding him his two hundred dollars plus interest.[20] Freedom replaced slavery and interference with basic rights of personal autonomy in this case. Although the terms of the manumission were probably rare in any century, the suit itself and the court's decision were a product of the new, postabolition environment.

Sidney and others who saw the abolition of the slave trade and gradual abolition as harbingers of expanding opportunity nonetheless were overly hopeful. Some free blacks advocated publicly on their own behalf, and at least a few experienced the material benefits of freedom, yet many others discovered that they were negotiating from distinctly disadvantaged positions. Rural free blacks wishing to establish their independence without financial resources or social infrastructure faced particular difficulties.[21] The availability of the temporary labor of individual blacks living a marginal economic existence could prove to be a profitable arrangement that might enhance the authority of the white employer. For example, James Hawxhurst, an enterprising white farmer in Flushing, Long Island, hired black men for short- and long-term agricultural projects. These men sometimes purchased foodstuffs or rented quarters from Hawxhurst, adding to the farmer's profits. Hawxhurst's diary records the repeated departure and return of an African American man named Lebulon Frost; needing work and plagued by debt, Frost was dependent upon and tied to his white employer.[22]

While many urban blacks seized opportunities to make a better way in the world for themselves, in the long run, black occupational aspirations did not enjoy favor. Thousands of African Americans, like the boys actually sweeping New York City's chimneys, continued the difficult, low-status work of laborers and domestic servants. Blacks were often isolated from one another in white households. Moreover, an 1830 history of the African Free School decried that no matter how well it trained its graduates for various occupations, whites were unwilling to employ them.[23] Freedom was conditional and circumscribed for a significant portion of blacks listed in the census as free; under the terms of the gradual abolition law young African Americans continued to serve their mothers' masters as indentured servants unless other arrangements had been privately negotiated.

From his 1809 vantage point, Joseph Sidney's embrace of political citizenship emphasized a positive aspiration and a projection forward of favorable trends that did not sustain their momentum. Although his Wilberforce Society hoped to address the needs of the black community, Sidney's speech offered not a sociological analysis but rather a political declaration. His putative allies among white abolitionists, however, were not nearly as appreciative as he might have imagined for his collegial gratitude. When circumstances suited them, Federalist operatives, like the more consistently antiblack Republicans, had shown a willingness to bait the white electorate on the basis of race.[24]

Indeed, black support and support for blacks had long represented a double-edged sword for Federalists. Prominent Federalists worked against slavery from a combination of moral principle and a desire to be seen as high-minded. Yet, as far back as the Jay-Clinton governor's race of 1792, Federalist politicians had been vulnerable to criticism for their antislavery leanings. Despite the potential benefits of receiving votes from blacks, some conservatives viewed the participation of blacks in elections as further evidence of a political process that had grown altogether too democratic.[25] In 1803, "A Citizen" wrote to the Federalist-leaning *New-York Gazette and General Advertiser* defending New York City's charter against the Democratic charge that it too narrowly restricted access to the political process. The conservative writer warned that proposed reforms would mean "the whole host of Africans that now deluge our City (Already too impertinent to be borne), would be placed upon an equal with the citizens." The writer offered the caveat, "Far be it from me to imagine that the *Blacks* are an inferior race of beings—yet let them be kept at a proper distance, and themselves and us will experience the benefits of it."[26] This white New Yorker struggled against incoherence as he attempted to fend off Jeffersonian populism, express his disdain for African Americans, and deny the sort of absolute racism that Jeffersonian democrats were increasingly embracing. Such a conservative juggling act could not consistently serve the political aspirations for African American New Yorkers which Joseph Sidney expressed six years later.

Forthright indications of the sort of black autonomy demonstrated by Sidney and his fellow black citizens severely tested the limits of interracial cooperation. John Teasman, the African American teacher hired in 1799 as principal of the NYMS-sponsored African Free School, found himself increasingly at odds with his employers. Free blacks, including Teasman, chafed at the white trustees' emphasis on social monitoring and morally condescending instruction. Teasman and other well-positioned blacks, including some of his older students, began to form organizations to oversee the material needs of the black community unmet by white abolitionist patrons. Teasman also sought out Republican politicians as an alternative to black Federalism. In 1809, the NYMS replaced him with a white teacher, whom they retained at twice Teasman's salary. The fine line that Teasman had walked between autonomy and service had apparently worn down his patience and that of his employers.[27]

Nonetheless, the praise lavished on white abolitionists in Sipkins, Williams, and Sidney's speeches suggests that it is possible to exaggerate the degree of alienation between blacks and antislavery whites. The emergence of free black institutions was a necessary and inevitable step, regardless of white condescension and skittishness about black politics.[28] The management of relationships between white and black leaders in the midst of gradual emancipation presented a new set of challenges to all involved.

Thus, despite and because of its identification of black and white interests, a Sidney-style exercise in historical commemoration, replete with speeches and parades through the public streets, provoked deep apprehension among white antislavery men. In November 1809, the NYMS dispatched six of its members to inform African Americans "that their method of celebrating the abolition of the Slave Trade was improper, in as much as it tended to injure themselves and cause reflection to made on the Society" and "that both their procession, and Politicks in their orations should be discontinued for the future." Federalist reformers in the NYMS may not have wished their party to be too closely associated with the black portion of its constituency, or perhaps the society preferred to represent its cause in a nonpartisan fashion. African Americans determined not to subordinate their desire to integrate political discourse and the public streets. In January 1810, the Manumission Society's minutes ruefully summarized the African American response "that they had incurred considerable expense in providing their Standards and other things, and that they could not think of relinquishing their proposed method of Celebrating the day." Public displays of communal joy over the progress of abolitionism was not merely a token of black cultural style or of the plebeian nature of the community. To act autonomously in public was, in some sense, the whole point, affirmatively linking past progress with present needs and future aspirations.[29]

II.

As the emerging free black community's white friends wavered, their enemies went on the attack. While partisan advantage was one motivation for the unfolding opposition to postemancipation black citizenship, over time a broader purpose emerged—to define democratic citizenship in explicitly racist terms. Thus, the momentum of emancipation rapidly moved beyond the point of reversal and even accelerated, but hostility toward an integrated postslavery democracy mounted as well.

A symbol of the troubled postemancipation politics of race and a harbinger of the difficulties that lay ahead was the republication in 1810 of Daniel Horsmanden's account of the 1741 "Great Negro Plot." Whether or not the reissue of the only documentary record of the alleged conspiracy of the city's slaves and their unscrupulous white leaders to burn the city to the ground was meant as a gesture of race-baiting politics, the publisher seized an opportune moment to bring out the first American edition of the trial transcript since its original publication in 1744. This record of thievery, treachery, and interracial sex—in sum, an account of the dangers of laxness in patrolling the boundaries of race and slavery—coincided with the emergence for the first time since the Dutch period of a significant free black community in New York City.[30] In addition, as at the time of the original "conspiracy," in 1810 the threat of war loomed, this time with the British, rather than the Spanish, as potential adversaries.

Much to the chagrin of many whites, this free black community was committed to exercising its rights of citizenship and to taking its place in the public sphere. As historians Shane White and Graham White have described in vivid detail, black "expressive culture" flourished in the streets of New York during the era of gradual emancipation. Black music, dance, and dress combined European materials with African American cultural sensibilities in widely noticed ways that attracted some whites and repelled others. While some whites found dance contests held by blacks from Long Island and New Jersey visiting Manhattan's markets an exciting diversion, flashy clothes and assertiveness annoyed those who were perhaps used to greater deference. The creative impulse of early-nineteenth-century black New Yorkers contributed to an "edg[iness]" in relations between whites and blacks. Black people, free and enslaved, were eager to demonstrate a sense of autonomy in the street and even in the white homes where many blacks still worked. One white response was to police black behavior through the legal system: African Americans found themselves prosecuted at a rate far greater than their proportion in the population. In sum, the urban milieu of emancipation-era New York City fostered an environment full of new opportunities for whites and blacks to associate and to clash.[31]

The 1810 edition of Horsmanden's *The New York Conspiracy* was a reminder that the early nineteenth century was not the first time in New York's history that blacks had tested the limits of racial decorum or that some people of European descent had declined to act from a sense of racial solidarity. Accordingly, the preface subtly affirmed the value of white solidarity, offering an open apology not so much for the overzealous prosecution of blacks but rather for the persecution of alleged Catholics as mid-eighteenth century New York authorities crushed the alleged conspiracy. The publishers of the second edition apologized for the "rancorous hatred" of Catholics, which fueled fears that a few white Catholics would deliver the city to the Spanish through the manipulation of local slaves. The brief preface quoted at length from provincial New York's antipapist statute, a law which, according to the preface, was prompted in part by the inroads Catholic missionaries had made among the Indians who menaced the colony from the north. The publishers urged readers not to allow the anti-Catholic "bigotry and cruelty of our predecessors" to preclude "filial affection" for New York's forefathers. Ancestral prejudice against blacks, however, brought no such appeal for understanding, presumably because latter-day New York readers held many of the same prejudices.

The emphasis on white solidarity is all the more apparent when the 1810 preface is read in conjunction with Horsmanden's original preface, which appeared immediately afterward in the newer edition. Horsmanden focused on race with no mention of religion. Horsmanden warned mid-eighteenth-century New Yorkers against a negro slave menace, not a Catholic one, leveling charges that the publishers of the 1810 edition made little effort to discount. Horsmanden offered his own hostility toward black witnesses and the "caballing" predisposition of the slave population. Expounding upon the problems he faced in compiling the journal, Horsmanden stated, "The difficulty of bringing and holding them to the truth . . . is not to be surmounted, but by the closest attention; many of them have a great deal of craft." He reported that "their unintelligible jargon" helped black suspects "to conceal their meaning; so that an examiner must expect to encounter much perplexity, grope through a maze of obscurity, be obliged to lay hold of broken hints, lay them carefully together, and thoroughly weigh and compare them with each other, before he can be able to see the light, or fix those creatures to any certain determinate meaning."

For Horsmanden, the alleged opacity of black speech was not a source of humor or derision, as was so often the case in post–Revolutionary War New York newspapers; rather, the judge viewed black speech as an obstacle to uncovering the conspiracy and recording it for posterity. Interestingly, Horsmanden did not try to recreate his perceptions of black speech patterns in the text but paraphrased black witnesses' testimony and the reports of the inculpatory statements of the accused, so that their alleged guilt was straightforward and clear. The moments in the massive transcript where black speakers most commonly seemed to talk directly were when they were cursing, as when, ironically, a Spanish-speaking slave was heard to say "*d—n that son of a b—h.* . . ." Indeed, translation, more than transcription, served Horsmanden's purpose of exposing all blacks, not just Spanish ones, as an alien menace. The lesson of the "plot" and its prosecution was manifest to Horsmanden: "for everyone that has negroes, to keep a very watchful eye over them and not to indulge them with too great liberty." Good treatment and relative freedom allegedly produced "the greatest villains" in this conspiracy. Thirty of these alleged villains paid dearly; they were burned at the stake or hung. Over seventy others were sold into slavery in the West Indies and Madeira. Although the second edition preface noted that white New Yorkers of Horsmanden's day "carried their apprehensions and resentments beyond all bounds," nineteenth-century white readers might still feel that they recognized in such a transcript a familiar black menace to their authority and perhaps even sympathized with Horsmanden's anxieties about the difficulty of comprehending black intentions through black speech.[32]

Those who would forge the political prerogatives of whiteness in the early 1800s did not anticipate an insurrection nor did they have to launch a vindictive rampage of torture against African Americans in order to heed Horsmanden's warnings as it echoed across the decades. Careful monitoring of black political activity and transportation of undesired slaves served as twin engines of white hegemony during the first two decades of the nineteenth century, as they had in Horsmanden's day. As discussed in section IV, grotesque caricatures of black speech also served to illustrate the need to further elaborate a racial divide.

The campaign to undermine black citizenship during the era of gradual abolition began in earnest in 1811. Driven by opportunism, political self-interest, and racially tinged partisan vindictiveness, Republican lawmakers launched an assault on black voting. Taking back the New York legislature from the Federalists after a brief interval as the minority party, Republican legislators passed an election reform law substantially aimed at harassing potential black voters. The 1811 "Act to prevent frauds and perjuries at elections, and to prevent slaves from voting" required "any black or mulatto" voter to offer written proof of his freedom. African Americans were to obtain their official certification for a fee. Moreover, the validity of the freedom "certificate" could be challenged at the polls, a successful challenge leading not only to disqualification but also prosecution for perjury. The first two clauses of the law established a more general procedure by which voters who were accused of not meeting the property, age, and residency requirements could take an oath affirming their legitimacy. Recruiting to the polls voters with insufficient property was a regular feature of the political landscape of this era, against which the oath and challenge provided weak protection. Nonetheless, the law allowed opponents of black voting to use racial restrictions as a symbol of their resolve against the wider problem of voter fraud.[33]

Opponents of the 1811 law denounced the prejudicial nature of these seemingly partisan provisions. Indeed, the Council of Revision, which included Governor Daniel Tompkins, Chief Justice James Kent, and three other state supreme court justices, initially vetoed the proposed law. The council objected to the manner in which the law capriciously singled out one portion of the population and, reversing legal norms, presumed free blacks to be guilty of fraud unless they could produce an unusual amount of evidence to the contrary. The lead item in the Federalist *New-York Evening Post* offered a more aggressive indictment of the law. The correspondent accused legislators of setting up a "gantlet" of regulations for the prospective black voter before "he is graciously put upon an equality with a white man." The law, the writer suggested, made a mockery of the New York constitution and

Republican pretensions of egalitarian populism. The contributor implicated the law as a nakedly partisan measure: "The truth is, that great majority of the coloured men of this city, probably nine out of ten, have always voted for the federal ticket, and those who dared not directly disfranchise them, have had recourse to the abominable artifice of throwing in their way, such numerous difficulties to be overcome, and such expences to be incurred, as amounts nearly, very nearly, to an insurmountable obstacle."[34] While it would be a gross overstatement to equate this ill-intentioned partisan harassment with the "judicial murder[s]" in 1741, New York lawmakers in 1811 did extend Horsmanden's principle of intense racial vigilance to the political sphere of the new republic.[35]

White New Yorkers more directly imitated their colonial forebears in the forced removal of blacks from the state during the early nineteenth century. In the eighteenth century, transportation out of the province was a legally sanctioned punishment. But after the American Revolution, critics of slavery had successfully fought the practice, making it illegal to sell New York slaves elsewhere, a restriction that remained on the books after the commencement of gradual emancipation. Gradual abolition, however, created strong incentives for New York slave owners to sell the indentured offspring of slaves out of state to cash in on an asset that, with emancipation looming, was rapidly depreciating. Meanwhile, kidnappers continued to seize New York blacks, as well as blacks in New England states, for sale southward, regardless of the law or the legal status of their victims.[36]

The actual number of black New Yorkers shipped out of the state to faraway slavery remains a matter of statistical projection rather than careful documentary reconstruction. Leading economic historians who have looked at the problem have concluded that exportation probably represented a significant factor in the decline of New York state's black population. The black population of New York, slave and free, declined by over 2 percent during the second decade of the nineteenth century, despite having grown during the previous decade. While some of the population decline could be accounted for by difficulties in counting free blacks and the material hardships of free black life during this transitional period, it appears likely that surreptitious sales out of state placed a heavy burden on the emerging black community.[37] Such statistical projections also suggest that some historians, in crediting African American resistance for the swiftness of slavery's post-1799 fall in New York, have painted an overly inspiring portrait of black agency.[38]

Whatever the extent of the illegal transportation of blacks out of New York, combating this problem provided an arena of continued cooperation between blacks and sympathetic whites. White reformers, slaves, and free blacks all sought the common end of extending freedom to as many individuals as legally plausible; the trading of blacks into and out of the state was a major obstacle to that goal. The threats facing African Americans in New York City in the wake of gradual abolition required a vigorous response. Indeed, enforcing existing abolition law in order to combat particular injustices aimed at particular black clients was a mainstay of "first wave" northern abolitionism. If, as Robert Fogel and Stanley Engerman charged a generation ago, the process of gradual abolition was really "philanthropy at bargain prices," it remains vital to understand that leading white abolitionists in New York and Pennsylvania actively fought the most negative aspects of the bargain. Moreover, the kidnapping of black New Yorkers encouraged the Manumission Society to work with political allies to accelerate the abolition process itself.[39]

Intervention required information, whether blacks fought illegal enslavement on their own or with the assistance of the Manumission Society. Fortuitous leads revealed a sordid business: in 1809 "a black man named Plato" reported to George Newbold that two white New Jersey artisans had been ferrying black women from a tavern to a ship in the waters between New York and New Jersey; Newbold presumed that the kidnappers conspired "with Some Southern Captain to carry them off. . . ."[40]

Upon receiving word of slaves being held for imminent export, local blacks or NYMS members might rescue victims. On October 31, 1800, the NYMS standing committee indicated that three black women "who were about to be shipped were forcibly taken by several black Men from on board the vessel and are now at Liberty." Combinations of good fortune and black action in two other cases illustrated the difficulties faced in preventing exportation. In September 1807, a black woman and her child narrowly avoided slavery in Havana because the mother raised enough noise from the ship that a bystander embarked and rescued them. A black man forced upon a New Orleans–bound ship only managed to report his case to the NYMS and win manumission because a mutiny by the ship's crew brought the vessel to Staten Island.[41] The standing committee discovered that the practice of illegal transportation combined systematic smuggling and personal exploitation. In April 1800, the standing committee noted that while pursuing one suspected shipment of New York blacks to the West Indies via southern U.S. ports, investigators "stumbled upon another" ship whose hold contained a group of illegally held blacks. The minutes from the same meeting recorded the story of a free mulatto boy who was lured on board a ship to fetch a parrot.[42]

Cruelty cases, especially those involving children, also contributed significantly to the Manumission Society's caseload. Sadistic abuse of a slave woman named Betty and her young child Sarah so shocked public sensibilities that a New York City printer published in pamphlet form the 1809 trial transcript, explicitly as an "example . . . to deter others." The abusive master Amos Broad brokered an agreement with the NYMS to free his slaves, and the court ordered $1,000 in fines and 120 days in jail.[43]

Unfortunately, reliance on intelligence and luck to combat the export of slaves left blacks and their allies at the mercy of a system predicated on a lack of moral scruples and an undependable public moral climate. News that the free black sailor John Brown had been sold into slavery in Georgia by one of his shipmates reached the NYMS, but the threads of many similar stories surely eluded their grasp. The standing committee acknowledged the dimensions of the challenge in an August 1815 report: "It is true that the acts of kidnapping and of other outrageous oppression have become more rare . . . popular opinion may be sufficient to prevent their becoming more frequent; but it is equally true, that the spirit of oppression is prevalent . . . and the sufferers of consequence numerous in proportion."[44]

Frustration with violations of the gradual abolition statute caused advocates to seek further reforms in New York's slavery and abolition laws. The Manumission Society's legislative committee lobbied to eliminate the possibility of transportation out of the state for slave convicts, a colonial-era practice that remained legal despite the initiation of gradual emancipation. Undeterred by the state legislature's initial inaction, the NYMS decided to lobby judges not to employ the "discretionary power of Transportation" against slaves. By late 1811, even as the state was stripping free blacks of political rights, the society determined to seek the "general abolition of Slavery throughout this State" as the ultimate solution to the ongoing weaknesses of gradual abolition.[45]

Governor Daniel D. Tompkins, perhaps prompted by the petition from his fellow NYMS members, placed slavery back on the state government's agenda in 1812. Tompkins challenged the legislature to enact "the gradual and ultimate extermination from amongst us" of racial bondage. As with eighteenth-century efforts to initiate gradual abolition, nineteenth-century legislative maneuvering over reformed and accelerated abolition dragged on through several sessions. Meanwhile, the ongoing war with Britain allowed Tompkins to combine expediency with principle in 1814, as he lobbied U.S. Secretary of State James Monroe to accept New York's offer of "coloured Regiments" raised by the state. Slaves entering with approval of their masters would receive their freedom at the termination of their service. This proposal repeated the Revolutionary-era pattern that linked black liberty to the hazards of military enlistment.[46]

Governor Tompkins's 1817 parting plea for terminating slavery was granted. Shortly before assuming his role as vice president of the United States, Tompkins requested that "slavery be expunged from our statue book" by granting freedom to all slaves not covered by the 1799 gradual abolition law. Tompkins invoked George Washington as well as the increasingly sacred date of the nation's birth to advance abolition as a token of progress. The governor proposed that slaves born before July 4, 1799, should gain their freedom no later than July 4, 1827. In making his pleas, Tompkins soft-pedaled the practical impact of the measure while emphasizing its symbolic importance. He suggested slaveholders mostly stood to lose the service of slaves past their working prime, while New York responded to "the dictates of humanity, the reputation of the state, and a just sense of gratitude to the Almighty." By putting a definite end to racial bondage, New York took the lead among northern states abolishing slavery by statute. Although under the terms of the law the children of slaves would continue to bear the brunt of forced indenture to their parents' masters, the institution of domestic chattel slavery soon would be confined to New York's past. Whether the memory of New York slavery's brutalities would become a fading memory too depended upon who would take custody of that memory and for what purposes.[47]

III.

As more and more black New Yorkers made the transition from slavery to freedom, momentum grew for decoupling black freedom and black citizenship. Prior to the passage of gradual abolition, whites projected their hopes and fears about the possible consequences of emancipation onto such ideas as a black electorate, black participation in political debate, and black social responsibility. In the 1780s, unresolved concerns over African American political participation helped to derail gradual abolition, while doubts about the economic wherewithal of potential freed people slowed progress in the 1790s and shaped the eventual gradual abolition settlement. In the new century, as free black voters, speakers, and petitioners became a reality, white politicians continued to evaluate the implications of abolition for a republican society undergoing rapid democratization. Facing a growing free black public presence, whites became increasingly disinclined to recognize African Americans as full citizens. Insinuations of racial difference from the eighteenth century became gradually transformed into a legally enforced racial orthodoxy.[48]

The debate over the future of black citizenship was in large part an argument over what claims memory and the history of slavery and abolition legitimately made on lawmakers. Proponents of an expanded, exclusively white electorate openly denied that the history of slavery and abolition in New York should have any bearing on the future definition of political rights in their state. White dissenters from the emerging racial orthodoxy, while objecting to disfranchisement, betrayed an ambivalence about history and memory, wishing to preserve some aspects of the liberating narrative of abolition but unsure how to account for the memory of slavery itself.

The state's 1821 constitutional convention was a conundrum for the past and future of New York and even American politics. Led by future U.S. president Martin Van Buren, Bucktail Republicans dominated the convention with an eye toward weakening rival Republican governor DeWitt Clinton and his allies among the remnants of the rapidly declining Federalist Party. The freehold requirement for voting, as well as unusual features of the 1777 constitution, such as the Council of Appointment and the Council of Revision, were among the top priorities for reform.[49] Issues of race, slavery, and black citizenship inexorably emerged as an essential part of the political settlement that the convention's Bucktail Republican majority worked out for their state. New York's ambitious political leaders ensured that as the state moved toward the vanguard of American democratic politics, race would be constructed as a presumptively disabling condition.

Expanding the size and scope of the electorate was a central priority of the convention. The convention's suffrage committee proposed to the delegates assembled in Albany that the property-holding restrictions on the franchise be eliminated. The committee's proposal extended voting rights "almost as far as the male population of the state." Under the committee's initial plan, twenty-one-year-old men with six months residence in New York should have the right to vote, as long as they had either paid taxes, worked on the public roads, or served in the militia. The one glaring exception, as committee member Dr. John Z. Ross acknowledged, was that blacks would be completely excluded from the franchise. The Bucktail Republican and physician from Genesee County in the far western part of the state frankly cited his belief in black mental incapacity and the prerogative of sovereign states to determine in accordance with the "public good" who should vote. Ross imagined that extending equal suffrage to blacks "would serve to invite that kind of population to this state," followed by the inevitable demand for actual black legislators. One of Ross's even less inhibited allies in the ensuing debate, Peter R. Livingston of Dutchess County, baldly stated of black voters, "when they approach the ballot boxes, they are too ignorant to know whether their vote is given to elevate another to office, or to hang themselves on the gallows."[50]

Despite clear expressions of contempt for free blacks, the case for disfranchisement did not rest on the development of the explicit definition of race itself. More than once, speakers drew invidious comparisons between blacks and Indians, whom no one proposed enfranchising.[51] But in advocating a constitutional color line, Saratoga delegate Samuel Young regarded the establishment of technical "criterion" for "determin[ing] questions of fact in relation to the various shades of colour" as an issue of little practical significance. In one speech, Young assured his fellow delegates, "This distinction of colour is well understood" and a few moments later he remarked, "Although there may be some difficulty in individual cases, yet that circumstance furnishes no argument against the establishment of the principle."[52]

Young and his fellow proponents of black disfranchisement were perfectly comfortable with race as a social construction, as long as the white majority or their representatives did the construction. The pitiable circumstances of free blacks in New York was sufficient to establish color as a suitable principle for determining full citizenship. Young even conceded the hypothetical possibility that at some future time blacks might "arrive at such a degree of intelligence and virtue" as to merit enfranchisement. But the convention's priority, according to Young, should be "to make a constitution adapted to *our* habits, manners, and state of society. Metaphysical refinements and abstract speculation are of little use. . . ."[53]

Those delegates who argued for disfranchisement declined to draw on the precedent for hounding potential black voters established by the New York legislature ten years earlier. Under the law first instituted in 1811, black men had to prove that they were legally emancipated before exercising the right of a free person to vote. The proposed constitutional color line actually worked according to the opposite principle from the existing antiblack voting law: freedom implied no political rights whatsoever for New Yorkers defined as black.

By contrast, for convention delegates seeking to stave off total black disfranchisement, history was the principle rhetorical defense. These delegates argued that a racial standard for voting would fly in the face of the state's constitutional and abolitionist history, as well as the core principles of liberty and equality set forth during the American Revolution. Their appeals to history were specific, direct, and even soul-searching.

Peter A. Jay dismissed as having been already discredited pseudo-scientific theories of racial inferiority. The eldest son of John Jay, former Manumission Society president, and principle author of the previous New York constitution, also suggested that the alleged gap between black and white abilities stemmed from habits learned in slavery. Conceding to his opponents that black New Yorkers currently lagged behind whites "in knowledge and in industry," Jay asked, "But will you punish the children for your own crimes; for the injuries which you have inflicted on the parents?" He also noted the rapid progress achieved by free blacks in the realms of education and religious organization. Jay set his critique of racism in the context not only of natural rights but also the recently concluded controversy over the admission of Missouri into the union as a slave state. Less than a year before the convention's present debate, New York chose the "high ground against slavery." Noted Jay, "There are gentlemen on this floor, who, to their immortal honour, have defended the cause of this oppressed people in congress, and I trust they will not now desert them."[54]

All the delegates understood that Jay referred to the stand New Yorkers had taken when Missouri sought admittance to the union as a slave state. The New York assembly passed, 117 to 4, a resolution in November 1820 urging the state's congressional delegation to oppose the Missouri constitution, which denied the right of free blacks to move there. One congressman from New York criticized Missouri by citing his own state's practice of black voting. Ten months later, Jay pointed out that under the proposed scheme for disenfranchisement a free black from Pennsylvania would be stripped of his right to vote upon arriving in New York. This would compromise the same principle of geographically portable citizenship that Missouri had attempted to violate.[55]

Other speakers resisted defining potential voters as white by recalling the Revolutionary era. Robert Clarke, a Bucktail from Delaware County, drew together the equality enshrined in the Declaration of Independence, the procedures annunciated by the U.S. Constitution, and the established practices of the state. Clarke reminded his listeners that the Declaration sanctioned the principle "all men are created equal." According to Clarke, "ever since the formation of your government" blacks had "constituted a portion of the people." Inserting the word *white* would "deprive a large and respectable number of the people of this state of privileges and rights which they have enjoyed in common with us." Indeed, New Yorkers, in accordance with the U.S. Constitution, had counted "Free people of colour" toward the apportionment of federal representation. No doubt Clarke exaggerated the "sense of justice" exhibited by "our venerable fathers," the framers, in 1787. Nonetheless, he offered the unseemly legacy of racial bondage as a reason why he opposed denying blacks "their most invaluable rights." Clarke acknowledged his "lament," shared with the budding colonization movement increasingly popular among early-nineteenth-century reformers, regarding the black presence in American society. Yet he headed off his own wish for an exclusive white society by stating that "restoring . . . natural rights" was necessary albeit "very partial atonement" for what African Americans had endured.[56]

Albany Federalist Abraham Van Vechten invoked the history of black voting. He wondered why, at a convention called to expand the franchise, New York stripped blacks of the vote after they had held the right of suffrage for almost fifty years, virtually since the nation's founding. Van Vechten recalled the history of slavery and its abolition. Whites had caused the "degradation" repeatedly attributed to blacks. Moreover, the Albany delegate argued that the principles upon which New York had designed gradual emancipation assumed black citizenship and enfranchisement.[57]

Such appeals to historically minded consciences were convincing to many delegates. The convention narrowly defeated the initial attempt to explicitly bar all blacks from suffrage. Joining a solid core of fifteen Federalists to defeat the proposal were approximately thirty-five Bucktail Republicans. Yet only a four-vote majority prevented the insertion of the word *white* to describe the state's eligible voters. Some delegates who felt uncomfortable with an explicit denial of interracial citizenship soon found another formula based on artful compromise and freshly synthesized principles.[58]

The majority view that doomed African American suffrage by slightly less direct means emerged from principles connected not to the past but rather to the perceived demands—political and ideological—of the present. No sooner had the strict prohibition of black voters failed then Erastus Root of Delaware County proposed that only those eligible for service in the militia, as defined by federal law, be eligible for the franchise. Such linkage would exclude all blacks from the polls.[59]

President of the convention Daniel Tompkins inflected his advocacy for the rights of former soldiers with racial denigration, suggesting that sympathy was a finite resource that should be spent in racially appropriate fashion. The sitting U.S. vice president and former governor of New York noted that Thomas Jefferson had substituted the word "*happiness*" for "property" in the Declaration of Independence. According to Tompkins, no one sacrificed their happiness for that of the nation more than soldiers, and for that they deserved a guaranteed franchise.[60] The claims of African Americans, Tompkins suggested, amounted to far less: "Gentlemen," he proclaimed, "were very sensitive the other day on the question of excluding the blacks—a class confessedly degraded, ignorant and vicious; and now little sympathy is felt for the white man—the patriot soldier, who shed his blood in the defence of your soil, and whose bones whitened the shore of a foreign enemy."[61] The soldiers' inner whiteness, in Tompkin's emotional economy of citizenship, made them far more meritorious recipients not only of sympathy but, more to the point, of voting rights.[62]

Tompkins invidious distinction was based on a shockingly selective historical memory. Tompkins himself, as governor of New York during the War of 1812, lobbied U.S. secretary of state James Monroe to accept "coloured Regiments" raised by the state. In passing the enabling legislation, New York's legislature had offered freedom to slaves serving in the war with the approval of their masters. After the war, then-governor Tompkins had urged the legislature to enact the statute that accelerated gradual abolition. In his 1821 remark, Tompkins shed previous actions and prior sympathies in a prejudicial cause.[63]

The disfranchisers effectively linked their dismissals of the slavery-and-abolition heritage with the principle that "certain limits" on the electorate legitimized its broad expansion.[64] Martin Van Buren and Jacob Sutherland mapped out political and philosophical grounds for this approach. While Van Buren scoffed at conservative fears about what would happen to political life if the convention failed to preserve existing property-holding restrictions, he warned his fellow delegates not to stumble carelessly into advocacy of "universal suffrage." Sutherland provided intellectual architecture for Van Buren's view, drawing on an abstract version of history divorced from specific examples, let alone examples connected to the actual history of slavery and abolition in New York. According to this delegate from Schoharie County, just west of Albany, "all history teaches, that there is and must be, in every great community, a class of citizens, who, destitute alike of property, of character, and of intelligence, neither contribute to the support of its institutions, nor can be safely trusted with the choice of its rulers. . . ." Once the "class of voters who cannot act intelligently and independently" had been identified, the franchise could be tailored to eliminate them.[65]

The convention zeroed in on black New Yorkers as that "class" whose explicit exclusion would provide legitimacy for expanded suffrage. It swept away the broad property requirements of the 1777 constitution, while affixing exclusionary restrictions on potential black voters. In the constitution ultimately adopted by the convention, twenty-one-year-old white men who lived in the state for a year could vote if they paid any tax or served in the militia. Black males had a state-residency requirement of three years. Only whites too poor to pay taxes but who worked on the public highways had to have a similar three-year residency. Unlike poor whites, potential black voters had to own and pay taxes on property, free and clear of debts, worth at least $250. Thus, the convention applied to black men alone the now repudiated formula of an electorate limited to male property holders.[66]

Van Buren's explanation of the racial double standard for voter eligibility neatly captured the practical racism that ultimately guided the convention. The future U.S. president noted that the convention had averted "total and unqualified exclusion," had released most blacks from paying taxes, and "held out inducements to industry" by allowing black men who accumulated sufficient property to vote. Thus, only those who "exercise[d] the right of suffrage in its purity" would vote.[67]

To Van Buren, and to more than two-thirds of his colleagues, this mix of practical compromise and seemingly principled moderation was sufficient to overcome historical scruples and historical precedent. Arguments that downplayed history's significance and stressed present-day concerns about race and the rights of the majority built a convention constituency for racial exclusion. Opponents of disfranchisement had sought a usable past, a past in which their opponents had little interest.

The convention's conservatives and Federalists were willing to act as the meeting's memory and conscience when it came to racial disfranchisement, but concerning the issue of slavery itself they were much more ambivalent about the role of historical memory in constitution making. Convention delegate James Tallmadge Jr. of Dutchess County twice attempted to convince his colleagues that the new constitution should accelerate certain aspects of the law officially ending slavery in the state on July 4, 1827. As a U.S. congressman, Tallmadge had been a pivotal figure in provoking the Missouri crisis when he attempted to insert a gradual abolition plan into Missouri's proposed constitution. Not surprisingly, his avidly prodisfranchisement colleague Peter R. Livingston chided Tallmadge for stirring up in New York the sort of trouble that had so recently roiled the nation.[68]

The delegates who had opposed disfranchisement and who championed Tallmadge's cause on the Missouri question were equally unenthusiastic about guaranteeing abolition, let alone accelerating the implementation of gradual emancipation, through the new constitution. Peter A. Jay stated, "The cause of humanity would gain nothing by instant emancipation." Rufus

King, who as U.S. senator from New York had fought hard against Missouri's admission as a slave state, spoke at the convention against a compromise proposal that the new constitution simply endorse the abolition law passed in 1817. It was odd and ironic for a venerable Federalist like King to invest his hopes not in historical memory but in historical forgetting. The veteran politician hoped that, absent any mention of slavery in the constitution, "it may hereafter be forgotten that slavery once existed in the state." He realized that some might find such a suggestion far-fetched; yet, he told his fellow delegates "that we may be as fortunate as our ancestors" in England, who now proclaimed that her very "air" made a man free, even though in that nation's benighted past Englishmen sold one another into bondage. Asked King, "Does not the circumstance encourage us to hope that the enslaving of black men may hereafter be forgotten: and should we not forbear to make our constitution a record thereof?"

King, in a sense, offered a reprise of the performance of the U.S. constitutional convention in which he had participated more than thirty years before. In Philadelphia, delegates resolved not to mention slavery by name, even as they embedded the institution in the document they produced. As the Missouri crisis demonstrated, the earlier approach to constitution writing had not succeeded in weakening slavery itself. But in New York, time seemed more clearly on the abolitionist side, slavery's end having been legislated already.

King's hopes aside, the urge to separate New York from its slave past was doomed to fail. As another delegate remarked the day before King spoke, it was too late. The provisions designed to deny black men the right to vote in New York had indelibly imprinted the legacy of slavery on the new constitution.[69]

What the convention of 1821 as a whole did renounce successfully was the collective responsibility for redressing the ongoing evils of slavery and mitigating its legacy with a commitment to interracial democracy. Disenfranchisement proponents felt even more strongly than King that minimizing the memory of slavery, even the memory of the just-concluded Missouri debate, served their political ends. While history was not impotent as a weapon against such arguments, it was also no match for the onrushing tide of white men's democracy.

IV.

In 1827 black activists and religious leaders commemorated abolition in New York, not simply as an anniversary but also as an ongoing struggle against the consequences of this profound yet partial achievement. For African

Americans, celebrating the official end of legal slavery in New York that July virtually required surveying in some fashion the history of slavery and the struggle for abolition in the state and the nation. The triumph, black leaders suggested, was predicated on a full appreciation of the evils of the slavery system and the allies blacks had acquired along the way in their quest to break the chains of permanent, inheritable bondage. To a significant degree northern black spokesmen thus sought to integrate the history of their liberation into a much broader story of American freedom and even global enlightenment.[70]

William Hamilton, who as a young man in the late 1790s had written a letter to New York governor John Jay calling for the state to take action against slavery, spoke with a lifetime of experience in the cause of black liberation when he addressed the African Zion Church on July 4, 1827. Against the backdrop of "the principles of liberty, such as are broadly and indelibly laid down by the glorious sons of '76," Hamilton proclaimed that "This day . . . the state of NEW-YORK regenerated herself. . . . I stand amazed at the quiet, yet rapid progress that the principles of liberty have made." He then reviewed the history of slavery in New York, touching upon such signal moments as the "Negro plot" of 1741, which he labeled as a witch-hunt, and speaking at more length on the fifty-year struggle for full emancipation. Hamilton proudly recited the names of the Manumission Society's founders and stalwarts, who from 1785 to the early decades of the nineteenth century advanced the banner of abolitionism; he included praise for Daniel Tompkins for his role in the passage of the last emancipation law in 1817, not mentioning the former governor's support of disfranchisement in 1821.

Upon this historicized foundation, Hamilton built the second half of his address, making demands on blacks and whites alike. Hamilton attacked racism, including a thinly veiled critique of Thomas Jefferson's inconsistent application of the concept of human equality. He also called on blacks to embrace education and self-discipline. Toward the end of his speech, Hamilton asked rhetorically, "Why look up to others, when we may obtain the highest standing ourselves?" While black people would have to cultivate their own inner resources to satisfy Hamilton's "ambition" for his community, achieving status, like the struggle for emancipation, was to operate across the color line based on the presumption of racial equality.[71]

Speaking in Albany the following day, Nathaniel Paul, a black Baptist minister, also claimed the profound historical significance of abolition in New York. Early in his July 5, 1827, address, he informed his listeners, "We will tell the good story to our children and our children's children, down to the latest posterity, that on the *fourth day of July,* in the year of our Lord 1827, slavery was abolished in the state of New-York." Paul's historical perspective was more consistently intermeshed with the workings of sacred time than Hamilton's while his style more openly evoked the poetic sentimentality of literary antislavery. Paul's speech projected a historical trajectory, from "the gloomy slave ship . . . [where] I see the tears which follow each other in quick succession adown the dusky cheek" to the actions of benevolent moralists on the slaves' behalf, "men whose compassions have long since led them to pity the poor and despised sons of Africa." The triumph of abolition in the North, as Paul projected his vision forward from 1827, would gain more and more historical significance as "universal and not a partial emancipation" replaced southern slavery, as freed people acquired for themselves a full range of moral and intellectual virtues, and even as the missionary zeal of African Americans worked to transform Africa in the spirit of Christian and material progress. Yet, however grand the spiritual future might be, it was rooted in the decisions of specific historical actors, a fact underscored in the published version of Paul's address. Appended to the end of his speech were the names of every state legislator who had voted to enact New York's final abolition law, including a few, like Martin Van Buren, who would play a less sanguine role in the cause of black freedom in 1821.[72]

It would be tempting to read Hamilton and Paul as overly deferential to the efforts of white abolitionists, overexuberantly embracing a moment more steeped in paradox than they acknowledged. Neither speaker paused to consider the 1821 constitution's brazen assault on equal citizenship. Indeed, particularly in comparison to Joseph Sidney's 1809 address, the 1827 addresses largely avoid conventional politics. Nor did Hamilton and Paul dwell on the more sobering reality that even under the newly operational laws, blacks still could be legally bound to the white masters of their mothers for years to come. Blacks born after July 4, 1799, continued to serve indentures. Technically, a boy or girl born as late as July 3, 1827 to an as yet unemancipated slave mother would not see his or her indenture terminated until 1848.

It was not, however, technicalities that celebrants of emancipation in 1827 marked but rather the principle of liberty and the demise of an institution already irretrievably beyond revival. A generation of men and women had been born since 1799 who by law could not pass on their status as slaves, while manumissions, runaways, negotiations, cultural institution building, and illegal exports had worked fundamental transformations in the very basis of northern black life. Thousands of slaves born prior to July 5, 1799, actually received their freedom on July 4, 1827. Black New Yorkers clearly seized upon this fact, as well as the legal symbolism, as profoundly meaningful.[73]

More specifically, what preoccupied Hamilton and Paul was not legal detail but rather the concept of liberty as a torch passed from the past to the present, with dramatic consequences for the future. If they deemphasized black agency in bringing about abolition, they did so to emphasize black power in shaping the future. They also offered the vision that black and white Americans ultimately shared a language of liberty and a historical and perhaps cosmic fate. Even the process of political disfranchisement in New York and much of the north during this era would not be allowed, in July 1827, to obscure their larger purposes. For these speakers, the legal abolition of slavery went hand in hand with the ongoing project of black self-emancipation. As Paul put it, "This day commences a new era in our history . . . it follows as a necessary consequence, that new duties devolve upon us, which if properly attended to, cannot fail to improve our moral condition, and elevate us to a rank of respectable standing within the community. . . ."[74] Implicitly, Paul seemed willing to take the bet insincerely offered by white politicians like Van Buren and Samuel Young at the 1821 convention, that if African American achieved suitable advancements, whites would revise their standing as citizens accordingly.

Hamilton and Paul's complementary versions of the past, present, and future were offered in the context of earthbound contemporary disputes that highlighted in other ways how complex commemorating the past and setting an agenda for the future could be. Even as community leaders agreed on the dramatic symbolic significance of abolition, there was disagreement as to how, when, and where the arrival at this historic milestone should be observed. The two essential issues were whether July 4 itself was an appropriate date and whether indoor speeches or outdoor parades were preferable. Some Albany blacks, viewing the fourth as "the day that the National Independence is recognized by the white citizens . . . deem[ed] it proper to celebrate the 5th." In New York City, plans were launched for speeches on the fourth and a parade the following day.[75]

The debate over the appropriate date for celebration highlighted the disparate beliefs about how to publicly model African American uplift, whether to make the views of whites on this matter a primary concern, and whether blacks should emphasize their distinctive history or integrate it with a broader national history. A letter from "R." to the June 29 *Freedom's Journal* decried the plan for a twofold celebration. The correspondent found "such a division . . . disgraceful." R. asserted that African Americans aided their "enemies" by not acting "as one man." This advocate for a single commemoration on July 4 bridled at the notion that that day belonged to whites only. Indeed, whites and blacks should be equally proud of abolition; "the whole people, coloured and white" should mark the occasion. R. was also hostile to the entire idea of parading in the street, which the writer viewed as an insult to the black community's white "benefactors," many of whom were Quakers and frowned upon public processions.[76]

As blacks wrestled with the appropriate time and manner of marking important historical moments such as domestic abolition and the ending of U.S. participation in the international slave trade, they considered the opinions not only of would-be white benefactors but also overtly hostile white detractors. Black parading during the early republic stimulated a further articulation of the tradition of lampooning black dialect. As historians Shane White, Joanne Pope Melish, and David Waldstreicher have detailed, starting in the second decade of the nineteenth century, broadsides circulating in northeastern cities heaped scorn on black parades under the heading "Bobaltion." Like the term *Bobaltion*—a corruption of *abolition*—the broadsides, which originated in Boston, drew on mock black dialect, the use of stock slave names like Cato and Cudjoe, as well as visual images exaggerating African American features. Illustrations of costumes worn by black marchers were also included in the broadsides, which packaged the black celebration of their own history of liberation as the absurd carryings-on of a contemptible group. The attempt to hound blacks from the public sphere and to deflate the historical memory of abolition through derision also included the publication of faux black dialect pieces in such newspapers as Republican functionary, publisher, and dramatist Mordecai Noah's *National Advocate*.

The determination of some whites to wall off the public sphere took on a particularly hard edge in the orchestrated harassment of the pioneering African Grove Theatre company, which in the early 1820s acquired a following among blacks and whites for, among other things, its performance of Shakespeare. Whether celebrating recent events or adapting aspects of the cultural history to which New York blacks were inevitably joined, blacks after abolition remained targets and participants in an intense struggle to determine the scope and meaning of freedom. As in the late eighteenth century, constructing and contesting the nature of the African American voice was integral to this struggle.[77]

Despite the coarseness and fierceness of opposition to black public performance, the 1827 holiday celebration was undeterred, carrying a variety of messages while accommodating multiple preferences and demands. As Hamilton and Paul's remarks illustrate, both July 4 and July 5 marked the arrival of abolition. A Manhattan parade on the fifth brought together the diverse urban black community in an impressive public gathering, with people of all ages marching and watching. Commemorations in Cooperstown on July 4 and Staten Island on July 5 further indicate that individual black communities ultimately set their own agendas for what was widely acknowledged to be an important event. At the symbolic birth of a new era, New York blacks would not speak with a single voice any more than could whites. The construction of historicized accounts of abolition would have to compete with the desire to assert the black presence in public life to the black community as well as to white onlookers.[78]

Freedom, of course, was not about a day or two days, nor speeches and processions, but rather it was an ongoing process of social and political struggle for place, recognition, and rights. No amount of white public scorn, moreover, could unilaterally halt this process. The founding in New York City of *Freedom's Journal,* the nation's first African American newspaper, just months prior to July 4, 1827, was emblematic of the new era and its demands. Samuel Cornish, a Presbyterian minister in New York City, and John Russwurm, who had recently become the nation's second recorded black college graduate, recognized that their newspaper represented a powerful new challenge to American slavery, complemented New York's imminent renunciation of domestic bondage, and directly challenged white race-baiters. Indeed, the newspaper would allow an ongoing black-controlled presence in a public discourse that still very much was concerned with the rights and conditions of black people.

Freedom's Journal undertook the interdependent missions of symbolic repudiation of racial prejudice, black self-assertion and self-help, and invigoration of a national campaign against slavery and racism. First and foremost, the editors wished "to come boldly before an enlightened publick," announcing in the paper's mission statement, "Too long have others spoken for us." It was neither desirable nor possible to rely on white people to speak for blacks if de jure freedom was to be defended and extended. Indeed, the editors declared, "we believe that the time has now arrived, when the calumnies of our enemies should be refuted by forcible arguments." African Americans, according to the journal's editors were to claim not only a voice but also a vote. The editors "urge[d] our brethren to use their right to the elective franchise as free citizens." Meanwhile, the editors hoped to prompt these citizens to acquire the education and "habits of industry" necessary "for becoming useful members of society."

The newspaper's self-proclaimed mandate to represent as well as inform its readers was national rather than local. Even before the first issue, the publishers had established a chain of sales agents from Maine to Washington,

D.C. But the stakes were higher than the numbers of newspapers sold or how many blacks went to the polls: as one supporter of the paper asserted within its columns, "The total annihilation of slavery in the Union, depends much, very much, on the conduct of the coloured population of New York."[79] In the former heart of slaveholding country north of the Mason-Dixon line, the community from which *Freedom's Journal* emerged was, at least in the estimation of this one correspondent, to speak for the black nation.[80]

In taking upon itself this improbable burden, the *Journal* indicated that black freedom also depended on cultivating historical memory. The roll call of historic black achievement offered within its pages included references to the literary talents Phillis Wheatley and Olaudah Equiano, whose work continued to serve as a response to assertions of black inferiority. Toussaint L'Ouverture, the subject of a three-part biographical retrospective reprinted in the *Journal*, was a towering reminder of the African American capacity for sublime political achievement. Closer to home, the first several issues of the *Journal* reprinted from the *Liverpool Mercury* a memoir of the Massachusetts-born shipping magnate Paul Cuffee.[81]

Questions that swirled around the prospect of abolition in the eighteenth century echoed in the postemancipation period, a fact also reflected in *Freedom's Journal*.[82] African Americans continued to fight long-standing, ongoing battles. The charge that free blacks placed an undue burden on the public relief funds required *Freedom's Journal* to marshal statistics proving the contrary. Consistent with the decades-old preoccupation of white Manumission Society members, the paper also felt obliged repeatedly to print commentaries cautioning against idleness and shows of pride that might damage the public image of black people. The use of West Indian sugar even still dramatized for the *Journal*'s readers how the ordinary consumer bore responsibility for the brutalities of slavery.[83] Despite all that had changed, there was no escape from the past in the nineteenth-century discourse of slavery and race. Indeed, drawing on and interpreting that past comprised a crucial part of the struggle to shape the future.

Epilogue
Inescapable

The connection of past and present helped to define the hazards and the pathos of free black life in the North. In 1830, Sally, a black woman from Ulster County, fell into the hands of an unscrupulous white trader. Her former master, George Tappen, wanted to assert the legal protection available to Sally under state law and wished to offer information to establish her identity. Tappen noted that one of the woman's sons still lived nearby but that he had lost track of another son; as Tappen explained, "there are no slaves in this State, the Blacks are all at liberty to go where they please. . . ." Black freedom and mobility made it harder for individual whites to assert their authority or, as in this instance, to extend their assistance. Thus, soberingly, the former master expressed the fear that Sally might find herself "in danger of being conveyed beyond our reach or knowledge," presumably into the thriving heart of American slave country.[1] Like disfranchisement, kidnapping was an unavoidable reminder of the immediacy of slavery's history in New York.

Thus, even as the battle over race and slavery in the north was transformed by the third decade of the nineteenth century, it reflected the lasting legacy of the previous half-century.[2] Events in New York laid the groundwork for and prefigured the post-1830 antebellum era in which free blacks and white abolitionists chafed against a hardening vision of racial difference. If black bodies were no longer legally traded and sold in New York, the image of African Americans was nonetheless thoroughly commodified and consumed through the growth of New York's minstrel stage. Packed audiences of working-class whites, many of them immigrants, learned the racial codes of America by mocking and embracing stage black speech and song. The ground had been well prepared for the popular theater of "whiteness" and "blackness" in anecdotes and letters pretending to recreate black speech in eighteenth-century newspapers, in hostile broadsides and taunts directed toward black parades, and in the early 1820s when the African Grove Theatre was driven out of business through a campaign of organized and orchestrated harassment. Developments in the realm of culture found their more concrete expression in antebellum New York in antiblack mob violence, segregation of public accommodations, and continued denial of the right of suffrage.[3]

Despite and because of these developments, on their newly free soil, citizens of New York state played a major role in creating new kinds of abolitionism. The "second wave" of abolitionism is often associated closely with the Garrisonians of Massachusetts, who made their mark through uncompromising immediatism and "mass action strategies."[4] As modern abolitionism found multiple forms of expression in the antebellum period, the road to the future literally and figuratively traveled through New York. Birthplace of Sojourner Truth and *Freedom's Journal,* New York became the home of Lewis Tappan's benevolent empire and center of a circle of influential Christian immediatists as well. Even Westchester County judge William Jay, whose father John was the archetype of New York–style gradualism, would embrace the cause of immediatism, a movement which took as an article of faith that the draining of the moral swamp of slavery could not be indefinitely postponed and that the passage of time strengthened rather than weakened the institution. Meanwhile, upstate New York would provide a generation of shock troops for various strains of radical abolitionism and elected one of the boldest advocates of political abolitionism and interracial cooperation, Gerrit Smith, to the U.S. Congress.[5]

Although only the most daring blacks and whites would forge meaningful friendships across the color line, hearing one another's voices in a different key than that offered on the minstrel stage became an essential element of the abolitionist crusade in the coming decades. Thus, the first-person runaway slave narrative emerged as a powerful form of sentimentalized antislavery discourse.[6] But sometimes the form of address was even more direct, sentiment leavened with accusation.

When Frederick Douglass gave his famous 1852 speech "What does the Fourth of July mean to the Negro" in Rochester, New York, he was not speaking to or for black people; he was challenging white people to rethink the implications of their history and to redefine the meaning of American freedom. Douglass drew distinctions between black and white historical memory in order to redefine the struggle blacks and whites had to engage in if American slavery was ever to be abolished. Having reviewed the revolutionary context of the anniversary, Douglass declared, "This Fourth [of] July is *yours,* not *mine. You* may rejoice, *I* must mourn." New York was free soil enough to provide a relatively safe platform for such statements, but, as an integral part of a slaveholding republic, it was appropriate ground upon which to deliver such a censure. In the midst of "the mournful wail of millions" of slaves, Douglass asserted, "America is false to the past, false to the present, and solemnly binds herself to be false to the future." The memories evoked by the fourth of July were, said Douglass, "a sham."[7]

Long before Douglass's famous speech and more than a decade before he escaped northward from Maryland, the memory of slavery in New York bound the fates of free black New Yorkers to those of southern slaves. *Freedom's Journal* proclaimed in its inaugural edition that southern slaves "are our kindred by all the ties of nature." Due to opportunistic masters and unscrupulous slave traders, southern blacks were sometimes literally sons and daughters of New York and in all cases were kindred to northern blacks by the ties of history.[8] New York, like the nation, had become "a house divided"—a bulwark of real and "sham" freedom—while the history of emancipation in the Empire state remained indivisible from the nation's intensifying struggle over slavery.

The shortcomings and unfinished accomplishments of northern abolition enabled such contradictions and their potential resolution. Between 1777 and 1827, white identity and black identity, white voice and black voice had developed dialectically, as part of the ongoing construction of the public sphere.[9] This discourse was by no means the exclusive province of political officeholders, let alone white New Yorkers, although power was always skewed to one degree or another. The anonymous and the imagined, the powerful and the abused, the humorist and the moral scold, the sentimental poet and the racist wag all had played a role. For any such voices to sustain an expansive discourse of emancipation and citizenship, the rudimentary yet incredibly difficult step of eliminating slavery in the North was crucial.

The bicentennial of the activation of New York's gradual abolition act passed with little fanfare in July 1999, perhaps a reflection of the ambiguous history behind that anniversary. A *New York Times* op-ed columnist—as it happens, an African American—marked July 4, 1799, with a column on nineteenth-century women's suffrage crusaders Elizabeth Cady Stanton and Susan B. Anthony, mentioning their abolitionist roots and their bitter response to the Fifteenth Amendment's enfranchisement of black men. The writer made no mention of the significance of July 4 to the history of race and slavery in New York itself.[10] Time will tell whether July 4, 2027, will be commemorated as a significant bicentennial or whether it will be another forgotten anniversary. What is certain is that American history was fundamentally altered by the process of gradual abolition in the North, creating a story driven by an inescapable discourse of slavery and freedom.

The story carries important lessons for today as well. We have witnessed the breathtaking multiplication of the sites and the speed of discourse, and yet our world still very much needs to be remade in the name of justice and equality. Change, of course, depends as much or more on what people do as what they say. Yet if history is any guide, we will have to construct our world out of liberating discourses or the globalization of human rights surely will continue to elude us.[11]

NOTES

ABBREVIATIONS

AANYLH	*Afro-Americans in New York Life and History*
ACent	*Albany Centinel*
AChron	*Albany Chronicle*
ACPAS	*The American Convention for Promoting the Abolition of Slavery and Improving the Condition of the African Race: Minutes, Constitution, Addresses, Memorials, Resolutions, Reports, Committees and Anti-Slavery Tracts* (New York, 1969)
AHR	*American Historical Review*
AJ	*Albany Journal*
CG	*Columbian Gazetteer* [New York City]
CJFR	*Country Journal and Dutchess and Ulster County Farmer's Register*
CJPA	*Country Journal and Poughkeepsie Advertiser*
CP	*Catskill Packet*
DA	*Daily Advertiser* [New York City]
Herald	*The Herald; A Gazette for the Country* [New York City]
JAH	*Journal of American History*
JER	*Journal of the Early Republic*
JNH	*Journal of Negro History*
LFH	*Lansingburgh Federal Herald*
MH	*Mott and Hurtin's New-York Weekly Chronicle*
NCLA	*Northern Centinel and Lansingburgh Advertiser*
NYJ	*New-York Journal*
NYM	*The New-York Magazine; or, Literary Repository*
NYMS	*Papers of the Society for Promoting the Manumission of Slaves in New York City, New-York Historical Society, New York City*
NYP	*New-York Packet*
NYWC	*New-York Weekly Chronicle*
NYWM	*New-York Weekly Museum*
OH	*Ostego Herald* [Cooperstown]
RT	*Register of the Times* [New York City]
SNC	*Salem Northern Centinel*
Spec	*The Spectator* [New York City]
TP	*Time Piece* [New York City]
WMQ	*William and Mary Quarterly*

NOTES TO INTRODUCTION

1. Joyce Appleby, *Inheriting the Revolution: The First Generation of Americans* (Cambridge, Mass., 2000), 45–46.

2. Abraham Lincoln, Speech to Republican state convention, June 16, 1858, quote in William E. Gienapp, ed., *This Fiery Trial: The Speeches and Writings of Abraham Lincoln* (New York, 2002), 43; Arthur Zilversmit, *The First Emancipation: The Abolition of Slavery in the North* (Chicago, 1967), 200. On "whiteness" see Peter Kolchin, "Whiteness Studies: The New History of Race," *JAH* 89 (2002): 154–73, and subsequent notes.

3. The best overview of northern abolition remains Zilversmit, *First Emancipation;* David Brion Davis, *The Problem of Slavery in the Age of Revolution, 1770–1823* (Ithaca, N.Y., 1975) is a classic study of early abolitionism in the Atlantic world.

4. Ira Berlin, *Many Thousands Gone: The First Two Centuries of Slavery in North America* (Cambridge, Mass., 1998); Peter Charles Hoffer, *The Great New York Conspiracy of 1741: Slavery, Crime, and Colonial Law* (Lawrence, Kans., 2003), 43–44, makes a strong case for the centrality of slavery in the development of colonial New York City.

5. Major recent studies of black life in New York City include Thelma Wills Foote, *Black and White Manhattan: The History of Racial Formation in Colonial New York* (New York, 2004); Leslie M. Harris, *In the Shadow of Slavery: African Americans in New York City, 1626–1863* (Chicago, 2003); Shane White, *Stories of Freedom in Black New York* (Cambridge, Mass., 2002); Craig Stephen Wilder, *In the Company of Black Men: The African Influence on African American Culture in New York City* (New York, 2001); Graham Russell Hodges, *Root and Branch: African Americans in New York and East Jersey* (Chapel Hill, N.C., 1999); and Shane White, *Somewhat More Independent: The End of Slavery in New York City, 1770–1810* (Athens, Ga., 1991). These studies should be supplemented by Vivienne L. Kruger, "Born to Run: The Slave Family in Early New York, 1626–1827" (Ph.D. diss., Columbia University, 1985), and Edgar J. McManus, *A History of Negro Slavery in New York* (Syracuse, N.Y., 1966). Other important studies of northern black life include Shane White and Graham White, *Stylin': African American Expressive Culture from Its Beginnings to the Zoot Suit* (Ithaca, N.Y., 1998), and James Oliver Horton and Lois E. Horton, *In Hope of Liberty: Culture, Community and Protest Among Northern Free Blacks, 1700–1860* (New York, 1997). For comparative purposes, see Gary B. Nash, "Forging Freedom: The Emancipation Experience in Northern Seaport Cities, 1775–1820," in *Slavery and Freedom in the Age of the American Revolution,* eds. Ira Berlin and Ronald Hoffman (Charlottesville, Va., 1983), 3–48; Gary B. Nash, *Forging Freedom: The Formation of Philadelphia's Black Community, 1720–1840* (Cambridge, Mass., 1988); and Leonard P. Curry, *The Free Black in Urban America, 1800–1850: The Shadow of the Dream* (Chicago, 1981).

6. Michael Edward Groth, "Forging Freedom in the Mid-Hudson Valley: The End of Slavery and the Formation of a Free African-American Community in Dutchess County, New York, 1770–1850" (Ph.D. diss., SUNY-Binghamton, 1994); Richard Shannon Moss, *Slavery on Long Island: A Study of Local Institutional and Early African-American Communal Life* (New York, 1993); Graham Russell Hodges, *Slavery and Freedom in the Rural North: African Americans in Monmouth County, New Jersey, 1665–1865* (Madison, Wisc., 1997); and Kruger, "Born to Run." See also several valuable articles cited in the next chapter.

7. Patrick Rael, *Black Identity and Black Protest in the Antebellum North* (Chapel Hill, N.C., 2002); Dickson D. Bruce Jr., *The Origins of African American Literature, 1680–1865* (Charlottesville, Va., 2001); David N. Gellman and David Quigley, eds., *Jim Crow New York: A*

Documentary History of Race and Citizenship, 1777–1877 (New York, 2003); David R. Roediger, *The Wages of Whiteness: Race and the Making of the American Working Class,* rev. ed. (London, 1999); Eric Lott, *Love and Theft: Blackface Minstrelsy and the American Working Class* (New York, 1993); James Brewer Stewart, "The Emergence of Racial Modernity and the Rise of the White North, 1790–1840," *JER* 18 (1998): 181–217; Lois E. Horton, "From Class to Race in Early America: Northern Post-Emancipation Racial Reconstruction," *JER* 19 (1999): 629–49; Joanne Pope Melish, "The 'Condition' Debate and Racial Discourse in the Antebellum North," *JER* 19 (1999): 651–72; and James Brewer Stewart, "Modernizing 'Difference': The Political Meanings of Color in the Free States, 1776–1840," *JER* 19 (1999): 691–712. See George Fredrickson, *The Black Image in the White Mind: The Debate on Afro-American Character and Destiny, 1817–1914* (New York, 1971), 61, on *"Herrenvolk* democracy" as applied to the South.

8. Leonard L. Richard, *The Slave Power: The Free North and Southern Domination, 1780–1860* (Baton Rouge, 2000); see also Richard H. Brown, "The Missouri Crisis, Slavery, and the Politics of Jacksonianism," *South Atlantic Quarterly* 65 (1966): 55–72.

9. Nell Irvin Painter, *Sojourner Truth: A Life, A Symbol* (New York, 1996); John Stauffer, *The Black Hearts of Men: Radical Abolitionists and the Transformation of Race* (Cambridge, Mass., 2001); Bertram Wyatt-Brown, *Lewis Tappan and the Evangelical War Against Slavery* (Cleveland, 1969); Whitney R. Cross, *The Burned-Over District: The Social and Intellectual History of Enthusiastic Religion in Western New York, 1800–1850* (Ithaca, N.Y., 1950), 217–26; David W. Blight, *Frederick Douglass' War: Keeping Faith in Jubilee* (Baton Rouge, 1989), esp. 28–31. Mitch Kachun, in *Festivals of Freedom: Memory and Meaning in African American Emancipation Celebrations, 1808–1815* (Amherst, 2003), 5, 53, writes of the broad influence of "northern values" on nineteenth-century black leaders and refers specifically to an antebellum "protest" model that emerged from New York; see also Foote, *Black and White Manhattan,* 232–33.

10. Although in many respects an excellent study, Richard S. Newman, *The Transformation of American Abolitionism: Fighting Slavery in the Early Republic* (Chapel Hill, N.C., 2002), largely skips over New York, as well as the public nature of the debate over northern abolition; see also Paul Goodman, *Of One Blood: Abolitionism and the Origins of Racial Equality* (Berkeley, 1998).

11. Gary B. Nash and Jean R. Soderlund, *Freedom by Degrees: Emancipation in Pennsylvania and Its Aftermath* (New York, 1991), 7. Rael, *Black Identity and Black Protest,* 86, 88, offers tables that neatly summarize the comparative demographic data on the African American population of the colonial and early-national north. The above comparison of percentages does not include Delaware, which sits next to Maryland and which did not abolish slavery until the Civil War. On Delaware's unique history, see William H. Williams, *Slavery and Freedom in Delaware, 1639–1865* (Wilmington, 1996), and Patience Essah, *A House Divided: Slavery and Emancipation in Delaware, 1638–1865* (Charlottesville, Va., 1996).

12. Nash and Soderlund, *Freedom by Degrees;* Joanne Pope Melish, *Disowning Slavery: Gradual Emancipation and "Race" in New England, 1780–1860* (Ithaca, N.Y., 1998); see also T. H. Breen, "Making History: The Force of Public Opinion and the Last Years of Slavery in Revolutionary Massachusetts," in *Through a Glass Darkly: Reflections on Personal Identity in Early America,* ed. Ronald Hoffman, Mechal Sobel, and Fredrika J. Teute (Chapel Hill, N.C., 1997), 67–95.

13. On political culture during the period, see Joseph J. Ellis, *Founding Brothers: The Revolutionary Generation* (New York, 2000); James Roger Sharp, *American Politics in the Early*

Republic: The New Nation in Crisis (New Haven, 1993); Stanley Elkins and Eric McKitrick, *The Age of Federalism: The Early American Republic, 1788–1800* (New York, 1993); Linda Kerber, *Women of the Republic: Intellect and Ideology in Revolutionary America* (Chapel Hill, N.C., 1980); Drew McCoy, *The Elusive Republic: Political Economy in Jeffersonian America* (Chapel Hill, N.C., 1980); Joyce Appleby, *Capitalism and the New Social Order: The Republican Vision of the 1790s* (New York, 1984); and Steven Watts, *The Republic Reborn: War and the Remaking of Liberal America, 1790–1820* (Baltimore, 1987).

14. On the rising political significance of newspapers in the new republic, see Jeffrey L. Pasley, *"The Tyranny of the Printers": Newspaper Politics in the Early Republic* (Charlottesville, Va., 2001), and below.

15. Elkins and McKitrick, *Age of Federalism*, 455–56; Winthrop D. Jordan, *White over Black: American Attitudes toward the Negro, 1550–1812* (1968; New York, 1977), 335–41; Richard D. Brown, *The Strength of a People: The Idea of an Informed Citizenry in America, 1650–1870* (Chapel Hill, N.C., 1996), 52–53, 84–86; Gordon S. Wood, *The Radicalism of the American Revolution* (New York, 1992).

16. Jay Fliegelman, *Declaring Independence: Jefferson, Natural Language, and the Culture of Performance* (Stanford, 1993), esp. 195.

17. Judith N. Shklar, *American Citizenship: The Quest for Inclusion* (Cambridge, Mass., 1991); see also Edmund S. Morgan, *American Slavery, American Freedom: The Ordeal of Colonial Virginia* (New York, 1975), and Dwight L. Dumond, *Antislavery: The Crusade for Freedom in America* (Ann Arbor, Mich. 1961), 120. On the dynamics of early nineteenth-century citizenship, see Robert H. Wiebe, *Self-Rule: A Cultural History of American Democracy* (Chicago, 1995), 17–40.

18. On slavery as a negative reference point, see Shklar, *American Citizenship*, 16–17, 22–23. Bernard Bailyn, *The Ideological Origins of the American Revolution* (Cambridge, Mass., 1967), 119–20, 122, 232–33, 312, explores the slavery metaphor during the Revolutionary era.

19. *NYP*, Sept. 9, 1784; see also *NYP*, June 10, 1784; see Shklar, *American Citizenship*, on "social standing" as a key concept. On positive conceptions of labor emerging in the wake of the Revolution, see Wood, *Radicalism*, 186, 276–86; and Gordon S. Wood, "Equality and Social Conflict in the American Revolution," *WMQ*, 3d ser., 51 (1994): 712–13. See Wiebe, *Self-Rule*, 23–27, on the notion of "self-directed work"; and Linda K. Kerber, *No Constitutional Right to Be Ladies: Women and the Obligations of Citizenship* (New York, 1998), 47–80.

20. Alexander Keyssar, *The Right to Vote: The Contested History of Democracy in the United States* (New York, 2000); Chilton Williamson, *American Suffrage from Property to Democracy, 1760–1860* (Princeton, 1960); Rogers Smith, *Civic Ideals: Conflicting Visions of Citizenship in U.S. History* (New Haven, 1997), esp. 1–16, and see 3, on "full citizenship"; Alfred F. Young, *The Democratic Republicans of New York: The Origins, 1763–1797* (Chapel Hill, N.C., 1967), 18–19; Kerber, *No Constitutional Right to Be Ladies*, xxiii–xxiv, 11–13, 15; Judith Wellman, "Women's Rights, Republicanism, and Revolutionary Rhetoric in Antebellum New York," *New York History* 69 (1988): 353–84.

21. Pasley, *"Tyranny of the Printers"*; Michael Warner, *The Letters of the Republic: Publication and the Public Sphere in Eighteenth-Century America* (Cambridge, Mass., 1990), 32, 51, 61, 68, 113, 125–28; Elkins and McKitrick, *Age of Federalism*, 456, 701, 848; Brown, *Strength of a People*, 61, 91, 103, 110; Taylor, "The Art of Hook and Snivey: Political Culture in Upstate New York during the 1790s," *JAH* 79 (1993): 1372, 1383, 1393–95; Carol Sue Humphrey, *The Press of the Young Republic, 1783–1833* (Westport, Conn., 1996); Donald H. Stewart, *The Opposition*

Press of the Federalist Period (Albany, 1969). For examples of New York newspapers describing their value to society, see *NYP*, Nov. 12, 1783, Feb. 24, 28, 1785, Nov. 21, 1786; *New York Independent Gazette*, Dec. 20, 1783; *NYJ*, Dec. 19, 1787; *CJPA*, Jan. 2, 1788; *LFH*, Apr. 19, 1790; *CP*, June 24, 1793; *New-York Evening Post*, Nov. 17, 1794; *OH*, June 5, 1795; see also Christopher Looby, *Voicing America: Language, Literary Form, and the Origins of the United States* (Chicago, 1996).

22. *Spec*, Feb. 14, 1798; *NYP*, Mar. 20, 1786, Aug. 10, 1787, Sept. 1, 1791; Samuel Williams, "Observations on the Nature and Preservation of Freedom," *NYM*, Aug. 1796, 407–8; *CG*, June 9, 1794; Colleen A. Sheehan, "The Politics of Public Opinion: James Madison's 'Notes on Government,'" *WMQ*, 3d ser., 49 (1992): 608–27; Elkins and McKitrick, *Age of Federalism*, esp. 451–56, 664, 701, 714, 717; Sharp, *American Politics in the Early Republic*, 44–46, 60–63, 66, 68, 85, 91, 113, 119, 120, 123–25, 131, 135; Michael Lienesch, "Thomas Jefferson and the American Democratic Experience: The Origins of the Partisan Press, Popular Political Parties, and Public Opinion," in *Jeffersonian Legacies*, ed. Peter Onuf (Charlottesville, Va., 1993), 316–39; Brown, *Strength of a People*, 61, 86–91.

23. Warner, *Letters of the Republic*, and Fliegelman, *Declaring Independence*, have been the most helpful works in formulating this perspective.

24. Jürgen Habermas, *The Structural Transformation of the Public Sphere: An Inquiry into a Category of Bourgeois Society*, trans. Thomas Burger (Cambridge, Mass., 1989). Critics and commentators have extended and modified Habermas's concept of the public sphere, highlighting, among other things, how the public sphere operated historically to exclude certain people and voices; see Warner, *Letters of the Republic*, throughout, and on race specifically, 11–14; and several essays in Craig Calhoun, ed., *Habermas and the Public Sphere* (Cambridge, Mass., 1992), including Harry C. Boyte, "The Pragmatic Ends of Popular Politics," 340–55, esp. 344; Mary Ryan, "Gender and Public Access: Women's Politics in Nineteenth-Century America," 259–88; Geoff Eley, "Nations, Publics, and Political Cultures: Placing Habermas in the Nineteenth Century," 289–339; Michael Warner, "The Mass Public and the Mass Subject," 377–401, esp. 382–83; and Jürgen Habermas, "Further Reflections on the Public Sphere," 421–61; "Concluding Remarks," 462–79.

25. Rael, *Black Identity and Black Protest*.

26. Bruce, *Origins of African American Literature;* Graham Russell Hodges, ed., *Black Itinerants of the Gospel: The Narratives of John Jea and George White* (Madison, 1993); Robert E. Desrochers Jr., "'Not Fade Away': The Narrative of Venture Smith, an African American in the Early Republic," *JAH* 84 (1997): 40–66.

27. Seymour Drescher, *Capitalism and Antislavery: British Mobilization in Comparative Perspective* (New York, 1987), 164.

28. White, *Somewhat More Independent;* Hodges, *Root and Branch;* Kruger, "Born to Run"; Nash, "Forging Freedom"; Judith L. Van Buskirk, *Generous Enemies: Patriots and Loyalists in Revolutionary New York* (Philadelphia, 2002), 147–54, 172–75.

29. Harris, *In the Shadow of Slavery*, makes important strides toward incorporating politics into the study of northern black life.

30. Newman, *Transformation of American Abolitionism*, esp. 16–38.

31. Young, *Democratic Republicans*, 587.

32. Despite the differences among them, Davis, *Age of Revolution;* Drescher, *Capitalism and Antislavery*, esp. 164, 166; and Thomas L. Haskell, "Capitalism and the Origins of Humanitarian Sensibility," *AHR* 90 (1985): 339–61, 547–66; and "Convention and Hegemonic Interest in the Debate over Antislavery: A Reply to Davis and Ashworth," *AHR* 92 (1987): 829–78, all

recognized abolition as a way of investigating broader ideological formations. See also Christopher L. Brown, "Foundations of British Abolitionism, Beginnings to 1789" (Ph.D. diss., Oxford University, 1994), esp. 14–24; and Philip Gould, *Barbaric Traffic: Commerce and Antislavery in the Eighteenth-Century Atlantic World* (Cambridge, Mass., 2003).

33. Stewart, "The Emergence of Racial Modernity" and "Modernizing 'Difference'"; Horton, "From Class to Race," 643–49; Melish, *Disowning Slavery* and "The 'Condition' Debate and Racial Discourse in the Antebellum North."

34. Wood, *Radicalism of the American Revolution;* Elkins and McKitrick, *Age of Federalism;* Sharp, *American Politics in the Early Republic;* admirably, Ellis, *Founding Brothers,* 81–119, placed a chapter on slavery, evocatively titled "The Silence," in the middle of his study. Roger Wilkins, *Jefferson's Pillow: The Founding Fathers and the Dilemma of Black Patriotism* (Boston, 2002) provides an intriguing angle of vision that moves these subjects beyond the sphere of academic history.

35. Academic critics have responded with no small amount of disgruntlement on the absence of slavery and race in leading syntheses on the early republic published in the 1990s. On Wood's work, see Jon F. Sensbach, "Charting a Course in Early African-American History," and Michael Meranze, "Even the Dead Will Not Be Safe: An Ethics of Early American History," *WMQ,* 3d ser., 50 (1993): 373–75, 404–5; see also the contributions to "How Revolutionary Was the Revolution? A Discussion of Gordon S. Wood's *The Radicalism of the American Revolution,*" *WMQ,* 3d ser., 51 (1994): 677–716, in particular, Joyce Appleby, "The Radical Recreation of the American Republic," 682; Barbara Clark Smith, "The Adequate Revolution," 688; and Michael Zuckerman, "Rhetoric, Reality, and the Revolution: The Genteel Radicalism of Gordon Wood," 698, as well as Wood's response, "Equality and Social Conflict in the American Revolution," 703–16. See also David Brion Davis, review of *The Age of Federalism: The Early American Republic, 1788–1800,* by Stanley Elkins and Eric McKitrick, *New York Review of Books,* May 12, 1994, 25–28; and James M. Banner Jr., review of *The Age of Federalism: The Early American Republic, 1788–1800,* by Stanley Elkins and Eric McKitrick, and *American Politics in the Early Republic: The New Nation in Crisis,* by James Rogers Sharp, *WMQ,* 3d ser., 52 (1995): 168. On the larger historiographic point, see David Grimsted, "Anglo-American Racism and Phillis Wheatley's 'Sable Veil,' 'Length'ned Chain,' and 'Knitted Heart,'" in *Women in the Age of the American Revolution,* ed. Ronald Hoffman and Peter J. Albert (Charlottesville, Va., 1989), 442; and the promising essay by François Furstenberg, "Beyond Freedom and Slavery: Autonomy, Virtue, and Resistance in Early American Political Discourse," *JAH* 89 (2003): 1295–1330.

NOTES TO CHAPTER 1

1. Graham Russell Hodges, ed., *The Black Loyalist Directory: African Americans in Exile After the American Revolution* (New York, 1996), 181–91, contains the ship's roster of African Americans. The Willis family appears on 188, and although it does not explicitly state the relationship between Samuel and Rachel Willis, and identifies their children Joseph, Charles, and Jenny as Rachel's, the arrangement of the names suggests conjugal ties. On the formation of black families during British wartime occupation of New York City, see Thelma Wills Foote, *Black and White Manhattan: The History of Racial Formation in Colonial New York* (New York, 2004), 216–21; Vivienne L. Kruger, "Born to Run: The Slave Family in Early New York, 1626–1827" (Ph.D. diss., Columbia University, 1985), 672–73; and Judith L. Van Buskirk, *Generous Enemies: Patriots and Loyalists in Revolutionary New York* (Philadelphia, 2002), 172–76.

2. *NYP*, Nov. 17, 1783.

3. Edwin G. Burrows and Mike Wallace, *Gotham: A History of New York City to 1898* (New York, 1999), 259–61, 265–87; Milton M. Klein, ed., *The Empire State: A History of New York* (Ithaca, N.Y., 2001), 243, 245; Alfred F. Young, *The Democratic Republicans of New York: The Origins, 1763–1797* (Chapel Hill, N.C., 1967), 3–105; Edward Countryman, *A People in Revolution: The American Revolution and Political Society in New York, 1760–1790* (Baltimore, 1981).

4. *The Constitution of the State of New-York* (Philadelphia, 1777).

5. Ira Berlin, *Many Thousands Gone: The First Two Centuries of Slavery in North America* (Cambridge, Mass., 1998), 177–94; James G. Lydon, "New York and the Slave Trade, 1700 to 1774," *WMQ*, 3d ser., 35 (1978): 375–94; Michael Kammen, *Colonial New York: A History* (New York, 1975), 167, 180–82, 205; James Oliver Horton and Lois E. Horton, *In Hope of Liberty: Culture, Community and Protest Among Northern Free Blacks, 1700–1860* (New York, 1997), 12; Edgar J. McManus, *A History of Negro Slavery in New York* (Syracuse, N.Y., 1966), 23–39, 199; Graham Russell Hodges, *Root and Branch: African Americans in New York and East Jersey* (Chapel Hill, N.C., 1999), 88.

6. McManus, *Negro Slavery*, 41–48; Graham Russell Hodges, ed., *"Pretends to Be Free": Runaway Slaves from Colonial and Revolutionary New York and New Jersey* (New York, 1994), xviii; Foote, *Black and White Manhattan*, 53–88; Thomas Davis, "New York's Long Black Line: A Note on the Growing Slave Population, 1626–1790," *AANYLH* 2 (1978): 44–45, 54–57; Shane White, *Somewhat More Independent: The End of Slavery in New York City, 1770–1810* (Athens, Ga., 1991), 16–23; Burrows and Wallace, *Gotham*, 118–29; Michael Kammen, *Colonial New York: A History* (New York, 1975), provides an excellent overview. In contrast to the above argument, Foote, in *Black and White Manhattan*, contends that race and slavery were pivotal in forging a racial unity among Europeans in colonial New York.

7. Peter Charles Hoffer, *The Great New York Conspiracy: Slavery, Crime, and Colonial Law* (Lawrence, Kans., 2003); Burrows and Wallace, *Gotham*, 159–66; Leslie M. Harris, *In the Shadow of Slavery: African Americans in New York City, 1626–1863* (Chicago, 2003), 46–47; Thomas J. Davis, *A Rumor of Revolt: The "Great Negro Plot" in Colonial New York* (New York, 1985), 225.

8. Carl Nordstrom, "The New York Slave Code," *AANYLH* 4 (1980): 9–17; McManus, *Negro Slavery*, 79–83, 91–98, 104–5, 125, 141–43; Michael Edward Groth, "Forging Freedom in the Mid-Hudson Valley: The End of Slavery and the Formation of a Free African-American Community in Dutchess County, New York, 1770–1850" (Ph.D. diss., Binghamton University, 1994), 129–31; Foote, *Black and White Manhattan*, 148–51; A. J. Williams-Myers, "The African Presence in the Hudson River Valley: The Defining of Relationships Between the Masters and the Slaves," *AANYLH* 12 (1988): 83.

9. McManus, *Negro Slavery*, 24; Hodges, *Root and Branch*, 10–18; Nordstrom, "Slave Code," 8–9; Foote, *Black and White Manhattan*, 80, 127–28, 133, 158; Williams-Myers, "The African Presence in the Hudson River Valley," 81–83. Hoffer, *Great New York Conspiracy*, 29–30. Hoffer (11–32) places New York's colonial slave law in their broader English and New World contexts. See also Winthrop D. Jordan, *White over Black: American Attitudes toward the Negro, 1550–1812* (1968; New York, 1977), 66–85; A. Leon Higginbotham Jr., *In the Matter of Color: Race and the American Legal Process* (New York, 1978); and William M. Wiecek, "The Statutory Law of Slavery and Race in the Thirteen Mainland Colonies of British America," *WMQ*, 3d ser., 34 (1977): 259–80.

10. James Oakes, *Slavery and Freedom: An Interpretation of the Old South* (New York, 1990), 38; Berlin, *Many Thousands Gone,* 177–94.

11. T. H. Breen, *Imagining the Past: East Hampton Histories* (Reading, Mass., 1989), 148, 58, 181–84; Davis, "New York's Long Black Line," 47, 50–53; Henry Lloyd II to Henry Lloyd, June 23, 1759, Bill of Sale, July 1, 1757, Bill of Sale, May 20, 1760, *Papers of the Lloyd Family of the Manor of Queens Village, Lloyd's Neck Long Island, New York,* Collections of the New-York Historical Society, vol. 60 (New York, 1927), 2:568, 501–2, 584–5; Richard Shannon Moss, *Slavery on Long Island: A Study in Local Institutional and Early African-American Communal Life* (New York, 1993); Jordan, *White over Black,* 66–71, on Puritans and slavery; Kammen, *Colonial New York,* 39–40, 43–44, 52–53, 82–84, 87.

12. By 1776, the percentage of blacks in Suffolk County had slipped to 8.4 percent; for demographic data, see McManus, *Negro Slavery,* 197–200; Davis, "New York's Long Black Line," 50–54; and Moss, *Slavery on Long Island,* 154–55.

13. Moss, *Slavery on Long Island,* xi–xvi, outlines the case for Long Island's distinctiveness and significance; McManus, *Negro Slavery,* 85–86, 197–200; Davis, "New York's Long Black Line," 46–47; Foote, *Black and White Manhattan,* 53–88.

14. Foote, *Black and White Manhattan,* 189–207; White, *Somewhat More Independent,* 92–93; McManus, *Negro Slavery,* 83–87, 98; Thomas Joseph Davis, "Slavery in Colonial New York City" (Ph.D. diss., Columbia University, 1974), 149–52; Williams-Myers, "The African Presence in the Hudson River Valley," 86.

15. Foote, *Black and White Manhattan,* 75, 79–85, 147–53, 216–17; McManus, *Negro Slavery,* 45, 81–82, 91–92, 97; White, *Somewhat More Independent,* 88–94, 113, 153; Thelma Willis Foote, "Black Life in Colonial Manhattan" (Ph.D. diss., Harvard, 1991), 90–91, 105, 224–25.

16. Kruger, "Born to Run," 200–201.

17. A. J. Williams-Myers, "The African Presence in the Mid-Hudson River Valley Before 1800: A Preliminary Historiographic Sketch," *AANYLH* 8 (1984): 31–39; A. J. Williams-Myers, "Hands that Picked No Cotton: An Exploratory Examination of African Slave Labor in the Colonial Economy of the Hudson River Valley to 1800," *AANYLH* 11 (1987): 25–51; Williams-Myers, "The African Presence in the Hudson River Valley," esp. 81, 88, 95; Carl Nordstrom, "Slavery in a New York County: Rockland County 1686–1827," *AANYLH* 1 (1977): 145–66; Groth, "Forging Freedom in the Mid-Hudson Valley," 6, 10–11, 31–34, 46–49, 54; Editor's Note, Baltus Van Kleek to Pierre Van Cortlandt, June 13, 1756, James Vaile to Pierre Van Cortlandt, Oct. 31, 1760, and Thomas Stilwell to Pierre Van Cortlandt, May 11, 1770, *Van Cortlandt Family Papers,* vol. 4, *Correspondence of the Van Cortlandt Family of Cortlandt Manor, 1815–1848,* ed. Jacob Judd (Tarrytown, N.Y., 1981), 433, 436–37, 438; McManus, *Negro Slavery,* 46–48; Anne Grant, *Memoirs of an American Lady with Sketches of Manners and Scenes in America Previous to the Revolution* (1808; New York, 1901), 1:265–66, 2:115; Foote, "Black Life," 2–4, 25–28; see also Edward Francis Countryman, "Legislative Government in Revolutionary New York, 1777–1788" (Ph.D. diss, Cornell University, 1971), 106–9 for a sociological tour of New York; and Kammen, *Colonial New York,* 58, 67–69, 112–17, 121, 124–25, 127, 179, for background on these various issues.

18. Davis, "New York's Long Black Line," 45–46, 48–51; Thomas J. Davis, "Three Dark Centuries Around Albany: A Survey of Black Life in New York's Capital City Area Before World War I," *AANYLH* 7 (1983): 8–9; White, *Somewhat More Independent,* 17; Groth, "Forging Freedom in the Mid-Hudson Valley," 37–39; see also Thomas S. Wermuth, *Rip Van Winkle's*

Neighbors: The Transformation of Rural Society in the Hudson River Valley, 1720–1850 (Albany, 2001), although Wermuth's study has surprisingly little to say about slavery.

19. Foote, *Black and White Manhattan,* 147–56, and on Manhattan slave demography, 69–70, 79–88; White, *Somewhat More Independent,* 88–89, 91, 95; Williams-Myers, "The African Presence in the Hudson River Valley," esp. 81, 85–87, 91; Moss, *Slavery on Long Island,* 72; Groth, "Forging Freedom in the Mid-Hudson Valley," 43–46; J. Hector St. John de Crèvecoeur, *Letters from an American Farmer* (New York, 1912), 163–64.

20. Henry Lloyd II to John Lloyd II, Aug. 15, Oct. 10, Dec. 28, 1767, July 29, 1769; James Lloyd II to John Lloyd II, July 31, 1769; Henry Lloyd II to John Lloyd II, July 29, 1769; John Lloyd II to Henry Lloyd II, Aug. 17, 1769; James Lloyd II to John Lloyd II, Sept. 24, 1770; Henry Lloyd II to Joseph Lloyd II, Oct. 1, 1770 [quotation]; Henry Lloyd II to Joseph Lloyd II, Sept. 5, 1772, *Lloyd Family,* 2:707–9, 716–17, 718–19, 722–23, 732, 735, 746, and n. 8 above; see also Foote, "Black Life," 150–51, 153, 157–58, 324; McManus, *Negro Slavery,* 81–82; Groth, "Forging Freedom in the Mid-Hudson Valley," 78–79.

21. Grant, *Memoirs of an American Lady,* 1:78–87, 264–70; Henry Lloyd II to John Lloyd II, June 4, Sept. 13, 1773 [quotation], *Lloyd Family,* 2: 735, 746. For additional related material on discipline and master-slave relations, see Foote, *Black and White Manhattan,* 147–56; Williams-Myers, "The African Presence in the Hudson River Valley," 83–84, 91–92; McManus, *Negro Slavery,* 94–95; Williams-Myers, "The African Presence in the Mid-Hudson Valley," 36. See also White, *Somewhat More Independent,* 88.

22. Hodges, *Pretends to Be Free,* xiii–xxxv; Graham Russell Hodges, "Black Revolt in New York City and the Neutral Zone: 1775–1783," in *New York in the Age of the Constitution, 1775–1800,* ed. Paul A. Gilje and William Pencak (Rutherford, N.J., 1992), 26; McManus, *Negro Slavery,* 101–19; White, *Somewhat More Independent,* 114–49; Foote, *Black and White Manhattan,* 189–98; Groth, "Forging Freedom in the Mid-Hudson Valley," 92; Kammen, *Colonial New York,* 285.

23. Hodges, *Pretends to Be Free,* 44, 46, 51 (*New-York Gazette,* Nov. 6, 1752, June 18, 1753, Mar. 3, 1755), appendix 1, tables 1, 2, 5, 6, 7–9; see also David Waldstreicher, "Reading the Runaways: Self-Fashioning, Print Culture, and Confidence in Slavery in the Eighteenth-Century Mid-Atlantic," *WMQ,* 3d ser., 56 (1999): 243–72; Hodges, *Root and Branch,* 130–33.

24. Jordan, *White over Black,* 115–16; Foote, *Black and White Manhattan,* 132–37; Hodges, *Root and Branch,* 65; McManus, *Negro Slavery,* 121–26; Kammen, *Colonial New York,* 225.

25. Hoffer, *Great New York Conspiracy,* makes a strong case for the existence of a conspiracy but is careful to draw boundaries around its extent and ideological impetus. Thomas J. Davis, in his introduction to *The New York Conspiracy* by Daniel Horsmanden (Boston, 1971), vii–xx, offers a valuable analysis of the challenges posed by the trial transcript and the conspiracy it appeared to document. For other arguments about whether a conspiracy actually existed in 1741, see Wallace and Burrows, *Gotham,* 159–66, who are skeptical, and Hodges, *Root and Branch,* 88–99, and Harris, *In the Shadow of Slavery,* 43–46, who are not. Foote, *Black and White Manhattan,* 159–86, offers a fascinating interpretation of the legal proceedings and the cultural context surrounding the "plot" which grants almost no credence to the possibility of an actual conspiracy; see also Thomas J. Davis, *A Rumor of Revolt: The "Great Negro Plot" in Colonial New York* (New York, 1985); and Jordan, *White over Black,* 116–20; Horton and Horton, *In Hope of Liberty,* 46–47; McManus, *Negro Slavery,* 87–91, 126–40; Kammen, *Colonial New York,* 120, 283–86.

26. Williams-Myers, "The African Presence in the Hudson River Valley"; Williams-Myers, "The African Presence in the Mid-Hudson Valley Before 1800," 33–34; and Foote, *Black and White Manhattan*, make a sustained case for the role of race in the construction of European identities and the maintenance of political order in colonial New York City.

27. McManus, *Negro Slavery*, 67–78; Foote, *Black and White Manhattan*, 47–49, 125–31, 140–47; see also Kammen, *Colonial New York*, 60, on the low incidence of Christian conversion to the Dutch Reformed Church by blacks in the seventeenth century. For opposing viewpoints on the timing of the African American–dominated Pinkster celebration, see A. J. Williams-Myers, "Pinkster Carnival: Africanisms in the Hudson River Valley," *AANYLH* 9 (1985): 7–17; and White, *Somewhat More Independent*, 95–106; see also Shane White, "Pinkster in Albany, 1803: A Contemporary Description," *New York History* 70 (1989): 191–99; Sterling Stuckey, *Slave Culture: Nationalist Theory and the Foundations of Black America* (New York, 1987), 80–82, 141–42; Horton and Horton, *In Hope of Liberty*, 30–32.

28. Hodges, *Root and Branch*, 47–53, 84–88, 115–17; Harris, *In the Shadow of Slavery*; Shane White and Graham White, *Stylin': African American Expressive Culture from Its Beginnings to the Zoot Suit* (Ithaca, N.Y., 1998), 5–36; Craig Steven Wilder, *In the Company of Black Men: The African Influence on African-American Culture in New York City* (New York, 2001), 9–35; Foote, *Black and White Manhattan*, 141–45.

29. Harris, *In the Shadow of Slavery*, 46–47; Davis, *A Rumor of Revolt*, 31–32, 44.

NOTES TO CHAPTER 2

1. J. Hector St. John de Crèvecoeur, *Letters from an American Farmer* (New York, 1912), 43–45, 19; Winthrop D. Jordan, *White over Black: American Attitudes toward the Negro, 1550–1812* (1968; New York, 1977), 340–41.

2. Crèvecoeur, *American Farmer*, 23; this passage from Crèvecoeur also excerpted in *NYP*, June 10, 1784.

3. Thomas Philbrick, *St. John de Crèvecoeur* (New York, 1971), 18–31.

4. Shane White, *Somewhat More Independent: The End of Slavery in New York City, 1770–1810* (Athens, Ga., 1991), 56.

5. David Brion Davis, *The Problem of Slavery in Western Culture* (1966; New York, 1988), 445.

6. Davis, *Western Culture*, 291–332.

7. Michael Kammen, *Colonial New York: A History* (New York, 1975), 155–56.

8. Kammen, *Colonial New York*, 60, 86, 118, 154, 239–40; Edwin G. Burrows and Mike Wallace, *Gotham: A History of New York City to 1898* (New York, 1999), 94; on Quaker slaveholding and antislavery in nearby New Jersey, see Graham Russell Hodges, *Slavery and Freedom in the Rural North: African Americans in Monmouth County, New Jersey, 1665–1865* (Madison, Wisc., 1997), 30, 71–75, 91–92.

9. Davis, *Western Culture*, 291–332, 483–91; David Brion Davis, *The Problem of Slavery in the Age of Revolution, 1770–1823* (Ithaca, N.Y., 1975), 213–54; Robert Duane Sayre, "The Evolution of Early American Abolition: The American Convention for Promoting the Abolition of Slavery and Improving the Condition of the African Race, 1794–1837" (Ph.D. diss., Ohio State University, 1987), 335–47; Arthur Zilversmit, *The First Emancipation: The Abolition of Slavery in the North* (Chicago, 1967), 55–93, 106–8; John Cox Jr., *Quakerism in*

the City of New York, 1657–1930 (New York, 1930), 55–58; Jordan, *White over Black,* 194–97, 271–75.

10. Yearly Meeting, 1746–1800, Archives of New York Yearly Meeting—Religious Society of Friends, Haviland Records Room, New York City; see entries for the years 1767, 1768, and 1771, on pages 55–58, 63–64; and Cox, *Quakerism,* 58–59. On the role of Dutchess County Quakers in encouraging attention to slavery in the yearly meeting, as well as the particulars of eliminating slavery among Dutchess County Friends, see Michael Edward Groth, "Forging Freedom in the Mid-Hudson Valley: The End of Slavery and the Formation of a Free African-American Community in Dutchess County, New York, 1770–1850" (Ph.D. diss., Binghamton University, 1994), 64–76.

11. Yearly Meeting, 1746–1800, Archives of New York Yearly Meeting; see entries for 1772, 1774–77, and 1781–83, on pages, 68, 73, 76, 79, 81, 82, 84–86, 88, 90, 91, 94, 129–30, 132–34, 149–52, 170–71 (quotations, 85, 133). For other accounts of the New York Yearly Meeting's handling of slavery, see Zilversmit, *First Emancipation,* 80–81; Jordan, *White over Black,* 357; and Cox, *Quakerism,* 59–60.

12. Davis, *Age of Revolution,* 213–54, esp. 216–17, 238–39; Cox, *Quakerism,* 60–64.

13. Davis, *Western Culture,* 118–21, 402–3, 412; Davis, *Age of Revolution,* 45, 168, 261, 263, 264, 488, 489, 559, 560; Jordan, *White over Black,* 287–94, 308–10, 350–52, 440; Jay Fliegelman, *Prodigals and Pilgrims: The American Revolution Against Patriarchal Authority, 1750–1800* (New York, 1982); Wayne Glausser, "Three Approaches to Locke and the Slave Trade," *Journal of the History of Ideas* 51 (1990): 199–216; Ari Helo and Peter Onuf, "Jefferson, Morality, and the Problem of Slavery," *WMQ,* 3d ser., 60 (2003): 589–93; and Edward Francis Countryman, "Legislative Government in Revolutionary New York, 1777–1788" (Ph.D. diss., Cornell University, 1971), 32.

14. For the Scottish intellectual influence on Hamilton, see Stanley Elkins and Eric McKitrick, *The Age of Federalism: The Early American Republic, 1788–1800* (New York, 1993), 83–87, 94–100, 102, 105–13; a recent forum on "The Madisonian Moment" in *WMQ,* 3d ser., 59 (2002): 865–956, extends and refines the ongoing scholarly conversation regarding the Scottish influence on American political thought.

15. David Hume, "Of Polygamy and Divorces," and "Of the Populousness of Ancient Nations," in *Essays Moral, Political and Literary,* ed. Eugene F. Miller (Indianapolis, 1987), 185, 383–84; on race, see Hume, "Of National Character," 207–8, 214–15, and "Of Commerce," 266–67. For Hume's thoughts on race, including their subsequent value to defenders of slavery, see also Jordan, *White over Black,* 253–54, 305, 307, 446, 450; Davis, *Western Culture,* 457–58, and *Age of Revolution,* 540; for hints of Smith's racial bias, see Adam Smith, *An Inquiry Into the Nature and Causes of the Wealth of Nations,* ed. Edwin Cannan (New York, 1937), 459, 599–600, 729.

16. Hume, "Of the Rise and Progress of the Arts and Sciences," 118, 124; "Of Refinement in the Arts," 270–80; "Of Commerce," 254–67, esp. 262–65; "Of Civil Liberty," 95, *Essays Moral, Political and Literary,* ed. Eugene F. Miller (Indianapolis, 1987); Smith, *Wealth of Nations,* 80–86, 363–66, 523–56, 648, 651; and "Extracts from Dr. Adam Smith, on 'The Wealth of Nations,' relative to the History of Slavery in Europe--of its Abolition in several Nations thereof; and Remarks on the Impolicy and Disadvantages of its Continuance both to Individuals and the State," *NYM,* Apr. 1793, 235–37; Elkins and McKitrick, *Age of Federalism,* 107–12; Davis, *Age of Revolution,* 266, 294 n., 347, 351–56.

17. Hume, "Of the Populousness of Ancient Nations," 397–464; on Hume, Smith, related Enlightenment thought, and its influence, see Davis, *Western Culture*, 417, 422–38, 485–86.

18. Leslie M. Harris, *In the Shadow of Slavery: African Americans in New York City, 1626–1863* (Chicago, 2003), 47; Graham Russell Hodges, *Root and Branch: African Americans in New York and East Jersey* (Chapel Hill, N.C., 1999), 122–28; Thelma Wills Foote, *Black and White Manhattan: The History of Racial Formation in Colonial New York City* (New York, 2004), 146–47; James Oliver Horton and Lois E. Horton, *In Hope of Liberty: Culture, Community and Protest Among Northern Free Blacks, 1700–1860* (New York, 1997), 42–43, 130; Albert J. Raboteau, *Slave Religion: The "Invisible Institution" in the Antebellum South* (New York, 1978), 128–29.

19. Davis, *Age of Revolution*, 287–99.

20. John Jea, *The Life, History, and Unparalleled Sufferings of John Jea, African Preacher,* republished in *Black Itinerants of the Gospel: The Narratives of John Jea and George White,* ed. Graham Russell Hodges (Madison, Wisc., 1993), 92. Jea was born in Africa in 1773 and brought to America as a slave when quite young; it is unclear precisely when this event occurred and is used here for its symbolic importance.

21. "Address to the People of Great Britain," Sept. 5, 1774, *The Correspondence and Public Papers of John Jay,* ed. Henry P. Johnston (New York, 1890), 1:17–31 (quotations, 18); John Jay to Susanna Philipse Robinson, Mar. 21, 1777, *John Jay: The Making of a Revolutionary, Unpublished Papers 1745–1780,* ed. Richard B. Morris (New York, 1975), 352–54; see also Letter from Congress to the "Oppressed Inhabitants of Canada," July 6, 1775, *Public Papers of John Jay,* 1:33–36.

22. Patricia Bradley, *Slavery, Propaganda, and the American Revolution* (Jackson, Miss., 1998).

23. James Otis, *The Rights of the British Colonies Asserted and Proved* (Boston, 1764), quoted in Jordan, *White over Black,* 292; [Richard Wells], *A Few Political Reflections . . .* (Philadelphia, 1774), 79–80, quoted in Bernard Bailyn, *The Ideological Origins of the American Revolution* (Cambridge, Mass., 1967), 239.

24. Horton and Horton, *In Hope of Liberty,* 55; Joanne Pope Melish, *Disowning Slavery: Gradual Emancipation and "Race" in New England, 1780–1860* (Ithaca, N.Y., 1998), 80; Dickson D. Bruce Jr., *The Origins of African American Literature, 1680–1865* (Charlottesville, Va., 2001), 40–61; Wheatley quotation, 45.

25. "A Dialogue; entitled, The Kind Master and the Dutiful Servant," in Stanley Austin Ransom Jr., ed., *America's First Negro Poet: The Complete Works of Jupiter Hammon of Long Island* (Port Washington, N.Y., 1970), 58–64. Hammon's work is explored further in chap. 6; see also Bruce, *Origins of African American Literature,* 51–52.

26. Ira Berlin, *Many Thousands Gone: The First Two Centuries of Slavery in North America* (Cambridge, Mass., 1998), 175.

27. Bailyn, *Ideological Origins,* 230–46; Pauline Maier, *American Scripture: Making the Declaration of Independence* (New York, 1997), 123–36, 146–47, 191–201; Jay Fliegelman, *Declaring Independence: Jefferson, Natural Language, and the Culture of Performance* (Stanford, 1993) 206, 79, 141–42; Jordan, *White over Black,* 290, 301, 362, 431, 453; Helo and Onuf, "Jefferson, Morality, and Slavery," 586–88, 591.

28. *The Constitution of the State of New-York* (Philadelphia, 1777), 7–12.

29. On Morris, see Leonard L. Richards, *The Slave Power: The Free North and Southern*

Domination, 1780–1860 (Baton Rouge, 2000), 28–31; Max M. Mintz, *Gouverneur Morris and the American Revolution* (Norman, Okla., 1970), vii–viii, 7, 14–15; Mary-Jo Kline, *Gouverneur Morris and the New Nation, 1775–1788* (1971; New York, 1978); Richard Brookhiser, *Gentleman Revolutionary: Gouverneur Morris—The Rake Who Wrote the Constitution* (New York, 2003), 3, 34; William Howard Adams, *Gouverneur Morris: An Independent Life* (New Haven, 2003), 4, 8–9.

30. *Journals of the Provincial Congress, Provincial Convention, Committee of Safety and Council of Safety of the State of New-York. 1775–1776–1777* (Albany, 1842), 1:887, 889, 897; Mintz, *Gouverneur Morris*, 76; *John Jay . . . Unpublished Papers, 1745–1780*, 402 n.; Zilversmit, *First Emancipation*, 139–40; John Jay to Robert R. Livingston and Gouverneur Morris, Apr. 29, 1777, *Papers of John Jay*, 1:136.

31. Michael A. Bellesiles, *Revolutionary Outlaws: Ethan Allen and the Struggle for Independence on the Early American Frontier* (Charlottesville, Va., 1993), 137–40, 160–62, 172; Melish, *Disowning Slavery*, 64; Zilversmit, *First Emancipation*, 116; Alfred F. Young, *The Democratic Republicans of New York: The Origins, 1763–1797* (Chapel Hill, N.C., 1967), 17–22.

32. Gary Nash and Jean Soderlund, *Freedom by Degrees: Emancipation in Pennsylvania and Its Aftermath* (New York, 1991), 3–136; Richard S. Newman, *The Transformation of American Abolitionism: Fighting Slavery in the Early Republic* (Chapel Hill, N.C., 2002).

33. Graham Russell Hodges, "Black Revolt in New York City and the Neutral Zone: 1775–1783," in *New York in the Age of the Constitution, 1775–1800*, ed. Paul A. Gilje and William Pencak (Rutherford, N.J., 1992), 21–40, esp. 27; James W. St. G. Walker, "Blacks as American Loyalists: The Slaves' War for Independence," *Historical Reflections/Reflections Historiques* 2 (1975): 51–67, esp. 53, 57, 66–67; Foote, *Black and White Manhattan*, 210–26; on slave resistance in Revolutionary-era Dutchess County, see Groth, "Forging Freedom in the Mid-Hudson Valley," 82–94.

34. Hodges, *Root and Branch*, 148.

35. *New-York Gazette: and the Weekly Mercury*, Mar. 6, 1775; see also *Rivington's New-York Gazetteer*, Mar. 2, 1775; Williams-Myers, "The African Presence in the Hudson River Valley: The Defining of Relationships Between the Masters and the Slaves," *AANYLH* 12 (1988): 84, 93; Edward Countryman, *A People in Revolution: The American Revolution and Political Society in New York, 1760–1790* (Baltimore, 1981), 171.

36. Cornelia Beekman to Pierre Van Cortlandt, Apr. 12, 1777, *Van Cortlandt Family Papers*, vol. 2, *Correspondence of the Van Cortlandt Family of Cortlandt Manor, 1748-1800*, ed. Jacob Judd (Tarrytown, N.Y., 1977), 184–86; Mary Clinton to her husband, Sept. 10, 1778, Letters, Museum of the City of New York; Peter Jay to John Jay and Sir James Jay, Sept. 22, 1779, *John Jay . . . Unpublished Papers, 1745–1780*, 642–43; Frederick Jay to John Jay, Apr. 10, 1781, Nov. 18, 1781; Estate of Peter Jay, May 27, 1782; John Jay to Robert R. Livingston, Aug. 13, 1782, *John Jay: The Winning of the Peace, Unpublished Papers 1780–1784*, ed. Richard B. Morris (New York, 1980), 183, 201–2, 211, 318; White, *Somewhat More Independent*, 122, 130–31, 142–43; Vivienne L. Kruger, "Born to Run: The Slave Family in Early New York, 1626–1827" (Ph.D. diss., Columbia University, 1985), 652–53; Graham Russell Hodges, ed., *"Pretends to Be Free": Runaway Slaves from Colonial and Revolutionary New York and New Jersey* (New York, 1994), xxxii–xxxiii; Graham Russell Hodges, ed., *The Black Loyalist Directory: African Americans in Exile After the American Revolution* (New York, 1996), xiv; Hodges, "Black Revolt in New York City," 28, 33–34; Williams-Myers, "The African Presence in the Hudson River Valley,"

91; Foote, *Black and White Manhattan*, 211–15; Ira Berlin, "The Revolution in Black Life," in *The American Revolution: Explorations in American Radicalism*, ed. Alfred F. Young (De Kalb, Ill., 1976), 355; Countryman, "Legislative Government in Revolutionary New York," 142–43.

37. Hodges, *Pretends to Be Free*, 234 (from *The Royal Gazette*, Aug. 19, 1780).

38. Sir Henry Clinton, June 3, 1800, quoted in Walker, "Blacks as American Loyalists," 54, see also 56, 57; Hodges, "Black Revolt in New York City," 27–38; Arnett G. Lindsay, "Diplomatic Relations Between the United States and Great Britain Bearing on the Return of Negro Slaves, 1783–1828," *JNH* 5 (1920): 392–93; Foote, *Black and White Manhattan*, 212–16; Berlin, "Revolution in Black Life," 353–54; Hodges, *Root and Branch*, 147–52; Thomas Jones, *History of New York during the Revolutionary War*, ed. Edward Floyd DeLancey (1879; reprint, New York, 1968), 1:334, 2:76, 84–85.

39. Judith L. Van Buskirk, *Generous Enemies: Patriots and Loyalists in Revolutionary New York* (Philadelphia, 2002), 150–53; Hodges, *Root and Branch*, 150–51.

40. "An Act for raising two Regiments for the Defence of this State, on Bounties of unappropriated Lands," Mar. 20, 1781, in *Laws of the State of New-York* (New York, 1792), 1:42; Solomon Close, Writ, Aug. 26, 1777, Miscellaneous Manuscripts, Hawley (photostat), New-York Historical Society, New York City; Hodges, "Black Revolt in New York City"; Hodges, *Black Loyalist Directory*, xiii, xx, approximates that "over five thousand black New Yorkers changed allegiances" during the course of the war; Foote, *Black and White Manhattan*, 215–16; Walker, "Blacks as American Loyalists," 52, 55; Berlin, "Revolution in Black Life," 353–55; Hodges, *Pretends to be Free*, xxxiii, xxxiv.

41. Hodges, "Black Revolt in New York City," 36; Jordan, *White over Black*, 302–3; Lindsay, "Diplomatic Relations," 393–94; Elkins and McKitrick, *Age of Federalism*, 99; Walker, "Blacks as American Loyalists," 51–67, esp. 53; Hodges, *Pretends to be Free*, xxxiii, xxxiv; Hodges, *Black Loyalist Directory*, xiv–xv; Berlin, "Revolution in Black Life," 353–55. To follow New Yorker Alexander Hamilton's advice to George Washington on the advantages of employing southern blacks in the war effort, see To the Committee of Congress with the Army, Jan. 29, 1778, *The Writings of George Washington*, ed. John C. Fitzpatrick (Washington, D.C., 1933), 10:401; Hamilton to John Jay, Mar. 14, 1779, *The Papers of Alexander Hamilton*, ed. Harold C. Syrett (New York, 1961), 1:421 n., 2:18–19; see also Hamilton to John Laurens, May 22, 1779; Laurens to Hamilton, July 14, 1779; Hamilton to Laurens, Sept. 11, 1779, *The Papers of Alexander Hamilton*, 2:35, 52, 102–3, 166–67; Laurens to Hamilton, July 1782, *The Papers of Alexander Hamilton*, ed. Harold C. Syrett (New York, 1962), 3:121.

42. Preliminary Articles of Peace, Article 7, Paris, Nov. 30, 1782, *John Jay . . . Unpublished Papers 1780–1784*, 435 (see also Richard Oswald to Thomas Townshend, Nov. 15, 1782, 420–21); Hodges, *Black Loyalist Directory*, xiv, xi; Lindsay, "Diplomatic Relations," 392, 394–95; Book of Negroes, 1, British Headquarters Papers, box 43, doc. 10427, Manuscript Division, New York Public Library, New York City; *NYP*, July 15, 1784; Walker, "Blacks as American Loyalists," 61–62; Foote, *Black and White Manhattan*, 217–19.

43. Van Buskirk, *Generous Enemies*, 172.

44. Book of Negroes, 47, 2–14, 16, 83, 142–43, British Headquarters Papers, box 43, doc. 10427; Hodges, *Black Loyalist Directory*, xvi–xix; Jones, *History of New York during the Revolutionary War*, 2:255–57; *NYP*, Sept. 9, 1784; Lindsay, "Diplomatic Relations," 395–400; Davis, "New York's Long Black Line," 56; Buskirk, *Generous Enemies*, 174–75; Walker, "Blacks as American Loyalists," 59–64; Foote, *Black and White Manhattan*, 221–26.

45. Hodges, *Black Loyalist Directory*, xxxix, 217–23; Hodges, *Pretends to Be Free*, xxxii;

Walker, "Blacks as American Loyalists," 66–67; Foote, *Black and White Manhattan,* 217–19, 221, 226; see also Kruger, "Born to Run," 654–75, for an analysis of blacks departing with the British.

46. *NYP,* Aug. 16, 1784; Van Buskirk, *Generous Enemies,* 154.

47. For a variety of perspectives regarding the Revolution's impact on slavery in New York see Foote, "Black Life," 376, 378; White, *Somewhat More Independent,* 4, 22, 27, 54; Hodges, "Black Revolt in New York City," 39–40; Kruger, "Born to Run," 636, 690–91; and Groth, "Forging Freedom in the Mid-Hudson Valley," 4, 58, 60–61, 94.

48. John Jay to Egbert Benson, Sept. 17, 1780, *Public Papers of John Jay,* 1 : 407; *New York Independent Journal,* Dec. 22, 1784 (essentially the same report of the facts of this Connecticut freedom case can be found in *NYP,* Dec. 23, 1784); on black patriot veterans, see also Walker, "Blacks as American Loyalists," 55; and Berlin, "Revolution in Black Life," 355.

49. [Samuel Hopkins], *A Dialogue Concerning the Slavery of the Africans . . .* (1776; reprint, with proceedings of the New York Manumission Society and an Appendix, New York, 1785), 8–10, 36–38, 63–64, 69–71; *NYJ,* Mar. 10, 1785; see also Davis, *Age of Revolution,* 294–95.

50. *NYP,* Dec. 29, 1786; Davis, "New York's Long Black Line," 55–57; Kruger, "Born to Run," 642–43, 688–89; Carl Nordstrom, "Slavery in a New York County: Rockland County 1686–1827," *AANYLH* 1 (1977): 150–52, 159; White, *Somewhat More Independent,* 3–55, esp. 22–23, 27, 54; McManus, *Negro Slavery,* 200; A. J. Williams-Myers, "The African Presence in the Mid-Hudson River Valley Before 1800: A Preliminary Historiographic Sketch," *AANYLH* 8 (1984): 35.

51. On free blacks in New York City, see White, *Somewhat More Independent,* 150–84; on free blacks and post-Revolution African American society throughout the nation, see Berlin, "Revolution in Black Life," 361–77; see also Gary B. Nash, "Forging Freedom: The Emancipation Experience in Northern Seaport Cities," in *Slavery and Freedom in the Age of the American Revolution,* ed. Ira Berlin and Ronald Hoffman (Charlottesville, Va., 1983), 3–48.

52. For the demographic information in this and the previous paragraph, see White, *Somewhat More Independent,* 3–113, esp. 17, on slaveholding patterns in various New York counties; see also Nordstrom, "Rockland County," 159, 164. Carl Nordstrom, "The New York Slave Code," *AANYLH* 4 (1980): 17; Williams-Myers, "The African Presence in the Mid-Hudson Valley," 35–36; Williams-Myers, "The African Presence in the Hudson River Valley," and "Hands that Picked No Cotton," suggests an essential continuity in the nature of New York slavery throughout the eighteenth century.

53. Crèvecoeur, *American Farmer,* 60, 45.

NOTES TO CHAPTER 3

1. *NYP,* Mar. 11, 1784; *Minutes of the Common Council of the City of New York, 1784–1831* (New York, 1917), Mar. 2, 23, Sept. 1, 1784, 1 : 11, 16–17, 68; *NYJ,* Apr. 15, 1784.

2. Judith L. Van Buskirk, *Generous Enemies: Patriots and Loyalists in Revolutionary New York* (Philadelphia, 2002), 154.

3. *Minutes of the Common Council,* Mar. 2, 1784, 1 : 11; see *NYP,* Mar. 8, 11, 18, 1784 for published texts of such laws. On New York City municipal regulations of the era, see also Paul A. Gilje and Howard B. Rock, "'Sweep O! Sweep O!': African-American Chimney Sweeps and Citizenship in the New Nation," *WMQ,* 3d. ser., 51 (1994): 507, 513–14.

4. It is difficult to produce precise population statistics for New York in this era, as Shane White discusses in "A Note to the Reader," in *Somewhat More Independent: The End of Slavery in New York City, 1770–1810* (Athens, Ga., 1991), xxv–xxvi. Edgar J. McManus, *A History of Negro Slavery in New York* (Syracuse, N.Y., 1966), 200, apparently relies on the state census of 1786 (see *NYP*, Dec. 29, 1786, and *CJPA*, Jan. 10, 1787), which indicates a New York County population approximately 8.9% black. According to McManus's figure, that proportion grew to approximately 10.5% in 1790, while White more recently has retabulated the census to arrive at 9.9% (p. 26).

5. *NYP*, Mar. 8, Apr. 8, May 3, 1784; see also on the state-government level, "An Act to lay a Duty of Excise on strong Liquors, and for the better regulating of Inns and Taverns," Mar. 1, 1788, *Laws of the State of New-York* 11 (New York, 1788), 104–5; "An Act for the more effectual Prevention of Fires in the City of New-York," Apr. 22, 1786, *Laws of the State of New-York* 9 (New York, 1786), 88–89 (*NYP*, May 8, 1786).

6. *Minutes of the Common Council*, Mar. 2, 23, Sept. 1, 1784, 1 : 11, 16–17, 68 (quotation); *NYP*, Mar. 11, 1784; Peter Charles Hoffer, *The Great New York Conspiracy of 1741* (Lawrence, Kans., 2003), 20–28, 30–32.

7. *NYP*, Mar. 25, 1784.

8. On the particular features of the law of citizenship in New York City during the period, including its political and economic qualities, see *The Burghers of New Amsterdam and the Freemen of New York, 1675–1866*, Collections of the New-York Historical Society, vol. 18 (New York, 1886), ix, 239–40, 274–75; and Graham R. Hodges, "Legal Bonds of Attachment: The Freemanship Law of New York City, 1648–1801," in *Authority and Resistance in Early New York*, ed. William Pencak and Conrad Edick Wright (New York, 1988), 226–44; and Robert Francis Seybolt, *The Colonial Citizen of New York City* (Madison, Wisc., 1918).

9. *NYJ*, Nov. 25, 1784.

10. *Journal of the Senate of the State of New-York* 7 (New York, 1784), Feb. 24, Mar. 2, 9, 1784, 38, 45, 54; Arthur Zilversmit, *The First Emancipation: The Abolition of Slavery in the North* (Chicago, 1967), 147.

11. *Journal of the Assembly of the State of New-York* 8, pt. 2 (New York, 1785), Feb. 22–23, 25–26, 1785, 48, 49, 53–55; *Journal of the Senate* 8, pt. 2 (New York, 1785), Feb. 4, 12, 16–18, 21, 1785, 8, 15, 20–23.

12. Joanne Pope Melish, *Disowning Slavery: Gradual Emancipation and "Race" in New England, 1780–1860* (Ithaca, N.Y., 1998), 68.

13. *Journal of the Assembly*, Feb. 25, 1785, 53. On the lack of support for immediate abolition more generally, see Winthrop D. Jordan, *White over Black: American Attitudes toward the Negro, 1550–1812* (1968; New York, 1977), 354, and David Brion Davis, "The Emergence of Immediatism in British and American Antislavery Thought," *Mississippi Valley Historical Review* 49 (1962): 209–30.

14. *Journal of the Assembly*, Feb. 26, 1785, 55–56; Carl Nordstrom, "The New York Slave Code," *AANYLH* 4 (1980): 19.

15. *NYP*, Jan. 24, 1785; on the 1780 Pennsylvania Gradual Abolition Act, see Gary B. Nash, *Forging Freedom: The Formation of the Philadelphia Black Community, 1720–1840* (Cambridge, Mass., 1988), 60–63; Gary B. Nash and Jean R. Soderlund, *Freedom by Degrees: Emancipation in Pennsylvania and Its Aftermath* (New York, 1991), 111–13. On Levi Hart and New England, see Melish, *Disowning Slavery*, 57–76; in analyzing gradual abolition laws in Con-

necticut and Rhode Island, Melish emphasizes the pragmatic, rather than the idealistic goals of the legislation.

16. *Journal of the Assembly,* Mar. 1, 2, 9, 1785, 62–64, 76; *Journal of the Senate,* Mar. 8, 1785, 39.

17. *Journal of the Assembly,* Mar. 9, 1785, 77; see Leslie M. Harris, *In the Shadow of Slavery: African Americans in New York City, 1626–1863* (Chicago, 2003), 58–59, and 148, 171–72, 191–94, 195–98 on the emergence, well into the nineteenth century, of more serious concerns over miscegenation in New York.

18. *Journal of the Senate,* Mar. 11, 12, 1785, 42, 45; *Journal of the Assembly,* Mar. 12, 1785, 86.

19. The Council of Revision, a constitutional innovation of Livingston's, included the governor and, at minimum, two supreme court justices or the chancellor and one justice; see Alfred B. Street, *The Council of Revision of the State of New York; Its History, A History of the Courts with which its Members Were Connected; Biographical Sketches of Its Members; and its Vetoes* (Albany, 1859), 5–7, 268–69; George Dangerfield, *Chancellor Robert R. Livingston of New York* (New York, 1960), 90, 451. For other accounts of the fate of gradual abolition in 1785, see Zilversmit, *First Emancipation,* 148–49; McManus, *Negro Slavery,* 162–65; Edgar J. McManus, "Antislavery Legislation in New York," *JNH* 46 (1961): 208–10; Edgar J. McManus, *Black Bondage in the North* (Syracuse, N.Y., 1973), 170–72; Harris, *In the Shadow of Slavery,* 59–61; see also Nordstrom, "Slave Code," 17–18; and Jordan, *White over Black,* 413.

20. *The Constitution of the State of New-York* (Philadelphia, 1777), esp. 16–21; Alfred F. Young, *The Democratic Republicans of New York: The Origins, 1763–1797* (Chapel Hill, N.C., 1967), 18–19, 84–85; David N. Gellman and David Quigley, eds., *Jim Crow New York: A Documentary History of Race and Citizenship, 1777–1877* (New York, 2003), 25–35.

21. *Journal of the Assembly,* Mar. 26, 1785, 119–20.

22. *Journal of the Assembly,* Mar. 26, 1785, 120; *Journal of the Senate,* Mar. 23, 1785, 55–56; Zilversmit, *First Emancipation,* 149.

23. Zilversmit, *First Emancipation,* 150; McManus, "Antislavery," 210; McManus, *Negro Slavery,* 166; Nordstrom, "Slave Code," 18; White, *Somewhat More Independent,* 85; *Journal of the Senate,* Mar. 31, Apr. 1, 2, 1785, 66, 68; *Journal of the Assembly,* Mar. 20, Apr. 7, 12, 1785, 126, 128, 142, 153.

24. "An Act granting a Bounty on Hemp to be raised within this State, and imposing an additional Duty on sundry Articles of Merchandize, and for other Purposes therein mentioned," Apr. 12, 1785, *Laws of the State of New-York* 8 (New York, 1785), 61–63; *NYP,* Nov. 28, 1785, and *NYJ,* Dec. 1, 1785, published by request the sections of this law relevant to slavery; Nordstrom, "Slave Code," 14–18, reviews the history of New York law governing manumission.

25. *NYP,* Mar. 28, 1785. This letter, although penned shortly before the council's veto and the failed override, was published after the override; Gracchus's next letter, condemning the exploitation of immigrants, appeared in the same paper on April 18, 1785. On the original Gracchus, see H. H. Scullard, *From the Gracchi to Nero: A History of Rome 133 BC to AD 68,* 5th ed. (New York, 1982), 7–8, 22–29. Gracchus and many of his adherents subsequently suffered violent deaths at the hands of enraged senatorial adversaries. My colleagues in the DePauw University Classics Department provided valuable assistance sorting through this material.

26. *NYP,* Apr. 4, 1785.

27. *NYP,* Mar. 31, 1785.

NOTES TO CHAPTER 4

1. NYMS, May 15, 1792, 6:165.

2. The NYMS, born officially on January 25, 1785, had held only three formal meetings by the time the new regulations governing manumissions and slave importation passed into law. In the midst of consideration of gradual abolition legislation, the state senate received a petition under the signature of John Jay, president of the new organization; see NYMS, Jan. 25, Feb. 4, 10, 1785, 6:1–17; *Journal of the Senate of the State of New-York* 8, 2 (New York, 1785), Feb. 17, 1785, 20; and Arthur Zilversmit, *The First Emancipation: The Abolition of Slavery in the North* (Chicago, 1967), 147–48; see also *NYP*, Feb. 21, 24, 1785.

3. Richard S. Newman, *The Transformation of American Abolitionism: Fighting Slavery in the Early Republic* (Chapel Hill, N.C., 2002), chaps. 1 and 3.

4. For an overview of the organization and its moderate approach, see Thomas Robert Moseley, "A History of the New York Manumission Society, 1785–1849" (Ph.D. diss., New York University, 1963). See also William Jay, *The Life of John Jay with Selections from his Correspondence and Miscellaneous Papers* (New York, 1833), 1:232; Edgar J. McManus, *A History of Negro Slavery in New York* (Syracuse, N.Y., 1966, 168–72; and Dwight L. Dumond, *Antislavery: The Crusade for Freedom in America* (Ann Arbor, 1961), v–125, for the broader context. For historical and scholarly critiques of early abolitionists, see Shane White, *Somewhat More Independent: The End of Slavery in New York City, 1770–1810* (Athens, Ga., 1991), 81–84; Rob N. Weston, "Alexander Hamilton and the Abolition of Slavery in New York," *AANYLH* 18 (1994): 31–45; and Newman, *Transformation of American Abolitionism*, 59.

5. David Brion Davis, *The Problem of Slavery in the Age of Revolution, 1770–1823* (Ithaca, N.Y., 1975), 213–54, esp. 238–42; Zilversmit, *First Emancipation*, 147, 166–67; Moseley, "New York Manumission Society," 27, 45–47, 82–90; Frederick William Pfister, "In the Cause of Freedom: American Abolition Societies, 1775–1808" (Ph.D. diss., Miami University, 1980), 12–16, 136–50; Robert Duane Sayre, "The Evolution of Early American Abolitionism: The American Convention for Promoting the Abolition of Slavery and Improving the Condition of the African Race, 1794–1837" (Ph.D. diss., Ohio State University, 1987), 11–44, 335–47; and Winthrop D. Jordan, *White over Black: American Attitudes toward the Negro, 1550–1812* (1968; New York, 1977), throughout, but esp. 359; see also NYMS, vol. 6; McManus, *Negro Slavery*, 168–69.

6. Yearly Meeting, 1746–1800, Archives of New York Yearly Meeting—Religious Society of Friends, Haviland Records Room, New York City.

7. Thomas Eddy, *Memoir of the Late John Murray, Jun. Read Before the Governors of the New-York Hospital* (New York, 1819); M. J. Heale, "From City Fathers to Social Critics: Humanitarianism and Government in New York, 1790–1860," *JAH* 63 (1976): 21–41.

8. Davis, *Age of Revolution*, 239–40; Weston, "Alexander Hamilton," 34–35; NYMS, Jan.–Nov. 1785, 6: 1–25; Edward P. Alexander, *A Revolutionary Conservative: James Duane of New York* (New York, 1938), esp. 186.

9. Thomas J. Davis, ed., *The New York Conspiracy by Daniel Horsmanden* (Boston, 1971), facsimile of the original appendix; John Jay to Benjamin Rush, Mar. 24, 1785, and John Jay to Dr. Richard Price, Sept. 27, 1785, in *The Correspondence and Public Papers of John Jay*, ed. Henry P. Johnston (New York, 1890–93), 3: 139–40, 168–69.

10. White, *Somewhat More Independent*, 82; Jan Horton, "Listening to Clarinda," a report

prepared for the John Jay Homestead State Historic Site, offers a detailed analysis of Jay's slave-holding practices.

11. NYMS, Feb. 4, 1785, 6:4.

12. White, *Somewhat More Independent*, 81, 86.

13. NYMS, Nov. 1785, 6:29–30.

14. Moseley, "New York Manumission Society," 263; Zilversmit, *First Emancipation*, 166.

15. NYMS, May 12, Aug. 18, 1785, 6:19, 22.

16. Davis, *Age of Revolution*, 213–54.

17. NYMS, Feb. 4, May 17, Nov. 15, 1785, Aug. 28, Sept. 24, 1788, 6:8–13, 66, 77, 114, 116; Granville Sharp to officers of the NYMS, May 1, 1788; Jay to the English Anti-Slavery Society, 1788; Jay to Society at Paris for the Manumission of Slaves, June 1788; Jay to Lafayette, Sept. 1, 1788; Jay to Sharp, Sept. 1, 1788, in *Public Papers of John Jay*, 3:329–32, 340–44, 344–45, 356, 357.

18. Jordan, *White over Black*, 371–74, makes too much of a distinction between the campaigns against the slave trade and domestic slavery.

19. McManus, *Negro Slavery*, 167–68.

20. [David Cooper], *A Letter from °°°°°°°°°, in London, to his Friend in America on the Subject of the Slave-Trade* (New York, 1784), 7, 17.

21. *NYJ*, Feb. 24, 1785; the prophecy's date was perhaps a reference to the vanquishing of Leisler's rebellion by British authorities; *NYP*, Feb. 23, 1786.

22. *NYP*, Apr. 17, 1786; see also *NYP*, Mar. 21, 1784, Mar. 31, 1785, Jan. 9, Mar. 20, 1787.

23. *LFH*, June 1, 1789 (*CJFR*, June 23, 1789); *NCLA*, Sept. 24, 1787; *NYJ*, Dec. 22, 1785.

24. *NYP*, July 4, 1785; NYMS, Aug. 18, 1785, 6:21; Thomas Philbrick, *St. John de Crève-coeur* (New York, 1970), 44–48, doubts that Crèvecoeur actually witnessed this scene.

25. *NYJ*, Mar. 9, 1786, June 22, 1786 (*NYP*, July, 6, 1786); *CJFR*, Mar. 10, 1789; McManus, *Negro Slavery*, 168. Two New York City newspapers carried the fanciful suggestion that natural disasters suffered by West Indian planters might have been divine punishment for the treatment of their slaves (*NYP*, Dec. 29, 1785; *NYJ* Jan. 5, 1786).

26. *NYP*, Feb. 13, 1786 (*NYJ*, Feb. 16, 1786); *CJFR*, Mar. 17, 1789; *NYP*, Jan. 9, 1787 (*CJPA*, Jan. 17, 1787); *NYP*, Aug. 24, 1787; see also *NYP*, Aug. 22, 1785.

27. On Rhode Island, see *NYJ*, Nov. 26, Dec. 21, 1787; *NYP*, Nov. 20, 1787; and *New York Independent Gazette*, Jan. 24, 1784; on New Jersey, *NYJ*, Mar. 9, 1786; on Virginia, *NYP*, Dec. 1, 1786 (*NYJ*, Nov. 30, 1786; *CJPA*, Dec. 6, 1786); on Cuba, see *LFH*, Aug. 3, 1789; and *NYP*, Dec. 18, 1787; see also on effort of New York and New England Quakers to protect free blacks in Connecticut, *CJFR*, Nov. 4, 1788; on Nova Scotia, see *NYP*, Feb. 10, 1785; for text of Pennsylvania's gradual abolition law, see *NYP*, Jan. 24, 1785; on a call for slavery's abolition from a New York and Pennsylvania synod, see *NYP*, June 13, 1788; for a petition to the Massachusetts legislature, see *NYP*, Mar. 24, 1785; for pointed criticism of the continuation of the slave trade in southern states, see *NYP*, Dec. 22, 1786; for reports placing West Indian slave law reform in a positive light, see *NYP*, Oct. 31, 1788 (*LFH*, Nov. 10, 1788), Dec. 5, 1788.

28. See Seymour Drescher, "The Breakthrough, 1787–92," in *Capitalism and Antislavery: British Mobilization in Comparative Perspective* (New York, 1987), 67–88.

29. See Frederick Cooper, "Race, Ideology, and the Perils of Comparative History," *AHR* 101 (1996): 1136, for an affirmation of this approach to the study of antislavery and other race-related political movements.

30. For the Clarkson excerpt, see *NYP*, Feb. 20, 1787; and Thomas Clarkson, "A Fancied Scene in the African Slave Trade," *NYM*, Aug. 1790, 464–67. *NYP*, Jan. 9, 1789, drew from a different Clarkson passage. Other mentions of the stir over Clarkson's essay include *CJPA*, May 30, 1787, and *NYP*, Sept. 26, 1785, Dec. 19, 1786, Feb. 6, May 25, 1787.

31. *LFH*, June 16, 1788; *NYP*, Sept. 8, 1785; see also *NYP*, Feb. 5, Nov. 15, 1784, Feb. 16, 1786, May 2, 1788; *DA*, Oct. 11, 1790; *AJ*, Aug. 25, 1788; *NYJ*, Apr. 11, 1792.

32. Dublin praises New Jersey, *NYP*, Oct. 30, 1786; letter from London to the New York Manumission Society, *CJPA*, May 30, 1787; London praise of American Quakers, *NYP*, Apr. 4, 1788; see also *NYP*, Feb. 24, 1789 (*CJFR*, Mar. 3, 1789); *NYP*, July 22 [really July 21], 1791, for a Philadelphian's commentary on Parliament; and *DA*, Oct. 12, 1790, which notes that a Charleston, South Carolina, newspaper deleted slavery remarks from an official British Quaker "epistle."

33. *NYJ*, Dec. 21, 1787 [italics removed from the original].

34. *NYJ*, June 14, 1787 [italics in original]; [Samuel Hopkins], *A Dialogue Concerning the Slavery of the Africans* (1776; reprint, with proceedings of the New York Manumission Society and an Appendix, New York, 1785), 12, 61; on Hopkins, see *Dictionary of American Biography*, ed. Dumas Malone (New York, 1961), 5:217–18, and Davis, *Age of Revolution*, 217–18, 275–76, 293–99.

35. "An Act further to amend an Act, entitled, An Act for the speedy Sale of the confiscated and forfeited Estates within this State, and for other Purposes therein mentioned," May 1, 1786, *Laws of the State of New-York* 9 (New York, 1786), 114; for the original statute, see "An Act for the speedy Sale of the confiscated and forfeited Estates within this State, and for other Purposes therein mentioned," May 12, 1784, *Laws of the State of New-York . . . Since the Revolution* (New York, 1792), 1:143. On these laws and details about the fate of confiscated slaves of loyalists, see Vivienne L. Kruger, "Born to Run: The Slave Family in Early New York, 1626 to 1827" (Ph.D. diss., Columbia University, 1985), 677–87.

36. NYMS, Aug. 10, 1786, Apr. 10, May 17, Aug. 16, Nov. 15, 1787, May 15, 1788, 6:48, 63, 65 (quotation), 68–69, 70, 75–6, 108.

37. NYMS, Feb. 8, May 11, 1788, 6:35, 37, 39, 41–45. See also Edgar J. McManus, "Antislavery Legislation in New York," *JNH* 4(1961): 211–12; White, *Somewhat More Independent*, 85; for broader background, see Duncan J. MacLeod, *Slavery, Race and the American Revolution* (London, 1974), 15, 40–43; and Donald L. Robinson, *Slavery in the Structure of American Politics, 1765–1820* (New York, 1971), 441, 446.

38. The text also can be found in NYMS, May 11, 1786, 6:41–45. See White, *Somewhat More Independent*, 79–113, on the "myth of the mild nature of the slave regime" in New York, although I question his interpretation (White, 84–86) that the petition discussed here contributed to the safeguarding of New York slavery.

39. *NYP*, Mar. 13, 16, 1786; for the related activity of registering manumissions, see *NYP*, Jan. 26, 1786 (*NYJ*, Feb. 2, 1786).

40. *NYP*, Mar. 6, 1786; see also a submission from Humanitas in *NYP*, Feb. 23, 1786.

41. John Jay received a letter from a South Carolina Quaker on a kidnapping case. Jay forwarded it to the NYMS before replying himself on Mar. 15, 1786 (John Jay to R. Lushington, Mar. 15, 1786, *Public Papers of John Jay*, 3:185); NYMS, Nov. 1785, Feb. 8, 1786, 6:27–28, 35–37. See also McManus, *Negro Slavery*, 169–70; and Moseley, "New York Manumission Society," 268–69.

42. *Journal of the Senate of the State of New-York* 9, pt. 1 (New York, 1786), Mar. 10, 24, 25,

27, Apr. 12, 21, 1786, 42, 56, 57, 77, 86; NYMS, May 11, 1786, Feb. 15, May 17, 1787, Jan. 26, 1788, 6:39, 41–45, 59–60, 66, 91; *Journal of the Assembly* 10 (New York, 1787), Feb. 28, 1787, 70; "An act concerning Slaves," Feb. 22, 1788, *Laws of the State of New-York* 11 (New York, 1788), 75–78; Zilversmit, *First Emancipation,* 151–52.

43. McManus, "Antislavery," 211; McManus, *Negro Slavery,* 169–71.

44. Newspapers up and down the Hudson River carried the text of the law subsequent to its passage; see *NYP,* Apr. 25, 1788; *LFH,* May 26, 1788; *CJPA,* Sept. 23, 1788. Carl Nordstrom, "The New York Slave Code," *AANYLH* 4 (1980): 18, 25, offers a brief and balanced assessment; Zilversmit, *First Emancipation,* 151–52, views the 1788 law in negative terms; McManus, "Antislavery," 210–11, and *Negro Slavery,* 166–67, provides an overly positive reading of the act's meaning; see also John P. Kaminski, *George Clinton: Yeoman Politician of the New Republic* (Madison, Wisc., 1993), 192–93.

45. NYMS, Feb. 21, 1788, 6:95; my reading of the evidence contradicts White, *Somewhat More Independent,* 85, in his assertion that the Manumission Society aimed more at the "reform" of slavery than its abolition.

46. *Journal of the Assembly of the State of New-York* 13, pt. 2 (New York, 1790), Jan. 20–22, 28, 1790, 12–15, 21; *Albany Register,* Feb. 1, 1790; *DA,* Jan. 21, 23, 1790, Feb. 4, 1790; *LFH,* Feb. 1, 22, 1790; Zilversmit, *First Emancipation,* 160–61, 165; Alfred F. Young, *The Democratic Republicans of New York: The Origins, 1763–1797* (Chapel Hill, N.C., 1967), 252–54; Kaminski, *George Clinton,* 192–93.

47. *Journal of the Assembly,* Feb. 15, 16, 24, 25, 1790, 37, 39, 52–54; Zilversmit, *First Emancipation,* 161; Young, *Democratic Republicans,* 253–54; Kaminski, *George Clinton,* 192–93; *Heads of Families at the First Census of the United States Taken in the Year 1790, New York* (Washington, D.C., 1908).

48. *Journal of the Senate* 13, pt. 2 (New York, 1790), Feb. 25, 26, Mar. 2, 3, 4, 11, 15, 1790, 26, 28, 29, 30, 35, 36, 37; *Journal of the Assembly,* Mar. 5, 9, 15, 16, 22, 1790, 64, 69, 70, 79, 81, 82, 89; Zilversmit, *First Emancipation,* 161.

49. Zilversmit, *First Emancipation,* 161, 165; MacLeod, *Slavery, Race and the American Revolution,* 142.

50. Remarks about the presence of individual slaveholders within various county delegations are based on a comparison of the assembly roster for the 1789–90 session and census data collected in *Heads of Families at the First Census of the United States Taken in the Year 1790, New York.*

51. Population ranks and percentage calculated from McManus, *Negro Slavery,* 200. Roll-call votes tabulated from the *Journal of the Assembly,* Jan. 21, 22, Feb. 24, Mar. 9, 1790, 13, 14, 52, 69, 70. See also Edward Countryman, *A People in Revolution: The American Revolution and Political Society in New York, 1760–1790* (Baltimore, 1981), 244, 248–49. To compare this analysis of the New York legislature to the Pennsylvania legislature, see Gary B. Nash and Jean R. Soderlund, *Freedom by Degrees: Emancipation and Its Aftermath* (New York, 1991), 104–10.

52. Leslie M. Harris, *In the Shadow of Slavery: African Americans in New York City, 1626–1863* (Chicago, 2003), 49, 64–65; see also Davis, *Age of Revolution,* esp. 238–42, as well as David Brion Davis, "Reflections on Abolitionism and Ideological Hegemony," *AHR* 92 (1987): 797–812; White, *Somewhat More Independent,* 84; and Moseley, "New York Manumission Society," 263, 354.

53. *DA,* Jan. 22, 1790.

54. Moseley, "New York Manumission Society," 45–47, 238–39. See Yearly Meeting,

1746–1800, Archives of New York Yearly Meeting; for references to educating or guiding former Quaker slaves, see the years 1781, 1784, and 1787, 133, 180, 217.

55. Zilversmit, *First Emancipation*, 163–64; Moseley, "New York Manumission Society," 242, 263, 276–77, on the link between monitoring blacks and public opinion, and 170–263, 357–358, on the NYMS and education; see also Sayre, "Early American Abolitionism," 152, 176; and White, *Somewhat More Independent*, 84, 86.

56. Harris, *In the Shadow of Slavery*, explores this theme in depth for the nineteenth century, with an emphasis also on the black middle class's role in directing black behavior.

57. NYMS, Aug. 18, 1785, May 11, 1786, Nov. 15, 1787, Jan. 26, 1788, 6:24, 39, 80–92. For the public announcement of school fundraising, see *NYP*, Nov. 17, 1786 (*NYJ*, Nov. 23, 1786).

58. NYMS, Nov. 15, 1787, 6:80–87.

59. NYMS, Feb. 21, 1788, 6:95–97; see also Harris, *In the Shadow of Slavery*, 62, 64–65.

60. NYMS, Feb. 21, Aug. 21, 1788, 6:97–98, 109–110.

61. NYMS, Nov. 20, 1788, 6:123; see also Feb. 21, 1788, Feb. 19, May 21, 1789, Feb. 15, 1791, 6:98, 127, 132, 152.

62. *NYP*, Nov. 17, July 20, 1786. Significantly, the assertion that women should receive formal education represented an early challenge to assumptions about the limitations on women in "public life" and even gender inequality (see *NYM*, "Essay on Education," Jan. 1790, 40–41; and "On Female Education," *NYM*, Sept. 1794, 569–70).

63. *NYJ*, Nov. 23, 1787 [italics in original]; see also *New York Impartial Gazetteer*, May 17, 1788; *LFH*, June 23, 1788; *Albany Register*, Feb. 1, 1790; *Kingston Farmer's Register*, Apr. 27, 1793; "On Education," *NYM*, Mar. 1794, 146–48.

64. *LFH*, Aug. 24, 1789; see also *DA*, Jan. 4, 1790; and "A Plain Dealer," *NYP*, July 20, 1786, cited above; see also Jay Fliegelman, *Prodigals and Pilgrims: The American Revolution Against Patriarchal Authority, 1750–1800* (New York, 1982), chap. 1, on the intellectual background and underlying philosophical premises of this discourse.

65. This is a major theme of Jordan, *White over Black* (see 287–94, 365, 445–57); see also Harris, *In the Shadow of Slavery*, 64–65. Jordan, 354–62, directly addresses black education and its relationship to the spirit of the times; in addition, see Sayre, "Early American Abolitionism," 154; and J. P. Brissot de Warville, *New Travels in the United States, 1788*, trans. Mara Soceanu Vamos and Durand Echeverria, ed. Durand Echeverria (Cambridge, Mass., 1964), 217–18.

66. NYMS, Feb. 21, 1788, 6:100–101.

67. Harris, *In the Shadow of Slavery*, 61, 64–65, 103, 130–33; White, *Somewhat More Independent*, 84; Pfister, "In the Cause of Freedom," 107–12; Sayre, "Early American Abolitionism," 152–56; Moseley, "New York Manumission Society," 354; Robert J. Swan, "John Teasman: African-American Educator and the Emergence of Community in Early Black New York City, 1787–1815," *JER* 12 (1992): 331–56, esp. 339–40.

68. Davis, *Age of Revolution*, 240–42; Pfister, "In the Cause of Freedom," 150; Moseley, "New York Manumission Society," 180. It should be noted that the NYMS did wish masters of children still enslaved to send them to the school; see NYMS, May 21, 1789, 6:133. Regulation is a common theme in the study of emancipation; see Harris, *In the Shadow of Slavery*. For a later period, see Amy Dru Stanley, "Beggars Can't Be Choosers: Compulsion and Contract in Postbellum America," *JAH* 78 (1992): 1265–93, esp. 1283–88.

69. NYMS, May 15, 1792, 6:166–67; *NYJ*, May 2, 1792; see also Zilversmit, *First Emancipation*, 228; and Jordan, *White over Black*, 350–52, on property rights as a hindrance to abolition.

NOTES TO CHAPTER 5

1. *NYJ*, May 4, 18, 1786. Drew R. McCoy, *The Elusive Republic: Political Economy in Jeffersonian America* (1980; New York, 1982), 49, 70–5, 77, 80–1, 96–7, 99–101, 133, discusses the mostly negative light in which late-eighteenth-century American commentators placed the Spartan model of political economy. See also Cathy D. Matson and Peter S. Onuf, *A Union of Interests: Political and Economic Thought in Revolutionary America* (Lawrence, Kans., 1990), 70.

2. Cathy Matson, "Liberty, Jealousy, and Union: The New York Economy in the 1780s," in *New York in the Age of the Constitution, 1775–1800*, ed. Paul A. Gilje and William Pencak (Rutherford, N.J., 1992), 112–50; Cathy Matson, "Public Vices, Private Benefit: William Durer and His Circle, 1776–1792," in *New York and the Rise of American Capitalism: Economic Development and the Social and Political History of an American State, 1780–1870*, ed. William Pencak and Conrad E. Wright (New York, 1989), 72–108; Mary-Jo Kline, "The 'New' New York: An Expanding State in the New Nation," and Michael Kammen, "'The Promised Sunshine of the Future': Reflection on Economic Growth and Social Change in Post-Revolutionary New York," in *New Opportunities in a New Nation: The Development of New York after the Revolution*, ed. Manfred Jonas and Robert V. Wells (Syracuse, N.Y., 1982), 14–23, 109–43, esp. 125; Edward Countryman, *A People in Revolution: The American Revolution and Political Society in New York, 1760–1790* (Baltimore, 1981), 287–96; and Anthony Gronowicz, "Political 'Radicalism' in New York City's Revolutionary and Constitutional Eras," in Gilje and Pencak, *New York in the Age of the Constitution*, 98–111.

3. David Brion Davis, "Reflections on Abolition and Ideological Hegemony," *AHR* 92 (1987): 800–801; David Brion Davis, *The Problem of Slavery in the Age of Revolution, 1770–1823* (Ithaca, N.Y., 1975), 241–42, 262–66, 339; Howard Temperley, "Capitalism, Slavery, and Ideology," *Past and Present* 75 (1977): 94–118. See also Philip Gould, *Barbarous Traffic: Commerce and Antislavery in the Eighteenth-Century Atlantic World* (Cambridge, Mass., 2003), esp. 3–4, 81; and Steven Mintz, "Models of Emancipation during the Age of Revolution," *Slavery and Abolition* 17 (1996): 1–21.

4. The exchange was a reprint; *American Museum* magazine originally published this debate.

5. *NYP*, Oct. 7, 1788.

6. *NYP*, Jan. 16, 1789; see Davis, *Age of Revolution*, 263–66, 273, on the role of slavery in marking the outer boundary of "rational order," and also 373, 377–85 on the relationship between hierarchy and antislavery in the British context; Davis, "Reflections on Abolitionism and Ideological Hegemony," 800; Winthrop D. Jordan, *White over Black: American Attitudes toward the Negro, 1550–1812* (1968; New York, 1977), 485.

7. John Locke, "The Second Treatise on Government," in *Political Writings of John Locke*, ed. David Wootton (New York, 1993), 269–73. David Brion Davis, *The Problem of Slavery in Western Culture* (New York, 1966), and Orlando Patterson, *Slavery and Social Death: A Comparative Study* (Cambridge, Mass., 1982), provide excellent treatments of this intellectual and social nexus; see also Joseph Miller, *Way of Death: Merchant Capitalism and the Angolan Slave Trade, 1730–1830* (Madison, Wisc., 1988), 53, 116–17, 123, 134; and David Brion Davis, "Preface" and "The Movement to Abolish Capital Punishment in America, 1787–1861," in *From Homicide to Slavery: Studies in American Culture* (New York, 1986), 17–40.

8. For the New York and New Jersey executions of African Americans, see *CJPA*, Sept. 29, 1785; and *NYWM*, Nov. 1, 1788. For instances of brutal West Indian punishments, see *NYP*,

Mar. 23, 1786; *LFII*, Nov. 23, 1789, May 10, 1790; *DA*, Jan. 6, 1790, May 3, 1790. For various comments in New York newspapers on punishment policy in the 1780s, see *NYP*, Mar. 9, 1786, May 15, 1787, Dec. 23, 1788, Feb. 13, 1789; *CJFR*, June 30, 1789; *NYJ*, Nov. 9, 1786; *NCLA*, Sept. 3, 1787; J. P. Brissot de Warville, *New Travels in the United States of America, 1788*, trans. Mara Soceanu Vamos and Durand Echeverria, ed. Durand Echeverria (Cambridge, Mass., 1964), 295–97 (a translation of Brissot de Warville's remarks was published as "Of the Prison of Philadelphia and Prisons in General," *NYM*, Dec. 1792, 213–14). See also Jordan, *White over Black*, 365–72.

Commentators continued to discuss criminal discipline in the 1790s: see *DA*, Apr. 12, 1790; *NYJ*, Nov. 1, 1790; *RT*, Nov. 4, 1796; Benjamin Franklin, "On the Criminal Law, and the Practice of Privateering, in a Letter to Benjamin Vaughan, Esq.," *NYM*, Oct. 1793, 603–7; and see more generally, *CG*, Dec. 2, 1793; *TP*, Apr. 7, Aug. 28, 1797, June 18, 1798; "On Imprisonment," *NYM*, Dec. 1791, 699–701; "Extract from Bradford's Inquiry how far the Punishment of Death is necessary in Pennsylvania," *NYM*, Apr. 1793, 226–30; *MH*, Mar. 12, 1795; *RT*, June 24, 1796; *Herald*, Dec. 28, 1796; see also Charles William Janson, *The Stranger in America, 1793–1806*, ed. Carl S. Driver (1807; New York, 1935), 188–90.

9. Stuart Banner, *The Death Penalty: An American History* (Cambridge, Mass., 2002); for statements about penal reform in New York, see *AChron*, Jan. 8, 1798 (*OH*, Jan. 11, 1798; *SNC*, Jan. 8, 1798); *Spec*, Jan. 12, 1799 (*OH*, Jan. 17, 1799). On the broader ethos of 1790s reform, see Davis, *Age of Revolution*, 240–41; Frederick William Pfister, "In the Cause of Freedom: American Abolition Societies, 1775–1808" (Ph.D. diss., Miami University, 1980), 150–54; Alfred F. Young, *The Democratic Republicans of New York: The Origins, 1763–1797* (Chapel Hill, N.C., 1967), 518–30; Shane White, *Somewhat More Independent: The End of Slavery in New York City, 1770–1810* (Athens, Ga., 1991), 84; Arthur Zilversmit, *The First Emancipation: The Abolition of Slavery in the North* (Chicago, 1967), 228.

10. "An Act granting a Bounty on Hemp to be raised within this State . . . and for other Purposes therein mentioned," Apr. 12, 1785, *Laws of New-York*, 8 (New York, 1785), 61–63; the text of this law was printed in *NYP*, Nov. 28, 1785, and *NYJ*, Dec. 1, 1785; see chap. 3 for further details.

11. *NYP*, Apr. 6, 1787; *NYP*, Feb. 19, 1788; see also *NYP*, Jan. 8, 1788. According to Matson, "Liberty, Jealousy, and Union," 127, personal debts in New York increased during the second half of the 1780s. For two modern scholarly definitions of slavery evoking the theme of civil death, see Patterson, *Slavery and Social Death*, and James Oakes, *Slavery and Freedom: An Interpretation of the Old South* (New York, 1990), 3–39; for a 1780s reference evoking this theme, see the closing lines of the poem "On the Death of an African Slave. Condemned for Rebellion in Jamaica," *NYP*, June 12, 1786 (*NYJ*, Aug. 17, 1786). For evocative discussions of debt's metaphorical and political implications in a different revolutionary era context, see T. H. Breen, *Tobacco Culture: The Mentality of the Great Tidewater Planters on the Eve of the Revolution* (Princeton, 1985), esp. 29–30, 91–93, 112, 132–34, 142, 161–76, 207. On the analogy between debt and slavery, see Herbert Sloan, "'The Earth Belongs in the Usufruct to the Living,'" in *Jeffersonian Legacies*, ed. Peter S. Onuf (Charlottesville, Va., 1993), 281–315, esp. 290.

12. *NYP*, June 13, 1788; "The Tradesman" commentary ran from May 30 through June 20 in the twice-weekly *Packet*.

13. See Thomas L. Haskell, "Capitalism and the Origins of the Humanitarian Sensibility," *AHR* 90 (1985): 339–61, 547–66; Gould, *Barbaric Traffic*, 31, 37, makes a related point; the conceptualization and implementation of postindependence commercial policy is the subject of Cathy Matson, "Liberty, Jealousy, and Union."

14. Without making an explicit connection, the New York Friends Yearly Meeting, devoted to ridding the sect of association with slavery, also urged its membership to avoid becoming debtors; see Yearly Meeting, 1746–1800, Archives of New York Yearly Meeting—Religious Society of Friends, Haviland Records Room, New York City; the following pages, covering the years 1783, 1786, 1787, 1790, 1791, 1800, are useful: 168, 204, 217, 256–57, 269–70, 437. For New York debt reform laws passed in the 1780s and early 1790s, see "An Act for the Relief of insolvent Debtors, with Respect to the Imprisonment of their Persons," Mar. 31, 1786; "An Act for Relief against absconding Debtors," Apr. 4, 1786; "An Act for the Relief of Insolvent Debtors," Apr. 13, 1786, *Laws of the State of New-York* 9 (New York, 1786), 23, 27–37, 56; "An Act for Relief in Cases of Insolvency," Mar. 21, 1788; "An Act for the Relief of Debtors, with respect to the Imprisonment of their Persons," Feb. 13, 1789; "An Act to repeal the first and second Sections of an Act, entitled, an Act for the Relief of Debtors with respect to the Imprisonment of their Persons. . . ," Mar. 31, 1790; "An Act Supplementary to the Act, entitled, An Act for giving Relief in Cases of Insolvency. . . ," Mar. 16, 1791, *Laws of the State of New-York . . . Since the Revolution* (New York, 1792), 2:204–11, 231–41, 318, 355–56; "An Act to repeal the Act, entitled, 'An Act for the relief of Insolvent Debtors,'" Feb. 8, 1788, *Laws of the State of New-York* 11 (New York, 1788), 45. For mention of debt imprisonment, as well as organizations to assist debt prisoners, in 1780s New York newspapers, see *NYJ*, Feb. 15, 22, June 28, July 5, 1787; *NYP*, May 25, Aug. 24, 1787, Feb. 8, June 24, 1788, *CJPA*, June 13, 1787. The intertwining of discourse and legislative action on debt imprisonment and slavery in the 1790s is further developed in chap. 8.

15. For two descriptions by American captives of Algerian slavery, see *NYP*, Nov. 21, 1785, Oct. 10, 1788 (see *LFH*, Oct. 20, 1788 for same report); for a concise history, see Gary E. Wilson, "American Hostages in Moslem Nations, 1784–1796: The Public Response," *JER* 2 (1982): 123–41.

16. *NYP*, Oct. 2, 1786; [Samuel Hopkins], *A Dialogue Concerning the Slavery of the Africans . . .* (1776; reprint, with proceedings of the New York Manumission Society and an Appendix, New York, 1785), 41, 43, 67, may have pioneered the antislavery argument linking Algerian and American slavery. See also Joanne Pope Melish, *Disowning Slavery: Gradual Emancipation and "Race" in New England, 1780–1860* (Ithaca, N.Y., 1998), 160; and Mukhtar Ali Asani, "Far from 'Gambia's Golden Shore': The Black in Late Eighteenth-Century Imaginative Literature," *WMQ*, 3d ser., 26 (1979): 362–63.

17. *CJPA*, May 16, 1787 [italics in original], May 13, 1788. For more instances in which the connection between American slavery in Algeria and African slavery in America are noted, see *CJPA*, Sept. 12, 1787 (*NCLA*, Sept. 17, 1787); and "A letter from an English Slave-driver at Algiers to his Friend in England," *NYM*, Oct. 1791, 584, reprinted several years later in *MH*, Jan. 22, 1795. See also the Pennsylvania Society for the Abolition of Slavery's petition to the Constitutional Convention, quoted in Brissot de Warville, *New Travels*, 243–44.

18. *NYP*, June 1, 1787.

19. This poem, and Algerian piracy more generally, prefigured some of the themes regarding nationalism, war, commerce, and identity explored with regard to the War of 1812 in Stephen Watts, *The Republic Reborn: War and the Making of Liberal America, 1790–1820* (Baltimore, 1987).

20. "A Poem, on the Happiness of America; addressed to the Citizens of the United States," *AJ*, Feb. 4–Mar. 15, 1788 (quotations from Mar. 3 and Mar. 15); see also *Dictionary of American Biography*, ed. Dumas Malone (New York, 1961), 5:373–75; David Humphreys, *The Miscellaneous Works of David Humphreys* (1804; Gainesville, Fla., 1968); and Gould, *Barbaric*

Traffic, 107. On Humphreys's Barbary hostage diplomacy, which continued for several years after he authored this poem, see Wilson, "American Hostages," 125, 129, 131, 137.

21. On the irreconcilability of white Americans to Algerian slavery see Susanna Rowson, *Slaves in Algiers; or, a Struggle for Freedom: A Play, Interspersed with Songs, in Three Acts* (Philadelphia, 1794), esp. 60; *CP,* Aug. 13, 1793; *CG,* Dec. 26, 1793; *MH,* Feb. 5, 12, 1795; *RT,* Feb. 17, 1797. See also Melish *Disowning Slavery,* 150–61; and Gould, *Barbaric Traffic,* chap. 3.

On seventeenth- and eighteenth-century hopes that capitalism might place international affairs on a more harmonious basis, see Albert O. Hirschman, *The Passions and the Interests: Political Arguments for Capitalism before Its Triumph* (Princeton, 1977); see also Cathy Matson, "Liberty, Jealousy, and Union," 112–13, 136; McCoy, *Elusive Republic,* 86–94; Matson and Onuf, *Union of Interests,* 149.

22. On Cowper, see Davis, *Age of Revolution,* 368–73.

23. *Address of a Convention of Delegates from the Abolition Society to the Citizens of the United States* (New York, 1794), 6, 7; Samuel Miller, *A Discourse Delivered April 12, 1797, at the Request of and Before the New-York Society for Promoting the Manumission of Slaves, and Protecting Such of Them as Have or May Be Liberated* (New York, 1797), 16; see also a poem "Addressed to the Consciences of Every American Citizen," *TP,* June 9, 1797; *DA,* Mar. 29, 1798; *Spec,* Apr. 4, 1798.

24. Hugh Williamson, Speech, Edenton, North Carolina, Nov. 8, 1787, printed in *DA,* Feb. 25–27, 1788, quoted from *The Debate on the Constitution: Federalists and Antifederalist Speeches, Articles, and Letters During the Struggle over Ratification,* ed. Bernard Bailyn (New York, 1993), 2:233.

25. *NYP,* Mar. 23, 1787 [italics in original]; this remark also demonstrated the porousness of geographical boundaries to political debate. The provocative commentary about a Western Massachusetts rebellion originated in Philadelphia. On Shays's Rebellion, see Robert A. Gross, ed., *In Debt to Shays: Bicentennial of an Agrarian Rebellion* (Charlottesville, Va., 1993).

26. See Matson, "Liberty, Jealousy, and Union," 126–41, for Federalist ideas about political economy.

27. NYMS, Aug. 16, Aug. 17, 1787, 6:72, 74.

28. Paul Finkelman, "Slavery and the Constitutional Convention: Making a Covenant with Death," in *Beyond Confederation: Origins of the Constitution and American National Identity,* ed. Richard Beeman, Stephen Botein, and Edward C. Carter II (Chapel Hill, N.C., 1987), 188–225; James Oakes, "'The Compromising Expedient': Justifying a Proslavery Constitution," *Cardozo Law Review* 17 (1996), 2023–56, esp. 2023, 2030–31, 2032, 2033, 2035–36. Donald L. Robinson, *Slavery in the Structure of American Politics, 1765–1820* (New York, 1971), offers a more even assessment of the convention's approach to slavery (170–246) but nonetheless in his essentials (201, 231–33, 246) supports Finkelman and Oakes. See also Davis, *Age of Revolution,* 122–31, 322–26; Jordan, *White over Black,* 323–24; William W. Freehling, "The Founding Fathers and Slavery," *AHR* 77 (1972): 83–84; William Wiecek, *The Sources of Antislavery Constitutionalism in America, 1760–1848* (Ithaca, N.Y., 1977), 81–82.

29. Leonard L. Richards, *The Slave Power: The Free North and Southern Domination* (Baton Rouge, 2000), 31–34; Max M. Mintz, *Gouverneur Morris and the American Revolution* (Norman, Okla., 1970), 76, 187–88, 197, 199.

30. *NYJ,* Jan. 18, 1788; *NYP,* July 1, 1788. For other Anti-Federalist enslavement metaphors, see *NYJ,* Sept. 6, Dec. 25, 1787, Jan. 1, 7, 1788, *CJPA,* Feb. 5, 1788, and [Mercy Otis Warren], "A Columbian Patriot, Observation on the New Constitution, and on the Federal and

State Conventions" (Boston, 1788), in *Debate,* 2:284–85. Alternatively, see *AJ,* Feb. 18, 1788, comparing Anti-Federalists to "negro thieves, in the night concert[ing] their despicable plans."

31. A Countryman from Dutchess County, *NYJ,* Nov. 23, 1787, quoted from *The Complete Anti-Federalist,* ed. Herbert Storing (Chicago, 1981), 6:52–53; on the vexed matter of the author's identity, see Storing, 6:49, 69–70; see also *CJFR,* Jan. 27, 1789.

32. Brutus No. 3, *NYJ,* Nov. 15, 1787; Cato No. 6, in *Complete Anti-Federalist,* 2:120; A Countryman from Dutchess County, *NYJ,* Jan. 22, 1788, in *Complete Anti-Federalist,* 6:62–63; see also "Address of the Albany Antifederal Committee," *NYJ,* Apr. 26, 1788, in *Complete Anti-Federalist,* 6:123; Oakes, "Justifying a Proslavery Constitution," 2039–43, 2052.

33. A Countryman from Dutchess County, *NYJ,* Nov. 21, 1787, quoted from *Complete Anti-Federalist,* 6:50–51; Centinel No. 3, *NYJ,* Nov. 20, 1787; Brutus No. 3, *NYJ,* Nov. 15, 1787; Cincinnatus No. 2, *NYJ,* Nov. 8, 1787; see also A Countryman, *NYJ,* Dec. 13, 1787, in *Complete Anti-Federalist,* 6:77–78; Oakes, "Justifying a Proslavery Constitution," 2033.

34. *NYP,* Mar. 31, 1785; see chap. 3.

35. Federalist Nos. 38, 42, in *Debate,* 1:780, 2:63, 65–66; *NYJ,* Nov. 21, 1787; in addition, see Pennsylvania Ratifying Convention, Dec. 3, 1787; Massachusetts Ratifying Convention, Feb. 4, 1788, *Debate,* 1:829–30, 931–33, for this viewpoint. See also [Noah Webster] A Citizen of America, *An Examination into the Leading Principles of the Federal Constitution Proposed by the Late Convention Held at Philadelphia. . . .* (Philadelphia, 1787), in *Debate,* 1:153, for a defense of the slave-trade clause by a person hostile to slavery. See also Oakes, "Justifying a Proslavery Constitution," 2024–25, 2035, 2043–51; Robinson, *Structure of American Politics,* 244; Davis, *Age of Revolution,* 130–31, 324–25, and Finkelman, "Covenant with Death," 191; and Jordan, *White over Black,* 322–23.

36. Federalist No. 54, quoted from *Debate,* 2:196–201, quotation 199; see also Mark Antony, *Boston Independent Chronicle,* Jan. 10, 1788, in *Debate,* 1:737–43, for a Bostonian's defense of the three-fifths clause; Oakes, "Justifying a Proslavery Constitution," 2049–50; and Robinson, *Structure of American Politics,* 184, 236–37.

37. Federalist No. 43, quoted from *Debate,* 2:76; see also Joseph J. Ellis, *Founding Brothers: The Revolutionary Generation* (New York, 2001), 114–15, on the "willful confusion" Madison created when discussing slavery.

38. Federalist No. 11, quoted from *The Federalist by Alexander Hamilton, James Madison, and John Jay,* ed. Garry Wills (New York, 1982), 49, 53, 55.

39. For observations on cotton's potential, see *NYP,* Apr. 29 (*CJPA,* May 6, 1788), July 18, Sept. 16, 1788; *CJFR,* Dec. 16–23, 1788, June 2, 1789; *LFH,* May 19, 1788; for related material, see Jordan, 316–21; Finkelman, "Covenant with Death," 213–14, 217–18, 220–21, 224; and Davis, *Age of Revolution,* 340–41.

40. *CJPA,* Mar. 11, 1788; and *NYJ,* Nov. 20, 1787.

41. For the New York ratifying convention, see *Complete Anti-Federalist,* 6:153; Harold C. Syrett, ed., *The Papers of Alexander Hamilton* (New York, 1962), 5:23–24; see also newspaper accounts in *CJPA,* June 24, July 15, 1788; *LFH,* July 28, 1788.

42. *NYJ,* Nov. 21, 1787, contains a reprint from Philadelphia responding to a twenty-three-part criticism of the Constitution, the twentieth of which concerned the slave-trade clause; Oakes, "Justifying a Proslavery Constitution," 2031–32, 2034; Jordan, *White over Black,* 325; Robinson, *Structure of American Politics,* 235, 239.

43. On support for a Bill of Rights, stressing "freemen," see *AJ,* July 21, 1788; Oakes, "Justifying a Proslavery Constitution," 2051–52.

44. Cecelia M. Kenyon, "Men of Little Faith: The Anti-Federalists on the Nature of Rep-

resentative Government," *WMQ*, 3d ser., 12 (1955): 3–43, provides a classic study of Anti-Federalist political ideology.

45. For these broader sentiments, see *NYJ*, Sept. 27, 1787; Hamilton, *Federalist Papers*, 49–55; *NYP*, Feb. 29, 1788; for an Anti-Federalist version of this vision, see *NYJ*, Dec. 5, 1787. For additional background, see Matson, "Liberty, Jealousy, and Union," 126–41; Oakes, 2046–48; Wiecek, *Antislavery Constitutionalism*, 73; and Robinson, *Structure of American Politics*, 171–77.

46. Matson, "Liberty, Jealousy, and Union," 141–42.

47. Jordan, *White over Black*, 325–31, and Robinson, *Structure of American Politics*, underscore how federal politics occasioned a new set of slavery controversies.

48. Maston and Onuf, *Union of Interests*, 45–49, 91–97, 150–51; Kline, "'New' New York," 14–23.

49. Alan Taylor, *William Cooper's Town: Power and Persuasion on the Frontier of the Early American Republic* (New York, 1995), 119.

50. *AJ*, Nov. 3, 1788; for additional optimism about sugar, see *DA*, Apr. 15, 1790; *CJFR*, July 7, 1789; and Michel-Guillaume Jean de Crèvecoeur, *Eighteenth-Century Travels in Pennsylvania and New York,* ed. and trans. Percy G. Adams (Lexington, Ky., 1961), 47.

51. *LFH*, July 20, 1789; see also *NYP*, Sept. 12, 1788; "Remarks on the Manufacturing of Maple Sugar . . . ," *NYM*, Jan. and Feb. 1791, 34–37, 71–72.

52. *DA*, Mar. 8, 1790; see also *DA*, Apr. 14 (*LFH*, Apr. 26, 1790), Aug. 24, Oct. 14, 1790; Brissot de Warville, *New Travels*, 246–49; and note 53 below.

53. *NYJ*, Mar. 14, 1792; see also *CP*, Feb. 25, 1793; *NYP*, Jan. 8, 13, Apr. 28, June 30, July 22, 1791; *Henry Wansey and His American Journal*, ed. David John Jeremy (Philadelphia, 1970), 70 n., 149–50, 150 n.

54. For Cooper's biography, see Taylor, *William Cooper's Town*, esp. 113–38, on Cooper and maple sugar.

55. William Cooper, "A Letter on the Manufacturer of Maple Sugar," *NYM*, Mar. 1793, 175–76; *DA*, Aug. 23, 1790; see also *LFH*, July 27, Sept. 21, 1789; *NYP*, Apr. 14, July 22, 1791.

56. *AJ*, Nov. 3, 1788; *DA*, June 18, 1790; see also *DA*, Apr. 14, 1790 (*LFH*, Apr. 26, 1790); *DA*, Apr. 15, 1790; and Brissot de Warville, *New Travels*, 247.

57. Taylor, *Cooper's Town*, 117, 120, 133–34; *CJFR*, July 7, 1789, carried an approving report from Philadelphia on the migration of New Englanders to Pennsylvania, where these "sober, industrious . . . citizens" cultivated maple trees; see also [Benjamin Rush], "An Address to the Inhabitants of the British Settlements in America, upon Slavery" (New York, 1773), 7–9. On slavery, emancipation, and free labor, see Davis, *Age of Revolution*, 305–6, 339–40, and on labor more generally, Gordon S. Wood, *The Radicalism of the American Revolution* (New York, 1992), 186, 276–86; and Gordon S. Wood, "Equality and Social Conflict in the American Revolution," 712–13, in "How Revolutionary Was the Revolution? A Discussion of Gordon S. Wood's *The Radicalism of the American Revolution*," *WMQ*, 3d ser., 51 (1994): 677–716.

58. Taylor, *William Cooper's Town*, 19, 20, 144, 299.

59. Taylor, *William Cooper's Town*, 121; Matson, "Liberty, Jealousy, and Union," 122. French travelers noted that even servants ate sugar in the United States (see Brissot de Warville, *New Travels*, 391–92; *Moreau de St. Méry's American Journey [1793–1798]*, trans. and ed. Kenneth Roberts and Anna M. Roberts [Garden City, N.Y., 1947], 298). On reminders of sugar's havoc-wreaking, morally suspect nature, see *NYJ*, Apr. 25, 1792; Benjamin Franklin, "Luxury, Idleness, and Industry," *NYM*, Aug. 1793, 481; "Negro Trade—A Fragment," *NYM*, Feb. 1797,

96; "Slavery—A Sonnet," *NYM*, July 1797, 387. On sugar substitutes, see *TP*, Nov. 15, 1797 (*ACent*, Nov. 21, 1797); "Cheap Substitute for Sugar," *NYM*, Dec. 1795, 747–48. Years after putting an abolition policy in place, the New York Friends Yearly Meeting repeatedly returned to the nettlesome problem of consuming slave-made products; see Yearly Meeting for the years 1792, 1794, 1799, 289–91, 301–2, 321, 412.

60. "A Fable for Sugar Eaters. The Bee and the Negro," *NYM*, Jan. 1792, 9. On Mandeville and his more "moderate" intellectual successors, see McCoy, *Elusive Republic*, 25–32. On images of the beehive, see Ann Fairfax Withington, "Republican Bees: The Political Economy of the Beehive in Eighteenth-Century America," and Jeffrey Merrick, "Royal Bees: The Gender Politics of the Beehive in Early Modern Europe," in John W. Yolton and Leslie Ellen Brown, eds., *Studies in Eighteenth-Century Culture* 18 (East Lansing, Mich., 1988): 7–77; more broadly, see Gould, *Barbaric Traffic*, esp. 3–4, 27–31.

61. See Taylor, *William Cooper's Town*, 117, 121–25, 131–35, 137, for an analysis of problems with plans for the mass marketing of maple sugar, and 431–32 for supporting statistics; see also *Henry Wansey and His American Journal*, 149–50.

62. On sugar production in Africa, see *NYP*, Feb. 23, 1786; *NYJ*, Feb. 3, 1785; *NYP*, Sept. 12, 1787; *TP*, Aug. 9, 1797; [Rush], "An Address to the Inhabitants of the British Settlements," 7–9; and Crèvecoeur, *Eighteenth-Century Travels*, 66; see also n. 21 above.

63. Jordan, *White over Black*, 512–41, 546–69. Jordan calls the colonization of blacks a "compelling fantasy" on 567. For an English version of "the fantasy of emancipation," see Davis, *Age of Revolution*, 373; and Christopher L. Brown, "Empire Without Slaves: British Concepts of Emancipation in the Age of the American Revolution," *William and Mary Quarterly*, 3d ser., 56 (1999): 274, 280, 306.

64. Edwin G. Burrows and Mike Wallace, *Gotham: A History of New York City to 1898* (New York, 1999), 118–29; Thomas Davis, "New York's Long Black Line: A Note on the Growing Slave Population, 1626–1790," *AANYLH* 2 (1978): 43–45; Graham Russell Hodges, *Root and Branch: African Americans in New York and East Jersey* (Chapel Hill, N.C., 1999), 77–82, 272–73.

65. *DA*, Mar. 1, 3, 4, 1790; on the Quaker appeal to the New York legislature, see *DA*, Jan. 23, Feb. 4, 1790; and chap. 4.

66. For the congressional speeches discussed in the next four paragraphs, see *DA*, Mar. 18, 19, 20, 22, 25; see also *Albany Register*, Mar. 1, 1790, and *LFH*, Mar. 22, 1790. Ellis, *Founding Brothers*, 81–119, describes the 1790 episode and deftly places it in the historical context of race, slavery, and abolition in the new republic; for additional descriptions of this episode, see Stanley Elkins and Eric McKitrick, *The Age of Federalism: The Early American Republic, 1788–1800* (New York, 1993), 142–43, 151–52; Robinson, *Structure of American Politics*, 301–12; and Jordan, *White over Black*, 325–27.

67. *DA*, Mar. 18, 20, 22, 1790, for references to Jefferson.

68. See *DA*, Mar. 20, 1790, for quotations; Robinson, *Structure of American Politics*, 306.

69. See *DA*, Mar. 18, 19, 1790, for quotations. The precarious public image of Quakers provides background for the suggestion by Arthur Zilversmit, *The First Emancipation: The Abolition of Slavery in the North* (Chicago, 1967), 166, that the New York Manumission Society functioned as a "front" for Quaker antislavery. On how Quakers were viewed in relation to the war for independence, see Thomas Jones, *History of New York during the Revolutionary War*, ed. Edward Floyd DeLancey (1879; New York, 1968), 1:282–84; Commissioners for Detecting Conspiracies to Pierre Van Cortlandt, June 18, 1777, in *Van Cortlandt Family Papers*, vol. 2,

Correspondence of the Van Cortlandt Family of Cortlandt Manor, 1748–1800, ed. Jacob Judd (Tarrytown, N.Y., 1977), 202; *NYP,* Nov. 18, 1784. For a defense of Quakers despite their image as "fanatics," see *NYP,* July 24, 1787 (*NCLA,* Aug. 6, 1787); see also Brissot de Warville, *New Travels,* 146, 165–67, 309–18, and xiv–xv, xxiv; J. Hector St. John de Crèvecoeur, *Letters from an American Farmer* (New York, 1912), 103, 114, 142, 192–97, had positive words for Quakers, in part because of their antislavery views, but see *Moreau de St. Méry's American Journey,* 302, 309, which casts Quakers in a poor light.

70. *DA,* Mar. 24, 1790; *FII,* May 3, 1790.

71. Rusticus's essay appeared in *DA,* Mar. 23, 25, 27, 30, 1790.

72. On serfdom, *DA,* Mar. 29, 1790; "E——" also submitted a defence of Quakers in the March 23 issue. "X.Y." appeared in the March 30 issue.

73. *DA,* Mar. 25, 1790; "Congressional Affairs," *NYM,* May 1790, 309–10; see also *Albany Register,* Mar. 29, 1790; and *DA,* Mar. 6, 1790. Congress ultimately entered into the record two reports, including one severely modified at the behest of slavery's protectors to say even less than the report discussed above; see Elkins and McKitrick, *Age of Federalism,* 152; Robinson, *Structure of American Politics,* 304–5, 310.

74. *DA,* June 3, 1790. A more speculative vision of the future U.S. capital imagined that 150 years hence the American dominion of "liberty" would spread southward from the Potomac all the way to the West Indies, "formerly the haunts of slavery and wretchedness" where "they have . . . restored the unfortunate race of men to the enjoyment of their natural rights" (*DA,* June 14, 1790).

75. *DA,* Mar. 30, 1790 [italics in original]; Ellis, *Founding Brothers,* 111–12.

NOTES TO CHAPTER 6

1. *MH,* Feb. 5, 1795; for a comment on newspapers as a marker of civilization, with regard to American Indians, see *ACent,* Apr. 19, 1799. The perceived absence of the tools of literacy among non-Europeans encountered during explorations provided a basis for Europeans to distinguish themselves from others; see Stephen Greenblatt, *Marvelous Possessions: The Wonder of the New World* (Chicago, 1991), 10; Henry Louis Gates Jr., *The Signifying Monkey: A Theory of Afro-American Literary Criticism* (New York, 1988), 129–32; and Charles T. Davis and Henry Louis Gates Jr., *The Slave's Narrative* (New York, 1985), xxiii.

2. For an introduction to a portion of this literature as published in early-national-era magazines, as well as suggestions about its importance to the antislavery cause, see Mukhtar Ali Isani, "Far from 'Gambia's Golden Shore': The Black in Late Eighteenth-Century American Imaginative Literature," *WMQ,* 3d ser., 36 (1979): 353–72; see Barbara E. Lacey, "Visual Images of Blacks in Early American Imprints," *WMQ,* 3d ser., 53 (1996): 137–80, for a view on white perceptions of blacks during this period informed by a different set of materials.

3. See Henry Louis Gates Jr., preface to *The Classic Slave Narratives* (New York, 1987), x–xi, on the racial representativeness of black speech and writing; see also Davis and Gates, *Slave's Narrative,* xvi. For commentary directly pertinent to the early-national North, see Robert E. Desrochers Jr., "'Not Fade Away': The Narrative of Venture Smith, an African American in the Early Republic," *JAH* 84 (1997): 43, 46–47. David Waldstreicher, *In the Midst of Perpetual Fetes: The Making of American Nationalism, 1776–1820* (Chapel Hill, N.C., 1997), esp. 231, 327–28. Dickson D. Bruce Jr., *The Origins of African American Literature* (Charlottesville, Va., 2001), brilliantly investigates the broad historical meanings of black voicings in early America,

see esp. xii, 49. See also Shane White, "'It Was a Proud Day': African Americans, Festivals, and Parades in the North, 1741–1834," *JAH* 81 (1994): 15–16, 49–50, for a related set of issues in a different public venue. On the concept of the public sphere developed by Jürgen Habermas, see *The Structural Transformation of the Public Sphere: An Inquiry into a Category of Bourgeois Society,* trans. Thomas Burger (Cambridge, Mass., 1989), and the introduction to this book.

4. Gates, *Signifying Monkey,* 132.

5. While accepting the general terms of the relationship among rhetoric, race, and citizenship set out in Jay Fliegelman, *Declaring Independence: Jefferson, Natural Language, and the Culture of Performance* (Stanford, 1993), 194–95, my reading of evidence and context leads to a much more contingent view of the discourse, which does not presume the inevitability of racial exclusion. For a philosophical exploration of antebellum abolitionism, with implications for the argument of this chapter, see David A. J. Richards, "Public Reason and Abolitionist Dissent," *Chicago-Kent Law Review* 69 (1994): 834; for another intriguing approach to blacks and print culture, see David Waldstreicher, "Reading the Runaways: Self-Fashioning, Print Culture, and Confidence in Slavery in the Eighteenth-Century Mid-Atlantic," *WMQ,* 3d ser. (1999): 243–72, esp. 258.

6. David R. Roediger, *The Wages of Whiteness: Race and the Making of the American Working Class,* rev. ed. (London, 1991); Peter Kolchin, "Whiteness Studies: The New History of Race," *JAH* 89 (2002): 154–73; Philip Gould, *Barbaric Traffic: Commerce and Antislavery in the Eighteenth-Century Atlantic World* (Cambridge, Mass., 2003), 67. See also Eric Lott, *Love and Theft: Blackface Minstrelsy and the American Working Class* (New York, 1993); Shane White, *Stories of Freedom in Black New York* (Cambridge, Mass., 2002).

7. *Albany New-York Gazetteer,* June 30, 1783.

8. The ideas posed in this and the preceding paragraph derive from Michael Warner, *The Letters of the Republic: Publication and the Public Sphere in Eighteenth-Century America* (Cambridge, Mass., 1990), 13, 16–17, and throughout; see also Waldstreicher, *Perpetual Fetes,* esp. 77–78, 85, 89; Benedict Anderson, *Imagined Communities: Reflections on the Origin and Spread of Nationalism,* rev. ed. (London, 1991); Christopher Looby, *Voicing America: Language, Literary Form, and the Origins of the United States* (Chicago, 1996), 1–45; also see note 1 above; and Shane White, *Somewhat More Independent: The End of Slavery in New York City, 1770–1810* (Athens, Ga., 1991), 116–19, with whom I disagree on the possibilities of racial discourse within print culture.

9. See Fliegelman, *Declaring Independence,* on "The Elocutionary Revolution," 28–42, 99–107, 128–29, and throughout; David J. Denby, *Sentimental Narrative and the Social Order in France, 1760–1820* (New York, 1994), esp. 2–3, 6, 95, 240–45; Waldstreicher, *Perpetual Fetes,* 73–79, 345–46; Elizabeth B. Clark, "The Sacred Rights of the Weak: Pain, Sympathy, and the Culture of Individual Rights in Antebellum America," *JAH* 82 (1995): 476–77; Janet Todd, *Sensibility: An Introduction* (New York, 1986), esp. 24, 29; Davis and Gates, *Slave's Narrative,* xvi; Gates, *Slave Narratives,* xiii.

10. See note 3 above on the racial representativeness of speech and writing. For Jefferson, the poetry of Phillis Wheatley, a Boston slave-turned-writer, had to be dismissed either as an aberration or as an achievement of a lesser sort. See Thomas Jefferson, *Notes on the State of Virginia,* ed. William Peden (New York, 1954), on Indians, including Logan's speech, see 58–63, 93; on blacks, 138–43; and on efforts at authenticating Logan's speech, 226–58; Fliegelman, *Declaring Independence,* 63, 97–99, 130–31, 138, 192–95; Davis and Gates, *Slave's Narrative,* xxvii–xxviii; Gates, *Signifying Monkey,* 66, 113, 119; Winthrop D. Jordan, *White over Black:*

American Attitudes toward the Negro, 1550–1812 (1968; New York, 1977), 283–85, 429–81, 486; David Grimsted, "Anglo-American Racism and Phillis Wheatley's 'Sable Veil,' 'Length'ned Chain,' and 'Knitted Heart,'" in *Women in the Age of the American Revolution,* ed. Ronald Hoffman and Peter J. Albert (Charlottesville, Va., 1989), 338–444; James T. Campbell, *Songs of Zion: The African Methodist Episcopal Church in the United States and South Africa* (New York, 1995), 18, 28–29. For public questioning of Jefferson's claims for the authenticity of Logan's speech, see *RT,* Apr. 21, 1797; and *Herald,* July 29, 1797.

11. Bearing out this point about the ability of blacks to avoid white "manipulation" in print is Desrochers, "Not Fade Away," 40–66, which offers an extended discussion of Venture Smith's narrative, published in Connecticut in 1798; on the broader issue of African American efforts to establish an enduring presence in the public life of the urban North, see Waldstreicher, *Perpetual Fetes,* 317–48.

12. For reflections on African American authorship during this era and beyond, see Lacey, "Visual Images of Blacks," 138, 170–79; Gates, *Signifying Monkey,* 127–69; Clark, "The Sacred Rights of the Weak," 470; Gates, *Slave Narratives,* ix–xvi; Davis and Gates, *Slave's Narrative,* xi–xxxi; see also Desrochers, "Not Fade Away," 43–45, 64–65; and Waldstreicher, *Perpetual Fetes,* 341.

13. Bruce, *African American Literature,* 50. Also consult Stanley Austin Ransom Jr., ed., *America's First Negro Poet: The Complete Works of Jupiter Hammon of Long Island* (Port Washington, N.Y., 1970), including Stanley Austin Ransom Jr.'s introduction; Oscar Wegelin, "Biographical Sketch of Jupiter Hammon"; and Vernon Loggins, "Critical Analysis of the Works of Jupiter Hammon," which, despite dated and anachronistic interpretations, provide useful background material. "A Dialogue; entitled, The Kind Master and the Dutiful Servant" (1782), in *America's First Negro Poet,* 58–64.

14. Ransom, *America's First Negro Poet,* 14, on Joseph Lloyd's suicide; Bruce, *African American Literature,* 52, highlights the issue of "authority" in Hammon's writing. Hammon has evoked a variety of critical assessments of the religious and political origins and meaning of his response to slavery; recent critics have been more likely to credit him with sophistication and a resister's spirit. For a sampling of religious, political, and artistic appraisals, see R. Roderick Palmer, "Jupiter Hammon's Poetic Exhortations," *CLA Journal* 18 (1974): 22–28; Bernard W. Bell, "African-American Writers," in *American Literature, 1764–1789: The Revolutionary Years,* ed. Everett Emerson (Madison, Wisc., 1977), 176–80, 183, 185, 192; Houston A. Baker Jr., *The Journey Back: Issues in Black Literature and Criticism* (Chicago, 1980), 3–6, 15, 22, 37; Erskine Peters, "Jupiter Hammon: His Engagement with Interpretation," *Journal of Ethnic Studies* 8 (1981): 1–12; Borgne M. Keith, "The Glory of Jupiter Hammon," *Negro History Bulletin* 45 (1982): 91–92; Sondra A. O'Neale, *Jupiter Hammon and the Biblical Beginnings of African-American Literature* (Metuchen, N.J., 1993); Philip M. Richards, "Nationalist Themes in the Preaching of Jupiter Hammon," *Early American Literature* 25 (1990): 123–38.

15. Graham Russell Hodges, ed., *Black Itinerants of the Gospel: The Narratives of John Jea and George White* (Madison, 1993); see editor's introduction, 18–39, and the narrative itself, esp. 89–102; and Bruce, *Origins of African American Literature,* 103–4.

16. See Hammon, "A Winter Piece" (1782), in *America's First Negro Poet,* 69, 73; see also "An Evening's Improvement," 94, in the same volume.

17. Jupiter Hammon, *An Address to the Negroes in the State of New-York* (New York, 1787); for quotations, see 8, 13, 19.

18. Hammon, "An Address to Miss Phillis Wheatley," in *America's First Negro Poet*, 48–53; Bruce, *African American Literature*, 50–51.

19. *NYP*, Mar. 21, 1784; Matilda, "On reading the Poems of Phillis Wheatley, the African Poetess," *NYM*, Oct. 1796, 549–50; see also Jordan, *White over Black*, 283–85, 437, 446, 460; and Grimsted, "Anglo-American Racism," 396, 426–28, 431–32, 434–38, on aspects of public reaction to Wheatley.

20. Olaudah Equiano, *The Interesting Narrative of the Life of Olaudah Equiano, or Gustavus Vassa, The African. Written By Himself* (New York, 1791); for an advertisement of this narrative, see *NYJ*, Feb. 1, 1792; Lacey, "Visual Images of Blacks," 168–73. Gates, "The Trope of the Talking Book," in *Signifying Monkey*, 127–69, offers an important analysis of the spiritual and literary emergence of Equiano and other early black autobiographers; see also Campbell, *Songs of Zion*, 5–7.

21. *NYP*, Feb. 16, 1786, Apr. 8, 1788; Bruce, *African American Literature*, 66–67; a Hammon-like, Bennington, Vermont, address published in Cooperstown in 1795, counseled slaves "to submit to the rod of affliction, with a Christian fortitude"; at the same time, the free should quietly display that they deserved their status. The meeting also rejected the notion that God or nations should distinguish people on the basis of "colour or complexion" (*OH*, Dec. 10, 1795). For other instances of newspapers recording or quoting voices of blacks, some more militant than others but all in standard English, see *DA*, Feb. 25, 1970; *TP*, Dec. 13, 1797 (*ACent*, Dec. 15, 1797); *NYP*, Nov. 3, 1785; *CG*, Nov. 4, 1793.

22. Sam Dennison, *Scandalize My Name: Black Imagery in Popular Music* (New York, 1982), esp. xii–xiii, 14–15, 26, 28, offers some useful remarks on allegedly black dialect in early American music and its broader cultural significance; see also White, "It Was a Proud Day," 26–28. On the use and meaning of black dialect in the nineteenth century, see Robert C. Toll, *Blacking Up: The Minstrel Show in Nineteenth-Century America* (New York, 1974), 67–68; John Edgar Wideman, "Charles Chestnutt and the WPA Narratives: The Oral and Literate Roots of Afro-American Literature," in *The Slave's Narrative*, ed. Charles T. Davis and Henry Louis Gates (New York, 1985), 59–78. Lott, *Love and Theft*, charts the ambiguities of blackface performance in antebellum America; see 24, 40–41, 94, 119, 122, for references to black dialect.

23. *NYP*, Mar. 31, 1785.

24. *NYJ*, Aug. 11, 18, 1785; see also *NYJ*, Aug. 25, 1785, for a complaint about blacks and whites gathering, as if at "a fair," to wash their filthy clothing in a city pond, thus polluting the water supply; in addition, see *NYP*, Feb. 3, 1785, on black and white ice-skaters; and *NYP*, Aug. 18, 1785, on an interracial street fight instigated by a white vendor; White, *Somewhat More Independent*, 116–17. See also White, "It Was a Proud Day," 34–37, 40; Waldstreicher, *Perpetual Fetes*, 295–348; Joanne Pope Melish, *Disowning Slavery: Gradual Emancipation and "Race" in New England, 1780–1860* (Ithaca, N.Y., 1998), 171–83; White, *Stories of Freedom*. Shane White and Graham White, *Stylin': African American Expressive Culture from Its Beginnings to the Zoot Suit* (Ithaca, N.Y., 1998), 85–124; much of this literature focuses on how objections to the public presence of blacks intensified in the early nineteenth century, including the public mocking of alleged black dialect. See chap. 9 of this book for a full discussion.

25. *NYP*, Sept. 11, 1786; *NYJ*, Sept. 21, 1786. Along these same lines, see a letter on black public preachers in Maryland published in New York City's *Daily Advertiser*, Aug. 2, 1790.

26. *NYJ*, Oct. 12, 1786; for an interesting comment on Rhode Island's rogue status which also mentions slavery, see *NCLA*, Sept. 17, 1787 (*CJPA*, Sept. 12, 1787); see also *LFH*, Apr. 26, 1790; J. P. Brissot de Warville, *New Travels in the United States of America, 1788*, trans. Mara

Soceanu Vamos and Durand Echeverria, ed. Durand Echeverria (Cambridge, Mass., 1964) 127–32; and Waldstreicher, *Perpetual Fetes,* 209–10, 230–32, on the deployment of faux black voices for Federalist partisan purposes. For a parable about the difficulties of French-style radical equality, in which the black servant Sambo acts beyond his station, see *OH,* Oct. 26, 1797 (*ACent,* Oct. 3, 1797). On black characters playing the role of social commentator in antebellum minstrel shows, see Toll, *Blacking Up,* 68–72. Lott, *Love and Theft.*

27. *CJPA,* June 17, July 8, 1788. The course of the Dutchess County debate can be followed as well in *CJPA,* Apr. 22, May 27, June 3, June 10, July 15, 1787; for related examples, see *OH,* Oct. 2, 1795; and *Spec,* Feb. 27, 1799 (*ACent,* Mar. 5, 1799); Waldstreicher, *Perpetual Fetes,* 209–10, 230–32, 327.

28. Brissot de Warville, *New Travels,* 134; *NYJ,* Sept. 20, 1787; see Jordan, *White over Black,* 283–85, 445–57, on the problem of "Talented Negroes"; see also Campbell, *Songs of Zion,* 29; and Grimsted, "Anglo-American Racism," 396, 426–28, 431–32, 434–38.

29. For a contemporary description of the various facets of newspapers, see *New York Independent Gazette,* Jan. 10, 1784. For an alternative reading to mine, see White, *Somewhat More Independent,* 56–75, esp. 68–73; White's allocation of anecdotes solely to the more plebian almanac literature shapes his largely nonpolitical interpretation of them.

30. *NYP,* Nov. 4, 1788 (*CJFR,* Nov. 25, 1788); *NYWM,* Dec. 13, 1788; see also *MH,* Jan. 29, 1795; and *NYJ,* Aug. 10, 1786. William D. Piersen, *Black Yankees: The Development of an Afro-American Subculture in Eighteenth-Century New England* (Amherst, 1988), traces black anecdotes, including the story of Cato and the crypt, to New England villages, 108–9, 132, 137, 156–57. For parallels to later minstrelsy routines, see Toll, *Blacking Up,* 73–74; White, *Somewhat More Independent,* 73; White, "It Was a Proud Day," 27–29, suggests that some features of eighteenth-century northern black festivals poked fun at white customs, foreshadowing aspects of the minstrel show; see also Wideman, "Charles Chestnutt and the WPA Narratives"; Lott, *Love and Theft,* 23, 119, 122.

31. *NYP,* Feb. 3, 1791; "An Act for raising two Regiments for the Defence of this State, on Bounties of unappropriated Lands," *Laws of the State of New-York . . . Since the Revolution* (New York, 1792), Mar. 20, 1781, 1:42.

32. *SNC,* Dec. 25, 1798; see *OH,* Mar. 14, 1799, July 6, 1797 (*ACent,* July 4, 1797; *Herald,* July 1, 1797); *CJFR,* Nov. 11, 1788 (*NYP,* Nov. 18, 1788); *Albany Gazette,* Apr. 5, 1790 (*OH,* Apr. 3, 1795); and see *AChron,* July 3, 1797, for a related news item. Donald H. Stewart, *The Opposition Press of the Federalist Period* (Albany, N.Y., 1969), 879–83, for partisan classification of newspapers.

33. *CJFR,* May 12, 1789; see also *ACent,* Dec. 26, 1797. For this and the previous paragraph, see Toll, *Blacking Up,* 67–75; Dennison, *Scandalize My Name,* 8–10; White, *Somewhat More Independent,* 69–73; Piersen, *Black Yankees,* 108–12, 156. Joining Piersen in a much more positive assessment of the anecdote than the one I offer is Desrochers, "Not Fade Away," 52; and White, "It Was a Proud Day," 27–29.

34. *ACent,* Jan. 26, 1798; Bruce, *African American Literature,* 70–71.

35. *ACent,* Oct. 12, 1798; for other derisive material, see *CJPA,* Aug. 19, 1788; *OH,* May 15, 1795; and *SNC,* Apr. 30, 1798. On the largely negative impact of the white use of alleged black dialect, see also Dennison, *Scandalize My Name,* 10, 14, 28; Toll, *Blacking Up,* 67; Melish, *Disowning Slavery,* 166–83.

36. "True African Wit," *NYP,* Dec. 5, 1788 (see also *CJFR,* Dec. 2, 1788, *OH,* Aug. 10, 1797, *CP,* Oct. 1, 1793).

37. Gary B. Nash, "Forging Freedom: The Emancipation Experience in the Northern Sea-port Cities, 1775–1820," in *Slavery and Freedom in the Age of the American Revolution,* ed. Ira Berlin and Ronald Hoffman (Charlottesville, Va., 1983), 20–27; Graham Russell Hodges, *Root and Branch: African Americans in New York and East Jersey, 1613–1863* (Chapel Hill, N.C., 1999), 176–86; White, *Somewhat More Independent,* 150–66; Piersen, *Black Yankees,* 108–9, 156–57. On black petitions for burial grounds, see *Minutes of the Common Council of the City of New York, 1784–1831* (New York, 1917), Oct. 27, 1794, Apr. 7, June 22, July 6, 1795, 2:112, 137, 158–59, 161.

38. For humor stigmatizing the Irish, see *DA,* Feb. 24, 1797; and *NYWC,* May 21, 1796; on Jews, including poetry, see *CJFR,* Mar. 24, 1789; *LFH,* Oct. 26, 1789; *NYP,* Aug. 11, 1791; on country bumpkins, *CG,* May 1, 1794; *OH,* Jan. 12, 1797; on the Dutch, *CJPA,* Dec. 26, 1787; *SNC,* Jan. 29, 1798; on Germans, *SNC,* Nov. 6, 1798; on American Indians, *AChron,* Sept. 4, 1797; *SNC,* June 4, 1798; *OH,* Nov. 9, Dec. 21, 1797; Waldstreicher, "Reading the Runaways," 257–59; see also Warner, *Letters of the Republic,* 16–17, on class; Lott, *Love and Theft,* 83–84, 94; and Roediger, *Wages of Whiteness.*

39. Bruce, *African American Literature,* 51–66; Dennison, *Scandalize My Name,* 11–26; Melish, *Disowning Slavery,* 167.

40. Jordan, *White over Black,* 365–72, quotation 370–71; White, *Somewhat More Independent,* 56–75; Karen Halttunen, "Humanitarianism and the Pornography of Pain in Anglo-American Culture," *AHR* 100 (1995): 303–34; see also Dennison, *Scandalize My Name,* 17, 25–26; Melish, *Disowning Slavery,* 183–84. Warner, *Letters of the Republic,* 12–17, 39–43, 48–49, indicates the racial and gendered barriers embedded in ostensibly disembodied print culture.

41. The editor's introduction and the massive collection of poems in James G. Basker, ed., *Amazing Grace: An Anthology of Poems About Slavery, 1660–1810* (New Haven, 2002), make a powerful case for the cultural significance of antislavery poetry in the English speaking world; see also Isani, "Gambia's Golden Shore," on the contemporary power of this type of literature.

42. Gould, *Barbaric Traffic,* esp. 3–9, 25, 37–81. Gould expressly seeks to leverage the antislavery–cultural hegemony debate between David Brion Davis and Thomas Haskell, cited elsewhere, and to extend their arguments; Gould focuses almost entirely on slave trading and, unlike this study, does not apply his inquiry to actual emancipations during this time period. For recent attention to the issue of sentiment and national identity, see Andrew Burstein, "The Political Character of Sympathy," *JER* 21 (2001): 601–32; Sarah Knott "Sensibility and the American War for Independence," *AHR* 109 (2004): 19–40; and note 43 below. Cathy N. Davidson's introduction to Susanna Rowson, *Charlotte Temple* (New York, 1986), is broadly suggestive as well.

43. Isani, "Gambia's Golden Shore," 354, 357–59; David Brion Davis, *The Problem of Slavery in Western Culture* (1966; New York, 1988), 473–82; Bruce, *African American Literature,* 20; and David Brion Davis, *The Problem of Slavery in the Age of Revolution, 1770–1823* (Ithaca, N.Y., 1975), 368–69 n. Clark, "The Sacred Rights of the Weak," 476–79, 482, 486–87. For more generally suggestive approaches to the political possibilities of sympathetic literature, see David J. Denby, *Sentimental Narrative and the Social Order in France, 1760–1820* (New York, 1994); Thomas W. Lacquer, "Bodies, Details, and the Humanitarian Narrative," in *The New Cultural History,* ed. Lynn Hunt (Berkeley, 1989), 176–204; and Sarah Maza, "Stories in History: Cultural Narratives in Recent Works in European History," *AHR* 101 (1996): 1498–1501, 1508, 1512, 1514; Fliegelman, *Declaring Independence,* 129; Todd, *Sensibility,* esp. 7, 29; Waldstreicher, *Perpetual Fetes,* 73–80.

44. *RT,* July 15, 1796 (*TP,* Jan. 22, 1798); *NYP,* June 19, 1786; for sentimental material on

debtors, see *RT*, Mar. 24, 1797; *TP*, May 7, Aug. 14, 1798 (*AChron*, Feb. 27, 1797); for a suggestive, stylized poetic dialogue between "distress" and "humanity," see *CG*, Feb. 3, 1794. On Algiers, see essays in *NYJ*, Aug. 24, 1786; and *NYP*, Oct. 2, 1786; poems in *AJ*, Mar. 3, 1788; and "The American Captive—An Elegy," *NYM*, Aug. 1794, 516–18; first person accounts in *CG*, Oct. 30, 1794; *MH*, Feb. 12, 1795; and *NYWC*, Aug. 13, 1795; and Susanna Rowson, *Slaves in Algiers; or, a Struggle for Freedom: A Play, Interspersed with Songs, in Three Acts* (Philadelphia, 1794). For an overview of "Humanitarianism and Sentimentality" and its relation to American slavery, see Jordan, *White over Black*, 365–70; and Bruce, *African American Literature*, 20; Isani, "Gambia's Golden Shores," 357–60. See also Todd, *Sensibility*, 2–3, 23, 41; *MH*, Jan. 15, 1795; and Denby, *Sentimental Narrative*, 116–38.

45. *CJPA*, Nov. 7, 1787.

46. Denby, *Sentimental Narrative*, 79, 95–115, 241; Gates, *Signifying Monkey*, 131, 156–57; Davis and Gates, *Slave's Narrative*, xvi; Todd, *Sensibility*, 49–64, esp. 58, 60, on the problematic relationship between style and sentimentality in British poetry. Isani, "Gambia's Golden Shore," 354, 372, offers a positive assessment of the literary artistry of creative antislavery writings.

47. *AJ*, Mar. 17, 1788.

48. George C. D. Odell, *Annals of the New York Stage* (New York, 1927), 1 : 151, 160, 170–71, 239, 245, 251, 259, 264, 316, 345, 2 : 132, 247.

49. Isaac Bickerstaffe, *The Padlock: A Comic Opera* (London, 1768); Basker, *Amazing Grace*, 183–86; Sylvia Wynter, "The Eye of the Other: Images of the Black in Spanish Literature," Carter G. Woodson, "Attitudes of the Iberian Peninsula (In Literature)," and John F. Matheus, "African Footprint in Hispanic-American Literature," in *Blacks in Hispanic Literature: Critical Essays*, ed. Miriam DeCosta (Port Washington, N.Y., 1977), 18, 37–38, 56; Dorothy Eagle, *The Oxford Companion to English Literature*, 4th ed. rev. (New York, 1967), 607. For a Boston, Massachusetts, performance of the play, which includes no reference to the English poem critiquing the characterization of Mungo, see [Isaac Bickerstaffe], *The Padlock: A Comic Opera: As it is Performed at the Theatre, Boston* (Boston, 1795).

50. *TP*, Jan. 22, 24, 1798. According to Basker, *Amazing Grace*, 509, "Quashy" was written by English scholar and former British army officer Capt. Thomas Morris.

51. *CJFR*, Nov. 18, 1788; *MH*, Jan. 22, 1795; see also *OH*, Mar. 7, 1799; Davis, *Age of Revolution*, 368–69 n.; Isani, "Gambia's Golden Shore," 368–69; Bruce, *African American Literature*, 81; Basker, *Amazing Grace*, 300–301.

52. Jordan, *White over Black*, 369; Dennison, *Scandalize My Name*, 15–18.

53. *New York Impartial Gazetteer*, June 14, 1788; *LFH*, Sept. 29, 1788 (*CJFR*, Oct. 14, 1788; *TP*, Mar. 12, 1798); *NYWC*, Oct. 1, 1795; Isani, "Gambia's Golden Shore," 353, 357, 359–360, 365; Jordan, *White over Black*, 371–72; see also White, *Somewhat More Independent*, 59–60.

54. *NYP*, Mar. 9, 1786; see also Mar. 20, 1787; Davis, *Western Culture*, 474; Isani, "Gambia's Golden Shore," 357–59; see Lacqueur, "Bodies, Details, and the Humanitarian Narrative," 179, 180, 204, on sentimentalism's ability in general to compress emotional distance; Clark, "The Sacred Rights of the Weak," 478–79; Todd, *Sensibility*, 29, 52; Jefferson, *Notes*, 138, on the significance of the ability to blush and the related racial implications for blacks; a letter by Antonetta, "For the New-York Magazine," *NYM*, June 1791, 338–39, responded to Jefferson's views on the racial basis of feeling; see also Fliegelman, *Declaring Independence*, esp. 129, 192–95; and Grimsted, "Anglo-American Racism," 419, 435.

55. NYP, Feb. 20, 1787; see also Thomas Clarkson, "A Fancied Scene in the African Slave Trade," *NYM*, Aug. 1790, 464–67.

56. *NYP,* June 12, 1786 (*NYJ,* Aug. 17, 1786). Ironically, Bryan Edwards, a Jamaica planter and proslavery apologist, authored this poem under a slightly different title in 1760 as a very young man, prior to launching his careers in commerce, politics, and literature. The poem provides strong evidence of how words lived a life of their own within eighteenth-century antislavery discourse, not entirely dependent on their authors for either context or meaning; see Basker, *Amazing Grace,* 131–32.

57. *TP,* Feb. 19, 1798; *MH,* Jan. 8, 1795 (*NYJ,* Oct. 16, 1793); Basker, *Amazing Grace,* 525. The dramatic narrative poem "Quashy: or, The Coal Black Maid," *TP,* Jan. 22, 24, 1798, mixed the story of a West Indian slave rebellion with the tragic romance of the title character and Quaco, who loses his life in a war for black freedom; "Ode on Seeing a Negro Funeral," *NYM,* Mar., 1796, 165–66, blends the themes of a life-after-death in Africa, "vengeance" against whites, and freedom for blacks rather than focusing on a specific act of rebellion; see also *NYP,* Oct. 28, 1788; Isani, "Gambia's Golden Shore," 361–62, comments on the more aggressive tone of some poems in this genre.

58. *LFH,* Oct. 13, 1788 (*CJPA,* Oct. 21, 1788); *RT,* Jan. 6, 1797; *LFH,* Sept. 29, 1788 (*CJPA,* Oct. 21, 1788); ; Quashy—see above—also took her life after the death in battle of her lover; see also *TP,* May 25, 1798; and *NYP,* May 29, 1786, Nov. 3, 1791; and Isani, "Gambia's Golden Shore," 358–60.

59. Jefferson, *Notes,* 139–43; Hannah More, *Slavery, a Poem* (New York, 1788), 6–8. See Todd, *Sensibility,* 53, 149, on themes of suicide and death as a sentimental trope.

60. *LFH,* Sept. 1, 8, 1788.

61. Gould, *Barbaric Traffic.*

62. More, *Slavery,* 8; White, *Somewhat More Independent,* 62–63; Gould, *Barbaric Traffic,* 67–70, 74.

63. William Hamilton to John Jay, New York, Mar. 8, 1796, in Frank Monaghan "Anti-Slavery Papers of John Jay," *JNH* 17 (1932): 491–93; Bruce, *African American Literature,* 81.

64. "Anti-Slavery Papers," 493.

65. Bruce, *African American Literature,* develops this theme throughout.

66. Donald L. Robinson, *Slavery in the Structure of American Politics, 1765–1820* (New York, 1971), 7. For a classic account of this compelling figure, see C. L. R. James, *The Black Jacobins: Toussaint L'Ouverture and the San Domingo Revolution,* 2d rev. ed. (New York, 1963); see also Davis, *Western Culture,* 479.

67. For L'Ouverture's military prose, see *RT,* May 12, 1797; *Herald,* May 10, 1797; on L'Ouverture as a force for order, *RT,* June 9, 1797; *TP,* May 19, Oct. 2, 1797; *Herald,* July 8, 1797.

68. Quotations from *Spec,* Oct. 11, 1797; see also *Spec,* Oct. 14, 1797; for the same reports, see *AChron,* Oct. 23, 30, 1797; for other instances of direct quotation of Toussaint L'Ouverture in the New York press, see *DA,* Mar. 13, 1799; and *ACent,* Mar. 22, 1799. See also James, *Black Jacobins,* 186–90, 197–98; and, for a different interpretation than mine, see Isani, "Gambia's Golden Shore," 361.

69. *ACent,* Mar. 22, June 4, 1799 ("Citizen Toussaint, with the black face, seems to be playing a deep game"); *DA,* Apr. 27, 1799; *Spec,* Dec. 29, 1798; *DA,* Apr. 5, 1799; for policy background, see Robinson, *Structure of American Politics,* 363–66; Jordan, *White over Black,* 377–78, 396; for Federalist views and the nuances of Anglo-American diplomacy toward Toussaint L'Ouverture's rebellious island colony, see also Rufus King to Lord Grenville, Dec. 1, 1798; King to Secretary of State, Dec. 7, 1798; King to Henry Dundas, Dec. 8, 1798; Dundas to

King, Dec. 9, 1798; King to Secretary of State, Dec. 11, 1798; King to Secretary of State, Jan. 10, 1799; Timothy Pickering to King, Mar. 12, 1799; Pickering to King, Apr. 22, 1799; Pickering to King, June 5, 1799; King to Secretary of State, June 14, 1799; King to Lord Grenville, Aug. 10, 1799, *The Life and Correspondence of Rufus King,* ed. Charles R. King (New York, 1895–96), 2 : 474–77, 483–88, 499–505, 556–58, 3 : 5–7, 30–31, 46, 86–87; and Pickering to Alexander Hamilton, Feb. 9, 1799; Hamilton to Pickering, Feb. 9, 1799; Pickering to Hamilton, Feb. 25, 1799, *The Papers of Alexander Hamilton,* ed. Harold C. Syrett (New York, 1975), 22 : 426 n., 427 n., 473–75, 500.

70. *Spec,* Feb. 27, 1799 (*ACent,* Mar. 5, 1799); see also *OH,* Oct. 2, 1795; Waldstreicher, *Perpetual Fetes,* 209–10, 230–32, 327–28; see also David Hackett Fischer, *The Revolution of American Conservatism: The Federalist Party in the Age of Jeffersonian Democracy* (New York, 1965), 165–67.

71. To review national trends in black suffrage during the early republic, see Jordan, *White over Black,* 412–14; and Alexander Keyssar, *The Right to Vote: The Contested History of Democracy in the United States* (New York, 2000), appendices.

72. James Brewer Stewart, "The Emergence of Racial Modernity and the Rise of the White North, 1790–1840," and Jean R. Soderlund, James Oliver Horton, and Ronald G. Walters, "Comments," in *JER* 18 (1998): 181–236; James Brewer Stewart, "Modernizing 'Difference': The Political Meaning of Color in the Free States, 1776–1840," in *JER* 19 (1999): 691–712; Melish, *Disowning Slavery,* 163–285; George M. Fredrickson, *The Black Image in the White Mind: The Debate on African-American Character and Destiny* (New York, 1971); Leonard L. Richards, *The Slave Power: The Free North and Southern Domination, 1780–1860* (Baton Rouge, 2000).

NOTES TO CHAPTER 7

1. *Spec,* Nov. 18, 1797; see New York City's *Spectator* in Oct., Nov., and Dec., 1797 for Webster's serialized argument. For background on yellow fever in urban America, see Susan E. Klepp, "Seasoning and Society: Racial Differences in Mortality in Eighteenth-Century Philadelphia," *WMQ,* 3d ser., 51 (1994): 473–506; Raymond Mohl, *Poverty in New York City, 1783–1825* (New York, 1971), 11–12, 105–7; and Charles William Janson, *The Stranger in America, 1793–1806,* ed. Carl S. Driver (1807; New York, 1935), 93, 100 n. See also Winthrop D. Jordan, *White over Black: American Attitudes toward the Negro, 1550–1812* (1968; New York, 1977), 528–30.

2. Noah Webster, *Effects of Slavery on Morals and Industry* (Hartford, 1793), esp. 6–14, 18–20, 37–38, 49; see also Jordan, *White over Black,* 283, 307, 443–48. Philip Gould, *Barbaric Traffic: Commerce and Antislavery in the Eighteenth-Century Atlantic World* (Cambridge, Mass. 2003), chap. 5, offers an extended analysis of the rhetorical parallels and actual intersection between discussions of slavery and yellow fever. On Webster's life and thought, see Joseph J. Ellis, *After the Revolution: Profiles of Early American Culture* (New York, 1979), 161–212, including p. 206 on yellow fever.

3. *Spec,* Dec. 16, 1797; on Webster's public health recommendations, see *Spec,* Nov. 25, Dec. 9, 16, 20, 23, 1797; Webster (*Effects of Slavery,* 35–36) wanted southern swamps drained.

4. Andrew Robertson, "'Look on this Picture . . . And On This!' Nationalism, Localism, and Partisan Images of Otherness in the United States, 1787–1820," *AHR* 106 (2001): 1263–80; Donald L. Robinson, *Slavery in the Structure of American Politics, 1765–1820* (New York,

1971), see esp. 248–94. See also James Roger Sharp, *American Politics in the Early Republic: The New Nation in Crisis* (New Haven, 1993); and David Waldstreicher, *In the Midst of Perpetual Fetes: The Making of American Nationalism, 1776–1820* (Chapel Hill, N.C., 1997).

5. On national politics, see Stanley Elkins and Eric McKitrick, *The Age of Federalism: The Early American Republic, 1788–1800* (New York, 1993); and Sharp, *American Politics in the Early Republic*. See also Joanne B. Freeman, *Affairs of Honor: National Politics in the New Republic* (New Haven, 2001); Jan Lewis, " 'The Blessing of Domestic Society': Thomas Jefferson's Family and the Transformation of American Politics," in *Jeffersonian Legacies,* ed. Peter Onuf (Charlottesville, Va., 1993), 109–46, esp. 117–23; and Joyce Appleby, *Capitalism and a New Social Order: Republican Visions of the 1790s* (New York, 1984).

6. Webster, despite his sponsors and his affiliation, carefully guarded his editorial independence amid the partisan fray; Ellis, *After the Revolution,* 198–207. Jeffrey L. Pasley, *"The Tyranny of the Printers": Newspaper Politics in the Early Republic* (Charlottesville, Va., 2001), esp. 46–47, 105–31. Carol Sue Humphrey, *The Press of the Young Republic* (Westport, Conn., 1996), 41–51, 59; Donald H. Stewart, *The Opposition Press of the Federalist Period* (Albany, 1969), esp. 11–13, 617, and a valuable appendix on the partisan affiliation of New York newspapers, 879–83; Alan Taylor, *William Cooper's Town: Power and Persuasion on the Frontier of the Early Republic* (New York, 1995), 205–8; Michael Lienesch, "Thomas Jefferson and the American Democratic Experience: The Origins of the Partisan Press, Popular Politics, and Public Opinion," in *Jeffersonian Legacies,* ed. Peter Onuf (Charlottesville, Va., 1993), 316–39; Milton H. Hamilton, *The Country Printer: New York State, 1785–1830,* 2d ed. (1936; Port Washington, N.Y., 1964), 98, 102, 213.

7. For New York politics, see Alfred F. Young, *The Democratic Republicans of New York: The Origins* (Chapel Hill, N.C., 1967), 13–14, 22–58, 42–58, 109–66, 281–82, and, more generally, 169–341; John P. Kaminski, *George Clinton: Yeoman Politician of the New Republic* (Madison, Wisc., 1993); Alan Taylor, " 'The Art of Hook and Snivey': Political Culture in Upstate New York during the 1790s," *JAH* 79 (1993): 1371–96. See also Staughton Lynd, *Class Conflict, Slavery, and the United States Constitution: Ten Essays* (Indianapolis, 1967), esp. 25–132; David Hackett Fischer, *The Revolution of American Conservatism: The Federalist Party in the Era of Jeffersonian Democracy* (New York, 1965), xv, 1–28, 52, 60; and Edward Countryman, *A People in Revolution: The American Revolution and Political Society in New York, 1760–1790* (Baltimore, 1981).

8. The details of Clinton's place in New York politics have been studied most recently in Kaminski, *George Clinton;* on the 1792 election specifically, see 201–17; see also Herbert Storing, ed., *The Anti-Federalist: Writings by the Opponents of the Constitution* (Chicago, 1985), 329.

9. *NYJ,* Feb. 4, 11, 1792. For a subsequent Africanus-Americanus exchange, see *NYJ,* Mar. 3, 10, 1792. On Jeffersonian racial thinking, see chap. 6; abolitionist environmentalism is taken up in chap. 8.

10. *NYJ,* Feb. 11, 1792.

11. *NYJ,* Mar. 10, 1792.

12. J. C. Dongan to John Jay, quoted in *The Correspondence and Public Papers of John Jay,* ed. Henry P. Johnston (New York, 1891), 3:413 n.; see also Jay to Dongan, Feb. 27, 1792, 3:413–15; Kaminski, *George Clinton,* 202, 204–5; Young, *Democratic Republicans,* 282, 289. On demography, see Edgar J. McManus, *A History of Negro Slavery in New York* (Syracuse, N.Y., 1966) 200; White, "Map 2: Slaveholding in New York State in 1790," *Somewhat More Independent: The End of Slavery in New York City, 1770–1810* (Athens, Ga., 1991), 17.

13. *NYJ*, Mar. 28, 1792. On Jay's reputation and portrayal during the campaign, see also *NYJ*, Mar. 31, Apr. 11, 1792; Young, *Democratic Republicans*, 281–82, 288–89, 291; Fischer, *Revolution of American Conservatism*, 6–10, succinctly describes Jay's political philosophy.

14. *NYJ*, Apr. 21, 1792; Kaminski, *George Clinton*, 206, implies that this piece exposed proslavery "bigotry," thus suggesting a less ambiguous meaning than that argued for above; see Taylor, "The Art of Hook and Snivey," for analysis of local electioneering in New York during the 1790s.

15. Josh Mersereau to Alexander Hamilton, Apr. 29, 1792, in *The Papers of Alexander Hamilton*, ed. Harold C. Syrett (New York, 1966), 11:344 [original italics].

16. Analysis of this election should make more room for race and slavery as a factor; see Kaminski, *George Clinton*, 215–27; and Young, *Democratic Republicans*, 300–303, 589; and on Ostego County, see Taylor, *Cooper's Town*, 170–96. Although not commenting on the Clinton-Jay election, Countryman, *A People in Revolution*, 244, 248–49, 287–88, is suggestive. Demographic calculations used here are based on McManus, *Negro Slavery*, 200.

17. Kaminski, *George Clinton*, 206; and Young, *Democratic Republicans*, 289; Duncan J. MacLeod, *Slavery, Race and the American Revolution* (New York, 1974), 141–42.

18. Young, *Democratic Republicans*, 308, 429–42, 589.

19. For a concise discussion of the issues surrounding the precipitation, negotiation, and ratification of Jay's Treaty, see Elkins and McKitrick, *Age of Federalism*, 375–449; see also Young, *Democratic Republicans*, 445–67.

20. *Argus*, July 17, July 10, 13, 1795 [original italics]; see also July 22, 25, 1795; George Dangerfield, *Chancellor Robert R. Livingston of New York, 1746–1813* (New York, 1960), 268–72.

21. Gould, *Barbaric Traffic*, 87–89, 104–5, is suggestive on the connections between the Jay Treaty, Algerian captivity, and Anglo-American commerce.

22. Camillus, "The Defence No. V," Aug. 5, 1795, *The Papers of Alexander Hamilton*, ed. Harold C. Syrett (New York, 1973), 19:93–94. For an overview of Camillus's arguments, see Elkins and McKitrick, *Age of Federalism*, 433–37; see also Robinson, *Structure of American Politics*, 356–57; *OH*, Sept. 11, 1795.

23. Camillus's remarks from "The Defence No. III," July 29, 1795, *The Papers of Alexander Hamilton*, ed. Harold C. Syrett (New York, 1973) 18:517–21, quotations on 519 [original italics]; see also "Philo Camillus No. 2," Aug. 7, 1795, *Papers of Alexander Hamilton*, 19:99–105, quotation on 102.

24. *Argus*, Aug. 1, 1795; see also Aug. 5, 10, 1795.

25. Hamilton's position can be traced in the following places in *The Papers of Alexander Hamilton*, ed. Harold C. Syrett (New York, 1961–87): "Remarks on the Treaty of Amity Commerce and Navigation," Alexander Hamilton to George Washington, July 9–11, 1795, 18:414–19, 431; Hamilton to George Clinton, June 1, 1783, 3:369; *A Second Letter from Phocion to the Considerate Citizens of New York* (New York, 1784), 3:540; Hamilton's Conversation with George Beckwith, Oct. 1789, 5:487; Hamilton's Conversation with George Hammond, Jan. 1–8, 1792, 10:494; Hamilton to Thomas Jefferson, May 20–27, 1792, 11:409–10. See also Elkins and McKitrick, *Age of Federalism*, 250–55; Arnett G. Lindsay, "Diplomatic Relations Between the United States and Great Britain Bearing on the Return of Negro Slaves, 1783–1828," *JNH* 5 (1920): 400–406; and Robinson, *Structure of American Politics*, 348–52. Nonetheless, Philo Cinna, "Camillus refuted by A. Hamilton," *Argus*, Aug. 10, 1795, claimed to have caught Hamilton in a contradiction based on his past position. Rob N. Weston, "Alexander Hamilton and the Abolition of Slavery in New York," *AANYLH* 18 (1994): 31–45, offers inconclusive remarks on whether Hamilton owned slaves.

26. *OH,* Apr. 28, 1796; see also *OH,* July 24, Aug. 21, Oct. 2, 1795; on partisanship and regionalization, including the Jay Treaty debate, see Robinson, *Structure of American Politics,* 357–61; Sharp, *American Politics in the Early Republic,* 128–29, 133–34; and Lindsay, "Diplomatic Relations," 406. To follow attempts to secure congressional funding of the treaty in April 1796, see Alexander Hamilton to Rufus King, Apr. 15, 1796; King to Hamilton, Apr. 17[-18], 1796, King to Hamilton, Apr. 20, 1796; Hamilton to King, Apr. 23, 1796; Oliver Wolcott Jr. to Hamilton, Apr. 29, 1796, *Papers of Alexander Hamilton,* ed. Harold C. Syrett (New York, 1974), 20:112–15, 121, 123, 124–25, 135–36, 146–49; see also Elkins and McKitrick, *Age of Federalism,* 431–49; Sharp, *American Politics in the Early Republic,* 127–33.

27. Lindsay, "Diplomatic Relations," 406; Elkins and McKitrick, *Age of Federalism,* 375, 415, 418, 441–42, 446, 449, 451; Sharp, *American Politics in the Early Republic,* 113, 119, 123–25, 131–32, 135–36; *NYWC,* July 30, 1795 (*OH,* Aug. 7, 1795); Alexander Hamilton to Rufus King, Apr. 15, 23, 1796, *The Papers of Alexander Hamilton,* 20:113, 135–36; Pasley, *"Tyranny of the Printers,"* 86, 91–92, 106–8; Stewart, *Opposition Press,* 177–283; Todd Estes, "Shaping the Politics of Public Opinion: Federalists and the Jay Treaty Debate" *JER* 20 (2000): 393–422.

28. Nonetheless, for the Jay treaty as a continuing political symbol, see *DA,* Apr. 24, 1798; *TP,* Apr. 25, May 21, July 16, Aug. 21, 1798; Linda K. Kerber, *Federalists in Dissent: Imagery and Ideology in Jeffersonian America* (Ithaca, N.Y., 1970), 30; see also Lindsay, "Diplomatic Relations," 407–8, for further U.S. attempts to secure compensation from the British for evacuated slaves.

29. See C. L. R. James, *The Black Jacobins: Toussaint L'Ouverture and the San Domingo Revolution,* rev. 2d ed. (New York, 1963), for a classic account.

30. On responses to the St. Domingue revolution, see Jordan, *White over Black,* 375–402; Robinson, *Structure of American Politics,* 361–76; MacLeod, *Slavery, Race and the American Revolution,* 92–93, 153–58, esp. 154; and White, *Somewhat More Independent,* 65.

31. Jordan, *White over Black,* 380, 386–91, 402; Elkins and McKitrick, *Age of Federalism,* 308–11, 335–36; David Brion Davis, *The Problem of Slavery in the Age of Revolution, 1770–1823* (Ithaca, N.Y., 1975), 327, 329; Robinson, *Structure of American Politics,* 361–63; Michael Zuckerman, "Thermidor in America: The Aftermath of Independence in the South," in *Prospects: The Annual of American Cultural Studies,* vol. 8 (New York, 1983), 364–65.

32. *NYP,* Oct. 6, 1791; *CP,* Aug. 6, 1792; see also *NYP,* Oct. 13, 1791.

33. *DA,* Jan. 29, 1796; *RT,* Nov. 18, 1796; *OH,* Dec. 15, 1796; *Spec,* Oct. 14, 1797; *ACent,* Oct. 20, 1797.

34. *CG,* Sept. 11, 1794; *TP,* June 23, 1797; see also *TP,* June 12, 1797.

35. *TP,* July 19, 1797 (*AChron,* Aug. 7, 1797); for an item expressing optimism about the prospects for St. Domingue's recovery, see *Herald,* July 8, 1797 (*TP,* July 10, 1797; *ACent,* July 11, 1797).

36. *Spec,* July 21, 1798, Apr. 3, 1799; *ACent,* Oct. 9, Dec. 11, 1798, Mar. 1, 1799; see also *ACent,* Dec. 28, 1798, for a more guarded analysis of American trade in St. Domingue. On U.S. policy, see Robinson, *Structure of American Politics,* 363–66; Jordan, *White over Black,* 377–78, 396.

37. On the interplay of region and political ideology in southern responses to St. Domingue, see Zuckerman, "Thermidor in America," 364–65; and MacLeod, *Slavery, Race and the American Revolution,* 92–93. On Albany arson, see *CP,* Dec. 3, 1793; and *CG,* Dec. 2, 1793; see also Don R. Gerlach, "Black Arson in Albany, New York: November 1793," *Journal of Black Studies* 7 (1977): 301–12; Stefan Bielinski, "Episodes in the Coming of Age of an Early American Com-

munity: Albany, N.Y., 1780–1793," in *World of the Founders: New York Communities in the Federal Period,* ed. Stephen L. Schechter and Wendell Tripp (Albany, 1990), 111–12, 118; and White, *Somewhat More Independent,* 65, 143–46, 155; on threats to the south, see *NYJ,* Oct. 16, 1793; *CG,* Oct. 31, 1793; rioting in New York City may also have borne an uncomfortable resemblance to events in St. Domingue; see *CG,* Oct. 17, 1793, *NYJ,* Oct. 19, 1793; also see Jordan, *White over Black,* 381–82, 392.

38. *Herald,* Dec. 17, 24, 1796; see also White, *Somewhat More Independent,* 65.

39. *TP,* Dec. 13, 1797 (*ACent,* Dec. 15, 1797); *RT,* Dec. 13, 1797.

40. *ACent,* Oct. 12, 1798; on the issue of sexually punctuated fears, see Jordan, *White over Black,* 398–99, and throughout; see also MacLeod, *Slavery, Race and the American Revolution,* 97, 158–61. On southern vulnerability, see *RT,* Dec. 30, 1796; *ACent,* Nov. 13, 1798, Dec. 11, 1798, Mar. 8, 19, 1799; *Spec,* June 27, 1798; *SNC,* July 2, Oct. 1, 1798; *TP,* Aug. 25, 1797; *Herald,* Aug. 19, 1797; *DA,* Mar. 22, 1799. See also George Washington to Alexander Hamilton, July 14, 1798, *The Papers of Alexander Hamilton,* ed. Harold C. Syrett (New York, 1975), 22 : 20; on fears of a general threat to the nation, see *ACent,* Sept. 5, 1797 (*AChron,* Sept. 11, 1797, *OH,* Sept. 14, 1797); *OH,* June 7, 1798.

41. *ACent,* Nov. 10, 1797; to follow congressional discussions, see *Spec,* Mar. 16, 20, 23, 27, 1799; and *DA,* Apr. 4, 1799; see also *Spec,* June 2, 1798; Robinson, *Structure of American Politics,* 364–65, 441.

42. Paul Finkelman, "Slavery and the Constitutional Convention: Making a Covenant with Death," in *Beyond Confederation: Origins of the Constitution and American National Identity,* ed. Richard Beeman, Stephen Botein, and Edward C. Carter II (Chapel Hill, N.C., 1986), 191, 211–12, 224–25.

43. Kerber, *Federalists in Dissent,* 41–50, indicates that these tendencies continued to typify Federalist-Republican debate over St. Domingue during the Jefferson administration; see also MacLeod, *Slavery, Race and the American Revolution,* 97, 155–58; Jordan, *White over Black,* 382–86.

44. White, *Somewhat More Independent,* 31–32, 155.

45. See White, *Somewhat More Independent,* 80–88, on the dubious nature of comparisons that New Yorkers made between northern and southern slavery.

46. On the slave ship disaster, see *TP,* Oct. 11, 1797. On strange judicial practices in Georgia, see *ACent,* Nov. 10, 1797; and *ACent,* Oct. 3, 1797 (*Herald,* Sept. 30, 1797; *AChron,* Oct. 2, 1797; *OH,* Oct. 12, 1797). Also see newspapers mentioning South Carolina's consideration of a reopening of the slave trade (*Herald,* Jan. 2, 1796) and Georgia's plans to ban it (*DA,* Feb. 24, 1798; *ACent,* Aug. 17, 1798).

47. Quotations from *OH,* Dec. 10, 1795; and *Herald,* June 17, 1797. For mention of violent black crime in the south, see *CP,* Dec. 31, 1792; *OH,* Aug. 21, 1795; *DA,* Feb. 17, 1797, Mar. 7, 1799; *ACent,* Aug. 15, 1797 (*OH,* Aug. 24, 1797), Feb. 20, 1798, Nov. 5, 1799; *NYWC,* July 30, 1795. For fears in North Carolina involving Quakers, see *RT,* June 24, Aug. 5, 1796, Feb. 24, 1797. On southern arson fears, see *RT,* Dec. 30, 1796, Jan. 6, 1797; *OH,* Aug. 4, 1796. On related southern concerns, see *SNC,* July 2, 1798; *ACent,* Oct. 12, 1798, Mar. 19, 1799; *OH,* July 3, 1795; see also Jordan, *White over Black,* 392–93; MacLeod, *Slavery, Race and the American Revolution,* 97; and White, *Somewhat More Independent,* 146. On the opportunities for slave resistance facilitated by the proximity of southern Indian tribes and the Spanish, see *DA,* Feb. 18, Sept. 11, Oct. 21, 1790; *NYWC,* July 30, 1795; *RT,* Sept. 16, 1796; *ACent,* July 4, 1797, May 3, 1799.

48. Quotations from two different accounts, *AChron,* Mar. 20, 1797, and *DA,* Mar. 14, 1797; see also *RT,* Mar. 17, 1797.

49. See David A. Copeland, *Colonial Newspapers: Character and Context* (Newark, Del., 1997), chap. 4, on newspaper coverage of crime during the colonial era, and chap. 5, on black slave rebellions.

50. *Herald*, Apr. 29, 1797 (*OH*, May 18, 1797; *AChron*, May 8, 1797); see also *AChron*, Feb. 27, 1797.

51. William Dunlap, *Diary of William Dunlap (1766-1839): The Memoirs of a Dramatist, Theatrical Manager, Painter, Critic, Novelist, and Historian*, Collections of the New-York Historical Society, vol. 62 (New York, 1930), 1:118–20. White, *Somewhat More Independent*, 146, cites the Maryland example to somewhat different effect, but see White, 86, on the larger point. See also T. H. Breen, "Making History: The Force of Public Opinion and the Last Years of Slavery in Revolutionary Massachusetts," in *Through a Glass Darkly: Reflections on Personal Identity in Early America*, ed. Ronald Hoffman, Mechal Sobel, and Fredrika J. Teute (Chapel Hill, N.C., 1997), 67–95. A reading of Henry Wiencek, *An Imperfect God: George Washington, His Slaves, and the Creation of America* (New York, 2003), suggests that Dunlap's anticipation of Washington's plans was close to the actual case.

52. *CP*, Dec. 10, 1792; *MH*, Feb. 26, 1795; see also Jordan, *White over Black*, 392.

53. *RT*, May 5, 1797; *ACent*, Sept. 26, 1797; see also *RT*, Dec. 13, 1797.

54. *Herald*, Dec. 14, 17, 24, 1796; *AChron*, Jan. 2, 1797.

55. Robinson, *Structure of American Politics*, 429–30, 441–42; and Waldstreicher, *Perpetual Fetes*, 251, 254, suggest a later emergence of these distinctive regional outlooks than I do, and do not emphasize New York's active role in defining its own regional identity.

56. Pasley, "*Tyranny of the Printers*," 105–43; Humphrey, *Press of the Young Republic*, chap. 4; Stewart, *Opposition Press*, esp. 466–86.

57. Elkins and McKitrick, *Age of Federalism*, 590–93, 694–95, 700–701, 703–13; Sharp, *American Politics in the Early Republic*, 176–77; Robinson, *Structure of American Politics*, 264.

58. Queens and Suffolk Counties in New York participated in petitioning against the Alien Act, which fomented the ironic response of Federalist congressmen; *OH*, Mar. 21, 1799 (*Spec*, Mar. 2, 1799; *ACent*, Mar. 12, 1799); *Spec*, Feb. 23, 1799; *ACent*, Mar. 1, Apr. 12, 1799.

59. *TP*, July 4, 1798. On the challenge to the Alien Act in the New York state legislature, see *Journal of the Assembly* 22, pt. 2 (Albany, 1799), Feb. 16, 1799, 119–23.

60. *ACent*, Jan. 1, 29, 1799. See also Robinson, *Structure of American Politics*, 264–65; Sharp, *American Politics in the Early Republic*, 187–88.

61. *ACent*, Mar. 5, 1799 (*Spec*, Feb. 27, 1799); see also *ACent*, Jan. 29, 1799; Waldstreicher, *Perpetual Fetes*, 209–10, 230–32, 327; Fischer, *Revolution in American Conservatism*, 165–66; and Sharp, *American Politics in the Early Republic*, 198.

62. *ACent*, Oct. 27, 1797; Davis, *Age of Revolution*, 338–39; Kerber, *Federalists in Dissent*, 23–32; Fischer, *Revolution in American Conservatism*, 167.

63. *DA*, Jan. 4, Feb. 4, 1799; see also *ACent*, Feb. 19, 1799.

64. Pasley, "*Tyranny of the Printers*," 125; the above-mentioned exchange on slavery is explored in chap. 8.

65. Young, *Democratic Republicans*, 529–32; Stewart, *Opposition Press*, chap. 9, esp. 346, 351; see also Sharp, *American Politics in the Early Republic*, 200; and Robinson, *Structure of American Politics*, 253.

66. Pasley, "*Tyranny of the Printers*," 126–31.

67. *DA*, Mar. 11, 1799 (*ACent*, Mar. 15, 1799); *ACent*, Apr. 6, 1798; *TP*, May 14, 1798; and Davis, *Age of Revolution*, 340–42; Sharp, *American Politics in the Early Republic*, 242.

68. Robertson, "Look on this Picture," esp. 1267, 1264. Waldstreicher, *Perpetual Fetes*, also develops the theme of localized nationalisms at great length.

NOTES TO CHAPTER 8

1. Michael Edward Groth, "Forging Freedom in the Mid-Hudson Valley: The End of Slavery and the Formation of a Free African-American Community in Dutchess County, New York, 1770–1850" (Ph.D. diss., Binghamton University, 1994), 96–100.

2. Judith N. Shklar, *American Citizenship: The Quest for Inclusion* (Cambridge, Mass., 1991); see Introduction for more on this concept; Leslie M. Harris, *In the Shadow of Slavery: African Americans in New York City, 1626–1863* (Chicago, 2003), 50.

3. Shortly after the turn of the century the organization adopted the name "The American Convention for Promoting the Abolition of Slavery and Improving the Condition of the African Race." See *ACPAS* 1:vii–viii. Henceforth, the text refers to the "American Convention" or "the ACPAS."

4. Edwin G. Burrows and Mike Wallace, *Gotham: A History of New York City to 1898* (New York, 1999), 376–78; Dumas Malone, ed., *Dictionary of American Biography* (New York, 1935), 17:259–60.

5. William Dunlap, *A History of the Rise and Progress of the Arts of Design in the United States* (1834; Boston, 1918), 317. The participation of Dunlap, Smith, and Webster in the operation of the NYMS can be traced in NYMS, Aug. 19, 1794, Feb. 17, May 19, Nov. 26, 1795, Jan. 17, Mar. 21, 1797, 6:192, 200, 204, 216, 243, 252. Joseph J. Ellis, *After the Revolution: Profiles of Early American Culture* (New York, 1979), 3–38, 113–212, esp. 120, 137–38, 140, 144–45, 157, 170–71, 184–85; William Dunlap, *Diary of William Dunlap (1766–1839): The Memoirs of a Dramatist, Theatrical Manager, Painter, Critic, Novelist, and Historian*, Collections of the New-York Historical Society, vol. 62 (New York, 1930), 1:ix, xi, xv–xvi, xviii, 51, 72–73, 148, 219, 221, 259, 263. This perspective is meant to complement but also to go beyond Richard S. Newman, *The Transformation of American Abolitionism: Fighting Slavery in the Early Republic* (Chapel Hill, N.C., 2002), esp. 16–32; see also Frederick William Pfister, "In the Cause of Freedom: American Abolition Societies, 1775–1808" (Ph.D. diss., Miami University, 1980), 3–5, 18, 107, 150; Thomas Robert Moseley, "A History of the New York Manumission Society, 1785–1849" (Ph.D. diss., New York University, 1963), 41–45; Graham Russell Hodges, *Root and Branch: African Americans in New York and East Jersey, 1613–1863* (Chapel Hill, N.C., 1999), 166–67.

6. E. H. Smith, *A Discourse, Delivered April 11, 1798, at the Request and Before the New-York Society for Promoting the Manumission of Slaves, and Protecting Such of Them as Have Been or May Be Liberated* (New York, 1798), 6.

7. *ACPAS*, 1:vii–x. See Robert Duane Sayre, "The Evolution of Early American Abolitionism: The American Convention for Promoting the Abolition of Slavery and Improving the Condition of the African Race, 1794–1837" (Ph.D. diss., Ohio State University, 1987), for an overview of this organization, its methods, and its goals; Newman, *Transformation of American Abolitionism*, 3, 19–20, 33–34.

8. *ACPAS*, Jan. 6, 1794, 1:22, 23.

9. *ACPAS*, Jan. 2, 4, 1794, Jan. 14, 1795, 1:8–9, 15–17, 59–60.

10. Samuel Miller, *A Discourse, Delivered April 12, 1797, at the Request of and before the New-York Society for Promoting the Manumission of Slaves, and Protecting Such of Them as Have or May Be Liberated* (New York, 1797), 32, see also 26, 27, 31; Winthrop D. Jordan, *White over Black: American Attitudes toward the Negro, 1550–1812* (1968; New York, 1977), 360, 362.

11. Jordan, *White over Black*, 285–311, 365–72, 487–88, 514–27.

12. *ACPAS,* Jan. 14, 1795, Jan. 6, 1796, May 9, 1797, 1:59–60, 77, 117; Sayre, "Early American Abolitionism," 22, 33, 36–37, 137–64; Smith, *Discourse Delivered April 11, 1798,* 28. See also Moseley, "New York Manumission Society," 276–77; Pfister, "In the Cause of Freedom," 5; M. J. Heale, "From City Fathers to Social Critics: Humanitarianism and Government in New York, 1790–1860," *JAH* 63 (1976): 28; James T. Campbell, *Songs of Zion: The African Methodist Episcopal Church in the United States and South Africa* (New York, 1995), 10–11, 25–26, 28, probes allied themes from the perspective of African Americans reformers.

13. *ACPAS,* Jan. 6, 1796, May 9, 1797, 1:74–77, 110–11; the convention's 1796 remarks were published in *Herald,* Jan. 23, 1796; NYMS, Nov. 15, 1796, Jan. 17, 19, 1797, Sept. 19, 1797, 6:241, 243, 246, 260; NYMS, Jan. 16, 1798, 9:2; Sayre, "Early American Abolitionism," 162.

14. *NYM,* May 1793, 258; *RT,* Nov. 18, 1796; see also *Spec,* Nov. 29, 1797; Sayre, "Early American Abolitionism," 176; Pfister, "In the Cause of Freedom," 7–9; Harris, *In the Shadow of Slavery,* 49, 61, 64–65, 101, 103, 130–32.

15. *Minutes of the Common Council of the City of New York, 1784-1831* (New York, 1917), Oct. 24, 1796, Oct. 30, Nov. 6, 1797, Jan. 29, June 25, 1798, Feb. 3, May 19, 1800, 2:296, 401, 404, 418, 452, 608, 628; NYMS, Nov. 15, 1796, Nov. 21, 1797, 6:239, 264–65; Sayre, "Early American Abolitionism," 177; for a different view, see Alfred F. Young, *The Democratic Republicans of New York: The Origins, 1763–1797* (Chapel Hill, N.C., 1967), 526.

16. NYMS, Apr. 5, 1796, 7:60; Sept. 19, 1797, 6:263; May 15, 1798, 9:10. See also Campbell, *Songs of Zion,* 7, 9, 10–12, 20–21, 28, for related experiences in Philadelphia; and Harris, *In the Shadow of Slavery,* 103, for similar tensions in the nineteenth century.

17. *Minutes of the Common Council,* June 22, 1795, 2:158–59; Hodges, *Root and Branch,* 183–84.

18. *ACPAS,* June 5, 6, 1798, 1:165, 170–73; Smith, *Discourse, Delivered April 11, 1798,* 29–30; see also Jordan, *White over Black,* 344; Sayre, "Early American Abolitionism," 79, 176; Shane White, *Somewhat More Independent: The End of Slavery in New York City, 1770–1810* (Athens, Ga., 1991), 84, 86; and Pfister, "In the Cause of Freedom," 5, 7–8.

19. *ACPAS,* Jan. 4, 6, 1794, Jan. 14, 1795, Jan. 7, 1796, June 5, 1800, 1:11, 18, 56, 85, 191; *Address of a Convention of Delegates from the Abolition Society, to the Citizens of the United States* (New York, 1794), 4. I differ with scholarly observers who sometimes question how much emphasis eighteenth-century opponents of slavery placed on abolition itself; see White, *Somewhat More Independent,* 81–86; Jordan, *White over Black,* 372–74; and *ACPAS,* 1:viii.

20. *ACPAS,* June 5, 1798, June 5, 1800, 1:162, 187–88.

21. Miller, *Discourse, Delivered April 12, 1797,* 36, and also 15–17, 31–33; Smith, *Discourse, Delivered April 11, 1798,* 21–26, 29–30; Dunlap, *Diary of William Dunlap,* 1:119–21.

22. *ACPAS,* Jan. 7, 1796, Jan. 9, 14, 1795, May 9, 1797, 1:89, 39–40, 58–59, 119–121; Miller, *Discourse, Delivered April 12, 1797,* 35, approvingly quoted this statement in his own address (see also 6, 32); Sayre, "Early American Abolitionism," 1, 33; Smith, *Discourse, Delivered April 11, 1798,* 5.

23. Smith, *Discourse, Delivered April 11, 1798,* 24–26.

24. White, *Somewhat More Independent,* 26–27, 114–49; Hodges, *Root and Branch,* 173–75; Graham Russell Hodges, ed., *"Pretends to be Free": Runaway Slave Advertisements form Colonial and Revolutionary New York and New Jersey* (New York, 1994); Edgar J. McManus, *A History of Negro Slavery in New York* (Syracuse, N.Y., 1966), 101–19, esp. 101, 118; Groth, "Forging Freedom in the Mid-Hudson Valley," 177–80, 202.

25. David Waldstreicher, "Reading the Runaways: Self-Fashioning, Print Culture, and Con-

fidence in Slavery in the Eighteenth-Century Mid-Atlantic," *WMQ*, 3d ser., 56 (1999): 243–72; White, *Somewhat More Independent*, 148–49.

26. Quotation from Milton H. Hamilton, *The Country Printer: New York State, 1785–1830*, 2d ed. (1936; Port Washington, N.Y., 1964), 159–60.

27. NYMS, June 2, Aug. 18, 1795, Feb. 16, 1796, Mar. 21, 1797, 6:209, 212, 220, 248; Jeffrey L. Pasley, *"The Tyranny of the Printers": Newspaper Politics in the Early Republic* (Charlottesville, Va., 2001), 52.

28. On the nature of runaway advertisements, see Jonathan Prude, "To Look upon the 'Lower Sort': Runaway Ads and the Appearance of Unfree Laborers in America, 1750–1800," *JAH* 78 (1991): 124–59; and White, *Somewhat More Independent*, 116, 119.

29. Walter Johnson, *Soul By Soul: Life Inside the Antebellum Slave Market* (Cambridge, Mass., 1999), brilliantly explicates the "chattel principle"; see esp. 2–44.

30. Waldstreicher, "Reading the Runaways," offers a fascinating account of the multiple meanings, for whites and blacks, contained in runaway advertisements.

31. Newman, *The Transformation of American Abolitionism*, esp. 60–85, emphasizes the technical, legal approach of early antislavery organizations, providing great detail on the operation of the Pennsylvania Abolition Society.

32. Harris, *In the Shadow of Slavery*, 49, 61–64, downplays the significance of interracial cooperation in this enterprise.

33. See White, *Somewhat More Independent*, 3–4, 14–22, on New York City slaveholding as part of a regional "system."

34. NYMS, vol. 7 (Minutes of Standing Committee, 1791–1807) provides the basis for these and subsequent remarks: see NYMS, June 19, July 12, 1792, Apr. 17, July 30, 1793, July 26, Dec. 1, 1796, Apr. 20, May 25, 1797, 7:11, 18, 21, 70, 79, 92, 94. See also an interesting case of interdiction of attempted slave importation via Connecticut in *CG*, June 30, 1794; for another account of this material, see Vivienne L. Kruger, "Born to Run: The Slave Family in Early New York, 1626 to 1827" (Ph.D. diss., Columbia University, 1985), 730–37.

35. On New England, see Arthur Zilversmit, *The First Emancipation: The Abolition of Slavery in the North* (Chicago, 1967), 103–5, 113–17; T. H. Breen, "Making History: The Force of Public Opinion and the Last Years of Slavery in Revolutionary Massachusetts," in *Through a Glass Darkly: Reflections on Personal Identity in Early America*, ed. Ronald Hoffman, Mechal Sobel, and Fredrika J. Teute (Chapel Hill, N.C., 1997), 67–95.

36. NYMS, Dec. 18, 1794, 7:38. For other cases involving the slaves of former loyalists, see NYMS, Sept. 9, 1791, Apr. 3, 1792, July 30, 1793, Mar. 27, 1794, June 4, 1795, Mar. 11, 1800, 7:2, 5, 21, 46, 145. For other types of cases, see NYMS, Oct. 9, 1792, June 3, July 30, 1793, Aug. 28, 1794, June 4, 1795, Oct. 25, 1796, 7:13, 16, 18, 21, 33, 46–47, 76; see also McManus, *Negro Slavery*, 170–71.

37. NYMS, Mar. 11, 22, May 31, 1796, 7:57–59, 64; *Herald*, Feb. 10, 1796 [italics in original]; see also Moseley, "New York Manumission Society," 108; Kruger, "Born to Run," 736; and Harris, *In the Shadow of Slavery*, 135–37, on how, in the mid-nineteenth century, the absence of black support sapped NYMS of the strength to continue functioning.

38. For cases involving white mothers, see NYMS, Mar. 7, 27, Apr. 3, 1794, Oct. 16, 1794, 7:25–27, 35.

39. NYMS, Feb. 13, Mar. 1, 1798, 7:107; and Register of Manumissions of Slaves, 1785–1809, Museum of the City of New York, 85–87. For other instances involving Indian ancestry, NYMS, May 18, Dec. 10, 1791, July 30, 1793, May 31, 1796, Dec. 15, 1796, Mar. 9, Sept. 28, 1797, 7:1, 3, 20, 64, 81, 89, 100. See also McManus, *Negro Slavery*, 103.

40. *ACPAS,* May 1797, June 5, 1800, 1:132, 189; Moseley, "New York Manumission Society," 71–72, 113.

41. Miller, *Discourse, Delivered April 12, 1797,* 17.

42. McManus, *Negro Slavery,* 101, 118, 167; White, *Somewhat More Independent,* 49, 108–12, 149, 151–52; Groth, "Forging Freedom in the Mid-Hudson Valley," 176–77, 181, 196; Shane White, *Stories of Freedom in Black New York* (Cambridge, Mass., 2002), 13–15.

43. White, *Somewhat More Independent,* 26–30, 222 n., and Kruger, "Born to Run," 746–48, 754–55, 1010–16, offer contrasting evaluations of manumission's effect on slavery prior to gradual abolition; a comparison of Harry B. Yoshpe, "Record of Slave Manumissions in New York During the Colonial and Early National Periods," *JNH* 26 (1941): 78–107, upon which White relies, and Register of Manumissions of Slaves, 1785–1809, Museum of the City of New York, suggests White's estimation of voluntary manumissions between 1791–1800 may be slightly low. See also Hodges, *Root and Branch,* 171–73.

44. ACPAS, Jan. 14, 1795, Jan. 5, 1796 1:59, 71; NYMS, Nov. 26, 1795, May 17, 1796, 6:217, 228.

45. William Jay, *The Life of John Jay: With Selections from His Correspondence and Miscellaneous Papers* (New York, 1833), 1:390–91; Jabez D. Hammond, *The History of Political Parties in the State of New-York, From the Ratification of the Federal Constitution to December, 1840,* 4th ed. (Syracuse, N.Y., 1852), 1:99–100; *Journal of the Assembly of the State of New-York* 19 (New York, 1796), Jan. 18, 1796, 27; Zilversmit, *First Emancipation,* 176.

46. *Journal of the Assembly,* Jan. 18, 19, 21, 25, 26, Feb. 2, 9, 1796, 27, 28, 35, 40, 41, 51–52, 64–65; Zilversmit, *First Emancipation,* 176–77; Young, *Democratic Republicans,* 531–32; Robert William Fogel and Stanley L. Engerman, "Philanthropy at Bargain Prices: Notes on the Economics of Gradual Emancipation," *Journal of Legal Studies* 3 (1974): 381.

47. *Journal of the Assembly,* Feb. 9, 1796, 64–65; Jay, *Life of John Jay,* 1:390–91; see also Hammond, *Political Parties,* 1:99–100; Carl Nordstrom, "The New York Slave Code," *AANYLH* 4 (1980): 19; and Zilversmit, *First Emancipation,* 176–77.

48. *Herald,* Feb. 13, 1796. On property rights as an obstacle to abolition, see Jordan, *White over Black,* 350–52; Zilversmit, *First Emancipation,* 167, 177–79, 199–200, 228; Nordstrom, "Slave Code," 19; and David Brion Davis, "The Emergence of Immediatism in British and American Antislavery Thought," *Mississippi Valley Historical Review* 49 (1962): 214–16. On public reaction, see Jay, *Life of John Jay,* 1:391; Zilversmit, *First Emancipation,* 177–79; and Young, *Democratic Republicans,* 530–31. The newspaper's interpretation of corporate law would not survive long into the next century; see Charles Sellers, *The Market Revolution, 1815–1846* (New York, 1991), 44–45, 54, 85–87.

49. Miller, *Discourse, Delivered April 12, 1797,* 15–16; Smith, *Discourse Delivered April 11, 1798,* 24–25.

50. *Herald,* Feb. 10, 1796 [italics in original].

51. The Peck-Morris controversy touches on slavery in *Ostego Herald,* Apr. 14, 21, May 11, 26, 1796; *The Political Wars of Ostego: or, Downfall of Jacobinism and Despotism: Being a Collection of Pieces, lately published in the Ostego Herald* (Cooperstown, N.Y., 1796), esp. 37; and Alan Taylor, *William Cooper's Town: Power and Persuasion on the Frontier of the Early American Republic* (New York, 1995), 235–49, give a full overview of the complex political feud that swept Ostego County in 1796. See also Young, *Democratic Republicans,* 508–13, 526, 530. On objections to funding compensation more generally, see Fogel and Engerman, "Philanthropy at Bargain Prices," 382.

52. In January 1797, when Jay ally James Watson, now in the state senate, placed a gradual

abolition bill before the upper house, that body dragged out consideration of the bill for two months before eventually voting to postpone the entire question until the next session. *Journal of the Senate of the State of New-York* 20 (Albany, 1797), Jan. 13, 14, 26, Feb. 8, 11, 16, 20, Mar. 11, 1797, 32, 33, 46, 56, 58, 63, 67–68, 88, 90; Jay, *Life of Jay*, 1 : 396; Zilversmit, *First Emancipation*, 180; Young, *Democratic Republicans*, 532.

53.   *TP*, May 26, 1797; James G. Basker, *Amazing Grace: An Anthology of Poems About Slavery, 1660–1810* (New Haven, 2002), xlv, 342; see also Henry Wiencek, *An Imperfect God: George Washington, His Slaves, and the Creation of America* (New York, 2003), for a brilliant exploration of Washington and slavery.

54.   *TP*, May 29, June 7, 1797.

55.   *TP*, June 2, June 12, 1797; this second poem also suggested that the bloodiness of St. Domingue might have been avoided had "SYMPATHY's emotions" flowered there.

56.   *TP*, June 7, June 9, 1797; see also *TP*, June 16, June 23, 1797.

57.   *New York Minerva*, June 9, 1797 (same item in *Herald*, June 10, 1797); Young, *Democratic Republicans*, 529–32; Davis, "Immediatism," 214–15; Burrows and Wallace, *Gotham*, 348–49.

58.   Edgar J. McManus, "Antislavery Legislation in New York," *JNH* 36 (1961): 214.

59.   Young, *Democratic Republicans*, 505–7, 532; White, *Somewhat More Independent*, 84.

60.   *Journal of the Assembly of the State of New-York* 21 (Albany, 1798), Mar. 22, 1798, 262–63; counties referred to as northern and western include: Clinton, Delaware, Herkimer, Montgomery, Onondago, Ontario, Ostego, Rensselaer, Saratoga, Schoharie, Steuben, Tioga, and Washington. Alternative breakdowns tell the same story. For counties formed since 1790 (Delaware, Herkimer, Onondago, Ostego, Rensselaer, Saratoga, Schoharie, Steuben, and Tioga; although Ontario does not fall into this category, its representatives were shared with Steuben, which does), the tally was 22 to 1; for western counties (Delaware, Herkimer, Onondago, Ontario, Ostego, Schoharie, Steuben, and Tioga), the vote was 14 to 1.

61.   *Journal of the Assembly*, Mar. 23, 1798, 267–68; alternative breakdowns of voting reveal a similar pattern of opposition to state funding for emancipated paupers: counties added since 1790 voted 19 to 4; western counties voted 11 to 3; see also Fogel and Engerman, "Philanthropy at Bargain Prices," 380, 382.

62.   *Journal of the Senate*, Apr. 4, 1798, 135; Zilversmit, *First Emancipation*, 180; see Young, *Democratic Republicans*, 19, on New York constitutional rules limiting the electorate in senatorial campaigns.

63.   *Journal of the Assembly*, Mar. 23, 1798, 267.

64.   McManus, "Antislavery Legislation in New York," 214; see also Kruger, "Born to Run," 942; and Benjamin Joseph Klebaner, "American Manumission Laws and the Responsibility for Supporting Slaves," *Virginia Magazine of History and Biography* 63 (1955): 443–53; and Carl Nordstrom, "Slavery in a New York County: Rockland County 1686–1827," *AANYLH* 1 (1977): 158–60.

65.   David Brion Davis, *The Problem of Slavery in the Age of Revolution, 1770–1823* (Ithaca, N.Y., 1975), 339–40; Raymond A. Mohl, *Poverty in New York, 1783–1825* (New York, 1971), 4–21; White, *Somewhat More Independent*, 24–26; Robert Cray Jr., "Poverty and Poor Relief: New York City and Its Rural Environs, 1700–1790," and Graham R. Hodges, "Legal Bonds of Attachment: The Freemanship Law of New York City, 1648–1801," in *Authority and Resistance in Early New York*, ed. William Pencak and Conrad Edick Wright (New York, 1988), 174, 234; Edward Countryman, *A People in Revolution: The American Revolution and Political Society*

in New York, 1760–1790 (Baltimore, 1981), 22, 24, 34–35, 189, 265, 283–96; Burrows and Wallace, *Gotham*, 332–46, 380–81, 385; David Montgomery, *Citizen Worker: The Experience of Workers in the United States with Democracy and the Free Market During the Nineteenth Century* (New York, 1993). In the Hudson River Counties, some dominated by the old manorial system and others by small freeholders, this process of transformation was very gradual and not without ambiguity: on Columbia County, see Martin Brugel, "Unrest: Manorial Society and the Market in the Hudson Valley, 1780–1850," *JAH* 82 (1996): 1393–1424; and, although surprisingly little is said about slavery in slave-heavy Ulster County, see Thomas S. Wermuth, *Rip Van Winkle's Neighbors: The Transformation of Rural Society in the Hudson River Valley, 1720–1850* (Albany, 2001).

66. Shklar, *American Citizenship*; Hodges, "Legal Bonds of Attachment," 226–44; see also Anthony Gronowicz, "Political 'Radicalism' in New York City's Revolutionary and Constitutional Eras," in *New York in the Age of the Constitution, 1775–1800*, ed. Paul A. Gilje and William Pencak (Rutherford, N.J., 1992), 98–111.

67. On the reformist energies of the era, see Young, *Democratic Republicans*, 518–45; White, *Somewhat More Independent*, 84; Heale, "From City Fathers to Social Critics," 22–24, 29; and Zilversmit, *First Emancipation*, 228. On various charitable endeavors and ideals, see "The Citizens of New-York Establishing a Society for the Relief of Emigrants, gave rise to the following lines," *NYM*, Nov. 1794, 703–4; Livingston, "Address to the Rich," *NYM*, Dec. 1795, 740–42; "New-York Dispensary," *NYM*, Apr. 1797, 193; *CG*, Feb. 3, 1794; *TP*, Dec. 18, 1797; *SNC*, Feb. 5, 1798; Thomas Eddy, *Memoir of the Late John Murray, Jun., Read Before the Governors of the New-York Hospital* (New York, 1819), 7–8; *Moreau de St. Méry's American Journey [1793–1798]*, trans. and ed. Kenneth Roberts and Anne M. Roberts (Garden City, N.Y., 1947), 151–53.

68. *NYWC*, Sept. 3, 1795; see also *AChron*, Jan. 2, 1797; *Herald*, Jan. 18, 1797; *Spec*, Nov. 3, 1798; "An Act to amend the act entitled, 'An act for the better settlement and relief of the Poor,'" and "An Act to enable the Mayor, Recorder and Alderman of the city of New-York, to order the raising of monies by Tax for the maintenance of the Poor," Apr. 1, 3, 1799, *Laws of the State of New-York* 22, pt. 2 (Albany, 1799), 803–6, 830; Minutes, Almshouse and Bridewell, N.Y. City, 1791–1797, Apr. 30, May 21, Dec. 12, 1792, Nov. 11, 1794, 25–27, 43–44, 139, Manuscript Room, New York Public Library; for more on changing attitudes toward poor relief, see Cray, "Poverty and Poor Relief," 173–201, esp. 183, 185, 189–90, 193; Robert Cray Jr., "White Welfare and Black Strategies: The Dynamics of Race and Poor Relief in Early New York, 1700–1825," *Slavery and Abolition* 7 (1986): 279; Groth, "Forging Freedom in the Mid-Hudson Valley," 227–28; see also Mohl, *Poverty in New York*, 64–65, for a critical appraisal on New York poor laws and the attitudes behind them.

69. Burrows and Wallace, *Gotham*, 333–34, 336, 343, 346, 351–52, 364–65, 368, 380–85. See also Cathy Matson, "Liberty, Jealousy, and Union: The New York Economy in the 1780s," in *New York in the Age of the Constitution, 1775–1800*, ed. Paul A. Gilje and William Pencak (Rutherford, N.J., 1992), 112–16, 131–33, 141; Milton M. Klein, ed., *The Empire State: A History of New York* (Ithaca, N.Y., 2001), 257–68; Mary-Jo Kline, "The 'New' New York: An Expanding State in the New Nation," and Michael Kammen, "'The Promised Sunshine of the Future': Reflections on Economic Growth and Social Change in Post-Revolutionary New York," in *New Opportunities in a New Nation: The Development of New York after the Revolution*, ed. Manfred Jonas and Robert V. Wells (Syracuse, N.Y., 1982), 14–23, 109–43.

70. Almshouse and Bridewell, Dec. 26, 1796, Jan. 2, 1797, May 29, 1797, 230, 231, 250;

see also entries on 76, 78, 102, 105, 110, 185–87, 188, 190–92, 203, 206, 207, 229, 230, 243, 247, 248, 249–50, 263; Cray, "White Welfare and Black Strategies," 279, 280; for background, see Steven J. Ross, "'Objects of Charity': Poor Relief and the Rise of the Almshouse in Early Eighteenth-Century New York City," in *Authority and Resistance in Early New York*, ed. William Pencak and Conrad Edick Wright (New York, 1988), 138–72.

71. *Spec*, Feb. 7, 1798 (*TP*, Jan. 29, 1798); on the Almshouse caseload, see also Almshouse and Bridewell, Feb. 2, 1795, Mar. 6, 1797, 149–50, 240.

72. For newspaper items relevant to this analysis of the opposition to debt imprisonment in the 1790s, see *CG*, Dec. 2, 1793, Mar. 6, Aug. 4, 1794; *Spec*, Feb. 21, 1798; *ACent*, July 24, Aug. 14, 1798; *AChron*, Sept. 11, 1797; *Herald*, Sept. 23, 1797; *TP*, Dec. 18, 1797; see also Burrows and Wallace, *Gotham*, 381. For poetry on debt imprisonment, see *RT*, July 15, 1796; and *TP* May 7, Aug. 14, 1798.

73. *Herald*, Feb. 10, 1796; Mar. 18, 1797; *NYP*, Sept. 22, 1791; *RT*, July 1, 1796; *TP*, Dec. 13, 25, 1797; *ACent*, Nov. 24, 1797; see also Drew R. McCoy, *The Elusive Republic: Political Economy in Jeffersonian America* (New York, 1980), 179–80.

74. A point made with regard to gradual abolition in New England in Joanne Pope Melish, *Disowning Slavery: Gradual Emancipation and "Race" in New England, 1780–1860* (Ithaca, N.Y., 1997), 97–99; and by Harris, *In the Shadow of Slavery*, 70–71, with regard to New York.

75. Fogel and Engerman, "Philanthropy and Bargain Prices," 377–91; Claudia Dale Goldin, "The Economics of Emancipation," *Journal of Economic History* 33 (1973): 68–70; Harris, *In the Shadow of Slavery*, 70; Nordstrom, "Slave Code," 19–20.

76. *Journal of the Assembly of the State of New-York* 22, pt. 2 (Albany 1799), Jan. 31, 1799, 77.

77. Zilversmit, *First Emancipation*, 181; Fogel and Engerman, "Philanthropy at Bargain Prices," 382; *Journal of the Assembly*, Jan. 18, 19, 31, Feb. 1, 6, 1799, 47, 49, 77–79, 79–81, 93–94.

78. *Journal of the Assembly*, Feb. 6, 9, 1799, 94–95, 99.

79. Goldin, "Economics of Emancipation," 68–69.

80. Zilversmit, *First Emancipation*, 181.

81. *Journal of the Senate*, Feb. 11, 12, Mar. 12, 25, 27, 28, 1799, 41, 43, 76, 102, 107–8, 109; *Journal of the Assembly*, Mar. 27, 29, 1799, 264–65, 271–72; *DA*, Mar. 19, 1799.

82. See 1799 roll-call votes, *Journal of the Assembly*, Feb. 6, 1799, 93–94, to reject gradual abolition; Feb. 16, 1799, 122–23, on Virginia and Kentucky Resolutions. See also Young, *Democratic Republicans*, 524–33; Zilversmit, *First Emancipation*, 182–83; McManus, "Antislavery Legislation in New York," 214. I echo Zilversmit's method, as well as his conclusion, regarding party affiliation. My numbers differ from Zilversmit's based on a different selection of votes to compare; his calculations show even more lopsided support for gradual abolition in each party.

83. "An Act for the gradual abolition of Slavery," Mar. 29, 1799, *Laws of the State of New-York* 22 (Albany, 1799), 721–23. For additional analyses of the law's provisions, see Zilversmit, 181–82; Nordstrom, "Slave Code," 19–20. For a survey of New York poor law and its priorities, see Mohl, *Poverty in New York*, 52–65; see also Cray, "Poverty and Poor Relief," 189.

84. Goldin, "The Economics of Emancipation," 72.

85. Mohl, *Poverty in New York*, 52–65.

86. See Harris, *In the Shadow of Slavery*, 70, on the paradox between the political and economic implications of the New York's gradual abolition law.

87. Nordstrom, "Rockland County," 158, 160.

88. Melish, *Disowning Slavery*, 68–78.

89. Harris, *In the Shadow of Slavery;* David N. Gellman and David Quigley, eds., *Jim Crow New York: A Documentary History of Race and Citizenship, 1777–1877* (New York, 2003).

90. Charles C. Andrews, *History of the African Free School* (New York, 1830), 117–22, reports on the problem of job discrimination in the nineteenth century; see also Harris, *In the Shadow of Slavery,* 77, 98–100, 142, 167, 237.

91. Nordstrom, "Slave Code," 19–23.

92. Harris, *In the Shadow of Slavery,* 61–66.

93. Harris, *In the Shadow of Slavery,* 70; Melish, *Disowning Slavery,* 76; see also François Furstenberg, "Beyond Freedom and Slavery: Autonomy, Virtue, and Resistance in Early American Political Discourse," *JAH* 89 (2003): 1295–1330. Jordan, *White over Black,* 350–51, and Zilversmit, *First Emancipation,* 200, 228, observe the paralyzing problem for antislavery of a Lockean rights discourse that championed equal rights and property rights; these observations contain a fundamental truth. Moreover, as Wiencek, *An Imperfect God,* shows throughout his exploration of George Washington's struggle to craft an emancipation plan, parsing the economic impact of manumission on masters and slaves was an issue that serious people of at least some good will took seriously.

94. Zilversmit, *First Emancipation,* 180; Nordstrom, "Slave Code," 19–20; Fogel and Engerman, "Philanthropy at Bargain Prices," 377–81; Goldin, "The Economics of Emancipation," 68–70; Groth, "Forging Freedom in the Mid-Hudson Valley," 112.

95. *Journal of the Assembly of the State of New-York* 25 (Albany, 1802), Jan. 26, Feb. 13, 15, 24, Mar. 8–9, Mar. 17–19, Mar. 23–25, 1802, 5–6, 24, 78, 86, 128, 174, 177, 210–211, 212, 217, 231–232, 233, 239; *Journal of the Senate of the State of New-York* 25 (Albany, 1802), Mar. 9–10, 13, 15, 24, 26, 1802, 61, 63, 71, 72, 73, 77, 93, 99; "An Act amending the Act, entitled 'An Act concerning Slaves and Servants,'" Mar. 26, 1802, *Laws of the State of New-York* 25 (Albany, 1802), 82–83; Zilversmit, *First Emancipation,* 183–84. For an example of the local administration of the finer points of the abandonment clause, see *Minutes of the Common Council of the City of New York, 1784–1831* (New York, 1917), July 25, 1803, 3:351–52; see also for examples of registered abandonment in the early 1800s, Book of Coloured People, 1785–1822, Town Clerk's Vault, Eastchester, New York (microfilm, New York State Archives); and *Manumission Book of the Towns of Huntington and Babylon, Long Island, New York, with some earlier manumissions and index, 1800–1804* (Huntington, N.Y., 1980), 1, 2, 4, 7, 10, 11, 12, 15, 16, 17, 20.

96. "An Act to repeal the tenth Section of the Act, entitled 'An Act concerning Slaves and Servants,'" Mar. 31, 1804, *Laws of the State of New-York* (Albany, 1804), 3:479–80; *Journal of the Assembly of the State of New-York* 27 (Albany, 1804), Feb. 10–11, 13–14, Mar. 9–10, 24, 26, 1804, 54, 57, 66–67, 151, 156, 157–158, 223, 232–235, 237; *Journal of the Senate of the State of New-York* 27 (Albany, 1804), Mar. 15–16, 22–23, 26, 28, 1804, 50, 51, 61–62, 67, 70, 78–79.

The public expense of the disavowed abandonment policy was as much perception as reality. Twenty thousand dollars in such payments represented a fraction of the total $340,000 in 1804 government outlays. Such outlays were half the cost of convening the state legislature itself. Under the new law, masters henceforth would have to wait until females reached the age of 18 and males 21 before manumitting the children of their slaves without financial liability. Slave owners could choose to command the labor of women until the age of 25 and men until the age of 28. On budgetary issues, see *Journal of the Assembly of the State of New-York* 28 (Albany, 1805), Jan. 24, 1805, 35; and *Journal of the Assembly of the State of New-York* 25 (Albany, 1804), Jan. 26, 1802, 17, 19; see also *Journal of the Assembly of the State of New-York* 26 (Albany,

1803), Mar. 12, 14, 16–17, 1803, 181, 186, 200, 202; *Journal of the Senate of the State of New York* 26 (Albany, 1803), Mar. 17, 22, 91, 103–4; see Zilversmit, *First Emancipation*, 184, who views state-supported abandonment as a skyrocketing expense; see also Kruger, "Born to Run," 843–50; and George Clinton to Pierre Van Cortlandt Jr., July 29, 1802, *Van Cortlandt Family Papers*, vol. 3, *Correspondence of the Van Cortlandt Family of Cortlandt Manor, 1800-1804*, ed. Jacob Judd (Tarrytown, N.Y., 1978), 3:70, for a private remark disparaging manumission and the ability of free blacks to support themselves.

97. Zilversmit, 184–89, 192–200; Graham Russell Hodges, *Slavery and Freedom in the Rural North: African Americans in Monmouth County, New Jersey, 1665–1865* (Madison, Wisc., 1997), 129, 134–36.

98. Zilversmit, *First Emancipation*, 183–84; Nordstrom, "Slave Code," 20. On the delaying of freedom to an adult age, see *Journal of the Assembly*, Mar. 23, 1798, 268; Harris, *In the Shadow of Slavery*, 70; Fogel and Engerman, "Philanthropy at Bargain Prices," table on 381; and chap. 3 of this book.

99. *Laws of New-York*, Mar. 29, 1799, 721; Fogel and Engerman, "Philanthropy at Bargain Prices," 377–81, 399; Jordan, *White over Black*, 354; Seymour Drescher, *Capitalism and Antislavery: British Mobilization in Comparative Perspective* (New York, 1987), 166.

100. Jordan, *White over Black*, 350–51; Zilversmit, *First Emancipation*, 167, 177–78, 199–200, 228.

101. *Journal of the Assembly*, Jan. 10, 15, 29, 30, Feb. 1, Mar. 8, 13, 15, 19, 30, Apr. 1, 1799, 25–26, 40–41, 66–68, 79–80, 183, 202–4, 213, 225, 274, 285; *Journal of the Senate*, Feb. 2, Mar. 18, 19, 20, 21, 28, 29, 30, Apr. 1, 1799, 32, 85, 86, 87, 91, 110, 112, 118, 121, 128; "An Act to amend the Act entitled n Act for the relief of Debtors with respect to the Imprisonment of their Persons," Apr. 2, 1799, *Laws of the State of New-York*, 817–18. For objections raised about retroactivity in debt prison relief, see *ACent*, Jan. 25, 1799.

102. *Journal of the Senate*, Feb. 2, 1799, 32; *Journal of the Assembly*, Jan. 9, 1799, 15; *Herald*, Mar. 18, 1797; *OH*, Jan. 25, Aug. 23, 30, 1798; *ACent*, Dec. 14, 1798; Young, *Democratic Republicans*, 533.

103. Actual support or opposition to each form of abolition does not itself correlate well. Although Federalists were more likely to oppose the abolition of debtor imprisonment and Republicans more likely to support it, each party was noticeably divided internally on the proposal to phase out this practice. For final roll-call vote on debt imprisonment abolition, see *Journal of the Assembly*, Mar. 19, 1799, 225; on Virginia and Kentucky Resolutions, see Feb. 16, 1799, 122–23. See also Young, *Democratic Republicans*, 524–33; Zilversmit, *First Emancipation*, 182–83; McManus, "Antislavery Legislation in New York," 214.

104. *Herald*, Sept. 23, 1797.

105. Smith, *Discourse Delivered April 11, 1798*, 25; Nordstrom, "Rockland County," 159–60.

106. White, *Somewhat More Independent*, 38, 149; White, *Stories of Freedom*; Goldin, "The Economics of Emancipation," 71; and chap. 9 of this book.

107. Melish, *Disowning Slavery*, is the leading work on gradual emancipation in New England; see also T. H. Breen, "Making History"; Zilversmit, *First Emancipation*, 103–5, 113–17; MacLeod, *Slavery, Race and the American Revolution*, 99.

108. "Notes of Gen. E. Root," in Hammond, *Political Parties*, 1:580–81; White, *Somewhat More Independent*, 27, 83–84.

109. Zilversmit, *First Emancipation*, 208.

110. *ACPAS*, June 5, 1800, 1 : 186–91, quotations on 191.

NOTES TO CHAPTER 9

1. The epigraphs to this chapter are from Samuel L. Knapp, *The Life of Thomas Eddy, Comprising an Extensive Correspondence with Many of the Most Distinguished Philosophers and Philanthropists of This and Other Countries* (1834; London, 1836), 209; Nathaniel H. Carter and William L. Stone, eds., *Reports of the Proceedings and Debates of the Convention of 1821, Assembled for the Purpose of Amending the Constitution of the State of New York* (Albany, 1821), 497–98; William Hamilton, *Oration Delivered in the African Zion Church, on the Fourth of July, 1827, in Commemoration of the Abolition of Domestic Slavery in This State* (New York, 1827), 5–6 [italics in original].

2. Hamilton, *Oration Delivered in the African Zion Church*, 5; *FJ*, July 27, 1827; for reports of commemorative meetings of blacks, see *FJ*, July 6, 13, 20, 1827.

3. The study of historical memory is a rapidly growing field. For a landmark study of memory related to post–Civil War emancipation, see David W. Blight, *Race and Reunion: The Civil War and American Memory* (Cambridge, Mass., 2001); Andrew Burstein, *America's Jubilee: How in 1826 a Generation Remembered Fifty Years of Independence* (New York, 2001), investigates American historical memory during the period discussed in this chapter. Joanne Pope Melish, *Disowning Slavery: Gradual Emancipation and "Race" in New England, 1780–1860* (Ithaca, N.Y., 1998), chap. 6, offers an intriguing discussion of memory and "amnesia" in postemancipation New England, a phenomenon, I argue here, which does not describe the situation in New York.

4. James Brewer Stewart, "The Emergence of Racial Modernity and the Rise of the White North, 1790–1840," and comments by Jean R. Soderlund, James Oliver Horton, and Ronald G. Walters, *JER* 18 (1998): 181–236. See also James Brewer Stewart, "Modernizing 'Difference': The Political Meaning of Color in the Free States, 1776–1840," *JER* 19 (1999): 691–712; and Lois E. Horton, "From Class to Race in Early America: Northern Post-Emancipation Racial Reconstruction," *JER* 19 (1999): 629–49.

5. Joanne Pope Melish, "The 'Condition' Debate and Racial Discourse in the Antebellum North," *JER* 19 (1999): 653, notes the frequency of the application of this term to free blacks by white and African American commentators during the antebellum period.

6. Mitch Kachun, *Festivals of Freedom: Memory and Meaning in African American Emancipation Celebrations, 1808–1915* (Amherst, 2003), highlights the historical dimension of African American celebration and oratory in the nineteenth century.

7. Graham Russell Hodges, *Root and Branch: African Americans in New York and East Jersey* (Chapel Hill, N.C., 1999), 180–85, 213–15; Leslie M. Harris, *In the Shadow of Slavery: African Americans in New York City, 1626–1863* (Chicago, 2003), 82–86; James Oliver Horton and Lois E. Horton, *In Hope of Liberty: Culture, Community and Protest Among Northern Free Blacks, 1700–1860* (New York, 1997), 130–50; John H. Hewitt, "Unresting the Waters: The Fight Against Racism in New York's Episcopal Establishment, 1845–1853," *AANYLH* 18 (1994): 7–30.

8. Patrick Rael, *Black Identity and Black Protest in the Antebellum North* (Chapel Hill, N.C., 2002), 47, 84–91, quotation on 90.

9. Peter Williams Jr., *An Oration on the Abolition of the Slave Trade, Delivered in the African Church in the City of New-York, January 1, 1808* (New York, 1808), 15, 21; Harris, *In the Shadow of Slavery*, 84, 89; Hodges, *Root and Branch*, 142, 183–84.

10. Williams, *Oration*, 24, 26, 27–28.

11. Henry Sipkins, *Oration Delivered in the African Church in the City of New York, January 2, 1809* (New York, 1809), 9–11; quotations on 16, 20, 21; Williams, *Oration*, 11, 13, 15, 20.

12. Hodges, *Root and Branch*, 187–188; Harris, *In the Shadow of Slavery*, 86–89.

13. Joseph Sidney, *An Oration Commemorative of the Abolition of the Slave Trade in the United States; Delivered Before the Wilberforce Philanthropic Association in the City of New-York, on the Second of January, 1809* (New York, 1809), 4, 8, 15–16; Paul A. Gilje and Howard B. Rock, "'Sweep O! Sweep O!': African-American Chimney Sweeps and Citizenship in the New Nation," *WMQ*, 3d ser., 51 (1994): 520.

14. Sidney, *Oration*, 16; Harris, *In the Shadow of Slavery*, 89–92, also offers a helpful account of the speeches discussed above.

15. Agreement between John Peter de Lancey and H. Purdy, regarding slave Jack Purdy, [Mar. 30?], 1803; Contract by James Hart, regarding Nan, Apr. 22, 1803; Agreement between John Peter de Lancey and Ruth Ward regarding Betty, Apr. 14, 1806; Agreement between John Peter de Lancey and Peter Underhill, May 14, 1807, de Lancey Papers, Museum of the City of New York; Vivienne L. Kruger, "Born to Run: The Slave Family in Early New York, 1626 to 1827" (Ph.D. diss., Columbia University, 1985), 725, 741, 746–48, 755–66. *Albany Gazette*, Nov. 14, 1808, May 6, 1816; Nicholas Schenck, Manumission Agreement with Harry Ferguson, June 7, 1819, Schenck Family Papers, New-York Historical Society, New York City; Shane White, *Somewhat More Independent: The End of Slavery in New York City, 1770–1810* (Athens, Ga., 1991), 29–30, 49, 108–12, 115, 149, 151–52; Shane White, *Stories of Freedom in Black New York* (Cambridge, Mass., 2002), 8–66, including 13–15, on slave-master negotiations; Michael Edward Groth, "Forging Freedom in the Mid-Hudson Valley: The End of Slavery and the Formation of a Free African-American Community in Dutchess County, New York, 1770–1850" (Ph.D. diss., Binghamton University, 1994), 147–202.

16. Claudia Dale Goldin, "The Economics of Emancipation," *Journal of Economic History* 33 (1973): 70–71; White, *Somewhat More Independent*, 26, 46–53, 111; Kruger, "Born to Run," 747, 924; Groth, "Forging Freedom in the Mid-Hudson Valley," 114–15, 121, 147; Harris, *In the Shadow Slavery*, 72–74.

17. White, *Somewhat More Independent*, 150–84, esp. 156–66, on occupational structure; White, *Stories of Freedom*, 32–34; Stefan Bielinski, "The Jacksons, the Lattimores, and the Schuylers: Three Albany Families and the Emergence of an African-American Middle Class in an Early American City," paper, Colonial Albany Social History Project, New York State Museum, 1993; Gilje and Rock, "African-American Chimney Sweeps," 506–38.

18. Gilje and Rock, "African-American Chimney Sweeps," 520–30.

19. *Minutes of the Common Council*, Aug. 4, 1806, Mar. 30, Aug. 10, 17, Dec. 28, 1807, Mar. 28, Sept. 26, Oct. 10, 1808, June 19, 1809, 4:256, 389, 522–23, 525, 682, 5:59, 272, 278, 586.

20. Ichabod Brush Estate Papers, Miscellaneous Documents, Long Island Room, Queensborough Library, Jamaica, Queens, New York.

21. Groth, "Forging Freedom in the Mid-Hudson Valley," 203–38; Jacquetta M. Haley, "The Van Cortlandt Family in a New Nation" (from the library collection of Historic Hudson Valley, Tarrytown, New York, 1984), 51–59; Gary B. Nash, "Forging Freedom: The Emancipa-

tion Experience in the Northern Seaport Cities, 1775–1820," in *Slavery and Freedom in the Age of the American Revolution,* ed. Ira Berlin and Ronald Hoffman (Charlottesville, Va., 1983), 10; Hodges, *Root and Branch,* 175–76, 220–23; Graham Russell Hodges, *Slavery and Freedom in the Rural North: African Americans in Monmouth County, New Jersey, 1665–1865* (Madison, Wisc., 1997), 147–70, on conditions for free blacks in neighboring New Jersey.

22. James Hawxhurst, Journal 1797–1815, Rare Book and Manuscript Room, New York Public Library, New York City (my observations are based on entries from 1801–1811). See also Jonah Willets, Account Book, Long Island Room, Queensborough Library, Jamaica, Queens, New York; White, *Somewhat More Independent,* 47–50; and Harris, *In the Shadow of Slavery,* 80–81.

23. On various aspects of free black life in the urban north, see Nash, "Forging Freedom," 3–48. On the decline of black economic opportunity, see Charles C. Andrews, *History of the New-York African Free-Schools* (New York, 1830), 117–22; see also Harris, *In the Shadow of Slavery,* 77, 98–100, 142, 167, 237; White, *Somewhat More Independent,* 208–9; White, *Stories of Freedom,* 34–38.

24. David Hackett Fischer, *The Revolution of American Conservatism: The Federalist Party in the Era of Jeffersonian Democracy* (New York, 1965), 165–66; David Waldstreicher, *In the Midst of Perpetual Fetes: The Making of American Nationalism, 1776–1820* (Chapel Hill, N.C., 1997), 230–32, 327; see also chap. 6 above.

25. On black voters and Federalism, see Fischer, *Revolution of Modern Conservatism,* 166–67; Dixon Ryan Fox, "The Negro Vote in Old New York," *Political Science Quarterly* 32 (1917): 254–57; Charles Wesley, "Negro Suffrage in the Period of Constitution-Making, 1787–1865," *JNH* 32 (1947): 155–56; Harvey Strum, "Property Qualifications and Voting Behavior, 1807–1816," *JER* 1 (1981): 360; Rael, *Black Identity,* 44, 240.

26. *New York Gazette and General Advertiser,* Jan. 3, 1803, quoted in *The Burghers of New Amsterdam and The Freemen of New York. 1675-1866,* Collections of the New-York Historical Society, vol. 18 (New York, 1886), 305–6.

27. Robert J. Swan, "John Teasman: African-American Educator and the Emergence of Community in Early Black New York City, 1787–1815," *JER* 12 (1992): 331–356; Harris, *In the Shadow of Slavery,* devotes much attention to the formation of African American organizations.

28. Craig Steven Wilder, *In the Company of Black Men: The African Influence on African American Culture in New York City* (New York, 2001), develops the subject of black organizational life in great detail, tracing the impetus for black organization to the period of colonial enslavement and to Africa.

29. NYMS, Nov. 14, 1809, Jan. 9, 1810, 9:223, 231; Harris, *In the Shadow of Slavery,* 88–89, 92, 102–3, 122–28; Timothy P. McCarthy, "'To Plead Our Own Cause': Freedom, Black Print Culture, and the Origins of Abolitionism in New York" (paper presented at the Annual Meeting of the Organization of American Historians, San Francisco, Apr. 1997), 15–18; Shane White, "'It Was a Proud Day': African Americans, Festivals, and Parades in the North, 1741–1834," *JAH* 81 (1994): 38–40, 43–46, 49–50; Swan, "Teasman," esp. 349; Kachun, *Festivals of Freedom,* 43.

30. Thelma Wills Foote, *Black and White Manhattan: The History of Racial Formation in Colonial New York City* (New York, 2004), 39–40.

31. Shane White and Graham White, *Stylin': African American Expressive Culture from*

Its Beginning to the Zoot Suit (Ithaca, N.Y., 1998), 85–96; White, *Stories of Freedom*, 5–58; Shane White, "The Death of James Johnson," *American Quarterly* 51 (1999): 753–95; see 778 for statistics on blacks and the New York City legal system.

32. Daniel Horsmanden, *The New York Conspiracy; or, A history of the negro plot, with the journal of proceedings against the conspirators at New-York, in the years 1741–2*, 2d ed. (New York, 1810), 3–4, 7–8, 11–12; *The New York Conspiracy by Daniel Horsmanden*, ed. Thomas J. Davis (Boston, 1971), 117; Peter Charles Hoffer, *The Great New York Conspiracy of 1741: Slavery, Crime, and Colonial Law* (Lawrence, Kans., 2003), 91, 116; Foote, *Black and White Manhattan*, 159–86, esp. 177–79, on the role that interpreting, or misinterpreting, black dialect played in the Horsmanden transcript.

33. "An Act to prevent frauds and perjuries at elections, and to prevent slaves from voting," Apr. 9, 1811, *Laws of the State of New-York* 34 (Albany, 1811), 370–73; *Journal of the Senate of the State of New-York* 34 (Albany, 1811), Mar. 26, 30, Apr. 6, 8, 1811, 143–44, 163–64, 196–97, 199–202; *Journal of the Assembly of the State of New-York* 34 (Albany, 1811), Mar. 9, 13, 23, 25, 30, Apr. 1, Apr. 8, 1811, 231, 251–52, 310–11, 315–16, 351, 358–60, 401, 404–6; Wesley, "Negro Suffrage," 148, 154–58; Strum, "Property Qualifications," 348–49, 360–66; Chilton Williamson, *American Suffrage: From Property to Democracy, 1760–1860* (Princeton, 1960), 159–61. For further adjustments to the 1811 law, see "An Act to amend an Act, entitled 'An Act for regulating Elections,' passed March 29, 1813," Apr. 11, 1815, *Laws of the State of New-York* 36–38 (Albany, 1815), 146–47.

34. *Journal of the Senate*, Apr. 5, 1811, 193; Alfred B. Street, *The Council of Revision of the State of New York; A History of the Court with which its Members were Connected; Biographical Sketches of its Members; and its Vetoes* (Albany, 1859), 362–64; *New-York Evening Post*, Apr. 16, 1811.

35. Foote, *Black and White Manhattan*, 160–61, 186.

36. Melish, *Disowning Slavery*, 101–6.

37. Robert William Fogel and Stanley Engerman, "Philanthropy at Bargain Prices: Notes on the Economics of Gradual Emancipation," *Journal of Legal Studies* 3 (1974): 392–93; see also Goldin, "The Economics of Emancipation," 70; and Philip Foner, *Blacks in the American Revolution* (Westport, Conn., 1975), 104.

38. See White, *Somewhat More Independent*, esp. 149–53.

39. Richard S. Newman, *The Transformation of American Abolitionism: Fighting Slavery in the Early Republic* (Chapel Hill, N.C., 2002), 16–49, 60–85; Fogel and Engerman, "Philanthropy at Bargain Prices."

40. NYMS, Mar. 21, 1809, 10:64–65.

41. NYMS, Oct. 31, 1800, 7:173; Sept. 17, 1807, Sept. 14, Oct. 2, 1810, 10:14, 107–108; June 10, 1800, May 23, 1806, 7:165–66, 312–13; *ACPAS*, June 5, June 6, 1800, 1:190, 195–96; and Harris, *In the Shadow of Slavery*, 92, 208.

42. NYMS, Apr. 25, 1800, 7:158–61.

43. *The Trial of Amos Broad and His Wife, On three several Indictments for Assaulting and Beating Betty, A Slave, And Her Little Female Child Sarah, Aged Three Years* (New York, 1809); for quotation see 3. The NYMS made plans to the lobby the state legislature to tighten restrictions against cruelty to slaves (NYMS, Nov. 17, 1807, 9:176); see also NYMS, Oct. 15, 1811, Feb. 3, 1812, 10:148–49, 162, for two complaints of master cruelty brought before the standing committee; see also White, *Stories of Freedom*, 17–19.

44. NYMS, May 6, 1806, 7:311–12; Aug. 22, 1815, 10:273.

45. NYMS, Jan. 9, Apr. 10, 1810, Jan. 15, Nov. 25, 1811, 9:230–31, 244, 268–69, 280; Goldin, "The Economics of Emancipation," 70–71; Harris, *In the Shadow of Slavery,* 108.

46. *Public Papers of Daniel D. Tompkins: Governor of New York, 1807-1817,* ed. Hugh Hastings (New York, 1898), 1:20, 2:446–47, 3:590, 595–96, 616; "An Act to authorize the Raising of two Regiments of Men of Colour," Oct. 24, 1814, *Laws of the State of New-York,* 36–38, 22–23; Jabez D. Hammond, *The History of Political Parties in the State of New-York, From the Ratification of the Federal Constitution to December, 1840,* 4th ed. (Syracuse, N.Y., 1852), 1:381.

47. Tompkins's 1817 request quoted in *FJ,* July 13, 1827. For accounts and analysis of these events, see Arthur Zilversmit, *First Emancipation: The Abolition of Slavery in the North* (Chicago, 1967), 208–14; *Papers of Daniel D. Tompkins,* 1:106–107; Hammond, *Political Parties,* 1:432–33; Harris, *In the Shadow of Slavery,* 94–95.

48. Richard D. Brown, *The Strength of a People: The Idea of an Informed Citizenry in America, 1650–1870* (Chapel Hill, N.C., 1996), 170–73; Rogers M. Smith on "full citizenship" in *Civic Ideals: Conflicting Visions of Citizenship in U.S. History* (New Haven, 1997); and see n. 4 above.

49. On the 1821 convention, see John Anthony Casais, "The New York State Constitutional Convention of 1821 and Its Aftermath" (Ph.D. diss., Columbia University, 1967); Williamson, *American Suffrage,* 195–206; David N. Gellman and David Quigley, eds., *Jim Crow New York: A Documentary History of Race and Citizenship, 1777–1877* (New York, 2003); Merrill D. Peterson, ed., *Democracy, Liberty, and Property: The State Constitutional Conventions of the 1820s* (Indianapolis, 1966); Hammond, *Political Parties,* 1:537, 539, 542–51, 558–61, 571, 2:1–85. Judith Wellman, "Women's Rights, Republicanism, and Revolutionary Rhetoric in Antebellum New York," *New York History* 69 (1988): 352–84, offers a valuable gendered analysis of the convention's debates.

50. Carter and Stone, *Debates,* 179, 181, 198.

51. Carter and Stone, *Debates,* 181, 190, 199.

52. Carter and Stone, *Debates,* 190, 191; for an interesting instance of the difficulties of determining race and how such problems might be solved, see *The Commissioners of the Alms-House, -vs- Alexander Whistelo, A Black Man; Being a Remarkable Case of Bastardy, Tried and Adjudged by the Mayor, Recorder, and Several Aldermen, of the City of New-York, Under the Act Passed 6th March, 1801, for the Relief of Cities and Towns from the Maintenance of Bastard Children* (New York, 1808).

53. Carter and Stone, *Debates,* 191 [italics in original]; Melish, "The 'Condition' Debate."

54. Carter and Stone, *Debates,* 184.

55. William Yates, *Rights of Colored Men to Suffrage, Citizenship and Trial By Jury* (1969; Freeport, N.Y., 1838), 38–50; Carter and Stone, *Debates,* 184, also 189; and Charles Z. Lincoln, *The Constitutional History of New York: From the Beginning of the Colonial Period to the Year 1805* (Rochester, 1906), 658–60.

56. In addition, Clarke juxtaposed the passion aroused by Missouri's antiblack immigration rules with the far more injurious process of disenfranchisement; Carter and Stone, *Debates,* 186–89. On the "fantasy" of black disappearance, see Winthrop D. Jordan *White over Black: American Attitudes toward the Negro, 1550–1812* (1968; New York, 1977), 512–41, 546–69; Melish, *Disowning Slavery,* esp. chaps. 5 and 6.

57. Carter and Stone, *Debates,* 193.

58. Carter and Stone, *Debates,* 202; John Langley Stanley, "Majority Tyranny in Tocqueville's America: The Failure of Negro Suffrage in New York State in 1846" (Ph.D. diss.,

Cornell University, 1966), 37; Peterson, *Democracy, Liberty, and Property,* 138; Casais, "Convention of 1821," 73–76, provides helpful classifications of the delegates political loyalties.

59. Carter and Stone, *Debates,* 202, see also 185–86, 199, 211–12; Fox, "The Negro Vote in Old New York," 257–58.

60. The desire to ensure that those who served in the military had the franchise expressed the martial spirit of nationalism aroused by the War of 1812. See Steven Watts, *The Republic Reborn: War and the Making of Liberal America, 1790–1820* (Baltimore, 1987), on the broad cultural impact of that war. Casais, "Convention of 1821," esp. 179 n., notes the long shadow cast by the War of 1812.

61. Carter and Stone, *Debates,* 235.

62. See Foote, *Black and White Manhattan,* 183, on the rhetoric of inner racial identities in the aftermath of the 1741 "Great Negro Plot"; John L. Brooke, who shared with me a portion of his manuscript "Columbia: Civil Life in the World of Martin Van Buren's Emergence, 1776–1821" as I finished this book, has helped me to see how to extend arguments about sympathetic politics.

63. See n. 46 above. Jabez Hammond, *Political Parties,* 1:381–82, noted the bitter irony that Young, an advocate of black disenfranchisement in 1821, was a key supporter of the black militia units during the war. Days before Tompkins spoke, Clarke had attempted to debunk the notion that blacks had not participated in the war effort (Carter and Stone, *Debates,* 187–88); see also Harris, *In the Shadow of Slavery,* 93–94, on the service of black New Yorkers during the War of 1812.

64. Carter and Stone, *Debates,* 288.

65. Carter and Stone, *Debates,* 255–56, 277, 279–81; Donald B. Cole, *Martin Van Buren and the American Political System* (Princeton, 1984), 70–73.

66. Carter and Stone, *Debates,* 329, 661. To ward off complaints of taxation without representation, the clause exempted from taxation the vast majority of blacks who fell below the $250 threshold; the militia service qualification was added later in the convention.

67. More practically, Van Buren also reminded northern and western county delegates that they had come to expand their own representation, not New York City's; Carter and Stone, *Debates,* 376; see also Cole, *Van Buren,* 70–71.

68. Carter and Stone, *Debates,* 167, 171, 485–87; see also Richard H. Brown, "The Missouri Crisis, Slavery, and the Politics of Jacksonianism," *South Atlantic Quarterly* 65 (1966): 55–72.

69. Carter and Stone, *Debates,* 485–86, 497–98. Melish, *Disowning Slavery,* 220–25, offers some intriguing comparative remarks about the memory and forgetting of slavery in the North, including New York. See also Joseph L. Arbena, "Politics or Principle? Rufus King and the Opposition to Slavery, 1785–1825," *Essex Institute Historical Collections* 101 (1965): 56–77.

70. Rael, *Black Identity and Black Protest,* 3; Kachun, *Festivals of Freedom,* 26, 31, 39–41, 42–43, 46–47.

71. Hamilton, *Oration;* quotations, 6, 14, 15; William Hamilton to John Jay, Mar. 8, 1796, in "Anti-Slavery Papers of John Jay, Collected by Frank Monaghan," *JNH* 17 (1932): 491–93; see also Kachun, *Festivals of Freedom,* 47.

72. Nathaniel Paul, *An Address, Delivered on the Celebration of the Abolition of Slaver, in the State of New-York, July 5, 1827* (Albany, 1827); quotations, 3, 10, 14, 16; see also Kachun, *Festivals of Freedom,* 49–50.

73. Vivienne Kruger, "Born to Run," 780–83, calculates that for the southern six counties of New York, as many as 2,866 slaves were freed as the 1827 law went into effect.

74. Paul, "Address," 18–19; Rael, *Black Identity and Black Protest*, 3, 5; Kachun, *Festivals of Freedom*, 26, 31, 32, 40–41.

75. *FJ*, Apr. 26, 1827; Hodges, *Root and Branch*, 223.

76. *FJ*, June 29, 1827; Rael, *Black Protest and Black Identity*, 55–81; White, "It Was a Proud Day," 38–39; Kachun, *Festivals of Freedom*, 13, 36, 39, 43–49.

77. White and White, *Stylin,'* 96–121; White, *Stories of Freedom;* Melish, *Disowning Slavery*, 171–83; Gellman and Quigley, *Jim Crow New York*, 87–89; Waldstreicher, *Perpetual Fetes*, 328–38; Foote, *Black and White Manhattan*, 232; Kachun, *Festivals of Freedom*, 26–27; Marvin Edward McAllister, "'White People Do Not Know How to Behave at Entertainments Designed for Ladies and Gentlemen of Colour': A History of New York's African Grove/American Theatre" (Ph.D. diss., Northwestern University, 1997).

78. White, "Proud Day," 49–50; Rael, *Black Identity and Black Protest*, 77–79; Hodges, *Root and Branch*, 223–24; *FJ*, July 13, 1827; Kachun, *Festivals of Freedom*, 36, 39, 42–43, 53; Kruger, "Born to Run," 782–83.

79. *FJ*, Mar. 16, July 13, 1827. McCarthy, "To Plead Our Own Cause," offers a penetrating analysis of *Freedom's Journal;* see also Edwin G. Burrows and Mike Wallace, *Gotham: A History of New York City to 1898* (New York, 1999), 549–51.

80. Rael, *Black Identity and Black Protest*, 49.

81. *FJ*, Mar. 16, 23, 30, Apr. 6, May 4, 11, 18, 1827.

82. McCarthy, "To Plead Our Own Cause."

83. *FJ*, Mar. 23, 30, Apr. 6, 26, May 4, 11, 18, June 29, 6, 13, 27, Aug. 17, 24, 1827 all contain relevant material; Harris, *In the Shadow of Slavery*, extensively explores the moral supervision of African Americans by black and white reformers; see also White, "It Was a Proud Day," 38–43, 46, 49–50.

NOTES TO EPILOGUE

1. George Tappen to J. Y. McKinney, Kingston, Ulster County, New York, Dec. 7, 1830, New-York Historical Society, New York City.

2. Richard S. Newman, *The Transformation of American Abolitionism: Fighting Slavery in the Early Republic* (Chapel Hill, N.C., 2002).

3. Shane White, "'It Was a Proud Day': African-Americans, Festivals, and Parades," *JAH* 81 (1994): 26–28, 36–38, 47; Patrick Rael, *Black Identity and Black Protest in the Antebellum North* (Chapel Hill, N.C., 2002), 72–75; Graham Russell Hodges, *Root and Branch: African Americans in New York and East Jersey, 1613–1863* (Chapel Hill, N.C., 1999), 197–98; James Oliver Horton and Lois E. Horton, *In Hope of Liberty: Cultures, Community and Protest Among Northern Free Blacks, 1700–1860* (New York, 1997), 158–72; David R. Roediger, *The Wages of Whiteness: Race and the Making of the American Working Class*, rev. ed. (London, 1999), chaps. 5 and 6; Eric Lott, *Love and Theft: Blackface Minstrelsy and the American Working Class* (New York, 1993); Robert C. Toll, *Blacking Up: The Minstrel Show in Nineteenth-Century America* (New York, 1974); Shane White, *Stories of Freedom in Black New York* (Cambridge, Mass., 2002), esp. 157, 185–14; Shane White and Graham White, *Stylin': African American Expressive Culture from Its Beginnings to the Zoot Suit* (Ithaca, N.Y., 1998), 106–22; David N. Gellman and David Quigley, eds., *Jim Crow New York: A Documentary History of Race and Citizenship, 1777–1877* (New York, 2003); see also James Brewer Stewart, "The Emergence of

Racial Modernity and the Rise of the White North, 1790–1840," *JER* 18 (1998): 181–217; and n. 4 of chap. 9.

4. Newman, *Transformation of American Abolitionism,* esp. chaps. 5 and 6.

5. Nell Irvin Painter, *Sojourner Truth: A Life, A Symbol* (New York, 1996); John Stauffer, *The Black Hearts of Men: Radical Abolitionist and the Transformation of Race* (Cambridge, Mass., 2002); Lawrence J. Friedman, "Confidence and Pertinacity in Evangelical Abolitionism: Lewis Tappan's Circle," *American Quarterly* 31 (1979): 81–106; William Jay, *Inquiry into the Character and Tendency of the American Colonization, and Anti-Slavery Societies* (1835), re-published in William Jay, *Miscellaneous Writings* (1853; Freeport, New York, 1972); David M. Reese, *Letters to the Hon. William Jay Being a Reply to his "Inquiry into the Character and Tendency of the American Colonization and American Anti-Slavery Societies"* (New York, 1835), vi–vii, 88–89; Whitney R. Cross, *The Burned-Over District: The Social and Intellectual History of Enthusiastic Religion in Western New York, 1800–1850* (Ithaca, N.Y., 1950), 217–27, 276–77.

6. Elizabeth B. Clark, "'The Sacred Rights of the Weak': Pain, Sympathy, and the Culture of Individual Rights in Antebellum America," *JAH* 82 (1995): 463–93.

7. Quotations from Frederick Douglass, "What to the Slave Is the Fourth of July?" in *The Oxford Frederick Douglass Reader,* ed. William L. Andrews (New York, 1996), 116, 117, 119 [italics in original]; see also Thelma Wills Foote, *Black and White Manhattan: The History of Racial Formation in Colonial New York City* (New York, 2004), 231–32.

8. *FJ,* Mar. 16, 1827; Rael, *Black Identity and Black Protest,* 21.

9. Dickson D. Bruce Jr., *The Origins of African American Literature, 1680–1865* (Charlottesville, Va., 2001); Rael, *Black Identity and Black Protest* 3, 47, 49.

10. Bob Herbert, "Stanton and Anthony," *New York Times,* July 4, 1799, 122. A letter to the editor penned that same day and printed on July 7 criticized a *Times* editorial for ignoring slavery in an editorial in praise of the Declaration of Independence, but the writer, Eric K. Washington, made no mention of New York. A search of multicultural, alternative, and mainstream journalism on-line databases for July 1999 turned up no coverage of the New York anniversary elsewhere, but see Martin C. Evans, "The Day New York Freed Its Slaves: July 4, 1827," *Newsday,* July 4, 2003 (accessed at www.Newsday.com).

11. Eric Foner, "American Freedom in a Global Age," *AHR* 106 (2001): esp. 15–16; Kenneth Cmiel, "The Recent History of Human Rights," *AHR* 109 (2004): 117–35.

INDEX

A.B., 133

Abolition, 1, 4, 42; debate over, 7, 9; in England, 213; and history, 207, 210, 213, 218, 222; in North, 2, 4, 215; William Hamilton calls for, 125. *See also* Abolitionism; Emancipation; Gradual abolition; Immediate abolition; specific state names

Abolitionism: American, 10; British, 8, 60, 63–64, 118, 133, 192; French, 60; Garrisonian, 4, 221; as nineteenth-century movement, 3; northern, 4; relationship to American Revolution questioned, 139; as a transatlantic phenomenon, 1, 2, 60, 64

Abolitionists: blacks as, 7, 216; critiqued in press, 81; from Pennsylvania, 95, 204; white, 215. *See also* Abolitionism; Convention of Delegates from the Abolition Societies Established in Different Parts of the United States (ACPAS); New York Manumission Society (NYMS); Pennsylvania Abolition Society (PAS)

Acadian refugees, 23

"Act concerning Slaves," 68–69

"Act for the gradual abolition of slavery," 1, 153, 177–84, 186. *See also* Gradual abolition law (1799)

"Act for the speedy Sale of the confiscated and forfeited Estates," 66

"Act to prevent frauds and perjuries at elections, and to prevent slaves from voting," 202

Adam (slave), 174

"Address of an Indian Chief, to a party of Slaves, previous to the midnight Massacre of their inhuman Masters," 121

"Address to Miss Phillis Wheatley . . . ," 107

Address to the Negroes in the State of New-York, 106–7. *See also* Hammon, Jupiter

Africa, 83, 84, 107, 108, 130, 193; as continuing influence on black culture in New York, 24, 191–92; potential for sugar cultivation in, 94; slave trade with New York, 16, 20, 22; as subject of literary antislavery, 117, 121; victimized by slave trade, 61

African Americans: and celebrations of emancipation and withdrawal from international slave trade, 189, 196, 198–99, 213–18; and Christianity, 23–24, 30, 106–8, 110, 114; and citizenship, 7, 216; in colonial New York, 19–25; compared to Romans, 113, 122; denial of opportunities for, 180, 197; development of identity among, 3, 191–92, 219, 221; dress of, 2, 200; evacuation from Manhattan (1783), 15, 38–39; families, 2, 8; housing, 2; laws offering protection to, 68; in New York, 1; in North, 2, 219; occupations of, 2, 195, 197; participation in Revolutionary War, 8, 36, 37–38, 39, 40, 141; petitions by, 32, 108; political protest by, 2; and relationship to New York Manumission Society, 57, 72, 75, 153, 159–65; resistance to slavery, 8, 21–25, 33, 36, 39, 144–46, 153, 159–65; role in bringing about abolition, 5, 9, 185, 216; rural, 2, 195–97; slavery-era names discarded, 114; and social advancement, 216, 218; voices and printed voicing of, 7, 103–4, 108–24, 201–2, 217, 218. *See also* Free blacks, Kidnapping, Resistance by blacks to slavery, Slavery, Slaves

African Free School, 58, 72–75, 155, 157, 197, 198. *See also* New York Manumission Society (NYMS)

African Grove Theatre, 217, 220

African Methodist Episcopal Zion Church, 192, 196